South Asia
Dynamics of Politics, Economy & Security

South Asia
Dynamics of Politics, Economy & Security

Edited by

Kulwant Kaur & Baljit S. Mann

Knowledge World

New Delhi

Knowledge World
5A/4A, Ansari Road, Daryaganj, New Delhi 110 002

Published in India by Knowledge World, New Delhi

ISBN: 81-87966-46-7

Published by Kalpana Shukla, Knowledge World
5A/4A, Ansari Road, Daryaganj, New Delhi 110 002
email: knowledgeworld@vsnl.net website:www.knowledgeworldonline.com

Typeset by Dharana, New Delhi; studiodharana@gmail.com
Printed at Chaman Offset Printer, New Delhi

Contents

Section III
Security in South Asia: Need for Rethinking

Section IV
Regionalism and Regional Cooperation

Preface

South Asia has witnessed cataclysmic changes in internal and external politics, which have initiated the process of political, economic and social transformation in the region. The process of socio-economic churning has posed a threat to the stability of the old state structures. These are either becoming irrelevant and unpopular or inefficient and corrupt, whereas the new structures are unable to withstand the pressures generated by this multi-dimensional process of change. However, the structures of governance are being diversified and differentiated but still governance is the last priority. The recent past has witnessed the rise of democratic grass roots movements throughout the region but the feudal mindset and bureaucratic attitude did not allow the governance to improve for the betterment of the people. Hence, the process of democratic transition is not only incomplete but it is also facing rough weather almost in the majority of South Asian countries. The economic transition is also in progress in the South Asian region. Since the 1990s, the majority of South Asian countries have introduced globalization as a measure to address their economic crisis by way of reducing poverty and thereby improving governance. However, globalization has accelerated the process of growth but development is still a mirage. The impact of globalization indicates that it has not been accompanied by a reduction in poverty or improvement in human development through the formation of social capital.

All the South Asian states are suffering from the syndrome of insecurity. Threats to their security are not only from within but also from outside the region. These states are being confronted by both the conventional and non conventional threats. India and Pakistan, the two core states, declared themselves as nuclear weapons states in the year 1998, but their new stature fails to provide them security or overcome their mutual mistrust and predicaments. Moreover, the understanding, approach and strategy regarding security in all South Asian states have remained largely conventional. Recently, the non-conventional security threats like poverty, governance, water, food, energy and environmental security have become more pronounced, whereas the hard and un-demarcated borders have remained the major source of conflict in the region. Though globalization has changed the nature of borders from hard to soft for the flow of capital, goods and technology, this region is still suffering from limitations of hard borders, which has jeopardized the process of regional integration. This could be due to the trust deficit in the region in general and India and Pakistan in particular.

Recent efforts to fill the trust deficit between India and Pakistan have a huge potential for the progress, prosperity and development of the entire South Asian region. The process of confidence-building measures that has been instituted between India and Pakistan particularly since 2003 has enlarged the constituency of peace and cooperation. Probably, both the countries have realized that in the changed global scenario, they cannot change the border but they can certainly change the nature of borders. The soft instead of hard borders had great promise for the people of this region. Now India and Pakistan are trying to convert their hard borders into soft by facilitating the movement of people and goods across the boundaries.

This volume is an outcome of the Seminar "**Conflict and Cooperation in South Asia**" organized by the Department of Political Science, University of Jammu, Jammu in 2004. Scholars from different parts of the country and Nepal attended the seminar and enriched the deliberations by their valuable comments and observations. In the light of extensive discussions, the contributors have revised and updated their papers. We are indeed grateful to all the contributors for their cooperation. It is in fact their endeavours that have made the publication of this volume possible.

We wish to acknowledge with gratitude the financial support provided by the Indian Council of Social Sciences Research (ICSSR), New Delhi, for organizing the seminar. The cooperation and support extended by colleagues, scholars and office of the Department of Political Science and Centre for Strategic Studies, University of Jammu deserve a word of special thanks. Mr. Ajay Singh Manhas and Mr. Sanjeev Magotra have made special efforts and helped in typing some part of the book.

We shall be failing in our duty if we do not express our gratitude to Professor Amitabh Mattoo, a Political Scientist of international repute and the Vice Chancellor, University of Jammu, for providing not only the administrative and financial support, but also encouragement, inspiration and academic inputs.

The final word of thanks must go to Ms. Kalpana Shukla of Knowledge World, New Delhi, for her sincere efforts in bringing out this volume.

Jammu
25 January 2006

Kulwant Kaur
Baljit S. Mann

Introduction

Kulwant Kaur and Baljit S. Mann

The South Asian region has been undergoing the process of transition, which is multi-dimensional, multi-faceted and complex in nature. The South Asian people have been experiencing political, economic and social transformation. Dynamics of internal politics in the South Asian countries is being shaped by their socio-economic and political universe apart from the forces and factors located outside their territorial jurisdiction. Under the impact of globalisation, the national identity and sovereignty are de-territorialized. Hence the domestic politics in the region is trans-nationalized, economics is commercialized and culture is commodified. Trans-nationalism has become the dominant factor in the domestic politics and foreign policies of the South Asian countries.

South Asia has been perceived to be a very volatile region of the world. The area is bedevilled by religious fundamentalism, sectarian and ethnic conflicts, terrorism, cross-border tensions, water and territorial disputes. Failure of governments in these states to control violence and provide efficient administration and good governance further deepened the crisis. Although the structures of governance in South Asian region are being diversified and differentiated, governance is still the last priority. This region has witnessed too much government and too little governance. The past couple of decades have witnessed the rise of democratic movements in every South Asian country but the feudal mindset and authoritarian tendencies do not allow them to bring about fundamental change in the society. The structures and institutions have been taken over by sectarian forces, which have created serious problems of survival and identity for the minorities and the deprived sections of society. Political and vested interests have played significant roles in creating and nurturing the monsters of communal, ethnic and sectarian violence.[1] The increasing reliance of the post-colonial state on the coercive measures indicates that all is not well with the health of the state in this region. The institutions of governance in South Asia generally bypass the voiceless who suffer multiple deprivations on account of their income, ethnicity, gender or religion or where they live. The larger question of how minorities of various kinds are given full participation in social services and governance structures in the multi-ethnic and multi-cultural societies in South Asia has remained largely unaddressed.[2]

South Asia's democratic transition is incomplete and is facing rough weather. These countries have limited understanding about democracy. It is primarily understood as a form of government in South Asia. Even as a form of government, it is reduced to the majority rule, which is described by J.S. Mill as a tyranny of the majority. Meaning thereby that democracy is not understood as a broader canvas in South Asia. Democracy has generally been understood and even practised in terms of political superstructure. It has not been related to socio-economic structures and the cultural dynamics of the South Asian societies. Consequently, there exists a clear hiatus between the political superstructure and socio-economic base of democracy in South Asia.[3] Hence democracy has failed to bring about fundamental socio-economic and political change in the society. Democracy has empowered the elites rather than the masses in this region.

The process of socio-political and economic churning in the region has posed a threat to the stability of the state structures in the region. The old structures are becoming irrelevant and unpopular and new structures are also unable to withstand the pressures generated by this multi-dimensional process of change. The monarchical and democratic state structures in Nepal are a classic case in point. Monarchy is becoming unpopular but the democratic state structures could not withstand the pressures of the change in the polity, economy and society of Nepal. Democratic state structures in Pakistan could not survive the pressures of change and the army ventured into politics and thereby established the authoritarian state structures in collaboration with bureaucracy, which are dominating its politics till date. An organized and powerful military, bureaucratic oligarchy and landlords have complete hold over the power in Pakistan.[4] The Maldives, a city-state of South Asia is also facing threat to its state structures, which were established under the constitution of 1968. It opted for the republican state structure under the leadership of President, elected through a circuitous process.[5] Under such a system, the incumbent can stay in power forever as happened in the case of President Gayoom. Consequently, the republican structure of state has developed the oligarchy tendencies because the same person had been elected President six times. Now, there is a movement for restructuring the Presidency of the Maldives. But there are larger issues to be addressed because at present state structures of the Maldives are republican but not democratic. Separation of powers and checks and balances can ensure the democratization of state structure. The pro-democracy movement has also revived the development vs. democracy debate.

South Asian countries, which had very open economies in the immediate post-independence period in the 1940s, had become some of the most highly protectionist in the world by the 1970s. While this region began to change gradually in the late 1970s, it was only in the 1990s that most South Asian economies initiated substantive reform efforts involving both trade and investment liberalization.[6] Since the last one and a half decades, the South Asian countries have introduced globalization as a measure to address their economic crisis by way of reducing poverty and thereby improving governance. However, the impact of globalization in this regard is neither positive nor constructive. According to the Human Development Report (2001), half a billion people in South Asia, or 40 per cent of its population, have experienced a decline in their income, despite a 5.4 per cent increase in the South Asian GDP during the 1990s. Meaning thereby that globalization has not been accompanied by a reduction in poverty or improvement in human development[7] since most South Asian countries have failed to maintain a balance between economic and social development policies. For most South Asians, the outcome of the globalization process has been higher prices, fewer employment opportunities, increased disparities in income and a higher incidence of poverty.[8]

Globalization has de-centred the state in the region. The state has not only become reductionist but is also losing touch with the ground reality. The state is de-centred because the national identity, which the post-colonial states have tried to construct in the region, is facing rough weather. Globalization has not only marginalized the national identities but has also reinforced the local cultural identities in the region. It has provided a new context, in which the national identities of South Asian countries are not only homogenized but are also de-territorialized and trans-nationalized. India is a classic case in point. Globalization in collaboration with Hindutva, has further accentuated the politics of identities in India. Under the impact of corporate globalization, the market has emerged an identity in the Indian politics. The size and significance of the market in the public domain has been expanding and the size of the state has been reducing. The market has created a context in which the rights of communities are being substituted by rights of corporations to commodify the private property. Private property rights in water, bio-diversity and knowledge are violating the Indian ethos and the customary, community rights of the people.

Though the whole world is moving rapidly in the direction of peace, stability and development, South Asia continues to be gravely threatened by conflicts and multiple security threats.[9] In the context of rapidly changing regional strategic, economic, political and social environment in South Asia, the ideas of peace, security and development have to be redefined in the broader framework.[10] Security has always remained a serious concern for the states in South Asia but the understanding about security is very limited at the conceptual as well as operational level. Here the connotation of security has by and large remained traditional, which does not take into account the non-traditional security threats.[11] The traditional notion of security and its operation in the South Asian region has done a major damage to the security of people in the region. The elite in these states are busy spending more and more on the purchase of arms and ammunition, which alone cannot ensure security. In this context, it may be pointed out that nuclearization of the Indian subcontinent failed to provide any security to the people.[12] The greatest threat to the security of the people in the region is poverty. A determined attack on poverty will require a new paradigm of security that recognizes the role of the state in protecting the rights of the poor people, which will ensure social security and peace as well. The alleviation of poverty is not only essential for human security and development but for the formation of social capital as well, which is vital for social peace and harmony.

In a globalized world, borders are progressively disappearing. However, the South Asian region has remained immune from the winds of change blowing across the globe for a long time. This region is still suffering from the syndrome of hard borders, which has proved a major obstacle to the process of regional integration. South Asian countries still believe in the hard borders because of the trust deficit the region is suffering from. This trust deficit is primarily between the two major countries of this region. Recent efforts to build confidence and trust between India and Pakistan have a huge potential for the progress, prosperity and development of the entire South Asian region. The process of confidence-building measures that has been instituted between India and Pakistan in the last couple of years has enlarged the constituency of peace and cooperation. It can be inferred that now India and Pakistan have realized that they cannot change the border but they can change the nature of borders. The soft, instead of hard border, has great promise for the people of this region. Now India and Pakistan are trying to convert their hard borders into soft by facilitating the movement of people and goods across the boundaries. In the wake of the earthquake on 8 October, 2005 in the subcontinent, India and Pakistan agreed to five openings in Jammu and Kashmir. The CBMs like opening of bus service between Amritsar and Lahore and the decision to start the Thar Express between Rajasthan and Sindh, besides starting the bus service between Srinagar and Muzaffarabad have brought about positive winds in the region.

The conflict has remained the dominant mode of inter-state politics in the region. In 1985 by establishing South Asian Association for Regional Cooperation, an attempt was made to translate the idea of regionalism into practice. However, the SAARC could not take off as a regional body. The disproportionate size of the economies of member states and the fear of unequal distribution of the cost and benefits of regional cooperation has often led to the indifferent behaviour of the South Asian countries towards SAARC. They have failed to realize that the benefits of regionalism would outweigh its dangers and shortcomings. If the South Asian states are able to forge an effective regionalism, built upon and around the strengths of the region, the rewards would be significant for each and all. It would be a win-win situation.

Now, the South Asian countries are gradually realizing that politics in the region cannot be pursued through conflict and confrontation. Of course, it is the dominant but not the only mode of politics. Cooperation is also a significant mode of politics, which can be bilateral as well as multilateral. Therefore, the sub regional cooperation has taken shape in the region in the recent past. India has played a leading role to promote that through the instrument of the Gujral Doctrine. The forces of globalization have also created the constituency of cooperation in the region. Agreements regarding the formation of SAPTA and SAFTA are classic cases in point. While SAFTA was seen as the route to opening up trade, it was always needed to address the problem of trade asymmetry in the region. To the extent that the SAARC process moved slowly to address these issues, bilateralism became a preferred option to stimulate intra-regional trade. India has already entered into bilateral free trade agreements with Nepal, Bhutan and Sri Lanka.[13] Consequently, the intra-regional trade has increased during the last couple of years in the region.

The Islamabad Declaration, by adopting the framework agreement on South Asian Free Trade Area (SAFTA) at the 12th SAARC Summit has provided a momentum to the process of regional economic integration in South Asia. Apart from this, it is significant to note that the 43-point Islamabad Declaration recognizes the importance of informal political consultations in promoting mutual understanding and reinforcing the confidence-building process among member states. The leaders in their Islamabad Declaration have jointly vowed to make South Asia a peaceful and stable region where each nation is at peace with itself and with its neighbours.[14]

The 9/11 happenings in the United States have changed the strategic scenario of the South Asian region. This was followed by the US war against terrorism and its main theatre is South Asia. Once again, Pakistan has emerged as a frontline state in the US war against terrorism. These developments led to a competition between India and Pakistan in showing loyalty to the United States. They forgot that controlling Afghanistan is basically controlling the gateway to South Asia. The leadership of this region has shown its myopic view on the situation prevailing in South Asia.[15] For protecting their long-term interests and security in South Asia, these states must cooperate to keep away the external powers and their armies from the region.

The thematic scheme of this book contains four sections ranging from dynamics of internal politics to Indo–Pakistan relations and from security to regional integration and cooperation in South Asia.

Section I: Dynamics of Internal Politics

The first section comprises six papers dealing with the different issues pertaining to the domestic politics of South Asian countries. Major issues analyzed in this section are: governance, revolt, Islamic fundamentalism, track five diplomacy and democracy in South Asia. The issue of democracy is discussed with special reference to the two small countries of this region, Nepal and Bhutan.

Governance in South Asia: Problems and Prospects is the title of Baljit Singh's contribution for this volume. In his paper, he examines the diversity of political systems in South Asia. He argues that post-colonial South Asia is in a multi-faceted and multi-dimensional political transition. South Asian states have failed to ensure proper governance in the region, though the area is gradually moving towards democracy. Their political systems are neither institutionalized nor sensitive to the concerns of masses, rather they are elite centric. The concentration and personalization of power have coincided with the parallel erosion of institution of governance. His perspective of governance is different from that of the Washington Consensus. He argues that the rolling back of state and creating more space for the civil society cannot ensure governance, as the latter cannot be a substitute for the former. It can be a facilitator to the state for ensuring governance. This paper is divided into four parts ranging from the present situation and problems to prospects and conclusions. It deals with the present situation regarding governance in the region. While talking about the future of governance, he argues that it lies in democracy not in authoritarianism, multiculturalism not in homogenization, accommodation not assimilation, decentralization not centralization of power, secular not sectarian state, rule of law not rule of rulers, politics as a service not as a business, institutional building not the institutional decay.

Karori Singh in his paper **Revolt in the Post-Colonial Sri Lanka Dynamics and Implications** argues that the Sri Lankan society being most peaceful in the past has recently turned out as most violent. In Sri Lanka main ethnic groups are on the path of revolt against state or each other, as a result of which the civil society is so impaired that all the communities and groups are involved in the vicious circle of fear, violence, unrest, terror and torture. The author opines that the revolts in Sri Lanka are almost controlled by the coercive power of the existing state apparatus though political settlement process is also continuing. In the case of the JVP, the killings of the main leaders during 1988–99 brought it under control, while the revolt by Tamil groups has also been weakened by internecine strife between different Tamil groups. However, LTTE emerged as a strong group and therefore, it is continuing over a long period of time with little hiccups as and when political process begins through peace initiatives of various kinds. Ultimately, IVP joined the mainstream democratic constitutional process but the revolt led by LTTE still forms a separate legal, political, administrative, socio-economic and cultural identity. It is aspiring to institutionalize and consolidate the new political order. Irrespective of the magnitude of the revolt by LTTE, the Sri Lankan society is not in regression. His analysis of the Sri Lankan situation goes beyond the established theoretical postulates and draws certain lessons for other such plural societies in other parts of the world.

B.C. Upreti in his paper titled **Democracy in Nepal: Bumpy Ground and Road Blocks** discusses the transition from absolute monarchy to democracy in the political system of Nepal. He argues that this process of democratic transition began in Nepal soon after the overthrow of the Rana regime in 1951, which is yet an unfinished agenda. It has not been smooth sailing and the decade of the 1950s was marked by political instability and disorder. The Nepalese ruling elite failed in developing a broad-based nationalism, which would have been supportive of democracy. In 1991, another attempt was made to establish democracy but its functioning was neither smooth nor stable. He argues that the multi-party system and factionalism within the political parties were the major reasons for the disorder and political instability in Nepal. The multi-party system resulted in coalition governments, which reduced the prospects of strengthening of democracy in the country. Since political parties have failed in providing stability to the government, they opened doors for political assertion by the monarchy. The author argues that the *royal coup* of February 2005 not only reversed the democratic process in Nepal but it also indicates that the traditional political forces are still capable of changing the course of politics in Nepal. He holds political parties and leaders responsible for the failure of democracy in the country. As they remained out of the political scene for a long time, this also resulted in their ineffectiveness and a narrow social base. Corruption has emerged as another roadblock in the smooth sailing of democracy besides the Maoist terrorism. The Maoists were unhappy with the democratic political parties reaching an understanding with the royalists and surrendering to the feudalistic forces apart from their failure to bring about fundamental socio-economic change.

Rise of Islamic Fundamentalism in Pakistan: An International Concern is the title of Surendra Chopra's article. Although it has become an issue of international concern after the 9/11 happenings in the United States its roots are traced back to the middle of the 8th century. The author argues that the contemporary Muslim world has also witnessed the revival of Islam and assertion of Islamic Fundamentalism. The examples of Pakistan, Iran and Afghanistan are cited to substantiate the argument. The deteriorating condition of the masses in some of the Muslim countries has prepared the fertile ground for Islamic fundamentalist movement because the poor and downtrodden, frustrated by the politics of the ruling classes have often sought refuge in the promise of the fundamentalists. He analyzed how the different rulers of Pakistan used Islamic fundamentalism to strengthen its relations with Muslim countries in order to stabilize their position at home. He concludes by saying that the Islamic factor has played a dominant role in the domestic politics as well as in the foreign policy of Pakistan.

Mathew Joseph C. in his paper titled **Struggle for Democracy in South Asia: Case of Bhutan**, discusses the democratic transition in South Asia. He touches upon the diversity of political systems in this region ranging from democracy to monarchy and from absolute monarchy to autocratic rule. The author argues that India and Sri Lanka are successful democracies in post-colonial South Asia and world as well, however, the struggle for democracy has remained the main thrust of this work. To understand the drive for democracy in a broader perspective, the author has given the demographic account of Bhutan. As Bhutan is having absolute monarchy, the king is the central figure in the Bhutanese political system. He exercises the legislative, executive and judicial powers. The Nepalis-dominated south and the Drupka-dominated north were cut off from each other till the beginning of the state-sponsored modernization process. The attitude of the Bhutanese authorities towards the demographic and cultural challenges posed by the Nepalis was not very receptive. The popular movement for the realization of political and economic rights for the people of Nepali origin has contributed substantially to struggle for democracy in the region. The Bhutanese authorities were taken by surprise by the enormity of the mass mobilization in pro-democracy demonstrations. It tried to suppress the wave of discontent through various means. From September–October 1990 onwards the struggle for democracy and human rights has been carried out from outside Bhutan. As the pro-democracy movement has grown in strength, the different trends dormant in the movement surfaced. In 1995 broad coalitions of political parties and human rights groups were formed to strengthen the struggle for democracy. The pro-democracy movement succeeded in compelling the king to surrender some of his powers to a cabinet in 1998 and initiate a process to draft a constitution. In contrast to the various contemporary experiences, the ethnic assertion of the people of Nepali origin in Bhutan has developed into a movement for the democratization of the Bhutanese polity and society.

Jane E. Schukoske and Manjri Sewak contributed their paper **Track-Five Diplomacy: Role for Higher Education in Conflict Transformation**. The authors have differentiated "conflict transformation" from "conflict resolution" and focused on the role of education in conflict transformation. The educational institutions comprise universities that offer education in conflict resolution as well as think tanks that include a variety of research, analysis and study programmes. They have tried to address a very pertinent question related with the role of institutions of higher education in the process of conflict transformation. Institutions of higher educations in India, Sri Lanka and Nepal have shown keen interest in providing training to their graduates, teachers and members of their societies to contribute to the emerging conflict transformation field. The traditional fields of study and their roles are discussed in this paper. The authors have also mentioned the nomenclature of the various courses designed by the different institutions regarding the conflict transformation.

Section II : Indo–Pakistan Relations—A Paradigm Shift

In this section, the various issues between the two countries are discussed. The wide range of issues are from: mediation to diplomacy, tension to normalization, traditional mindset to new approach, inter-continental missiles to confidence-building measures and process of composite dialogue besides Indus Water Treaty have prominently figured in this section.

A.S. Narang in his work **Indo–Pak Relations and SAARC: Retrospect and Prospect** analyzes that notwithstanding the positive developments which have accompanied the end of the Cold War, South Asia has remained susceptible to tensions and conflicts originating from the unique history of the region. The author argues that given close co-relation between the fortunes of SAARC and the state of Indo–Pak relations, the big question is, can India and Pakistan set aside their history of conflict and animosity. There are vested interests that have benefited from the continuous tension between India and Pakistan, like the weapon dealers, the smugglers and conflict entrepreneurs. It is a fact that whenever some progress is being made on the Indo–Pak front, the military picks up. It is a question of the survival of the fundamentalist elements. He argues that if history of the last 55 years and the resultant mindset in the two countries are hindrances in ways of peace offensives, the changed geo-strategic and global environment do provide optimism. The dynamic of changes in the global economic environment due to scientific and technological progress has been such that the need for a vibrant and effective regional cooperation for South Asia has now become an imperative. India and Pakistan can ignore this only at the cost of their own peace, progress and stability as also of all member states of SAARC. The 12th SAARC Summit made it clear that there is realization by all member states about necessity for economic cooperation to strengthen their competitive position, both individually and as a group. And for that they are prepared for mutual compromises. The success of regional cooperation would be a win-win situation for all SAARC countries. Civil society in both countries is tired of the bad blood. The new generation both in India and Pakistan wants to make it good in life and is convinced that the only way to make the economy grow is to ensure peace. There is also a great deal of consensus among political parties for improving relations. He further argued that India must shed its obsession with Pakistan and devote more political and diplomatic energies towards tendering its relationship with other neighbours. The author concluded his paper with a pertinent question that what has stopped the region from developing into a major player primarily is Indo–Pak tension. Resolution of this tension would result in prosperity of the entire region. India and Pakistan, therefore, have to take lead. This aspect is gaining ground on both sides and needs to be consolidated further.

P. Sahadevan in his paper **Relevance of Mediation for India–Pakistan Peacemaking** has dealt with the contrasting approaches to peacemaking. He argued that India has insisted on a bilateral approach, whereas Pakistan has desired third-party mediation. The complexity of the Indo–Pakistan conflict and inherent difficulties in conflict resolution, have prominently figured in this work. The Indo–Pak conflict has not resulted from their single incompatible goal but a variety of competing interests, which are linked to each other in a manner that solution or difficulty in resolution of one issue influences the other. The author stated that terrorism is an offshoot issue of the fundamental conflict over the territory like Kashmir. Of course, Siachen and Sir Creek are the other territorial issues between the two countries and one issue has linkages with another. The conflict resolution process entails a composite framework for negotiations. Their conflict goals are linked to their national ideology. Hence the incongruent ideological position of India and Pakistan is an important source of conflict formation. He is of the view that the CBMs have a limited role in the resolution of Indo–Pak conflict because these can only facilitate the peace process. He argues that mediation could become successful if there exist the required conditions besides a major change in the mindset of both the countries.

Mohd. Tajuddin and Muzaffar Ali in their paper entitled **Two States in One River Basin System: Conflict to Cooperative Co-Existence**, argue that the states of the contemporary world are equipped in terms of knowledge and technology to utilize their natural resources to the maximum limits for their economic development. This goal of maximum utilization of the natural resources is resulting in environmental threats of different types to the very existence of life on this planet and new areas of conflicts on trans-national common resources like river waters. Indus River Basin has provided a congenial atmosphere for the organization and development of one of the oldest civilizations of the world and an unbroken continuity thereafter. The British Indian empire was the first state in the basin with sovereignty or suzerainty over all the territory and has the technology and resources to develop a network of river-based canal irrigation system for optimum utilization of the fertility of the soil for agricultural growth. Economic and political reasons induced the empire to launch the construction of the largest river-based irrigation system in the third quarter of the nineteenth century, which continued till de-colonization in the subcontinent. The partition divided, along with other things, the canal irrigation system of the Indus

Basin, which added one more serious dispute between the two newly independent states. This paper attempts to understand the origin and intensification of Indo–Pak river water dispute and all the bilateral and multilateral initiatives taken to resolve it. It analyzes each aspect of the protracted negotiation for settlement of the dispute—first at bilateral level from 1948 to 1950 and afterwards with the good offices of the World Bank from 1952 to 1960. The irrigation development projects undertaken by the two states during the period of dispute have been examined. The dispute was resolved in the form of a treaty that permanently decided the principles and the procedure for sharing the common waters between the two states and also devised the ways and means to settle any future dispute in the area. The study analyses the content of the treaty from preamble to signature along with the annexures. The working of the treaty from 1960 till 2004, post-treaty Indus Basin development projects undertaken in each country and hydroelectric generation-related disputes that began to emerge in the 1980s and multiplied in the 1990s when India took up the construction of hydel projects on the Western Rivers in J&K have also been examined in this paper. In the concluding part of the paper the rationale for the uninterrupted working of the treaty even during war situation has been reviewed. Some suggestions have also been given for keeping the treaty relevant in the twenty-first century in the context of the fast increasing energy demands of the two parties when the energy generation potential of these rivers are utilized at the lowest level.

K.P. Vijaylakshmi in her paper **The Changing Policy of US in South Asia: Impact on Indo–Pak Relations** has discussed the changing perception of the United States towards the South–Asian region and its impact on the Indo–Pak Relations. The US policy towards South Asia as a whole and Indo–Pak conflict in particular have changed since 9/11. She argues that the re-emergence of South Asia on the foreign policy agenda of United States, has brought about change in the latter's policy towards the former. The US is concerned about terrorism and in its war against terrorism Pakistan is a frontline state. It is also concerned about the role of China in the subcontinent and the stability and viability of the state of Pakistan. The author argues that the hallmark of changing US policy towards South Asia is to develop relations with both the powers of this region, i.e. India as well as Pakistan. The US wants to improve its relations with India. It has played a significant role in the crisis of 2001 and 2002 between India and Pakistan and has certainly assumed the role of a discreet facilitator.

Happymon Jacob in his contribution discusses the significance of **Track-Two Diplomacy in Indo–Pak Relations: Problems and Prospects**. He has analyzed the present state of track-two initiatives between India and Pakistan apart from addressing a very pertinent question, viz. what ails the track-two initiatives between India and Pakistan and how these initiatives can be given a new lease of life. The track-two diplomacy has played a significant role to demolish deeply entrenched enemy images, which have been given to people about enemy countries. He argues that these images cannot be addressed and demolished by track-one processes and mainstream official dialogues, hence the importance of track-two diplomacy. It also prepares the societies at large for accepting strong decisions. The author states that track-two initiatives between India and Pakistan could not succeed in the past because these suffer from extreme elitism and do not have any participation from the younger generation. Besides this, there should be more representation of parliamentarians and media representatives in track-two initiatives. The author highlights the nature of track-two by pointing out an acute lack of participation from the larger non-Islamabad–New Delhi-based civil society. He is of the view that the track-two diplomacy in South Asia can survive only if it becomes part of the civil society movement both in India and Pakistan.

Harmeet Singh in his paper entitled **Genesis of Indo–Pak Dialogue on Sidelines of SAARC-2004** points out that the two major powers of South Asia, India and Pakistan have been at loggerheads with each other. He has substantiated his argument by citing the facts that they had already fought three full-fledged wars besides the ongoing proxy war. The acquisition of nuclear power status by both the countries further indicated the gravity of the situation. He argues that various efforts were made to normalize their relations but the track record of conflict resolution has not been impressive. The divergence in their policy priorities could be the major reason for that. For instance, for India the most important issue is cross-border terrorism, whereas Pakistan wants to focus on Kashmir because it is a core issue for it. The major argument of this research paper is that a congenial atmosphere exists now for India to strike a political deal with Pakistan. The first part of this paper discusses Indo–Pak dispute in the historical perspective, whereas part two highlights the easing of tension between India and Pakistan after Prime Minister A.B. Vajpayee launched his famous "Peace Initiative" in Kashmir in April 2003. The last part contains the analysis of the situation and suggestions made by the author. The various confidence-building measures announced by two countries also prominently figure in this paper.

Section III: Security in South Asia: Need for Rethinking

As the title suggests, this section deals with the existing paradigm of security and argues the case for a new paradigm of security for this region. The variety of issues dealing with the conventional and unconventional idea of security is discussed here. The ideas of human security, energy security have been discussed at length. The impact of Afghanistan crisis and the 9/11 happenings on the South Asian security also form part of this section.

South Asian Security: India–Pakistan Factor is the title of Karamjit Singh Sidhu's contribution for this book. He has argued that the shift of power equation from military to economic seems to be gradually recognized in the South Asian region. The security scenario in the region is dominated by the power position in the region, which has largely been determined by the intrusions from external forces with a motivation provided by internal factors. However, the military power continues to be deeply and intimately linked with national security at the cost of their social and economic needs. Motivated by the desire to accumulate power at the expense of each other, both India and Pakistan are known to be deriving strength from their respective inherent Hindu and Islamic beliefs. The author is of the view that while India strives to reduce the extra-regional influences and challenges to its power equation, as it perceives South Asia's natural balance of power to be one which is lopsided in its favour, Pakistan seems to work to reduce the imbalance through alliances and aid efforts to internationalise the bilateral issues related to national power and security. A profound strategic dissonance is clearly evident in the security postures of India and Pakistan. They are locked in a state of mutual distrust over the last more than fifty years. The Indo–Pak relationship seems to be based primarily on the self-contradictory perception of balance of power, which may not be rational due to the inequality of two states in terms of size, resources, threats and achievements, therefore, untenable. The author states that the real potential of the new confidence and security-building measures (CSBM) will be put to the ultimate test when critical issues will be discussed between India and Pakistan in the composite dialogue.

Bishnu Hari Nepal in his contribution entitled **Foreign Power Involvement and Regional Security in South Asia: A Roadmap to Peace, Development and Balance of Power System** has stated that alien rule in the region damaged the ethno-cultural, socio-economic, politico-strategic and above all the value system of South Asian region. He is of the view that the hangover of the Cold War still persists and almost all the conflicts in the region have remained Indo-centric so far. While talking about the Indo-centricity of this region, he argues that South Asia without India is incomplete. He has argued that the 9/11 happenings and developments thereafter have changed the strategic landscape of the South Asian region. The US policy towards India and Pakistan also figured in this paper. The author argues that contemporary South Asia needs new thinking as well as approach to ensure peace in the region because the major threat to peace in the area is poverty. In order to ensure peace in South Asia, there is need to reach the unreachable through a variety of means suggested by the author like trade, cooperation, disarmament, reconciliation and solidarity.

Surinder K. Shukla in her article titled **Impact of Afghanistan Crisis on South Asia**, argues that Afghanistan forms a part of the extended neighbourhood of South Asia. The significance of Afghanistan lies in its strategic location because it connects South Asia with Central Asia and the latter has emerged as a very important region for the energy requirements of the former. Shukla contends that Afghanistan remained underdeveloped and landlocked, but not impregnable for the large part of the 20th century. During this period, Afghanistan's internal politics underwent a series of changes. Due to its strategic importance in the changing regional and global scenario, India cannot absolve itself from its responsibility towards Afghanistan. The changed conditions in the north-western part of the subcontinent provide an opportunity for rethinking many of the traditional premises of enduring rivalry between India and Pakistan in Afghanistan. She states that India couldn't wish Pakistan away in Afghanistan because the geo-political reality of a long and uncontrolled border between two nations will always provide political opportunities for Pakistan. The author concludes by saying that India needs to take a pragmatic view regarding Afghanistan because its vital interests are at stake not only in South Asia but also in Central Asia.

Monir Alam in his contribution **Energy Scenario in South Asia: A Case Study of India's Energy Policy** discusses the energy security scenario of this region and argues that the rapid economic and population growth has increased the demand of energy in the region. South Asia is facing scarcity of energy, which has forced all the South Asian countries to diversify their sources of energy. After analysing the energy security profile of the entire region, it concentrates upon India's growing energy demand and different mechanisms adopted by government to ensure its future energy security. In recent years, natural gas identified as the fuel of the 21st century, has been growing in importance as a source of energy in India, especially for use in power generation, fertilizer and petrochemical production. Indian consumption of natural gas has risen faster than any other fuel. Now, it accounts for around 6 per cent of the country's energy demand. India ranks sixth in the world in terms of energy consumption and has formulated multiple strategies to meet its energy requirements.

The last contribution in this section has been made by Kulwant Kaur on **Proliferation of Small Arms and Light Weapons in South Asia: Impact on Human Security**. She has observed that in recent times, human security is threatened more by proliferation of small arms and light weapons than the nuclear weapons, as the highest number of casualties, since World War II, have occurred due to the use of small weapons. In this paper, the issue of small arms and light weapons, their production, causes of proliferation in South Asia and their impact on human security have been examined besides suggesting the measures to control this menace. Explaining the meaning of small arms and light weapons, the author points out that small arms are weapons for use by individuals and light weapons are those that require a crew or team to operate. Regarding their production and proliferation, she has mentioned that 90 per cent of proliferation is being done by P-5 of the United Nations and the US, China and Russia are the top three producers in the world.

Regarding South Asia, the author contends that the region has reached a saturation point because of the ongoing conflicts and the Afghan crisis. The proliferation of small arms and light weapons affects the intensity and duration of violence and encourages militancy rather than a peaceful resolution of unsettled differences. The author mentions that the human cost of proliferation of small arms has enhanced because of the nature of post-colonial states and their failure to govern in South Asia. She has also observed that one of the reasons for persistent violence and failure to have successful dialogue and reconciliation in J&K in India and in North-East Provinces of Sri Lanka is the large-scale availability of arms. The author has also analyzed how the task of post-conflict peace building and reconstruction becomes difficult with the large-scale availability of these weapons and the power and legitimacy of the state are eroded. In the end, the author suggests a few measures to control the proliferation and misuse of small arms and light weapons.

Section IV: Regionalism and Regional Cooperation

Now, the debate is going on between the old and new regionalism. The former took shape in the 1960s and 1970s and the latter has been taking shape over the last couple of decades. A distinction is drawn between the old and new regionalism on the basis of three features: the multi-polar context of the latter as opposed to the bipolar context of the former; the dominant role of hegemonic actors in the creation of old as opposed to the autonomous nature of new regionalism; and the comprehensive and multi-dimensional nature of new regionalism as opposed to the narrow and specific focus of the old.[16]

The last section of this book interrogates the idea of regionalism and regional cooperation in the context of the South Asian region. Contours of conflict, cooperative regimes, regional cooperation in a comparative perspective, political economy of trade and emerging trends in regional cooperation comprise this section.

Ranjit Singh Ghuman examines the **Political Economy of Indo–Pakistan Trade Relations and SAARC**. He explores the impact of hostile relations of two neighbours on their trade. The political and religious leadership of both sides of the border were suspicious of the designs of each other. The author has divided the trade relations between India and Pakistan into three phases. During the initial stage of first phase, the "Stand Still Agreement" governed their trade relations. The normal licensing and tariff restrictions on trade between the two countries came into force on the expiry of the Stand Still Agreement w.e.f. 1 March 1948. Thereafter, trade between India and Pakistan was conducted on the basis of bilateral trade agreements. Till 1965, about twelve trade/payments agreements were signed between India and Pakistan. The process of normalization of political relations between the two countries has also figured in this phase. The second phase covering the period of nine years (1966–1974), witnessed a trade embargo between India and Pakistan. There was absolutely no legal trade between the two countries during this phase. Politically, both the countries remained hostile to each other throughout this period. In spite of several efforts, the trade could not take off between India and Pakistan. However, the compulsions of national reconstruction and development did not allow acute belligerency between the two neighbours for a long period. The Simla Agreement paved the way for normalization of relations between India and Pakistan; however, it took more than two years to sign a trade protocol in pursuance of Article 3 of the Simla Agreement. Though the trade was resumed between India and Pakistan the relations between them and for that matter trade relations between the two passed through many ups and downs. During the third phase, that comprises the period of 29 years (1975–2004), the author argues that the formation of SAARC in 1985 was a major step to normalize relations amongst its members and promote trade and other economic relations. He has also given the data to show the reverse trend in Indo–Pak trade since 1947. Ghuman argues that the full potential of their mutual trade has never been realized so far, mainly owing to the predominance of political irrationalities over the economic rationalities. The situation has reached such a stage not because of the lack of potentialities but because of the hostile and hatred-loaded political relations, historical mistrust and fear psychosis.

Anand Aditya in his paper entitled **Contours of Conflict, Co-operative Regimes and Critical Mass: A Study of South Asian Region**, argues that South Asia is restless today because of the failures of its development in the post-colonial period. Instead of prosperity, the millions of people in the region today hang on the tenterhooks of poverty. He remarks that the traditional order of cooperation, growth and security has failed. This paper is divided into various parts, which include the conceptual framework, security profile of the region, evolution of regionalism and security developments, comparison of regional cooperation regimes, features and analysis of South Asian security regimes, scope for regional cooperation, changing regional scenario, stakeholders in the regional security and concluding observations. While concluding he argues that South Asia is at the threshold of change and a new order seems to be in the process of formation. More than five decades ago, the leaders and people of South Asia fought for political freedom, which has proved deficient in due course of time. Therefore, the present restlessness around the region heralds a new movement for four freedoms—freedom from fear, freedom from hunger, freedom from ignorance and freedom from disease—for all members of society. He argues that the freedom struggle was their tryst with destiny whereas the aforesaid four freedoms would be a tryst with the people in the real sense.

The Prospects of Regional Cooperation through SAFTA with Special Reference to India, is the major thrust of Jasbir Singh and Aroon Sharma's paper. They argue that the 12th SAARC Summit held in Islamabad was a path-breaking and historic attempt in the area of economic cooperation in the South Asian region. Their major argument is that with the Islamabad Declaration a new era of cooperation has started in the region, despite the fact that SAARC had remained the hostage of Indo–Pak conflict in the past. They argue that a strong association of South Asian countries is required to deal with regional and international problems like terrorism and regional economic imbalances in an effective way. They appreciate the role played by the Bhutanese state to crack down on the insurgent groups operating from its land against India, the same is expected from Pakistan and Bangladesh. Terrorism has been identified as a major stumbling block in the progress of cooperation in the region. It is argued that SAFTA will facilitate free trade, enhance infrastructural connectivity, free movement of business representatives and skilled personnels and work towards a common tourism policy. The whole system of free trade will be achieved over a period of ten years. In order to make this agreement (SAFTA) a success, both

India and Pakistan have taken a few more steps to build confidence among the smaller nations. It is well argued that the economic, political and social prospects of SAARC increasingly depend on the peaceful interaction of all member nations. The year 2005 was designated as South Asia Tourism Year to develop tourism within the region to bring economic, social and cultural benefits to the region.

Gurmeet Kaur in her piece of research work on **Regional Cooperation in South East Asia: Lessons for SAARC**, has given a comparative perspective of the two regional organisations. She is of the view that there has been a perpetual quest for regional cooperation in South East and South Asia in the contemporary past. Both the regions have civilizational ties that are many centuries old, though their political growth has tended to differ, especially with the onset of different colonial rules in their states. The author states that as compared to South East Asia, the efforts towards regional cooperation in South Asia are of recent origin. Before the creation of SAARC, the countries of South Asian region cooperated mainly at the international forums like the Non-Aligned Movement (NAM). However, at the regional level these states had largely experienced tension, conflict and even open warfare. Therefore, the formation of SAARC heralds a new dawn, which has given rise to a new set of expectations of cooperation, peace and eventual prosperity in the region. It works according to the principle of unanimity for decision making, exclusion of bilateral and contentious issues. The 12th SAARC Summit held in Islamabad has become a turning point in the history of South Asia. With all humility India has made it known to its neighbours that it can share its fortunes with others.

Although the aims and purposes of both the organizations are similar, SAARC as a newly emerged organization will define its own course in its quest for mutually beneficial cooperation for its member states. The reason is too obvious; conditions are different in both the regions. Some of the ASEAN experiences will, however, be of interest to SAARC, in some cases as positive knowledge while in others as kinds of things to be avoided. She argues that SAARC could learn the lesson from ASEAN that strained inter-state relations should not stand in the way of initiating regional cooperation for socio-economic development. ASEAN was born and nourished at a time when the politico-strategic environment and inter-state relations in South East Asia were seriously distorted. The ASEAN experience of regional cooperation shows that the association appears to have concentrated more on cooperation in politico-security and strategic matters. She states that innovations had hardly been witnessed in the case of SAARC. In her work, she argues that the prospects of cooperation between SAARC and ASEAN are promising and are likely to be beneficial to each other.

Parmjit K. Gill in her contribution on **Regional Cooperation in South Asia–Emerging Trends** discusses the various issues pertaining to regional cooperation in the region. She divides her paper into three parts. In the first part, she examines the ideas of regional cooperation, regionalism and new regionalism. She argues that the old concept of regionalism needs to be redefined in the light of recent development in the arena of international politics. According to her, globalization has been affecting the regional cooperation positively as well as negatively. In the second part, the regional cooperation in South Asia is the major focus. She has argued that as compared with the other regions, the experiment of regional cooperation has not remained very successful in this region. The various factors like Cold War politics, Indo–Pak rivalry, partition of the sub-continent and presence of extra-regional power in the region are responsible for that. The emerging trends have figured in the last part. She has observed that the end of Cold War, 9/11 incident and globalization are largely responsible for creating a conducive environment for cooperation in the region. She has concluded with an optimistic note that the ongoing process of normalization of relations between India and Pakistan will enlarge the constituency of peace and cooperation in the region. ■

Notes & References

1. Inder Kumar Gujral, "South Asia and the World", Ramesh Thakur and Oddny Wiggen, eds., *South Asia in the World: Problem Solving Perspectives on Security, Sustainable Development and Good Governance*, New Delhi, 2004, p. 23.
2. Manzoor Ahmed, "Human Security: The Perspective of Children and Women in South Asia", Ramesh Thakur and Oddny Wiggen, eds., n. l, pp. 304–305.
3. S.D. Muni, "Democracy, Development and Discontent in South Asia: The Problems and the Issues", Gopal Singh and Ramesh Chauhan, eds., *South Asia Today*, New Delhi, 2005, p. 23.
4. For details see T. Y. Tan and G. Kudaisya, *The Aftermath of Partition in South Asia*, London, 2000.
5. In the Maldives, the President is elected through a circuitous process. According to this process, Presidential aspirants have to secure their mandate from Parliament, which puts forward one name to be endorsed or rejected at a public referendum. Under such a system the incumbent can stay forever. See for detail, V. S. Sambandan, "A Cry for Democracy", *Frontline*, Vol. 21, No. 20, September 25–October 8, 2004, p. 60.
6. Dushni Weerakoon, "Globalization and South Asia: The Role of Foreign Direct

Investment in Economic Development", *South Asian Survey*, Vol. 11, No. 1, January–June 2004, p. 3.

7. In South Asia, about 40% of the people are still living below the poverty line (of a dollar a day) which is even higher than the sub-Sahara African region. Around 43% are still illiterate and a majority of them are without even having an access to safe drinking water.
8. Mehbub-ul-Haq, *Human Development in South Asia 2001—Globalization and Human Development*, Islamabad, Human Development Centre, 2001.
9. Niaz A. Naik, "A Security Organization for South Asia: Mechanism for Conflict Resolution in South Asia", Ramesh Thakur and Oddny Wiggen, eds., n. 1, p. 278.
10. For a new perspective see P.R. Chari, ed., *Security and Governance in South Asia*, Colombo, 2001.
11. Kanti Bajpai, 'Beyond Comprehensive Security: Human Security' in Delhi Policy Group Comprehensive Security: Perspectives from India's Regions, Delhi, 2002.
12. For details see Shikha Malhotra, *Challenges to India's Security: A Study of its Perception and Nuclear Response*, Unpublished Ph.d. Thesis, Deptt. of Political Science, Jammu University, Jammu, 2005.
13. Rehman Sobhan, "The Twelfth SAARC Summit: Charting a Road Map for South Asian Cooperation", *South Asian Survey*, Vol. 12, No. 1, January–June 2005, p. 6.
14. Islamabad Declaration was adopted at the 12th SAARC Summit held in Islamabad from January 4–6, 2004. Along with the framework agreement regarding SAFTA, it also contains an Additional Protocol to SAARC Convention on Suppression of Terrorism, as well as a Social Charter of SAARC. See for detail, Mohsin Mohammed, "The Twelfth SAARC Summit: Quest For Durable South Asian Cooperation", *South Asian Survey*, Vol. 12, No. 1, January–June, 2005, p. 39.
15. R.K. Barik, "Fundamentalism in South Asia Politics in the Era of Globalization", Gopal Singh and Ramesh Chauhan, eds., *South Asia Today*, New Delhi, 2005, pp. 80–81.
16. Sonu Trivedi, "Politics of Regionalism in the World Economy", *India Quarterly*, Vol. 61, No. 2, April–June 2005, p. 96.

Section I
Dynamics of Internal Politics

Governance in South Asia: Problems and Prospects

"In South Asia, there is too much government but too less governance."

Baljit S. Mann*

South Asia is marching towards democracy in the post-colonial period. The classic case in point is the transition from absolute monarchy and military dictatorship to formal democracy in Nepal and Bangladesh respectively in the 1990s. Most South Asians are now citizens of democratic states and the region is gradually graduating to democracy. Currently, South Asia can boast of two long-standing democracies including the world's largest and one recently established democracy. The other countries either have a constitutional or traditional monarchy or an authoritarian regime camouflaged with democracy. It indicates the prevailing political diversity in the region in terms of the nature of the system of governance. Despite this, the governance in the region is not free from problems. In this research exercise, a modest attempt has been made to explore the problems and prospects of governance in the region. This paper is divided into four parts ranging from the present situation and problems to prospects and conclusion.

I

The Present Situation

Post-colonial South Asia is in multi-faceted and multi-dimensional political transition. South Asian states have failed to ensure rule of law to a large extent. Instead, there is rule of rulers. Laws are twisted and bent to benefit those who are in power. Their political systems are neither institutionalized nor sensitive to the concerns of the masses. The state, projected as a universal institution, could

* Reader, Department of Political Science, University of Jammu, Jammu.

not live up to the expectations of its citizens. For the majority of politicians, the state is a profit-making venture. They invest money during election time and thereafter they appropriate public money. Politics is no more the noble domain of public service, rather, it has become a profession for the greedy elements of politics. It has become a profitable business for politicians and a liability for society. Corruption has become the dominant code of public life in these countries. It has not only been institutionalized but has also acquired legitimacy and social acceptability, whereas the processes and institutions of governance are yet to be institutionalized. The concentration and personalization of power has coincided with the parallel erosion of institutions of governance.

As argued in *Human Development in South Asia Report* (1999), this region is one of the most poorly governed regions in the world. This report highlights the governance failures in South Asia on several fronts. The formal institutions of governance in the region often bypass the many unfortunate people who suffer from multiple deprivations on account of their income, religion, gender and ethnicity. The poor have not only been excluded from the benefits of growth, they have failed to gain political empowerment. Some of the worst consequences of their exclusion are seen in the high rates of crime, violence, terrorism and ethno-nationalism throughout the region. Besides, poor governance has not only posed a major security threat but put a question mark on the survival of states in the region.

Before discussing the subject in detail let me clarify that my perspective of governance is different from that of the Washington Consensus as well as the World Bank because my understanding of the ground reality prevailing in South Asian region is different from that of the World Bank. As a policy prescription, the World Bank recommends that wherever civil society institutions are weak, they need to be strengthened and the role of state needs to be limited to provide civil society greater space to act. Civil society is seen as filling the gap of the withdrawal of the state, in promoting market as well as democracy. Good governance agenda then underlines the curbing of the role of state and expanding the space for market and competitions[1]. My understanding of governance is located in the socio-economic and political context of South Asia. Rolling back the state can neither ensure governance, nor can create more space for civil society because it is argued that civil society cannot be a substitute for state. Of course, civil society can be a facilitator to the state for ensuring governance. Although the three actors like state, civil society and economy are involved in the overall process of governance, the state is in the driving seat and always enjoys a privileged position. Both economy and civil society are subjected to state regulation as well as control as a facilitator to the overall process of governance. However, they are also rationalizing the functioning of state from the perspective of the well-being of people.

II

Problematic Areas

The poor governance in the region is the accumulated effect of the various developments that have taken place in the region during the last fifty-seven years. There are various factors responsible for the prevailing situation regarding governance in South Asia. As the marginalized sections are alienated from the process of governance, state institutions have began to lose legitimacy and social tensions have become inevitable. Therefore, the problem of governance has to be located more within the state and less within the civil society and economy.

The State

Usually, to ensure governance is the prime responsibility of the state. Being a legitimate political institution, the state has to accommodate all constituents of society in the political landscape of the country. The problem of governance in the region lies in the emergence of a majoritarian and sectarian state, instead of a plural and multicultural state. In South Asia, this problem is alarming because of overwhelming number of the majority groups: Punjabis in Pakistan, Bengalis in Bangladesh, Sinhalese in Sri Lanka and Hindus in India. There has been a rise in majoritarian and sectarian states in almost all the countries, which has resulted in the rise of ethno-nationalism as a major problem of governance in the region. It is the majoritarian and sectarian state which isolates and marginalises minority group and identities, provoking them to react. The sectarian state also emboldens the majoritarian ethnic groups to exploit and oppress the minorities, forcing them to react[2]. Relationship between the minority and majority is not only the test of democracy but a yardstick to judge the nature of state in a particular society. Although the majority governs, it has to recognise that there are limits to the restraints it can impose on the minority. But the state in this region is suffering from the tyranny of the majority. Consequently, the post-colonial state in South Asia has failed to ensure distributive justice in society. The state in the region is soft on the rich but hard on the poor. In some countries of this region the state is democratic in appearance but authoritarian in nature, whereas in other countries, it is authoritarian and theocratic in appearance as well as nature. Besides this, the state has also suffered from a host of other problems like institutional decline, defective electoral politics, dynastic politics, erosion of democracy and democratic values, etc.

Institutional Decline

One of the major institutions established for the purpose of governance was democracy. This institution has been running through rough weather since its inception in the region. Despite the fifty-seven years' history of independent South Asia, all countries of this region do not have even formal democracy; the question of substantive democracy does not arise at this moment. A formal democracy is a genuine democracy so far as it guarantees, among other things, the right to vote and freedom of expression. Democracy here refers to more than the exercise of citizens' voting rights in elections or even the right to free speech. Elections are only the political manifestation of democratization in the wider social sphere. Democratization is a substantive appeal derived from the empowerment of the people, not as abstract legal citizens but as concrete and active agents capable of pursuing their interests with a measure of autonomy from entrenched structures of dominance and privilege[3]. Democracy in the region has failed to bring about fundamental socio-economic change that is desired in the interest of effective governance in the region. Democracy as expressed in the formalization of regular elections can and often does co-exist with the inherently authoritarian tendencies of the state.

Democracy in this region is either camouflaging covert or overt authoritarianism. The dominance of the narrow brand of elite reflects the concentrated nature of political power. Elites are few in number and comprehensive in their powers in almost all the South Asian states. In many South Asian countries, democracy is fast turning into an empty ritual. Elections are often the only bridge between the elite and the masses in particular and state and society in general. People continually feel excluded from the larger political process through which decisions that directly affect their livelihood are made[4]. Democracy in the region is operating in the feudal mindset and has acquired a plebiscitary character. The elections are not contested on the basis of well-defined policies and programmes. In every election, in each South Asian country, an issue is submitted to the people for their electoral verdict. In many cases, elections are not contested but managed. In South Asia, the challenge to the process of governance is weak democratic institutions. These do exist and elections do take place, but their performance is uneven at best.

India is a functioning democracy, but increasingly it is not well governed. The evidence of eroding political order is everywhere and the state's capacity to govern has declined. Along with this decline, order and authority have been eroding[5]. Pakistan's abject failure to institute even a formal democracy with regular elections at the national and provincial level provides the obverse side of the British colonial legacy in South Asia. Even after fifty-seven years of its birth, Pakistan is struggling to build a democratic polity. Authoritarianism did not allow democracy to flourish in the country. It took no less than twenty-four years to hold the first general elections on the basis of universal adult franchise in 1970[6]. The process of democratization has had both positive as well as negative impact upon the political developments in Nepal. Democracy appears to be functioning more as a closed clique of altruistic politicians. Viable political institutions with strong democratic foundations are yet to be developed[7]. The visible impact of democracy on the life of Nepalese society is yet to be seen. The political, social and economic situation of the country is yet to be transformed. The country is facing problems like rising unemployment, poor law and order, rampant corruption and ailing economy, which are threatening the democratic process[8]. Internal conflicts, like those in Pakistan and Nepal, are difficult to prevent without stability of strong democratic institutions. Democracy in the region is identified with the form of government only, whereas it is a broader canvas. Even democracy as a form of government is confined to rule of majority in which the minorities do not have any role to play. Narrowing down the domain of democracy in South Asia is a major setback to the whole process of governance.

The other institutions established for the purpose of governance are in bad shape. Legislature tends to be an arena for rhetorical exchanges rather than a vehicle for consensus building[9]. In South Asia, the responsiveness of the legislatures to the demands of people continues to be dictated by political exigency, personal ties and patronage. Legislatures are often perceived to be nothing more than a collection of those who have brought their way to positions of power[10]. In Pakistan, Bangladesh and Nepal with a long tradition of autocracy, originating in the unchallenged power of the chief executive, there were no institutional mechanisms of accountability where parliament itself functioned at the will of the chief executive. The executive in South Asia is neither very efficient nor effective in discharging its prime function of serving the people.

The civil service, another institution of governance, is also facing rough weather. The constitutional safeguards provided to civil services in South Asia have been eroded over a period of time, which has seriously damaged the public image of the civil service. A civil servant is now a rent seeker and exploiter who has no respect for the rule of law. The civil servant has ceased to be either civil or a servant of the society. Instead of resisting the excessive political interference in their working, civil servants have welcomed it for the sake of personal benefits. Civil servants and politicians have indulged in a marriage of convenience.

Consequently, the public interests and institutions are bypassed and sacrificed for the purpose of personal gains.

Politics in South Asia

Dynastic politics, is another factor that jeopardises governance. South Asian states have become the victim of dynastic politics. In every South Asian country, a few families dominate politics. Their hold on politics is so strong that even democracy has failed to dismantle it. The number of sons, daughters and widows that has been elected to power in India, Pakistan, Bangladesh and Sri Lanka suggests that there is something in the air of the subcontinent that lends itself to political dynasties. The recent elections in India have further substantiated this thesis. In these elections, the sons and relatives of various politicians got elected to the newly constituted House of People. The dominance of political dynasties is symptomatic of the widespread belief that political power is derived from patronage rather than performance. One can imagine the fate of governance in such a situation. The system of government is often used to enrich rulers and their family friends, rather than the nation[11]. Hence, the casualty is the well-being of the people or common good and governance at large.

Electoral politics has also complicated the process of governance in the region. Instead of improving the health of democracy in the region, it has made democracy majoritarian and plebiscitary in character. During elections, the people are mobilized on the basis of parochial considerations like caste, religion, gender and ethnicity, instead of genuine concerns pertaining to the performance of the governments. From the South Asian experience, it appears that electoral politics has also become a liability to the process of governance in the region. It is being shaped by considerations other than the common good. Nowadays, politicians in every country draw upon the business sector to finance their election campaigns and in the process incur political debts. These debts are repaid through patronage when in office or when in opposition by their failure to take business groups to task for particular acts of malfeasance. This rent-seeking between business and politics has served to fuel corruption and violence in the body politic of South Asia[12].

The role of political parties in the electoral politics is neither healthy nor constructive. They have polluted the whole electoral politics by infusing money and muscle power in it. The increasing role of money and muscle power initially resulted in the politicization of criminals, and the criminalization of politics thereafter. The electoral politics in the region has failed to ensure democracy within the party. Almost all the political parties in the region are governed by the principle of "Iron Law of Oligarchy" instead of democratic norms. The electoral politics neither ensures the within-party democracy nor prevents the mobilization of people on the basis of parochial considerations during elections.

Most political parties in the region are personality-based organizations. Therefore, the authority of leadership is rarely questioned within their respective parties and leaders are treating political parties as their fiefdoms rather than a democratic organization. The role of Nehru and Indira for the growth of Congress, of Jai Prakash Narain for Janata Party in India, Bandarnaike for SLFP in Sri Lanka and Z.A. Bhutto for PPP in Pakistan and Sheikh Hasina for Awami League in Bangladesh are only some of the illustrative cases[13]. The tendency to vest absolute power in such party leaders, without accountability to their rank and file, perpetuates their lack of accountability within their party when they assume state power and accounts for the weak foundations of the democratic system in South Asia. This move towards absolutist leadership, even within a working democratic system in turn contributes to the weakening of any system of accountability within the system of governance. Such a system breeds weak governance not just within the administration but also within political parties, which remain organisational weak and financially non-transparent in their practices[14]. The political process remained largely personalized. There is a disturbing tendency amongst both the state and civil society to bend rules and to operate outside institutions. This is how too much personalization instead of institutionalization brings about decline in governance in South Asian countries.

Political apathy has also been growing in the region. It is increasingly reflected in low voting percentage in every general election concluded in each South Asian state. Though people say that the governments are inefficient, incompetent and corrupt, the moot question is: who is to be blamed. The situation in South Asia is paradoxical. People's participation in electoral politics is neither active nor meaningful, rather they have developed the tendency of political apathy whereas they should now expect more responsiveness, better performance, more accountability and less incompetence and corruption from the state or government[15].

The confrontational politics has further damaged the system of governance in South Asia. Generally, the opposition is for the sake of opposition only. This region has sacrificed some of the positive features of governance because of its confrontational approach to politics, which has introduced a sense of uncertainty in the style of governance. Politics of elimination is another feature of governance in South Asia.

Another setback to governance in the region is corruption. It has eaten into the vital core of the process of governance. Consequently, every South Asian country is gradually becoming ungovernable. It has derailed the whole process of economic development in the region, which has serious implications for governance in the region. While talking about corruption in South Asia, Mehbub-ul-Haq argued that corruption occurs upstream, not downstream. Corruption at the top distorts fundamental decisions about development, priorities, policies and projects. In developed countries these core decisions are taken through transparent competition and on merit, even though petty corruption may occur downstream. Moreover, corruption money in South Asia has wings, not wheels. However, there is some capital flight in some other countries as well, a greater proportion of which goes into investment. Corruption in South Asia often leads to promotion, not prison. Developed countries often have a process of accountability wherein even top leaders are investigated and prosecuted. Finally, corruption in South Asia occurs with 515 million people in poverty[16]. This is not true in the case of developed countries.

Society: Erosion of Civility

State operates in the social economic context, which is always in a constant process of change. The social context is provided by the society, which is in the process of transition from traditional to modern. The state–society interface is taking place through civil society. Actually it is a modern concept and associated with the idea of the rational human subject. It believes in reasoned debate, accommodation and tolerance, and above all the idea of a universal public discourse which is forged across particularistic loyalties. Civil society is the home of this concerned individual, who cares about participation, debate and limiting the state and who cares about rights and mutual respect in society. At present this concerned individual is engulfed by influences from two spheres: one that emanates from particularistic loyalties such as religion, caste, tribe, ethnicity and linguistic affiliations. Two, the state which constantly seeks to speak directly with the individual and calls upon him to commit himself to great causes, such as war, national honour and prestige or defending the sanctity of national boundaries.[17] These two threats have eroded the civility of society in many parts of the world including South Asia which has not only created the problem of governance but also put a question mark on the survival of nation-state as a viable political unit throughout the world.

In South Asia, civil society is stratified both horizontally and vertically. Largely the bases of stratification are caste, religion, ethnicity, gender, region, language, culture and race. Civil society gives importance to associational life and construction of informal sector to harness the people's initiatives through community institutions for the benefits of society and governance at large. In this region, there are associations based on caste, class, religion, ethnicity and they pursue sectarian and narrow interests. Some associations having an authoritarian ideology are pursuing undemocratic strategies and goals, whereas others are using violence as an instrument of their policy. When the state withdraws and allows voluntary associations to step in, intensification of particularism and parochialism is inevitable. Associations based on caste, religion and ethnicity may like to strengthen their own solidarity to compete with another. Particularistic identities are dominating the social fabric of society instead of universalistic loyalty in the region. Consequently, society is being gradually hegemonized and its civility has become the major casualty.

Almost all the South Asian states are suffering from the phenomenon of hegemonization of society. Despite its heterogeneous nature, society could neither promote multiculturalism nor democracy as its philosophy as well as operational principle. It is not a hegemonized civil society but a democratic civil society that is required for governance because the latter can ensure a democratic state. The former is detrimental to the process of governance whereas the latter is a great facilitator for proper governance.

A newly emerged constituent of civil society is Non Governmental Organizations (NGOs). These are voluntary organizations committed to the common good and well-being of society. Their performance is better than the departments of government because they operate at the small-scale level and enjoy flexibility in their working. But the role of NGOs has also become controversial because of three main reasons. First, in this region, there is a mushrooming growth of these NGOs in the recent past. Second, there is hardly any small-level NGO committed to public and social good at the local level. Their size has become large and complex and their structure is bureaucratized. Third, the majority of NGOs are receiving funds from outside and are pursuing the agenda of their funding agencies. Therefore, the role of NGOs needs the scrutiny and regulation of the state. Of course, there are some NGOs doing extremely well but their number is small.

The social movements constitute another constituency of civil society in the region. Some of them are talking about the rolling back of state and the space vacated by the state to be occupied by the civil society to ensure governance in the region. They consider state an illegitimate institution. By arguing that the state is an illegitimate institution, the social movement might side with the global capitalist forces[18]. The failure of the state to deliver does not mean that the state should be marginalized or done away with. Rather, it needs to be confronted in order to bring the state back on track. The social movements as a constituency of civil society can play a constructive role in the reconstruction of state because state and civil society do not constitute two totally independent spheres of operation in the developing countries, including South Asia. Both can contribute to the development of one another. Regarding the role of civil society in the South Asian region, it can be argued that not all civil society organizations are good. The extremists and terrorist organizations that fuel violence and intolerance are also part of civil society. This is a common trait of civil society throughout this region. In Bangladesh, several well-financed NGO delivery systems are notoriously corrupt—exploiting donor funds without providing the services promised[19].

The socio-economic change in the region has brought awakening among the people. New social groups have entered into the political landscape of this region. Their expectations from the state are enormous. But in the absence of a well-differentiated and institutionalized polity, the state is unable to respond to the rising expectations of the people. Rather, it has resulted in the politics of bargaining, opportunism and blackmailing. Instead of healthy politics, there is destructive and negative politics.

The Economy

The economy is the third major partner in the process of governance. Growth of the economy in a balanced way is an asset to the process of governance in society. It should be in a position to cater to the needs of the society and state. At present, the South Asian economy is in the process of transition from a state-controlled economy to a market-friendly economy. Some of the South Asian countries initiated this process of economic transition in the 1980s, whereas the other started the same in the 1990s. This economic transition is popularly known as liberalization, privatization and globalization. The South Asian states are trying to treat the ailment of their economies through globalization.

The South Asian countries' approach to solve their economic predicament through globalization has further aggravated the case of governance in the region. These countries, while reviewing the cost and benefits of their development process, found that the system of governance, which heavily relied on unwieldy bureaucracy within the framework of public sector dominance resulted not only in rising costs but also in an inefficient economic system. In the process, the delivery mechanism and accountability became the victims. As the organs of governance became increasingly insensitive to the needs of the people, the only option left was privatization and a steady downsizing of the bureaucracy[20]. That was the context in which globalization was introduced in the region. As globalization is in progress for the last 14 years, the governance is yet to be improved in the region. It is argued that the benefits of globalization cannot be achieved without proper governance. The latter deals with a host of issues like the rule of law, accountability, transparency and democracy at large. In its absence, undesirable by-products of globalization and liberalization such as non-compliance, corruption, organised crime and drug trafficking may negate the benefits of these processes. Governance has always grown mainly from within each society and has corresponded to firm policy commitments on the part of the states[21].

South Asia's experience of globalization has not been encouraging so far. In fact, instead of resulting in any improvement in the people's well-being, which after all is what is conventionally expected of such a process, globalization has only impoverished people further. The benefits go to only a marginal section—the educated urban population. The first message is that at least half a billion people in South Asia have experienced a decline in their real incomes. The social costs in this period of globalization have been borne almost entirely by the poor. Essentially, in South Asia, the globalization process has focused almost entirely on market integration without improving the conditions of the majority of the people. Therefore, while capital has moved freely, labour has not[22].

Instead of strengthening the ongoing process of globalization has further eroded it. There are instances where national governments have been reduced to the status of clients of multinational companies investing capital, and of multinational and international banks financing vast projects of modernization. Therefore, the globalization project has revived nationalist aspirations and agenda. A major consequence of this phenomenon has been the emergence of ethno-nationalism in the multi-ethnic societies[23]. The crucial issue, therefore, relates to the capability of the national governments in South Asia to effectively deal with the resultant tensions, particularly in the context of sharp erosion in their command over political means and economic resources. The adverse impact of globalization project, if not dealt with in an effective manner, may make the situation worse, thereby creating a series of conflictual situations in an already vulnerable region[24]. Regarding the major power of this region (i.e. India), one study said that whereas the decade of the 1990s was being celebrated as one of a high rate of growth as well as one in which a fair amount of reform of the economy was taking place, it was also a decade when poverty was on the increase. There is considerable growth in unemployment, homelessness and increase in the frequency of natural disasters[25]. One can imagine the situation prevailing in the other countries of the South Asian region.

The process of globalization might have brought prosperity for a small minority but it has proved detrimental to the interest of the majority. The number of people living below the poverty line has been constantly increasing in the region, despite globalization. The economic globalization process itself may exacerbate this latent tendency towards Balkanization. As some regions and states respond more positively to growth impulses, and have a better social and economic base to enlist mass participation in the production process, they will be far ahead of the rest of the country. The disparity between 12 per cent annual growth rate in one region and 2 per cent growth rate in another may not at first appear to be democratic, but within a decade it will be very great. Such disparities among regions are unsustainable in a democratic society[26]. Their consequences for governance will be far reaching, if these disparities are not taken care of in time. The social cost will be very hefty if this trend is not arrested well in time.

III

Prospects

The prospects of governance in the region lie in the move towards democracy, whatever may be its form in the initial stage. One, there is a visible transition in the region from authoritarian regimes and absolute monarchy to democracy. Democracy is facing rough weather in the region but it is surviving against all odds. This is an achievement in itself. Of course democracy in South Asia will take some time to consolidate its roots and to develop a democratic culture for its smooth functioning. Two, despite the majoritarian character of state in the region, it has tried to accommodate the ethnic diversities to some extent in some of the South Asian countries, perhaps under compulsion. In South Asia, in almost all countries, there has been more than one culture. The South Asian societies are multicultural in their composition but do not adhere to the philosophy of multiculturalism in their working. The need of the hour is to promote multiculturalism instead of the culture of majority. Multiculturalism would bring about stability of political order and a better sense of belonging, resulting in better functioning of democratic institutions and governance at large throughout the South Asian region. What is required is to revive the state because it cannot be bypassed as far as governance in a society is concerned. Its role needs to be analyzed more carefully at this juncture. The idea of bypassing the state, although unintentionally, might become a part of the contemporary neo-liberal agenda of forcing the state to roll back in order to promote the market[27]. Three, the reluctant move towards the decentralization of powers in some parts of the region is a healthy sign as far as governance is concerned. Decentralization should not be for the sake of it. Rather, decentralization should be promoted with a purpose to ensure the participation of the people in the political set-up of their country. Four, the move towards empowerment of women in the region, is another significant development. The classic case in point is 33 per cent reservation to women in the local bodies in India. But this is just a beginning. Moreover, there are various other means to empower women in the region for example, education and employment. Five, the era of coalition politics in the region has made politics more broad based, representative and accommodative in the region. Although the coalition politics has a negative impact on the process of governance, it has provided the opportunity for diverse interests to participate in the process of governance. Six, the emergence of people's movement in the region is another ray of hope. There are movements for the eradication of poverty, protection of environment and women's rights and above all the movement against indiscriminate globalization. They are trying to project the marginalised people's agenda and interests in the mainstream politics on the one hand and are strengthening the role of civil society on the other. Seven, the changing regional scenario can be a great help for improved governance in the region. It will shift the focus of states in the region from inter-state conflicts to real problems pertaining to governance like poverty, unemployment, deprivation, development and above all people's agenda.

IV

Conclusion

In a nutshell, it can be submitted that the future of governance in South Asia lies in democracy not authoritarianism, multiculturalism not homogenization, accommodation not assimilation, decentralization not centralization of power, a secular not sectarian state, rule of law not rule of rulers, politics as a service not as a business, in institutional building not in institutional decay. Democracy can solve the various problems pertaining to governance in South Asia. Here, democracy does not mean merely a form of government but a way of life. It is not a formal but substantive democracy, which will empower the people and ensure their active participation in the process of governance. This will inculcate a sense of belongingness among the people and bring coherence in governance. Therefore, the need of the hour is to promote genuine democracy, not tyranny of majority in the garb of democracy. Apart from this, South Asia needs discriminate globalization, which suits its own requirements. Globalisation with a human face which aims at a humane society not market as an end in itself can serve a great purpose. It should evolve into an economy in which well-being of the people instead of profit should be the focus. A conducive regional environment can be a great facilitator for improving governance in the region. Multiculturalism, democratic state and human economy can improve governance in the region. ■

Notes & References

1. Kuldeep Mathur, "Good Governance State and Civil Society in India", *Man & Development*, 2002, pp. 73–74.
2. S.D. Muni, "Conflict and State in South Asia", *International Studies*, Vol. 40, No. 4, October–December 2003, p. 401.
3. Ayasha Jalal, *Contemporary South Asia, Democracy and Authoritarianism in South Asia: A Comparative and Historical Perspective*, Cambridge, 1995, p. 3.
4. Document, "Overview, Human Development in South Asia 2000: The Gender Question", *South Asian Survey*, Vol. 9, No. 1, 2002, p. 131.
5. Atul Kohli, *Democracy and Discontent*, Cambridge, 1990, pp. 3–22.
6. Ayasha Jalal, n. 3, p. 48.
7. S.N. Jha, "Democratic Developments in Nepal", M.S. Dharamdasani, ed., *Multi-Party Democracies in South Asia*, New Delhi, 2001, p. 118.
8. Sudhakar Singh, "Nepalese Democracy: Challenges that Lie Ahead", M.S. Dharamdasani, ed., *Multi-Party Democracies in South Asia*, New Delhi, 2001, p. 92.
9. Rehman Sobhan, "Reprioritising South Asia's Development Agenda: Role of Governance", Hasnat Abdul Hye, ed., *Governance: South Asian Perspectives*, New Delhi, 2000, p. 348.
10. Navin Mishra, *Poverty in South Asia*, Delhi, 2001, pp. 236–237.
11. Ibid., pp. 226–227.
12. n. 9, p. 345.
13. M.S. Dharamdasani, "Democracy in South Asia: Challenges and Achievements", M.S. Dharamdasani, ed., *Multi-Party Democracies in South Asia*, New Delhi, 2001, p. 28.
14. n. 9, p. 357.
15. Ashok Kumar Upadhyay, "Multiculturalism and the Crisis of Democratic Governance", *The Indian Journal of Political Science*, Vol. 63, No. 4, December 2002, p. 226.

16. HDC, *Human Development in South Asia: The Crisis of Governance*, Oxford, 1999.
17. Neera Chandhoke, *State and Civil Society: Explorations in Political Theory*, New Delhi, 1995, pp. 224–225.
18. Rajeshwari Deshpande, "Social Movements in Crisis", Rajendra Vora and Suhas Palshikar, eds., *Indian Democracy Meanings and Practices*, New Delhi, 2004, p 406.
19. n. 10, p. 284.
20. Mahendra P. Lama, "Globalisation and South Asia: Primary Concerns and Vulnerabilities", *International Studies*, Vol. 38, No. 2, 2001, p. 150.
21. Ibid., p. 149.
22. T. K. Rajalakshmi, "Globalisation in South Asia", *Frontline*, May 10, 2002, p. 75.
23. T. V. Sathyamurthy, "Nationalism in the Era of Globalisation", *Economic and Political Weekly*, Vol. 34, No. 33, August 15–22, 1998, p. 2251.
24. n. 20, p. 152.
25. Rajni Kothari, "Issues Before Indian Democracy: An Overview", Rajendra Vora and Suhas Palshikar, eds., *Indian Democracy Meanings and Practices*, New Delhi, 2004, p. 47.
26. Jayaprakash Narayan, "The Crisis of Governance", Rajesh Tandon, & Ranjita Mohanty, eds., *Does Civil Society Matter? Governance in Contemporary India*, New Delhi, 2003, p. 110.
27. Bjorn Beckman, "The Liberation of Civil Society; Neo Liberal Ideology and Political Theory in an African Context", Manoranjan Mohanty, Partha Nath Mukherjee and Olle Tornquist, eds., *People's Rights—Social Movements and State in the Third World*, New Delhi, 1998, p. 145.

Revolt in Post-Colonial Sri Lanka: Dynamics and Implications

Karori Singh*

The history of humankind has witnessed violent protest movements throughout the world. Such protest movements have been described as "destructive construction" or "locomotive of history". The Indian sub-continent being the cradle of the oldest civilization experienced a large number of revolts, which had diverse bases ranging from the socio-economic to the psycho-genetic. The question still remains as to why the collective identity called community gains violent orientation and uses revolt as a means to achieve its collective goals. There are many explanations theorizing the nature and character of revolt in the island-society. Social scientists often used the historicist approach and propounded the discrimination theory or conspiracy theory to understand the nature and character of revolt. Some others like psycho-genetic, phrenologist and geo-climatic theories did not find much ground in conceptualizing and theorizing the violent and volatile situation in the island society. There is hardly any study which applies an integrated approach for deducing an all-encompassing theory which might explain the South Asian social reality (includes both realized and potentials). The lack of such a study and analysis made it difficult to identify a sound basis for appropriate policy planning. In the past, social understanding and policy planning had been partial and uni-dimensional, primarily based on a discrimination theory and historicist approach while the other dimensions of acquiring social understanding received very scant attention both in understanding and policy planning, whereas the revolt got a momentum of which both civil society and state were victims and no theory was sufficient to explain the agony and anxiety of the region.

---

* Former Director, South Asia Studies Centre, University of Rajasthan, Jaipur.

There are several violent protest movements in the South Asian states. Most of these movements are using extra-constitutional means for achieving their objectives. They are called sub nationalist and ethnic movements, with a multiplicity of manifestations, objectives and causes. Such revolt is visible in every organization or group. The nation-state being a pre-eminent organizational set-up is also facing revolts of various kinds. The Sri Lankan society being the most peaceful in the past has recently turned out as the most violent in this part of the world. In Sri Lanka the main ethnic groups are on the path of revolt against state or each other. As a result, the civil society is so impaired that all the communities and groups (Tamil, Sinhalese, Muslims, etc.) are involved in a vicious circle of fear, violence, unrest, terror and torture. The ideology, organization and techniques of various kinds of revolt are well defined. However, society needs its fast reversion to the first principle i.e. the recreation and re-earning of the faith for a peaceful and prosperous order, for which such a theory defying experience of revolt in the island nation has to be conceptualized and theorized. Attempt has, therefore, been made in this paper to understand the nature and character of revolt in Sri Lanka. The analysis goes beyond the established theoretical postulates and draws certain lessons for other such plural societies in other parts of the world.

While explaining why the collective identity called community gains violent orientation and acquires a shape of revolt, one has to look at the micro-level—children's revolt against parents or individual revolts against collectivity, institutional structures, historical interpretations and cultural values. Perhaps one group in any nation-state is against the concept or institution of state but certain groups are aspiring to form their own state. When it is not allowed, they revolt against the existing scheme of institutions, rules, values and historical interpretations. This becomes a serious problem when no nation-state in South Asia is homogeneous. All have a plural character and face different types of protest movements and revolts. The ethnic and sub nationalist reassertion in India, Pakistan, Bangladesh, Sri Lanka is obvious. The two major nation-states—India and Pakistan—have celebrated the "Golden jubilee" of their "tryst with destiny" while all the South Asian states are facing a "tryst with revolt" in everyday life. The military, which is supposed to be used in case of external threat, is frequently being used in dealing with domestic conflicts and revolts. The gendarome role of military has its own implications and consequences. The question remains as to why certain ethnic communities resort to violence or for that matter "the ethnic community in itself"' turns out to be the "ethnic community for itself only". The very simplistic and journalistic explanation would be that oppression, discrimination, lack of channelization of grievances, political awakening and injustices lead to revolt.

Why is there revolt by an individual or community? There are very simplistic explanations: discrimination, oppression, injustices historical hangovers by certain communities, higher level of peoples' participation and consciousness or lack of it lead to revolt. The movement in Kashmir, North-east and Punjab in India, North, North-east and Southern insurgents in Sri Lanka, Baluch and Sindh problems in Pakistan and Chakma problem in Bangladesh are cases in point. Some people term these revolts as "people against state". However, the people in these areas are not against the state; in some cases they either aim at a separate state of their own or demand a legitimate role in the existing state or a greater say in the decision-making process. Whatever may be the case, revolt is the "order of the day". If there are injustices, oppression, discrimination, why do certain types of individuals and communities choose to revolt while others remain docile or prefer servitude? Certainly, oppression, discrimination, geographical integration and functional aggregation provide certain objective conditions for making revolt effective.

Quite often we use the term "nation-state" for some politico-administrative boundaries defined as state through which the world is structured. However, the boundaries of the states do not coincide with the boundaries of the communities called 'nations', therefore the 'right to self-determination' is an elusive proposition provided in the UN Charter unless the politico-administrative boundaries are sustained by the communities called 'nation'. If it is not possible, how can there be a world free of revolt?

Revolts in Sri Lanka are rooted in the policies pursued by the state apparatus. They have strong roots in areas which are peripheral to the developmental process and also reflect a lack of liberal democratic values. It is therefore, essential to impart democratic values and expand the developmental process for preventing revolt in future. Both ethnic intolerance and rationalist dogmatism provided impetus to revolts during the post-colonial period. There is no dichotomy between the two. Rather, it is a dialectics of the evolutionary process. Revolt is not an evolutionary change. It is an eruptive change and accelerated process, which precedes an acute crisis. Successful revolt is an abrupt occurrence and forcibly severs the institutional, legal and personal links between new and the previous phases. It is invariably aimed at destroying the existing legal framework. It therefore, implies the acceleration of normal process of change and intends the replacement of one set of dominant social ruling groups by another. All civilization and political systems exhibit the instance of revolt of one kind or the other.

Why do people revolt at all in Sri Lanka? Several propositions have been given in volumes like Fratricidal War and Dismantling of Democracy, Betrayal of Buddhism, Indian intervention in Sri Lanka, Only Man is Vile, The Broken Palmyara, The Tears of Terror, The Tamil Homeland, Collective Identities Nationalism and Protest in Modern Sri Lanka, etc. However, these propositions could not satisfy me. All these volumes explained the half-truth or illuminated one corner of the amphitheatres, either laying emphasis on the maintenance of order or justifying the revolt. Regrouping of the propositions advanced in different studies reveals that whenever a particular scheme of structures, cultural values and historical interpretations is imposed on a plural society without providing proper ventilation and channelization of grievances of different communities, a revolt is likely to occur. Still, there are several explanations of the post-colonial experiences of revolt in the island society. These explanations may be regrouped in several theoretical postulates.

Discrimination Theory

Both the Marxists and non-Marxists believe in this theory. While the Marxists lay emphasis on socio-economic contents like exploitation and alienation, the non-Marxists explain the political super-structure, inequality and dominance. According to this Theory, the Tamils have been discriminated against. Most of the government policies since the 1980s have benefited the Sinhalese ethnic groups. The policies regarding colonization schemes, education system, language and employment have discriminated against the Tamils. The colonization scheme initiated after the Land Development Ordinance of 1935 has benefited the Sinhalese. The Colonization Scheme has been intensified after the implementation of the major irrigation project—the Mahaweli Development Project. The scheme has substantially changed the demographic pattern, particularly in the North-eastern region. In fact, the Tamil continuity between North and North-eastern areas has been disturbed because a large number of Sinhalese has been allotted land in the Trincomalee area. The settlement has altered the demographic compassion and disturbed Tamil majority in this area. It naturally invited sharp reaction from the Tamil stock of population. Similarly, educational and language policies since 1956 have virtually blocked the educational avenues and employment opportunities for Tamils. Even the Chelavenayake–Bandarnaike pact has not been implemented sincerely.

Conspiracy Theory

Those who believe in the conspiracy theory, raise suspicion over the role of the USSR, China and India. The USSR and China inspired both the Tamil and Sinhalese revolt during the 1960s and 1970s and India started working on its hegemonic projects since the 1970s when Indira Gandhi attempted to impose an India-sponsored order on the neighbouring smaller South Asian states. It led to sharp reaction in smaller states, which resisted the intention of India's hegemonic project and therefore, India inspired the revolt in these states. It has often been accused of aiding and abetting the Tamils in Sri Lanka and the Chakmas in Bangladesh. This theory was dominant during the early 1980s when bloody violence erupted after 1983 riots. Apart from the international dimension, this theory has a domestic aspect. The extremist groups have assassinated several political leaders in Sri Lanka during the late 1980s and 1990s. Leaders like Vijay Kumartunga, Ranjan Wijeratna, Lalith Atulathmudali, A. Amiratlingam, R. Premadasa, Gamini Dissanayake, the Sri Lankan industrialist Uppali Wijewardane and several others have been killed in political violence. Often, it has been explained that the political leaders conspired against each other, which led to the killings of these leaders. R. Premadasa has often been accused of such conspiracies to kill his rivals.

Other theories like the revivalist theory which lays emphasis on glorification of the past and generates nostalgia of one community; the Gandhian theory which is highly moralistic and emphasizes truth and non-violence; the Geo-Climatic theory which stresses on impact of various climatic conditions on human behaviour; the Phrenologist theory which implies different conditions of the brain, and the Psycho-genetic theory which explains the human and social psychology are rarely employed in explaining the conditions of revolt in Sri Lanka.

Historically, the post-colonial development path can be explained in three main phases: the first phase (1948–77), the second phase (1977–89) and the third phase (since 1989). The first phase symbolizes the recorrection exercise in which the development strategy was aimed at correcting certain imbalances created by the colonial rule and, therefore, nationalization (maybe around nationalist myths) and redistributive policies were the main component of the development strategy. Such a strategy helped in achieving greater income parity across groups and sections. However, it has slowed down the economic growth. Moreover, certain policy measures directly affected the privileged sections of the society, as a result of which the regime rapidly lost the support of the privileged section. The poorer section could not provide the support and legitimacy in proportion to the losing support of the privileged. Although the regime attempted patrimonialism as a resort to the losing support of the rich, it could not help much.[1] The regime remained in a catch-22 situation and was ultimately thrown out in the electoral battle of 1977. This was the inception of the second phase in which the Executive Presidency system was introduced as a political calculation of President J.R Jayawardene to keep his political party (UNP) in power for a longer period. Apparently, it was considered in consonance with the objective of accelerated economic growth and, therefore the island nation became the first country to embrace globalization and liberalization in South Asia as early as in 1978. However, the development strategy has reproduced different types of imbalances during this phase. Moreover, the island remained gripped by the worst kind of terrorist activities and authoritarianism of the state apparatus during the decade of the 1980s. Such a situation has inflicted many wounds on the civil society and people at large. Eventually, the focus of development strategy took a slightly different turn, which became tangible through the 1990s.[2]

The latest and third phase is harmonization of the good points of the earlier two phases. Economic growth, removal of disparities and employment generations are considered necessary components of the development strategy. It was declared that economic growth must be achieved with a human face. How far the island nation has treaded the path and how to enter into the millennium is still a million-dollar question. However, the initial trends show that along with accelerated growth, disparities across provinces, sectors and groups are increasing, barring a slight improvement in curbing income disparities. However, attainment of parity is still a distant goal. Such a situation is proving to be a breeding ground for revolts, which in the past were caused by limited effort for social capital formation, imperfect federalization and centric development.

Diminishing Social Capital

There are four main ethnic groups in Sri Lanka: Sinhalese (about 74 per cent), Tamils (about 18 per cent), Moors (about 7 per cent) and Burgers (about 0.5 per cent). The latter two are scattered all over the island. They are not geographically integrated and functionally aggregated while the former two are concentrated in different geographical areas but are functionally disaggregated. The geographical concentration and cultural separation have inspired them to political action. Under such a historical background of the island society wherein the ethnic composition as a social reality has been transformed into a political force for secession over a period of time, because the parity of status has not granted. As a result of this and other disparities, a worse type of ethnic crisis erupted which had its roots in the policies pursued by the state apparatus and politico-administrative changes taken place over a long period of time.[3]

Historically, nationalism in Sri Lanka got political manifestation like in India as a form of a movement for independence and, therefore, may be called a progressive force. It was smooth because the alien art, culture, literature and even feelings were different from both Sinhalese and Tamil communities, which came together during that period. However, the seeds of suspicion were sown or cracks in such a unity surfaced during the later phase of the colonial rule. The last fifty years are in a way competition between assertion of the nationalism of the majority community with minority complex and its antidote, that is Tamil nationalism. The left forces had limited scope or space and remained an ally of one of these competing nationalities.

There was, by and large, a consensus for sharing of power among the ethnic communities in Sri Lanka but it broke down immediately after it had achieved independence. The Sinhalese ethnic group increased its representation in successive general elections leading to the pursuance of policies beneficial to the Sinhalese community. This reinforced 'Sinhala–Sri Lankan Nationalism' and proved counter-productive as it alienated the Tamil community. The Bandaranaike–Chelvanayagam pact of 1957 and Senanayake–Chelvanayagam pact of 1968 did not prove effective enough to curtail the feeling of alienation. Simultaneously, the social unrest among the Sinhalese also grew. Obviously, the social unrest among the Tamils and Sinhalese grew and the state attempted to strike a balance by introducing several policy measures with regard to language, education, employment, colonization and constitutional reforms about which much has been written elsewhere. These measures were perceived by the Tamil stock of population as discriminatory against Tamil community while the extremist elements among the Sinhalese expected more benefits through state policies.

The post-independence developments in the democratic polity and society in Sri Lanka have remained a competition between two different models of national reconciliation and economic development. The political forces led by the United National Party (UNP) reinforced the Western-liberal-democratic model with capitalist inclination while forces led by Sri Lanka Freedom Party (SLFP) and supported by left parties reinforced the national democratic model with its socialist inclination. The forces led by Tamil-based political parties like Ceylon Tamil Congress and Federal Party played a bargaining role as and when possible.

Apart from the democratic polity, there remained two extremist forces, one representing Sinhalese grievances led by Janatha Vimukthi Peramuna (JVP) which incited the first ever insurgency aimed at overthrowing the government in 1971 and since then it has been continuing its fight against democratic government, the other represented Tamil interests led by Tamil Five, namely, the TELO, (1974), EROS (1975), LTTE (1976), PLOTE (1979) and ERRLF (1980). In the beginning they aimed at having a separate Tamil homeland, but ultimately, LTTE became the sole Tamil extremist force to fight for division of the island on an ethnic basis. Compelled by internal strife and deteriorating economic situation, the managers of polity and economy initiated serious efforts for national reconciliation and economic restructuring which are still major challenges before them.

National reconciliation has remained a great challenge right from the final phase of the colonial rule, but it became rather acute with a serious threat of division of the island during the 1980s. In the past, the fight had been between the government of Sri Lanka and Tamil and Sinhalese extremists led by LTTE and JVP respectively. The JVP was virtually wiped out, howsoever temporarily, in 1989. Hence, the problem of reconciliation has existed between LTTE and the government of Sri Lanka. It has often been defined as Sinhalese versus Tamils in which Muslims till recently were either indifferent or were with Tamils on account of their linguistic affinity. But now a new dimension has been added to the strife. Hindu–Muslim conflict has also surfaced. A large number of civilians has been killed in sporadic incidents of fighting between the two.

In essence, the nation-state has been proved a myth and nationalism became a divisive force. The state-nation society failed to transform itself into a nation-state through the mechanism of state. Rather, the state has inflicted wounds on the nation precluding the social capital formation. This is a major cause of revolt. Moreover the process of state formation and pursuance of certain policies with regard to language, education, employment and colonization in post-colonial Sri Lanka have reinforced disparities and thereby deepened the suspicion and distrust among various ethnic groups, which already have international connections with Sri Lankan diasporas and also socio-cultural linkages across the borders. Under such a situation national consolidation became very difficult.[4]

Lack of Federalization

Historically three different kingdoms—Jaffna (Tamil), Kandy (up-country Sinhalese) and Galle (low-country Sinhalese) were brought under one centralized political authority and administrative unit through Collebrooke Reforms in 1833. It provided a way for the "unifying national consciousness" though it could not take a form or manifestation of strong freedom struggle and independence movement through mass participation, as has been visible in other British colonies. Therefore, Sri Lanka continues to remain and opted for unitary state even after independence in 1948 whereas other colonies opted for a federal-democratic-political-system as a national unity path. Social forces are still in desperate discontent because the unitary political system in Sri Lanka became an instrument of Sinhala–Buddhist nationalism and the federal polity in other countries is not cemented with "pluralist authority" and conciliar communitarianism. Therefore, sectional consciousness remains pre-eminent in almost all the erstwhile colonies-turned-independent "nation states". Such a sectional consciousness led to socio-cultural reassertion which is being strengthened by linguistic, ethnic and religious composition and demographic patterns. It has created a chronic crisis in most of the countries and generated violent secessionist movement in Sri Lanka. Such a situation has direct bearing on the peace, prosperity, freedom and empowerment of the people as well as survival, security legitimacy and strength (not only in terms of increasing coercive power) of the nation-state system in the resplendent island.

The island has separate politico-administrative units since the ancient period during which separate kingdoms, quite often hostile, were in existence. The colonial masters brought the island under a single politico-administrative unit but the traditional division could not be eliminated. The dormant and explicit existence of separateness has been reinforced with the introduction of the representative system. The first ever election under the Donoughmore Constitution was boycotted by the Tamil ethnic group. Subsequently, the demand for the parity of status was consolidated even during the colonial days. The policies of the successive governments in the post-colonial period have aggravated the traditional separateness and social division in the island. The representative system, which is based on reconciliation and liberal democratic values, has rather proved discriminatory.[5] Other ethnic groups have perceived it as Sinhala ascendancy. Moreover, the organization and support base of the political parties is based on ethnic lines. They are sharply divided in their programmes and political agenda. Such a sharp division is the result of wide disparities of various kinds and a challenge not only to the survival of democratic institutions but also the very existence of the island nation-state.

Administrative and structural dimension in which centralization/ concentration of power and authority has taken place resulted into lopsided development. Therefore, devolution of power is necessary for development administration. Such a developmental approach is likely to mitigate the crisis in Sri Lankan polity but practice disproves it. Political and functional dimension is

Figure 1

Administrative and Structural Dimension of Federalization

Period	Unit of Administration	Extent of Devolution of Power	Aims and Objectives	Results
Pre-colonial	Three separate kingdoms—Jaffna, Kandy and Galle	No need for devolution	Preserve the Monarchic feudal power	Continuous war for expansions of Kingdom
Colonial advent	Province as unit and centralized unitary system	No need for devolution	Administrative efficiency and control or bureaucratization	Perpetuation of colonial rule through excessive bureaucratization and administrative decentralization up to village level for administrative control
Donoughmore Constitution 1931–48	Province as unit and centralized unitary system	Administrative decentralization at the centre, vertical department control	Democratization at the central level	Process of marginalization of Tamils begun
Post-colonial 1948–87	District as unit	Collective responsibility administrative coordination at the centre	Democratization at the central level	Cultural revolution and ethnic polarization
Indo–Sri Lanka Accord	Province as unit but unitary state	Three lists of subjects under devolution, provisions for Provincial Council and 13th Amendment in the Constitution	Power-sharing within unitary state	Towards federalization and reopening of national question, controlled devolution.

Figure 2

Political Dimension of Federalization

Period	Need/ Demand	Steps/ Responses	Results
Colonial	For unified administration, growing political awareness and demand for democratic reforms and even federalism	Colebrooke Reform 1833, Donoughmore Constitution 1931 and land Development Ordinance 1935	Initially isolation of Kandyan Sinhalese and marginalization of Tamils after 1931
Post-colonial	Aggregation of Tamil grievances demand for redressal. Simultaneously Sinhala Buddhist Revivalism and cultural revolution	B. C 1957 and D.C. 1965 Pacts, Republican Ethnic Constitution 1972	Polarization leading to militancy and chauvinism, concentration of power in executive presidency
Tamil insurgency since 1983	Violent struggle for separate Tamil Eelam	Indo–Sri Lanka Accord 1987, provincial councils for power sharing, offer of devolution package by P.A. government in 1995 and stern military action against errant LTTE continuing	Sinhalese backlash under JVP which was crushed through military action, however,Tamil struggle continuing

Figure 3

Devolution Package of 1995

	Unit of Devolution	Extent of Devolution	Short Comings	Aims and Objective
Provision	Region/Province with "Union of Regions" instead of Unitary state	Extensive Devolution with Regional list containing 45 and Reserved list 58 subjects	No provisions for second chamber and electoral system at the regional level	Political reconciliation for bringing about peace, harmony, security and prosperity in the island and restoring credibility and legitimacy of the political system
Hurdles	Need for redemarcation of regional boundaries keeping in view ethnic concerns and developmental requirements	Overlap in the subjects in Regional and Reserve lists, there is apprehension of conflict between centre and region	Not easy to pass it through parliamentary select committee, 2/3 majority and national referendum	Conflict resolution appears difficult under the given highly polarized society

subtle in the ethnically polarized society wherein the political system is losing its credibility and legitimacy and thus crisis and revolt are continuing.[6] Both the dimensions are intertwined.

The above-mentioned aspects of disparities have reinforced, rather created political myths, which resulted in vengeance. It was further aggravated when power sharing became difficult due to majoritarian rule. The recent measures for devolution and creation of institutional structures could not prove palliative. So much violence and distrust has erupted that the social and psychological fabric of the society has been disturbed in the island once known as resplendent. Even the Tamil community has come to the brink of refusal to accept themselves as a constituent part of the nation-state and put forward unacceptable demands, which proved counter-productive, resulting in severe crisis and violence. Naturally, though unfortunately, the process of federalization and devolution of power in Sri Lanka has often been viewed in the context of prevalent ethnic groups, i.e. Sinhalese and Tamil. It has hardly been viewed or understood in the context of the process of bureaucratization to politicization or, to be more precise, democratization of politico-administrative structures, which in turn reinforced the need or to some extent consolidated the demand from decentralization to devolution of power (sharing of power) or federalization. The disparities are such that no European models prevalent in Switzerland and Belgium wherein different ethnic groups and communities live in harmony could lead to reconciliation.

Centric Development

Sri Lanka is a classic case of "Centric Development" which is reflected in inter-ethnic, inter-sectoral and inter-regional disparities of various kinds. The disparity in economic development in the various provinces in the country, therefore, is manifest in regional pockets of poverty and varying standards of living. Some areas produce more but remain poor because the surpluses are siphoned off to develop the centre by way of internal terms of trade, banking system and the marketing structure.[7] The unemployment problem is most acute in the western, southern, central north-western and northern provinces. These areas suffer from unemployment malnutrition and other connected problems in the areas, which generate most of the income to the country.[8] For instance, Nuwara-eliya having the higher estate acreage producing tea and vegetable is the heaviest poverty-ridden area. In the southern province (three districts—Galle, Matra and Hambantota) there is only one major industry (a cement packing plant at Galle). There are sixteen major rivers flowing to the sea but only the Lunugamvhera project has been launched for colonization purposes.

Another reason for the disparity in development between provinces is the irrational manner in which provinces have been demarcated with obsolete boundaries that do not meet the economic development need of today. There are arguments in favour of demarcating boundaries based on watersheds and for amalgamation of several provinces to make them economically viable, socio-culturally desirable and politically acceptable units. These lopsided economic development programmes since 1948 have brought about an imbalance in the levels of socio-economic development. It is now time to devolve power for socio-economic development of the regions through regional planning and provincial industrialization. Economic devolution will be meaningless unless political decentralization is available. Here provincial councils may prove to be a step in the right direction.

It is evident that GDP contribution by different provinces, the unemployment situation and income received by the poorest 40 per cent of the people are largely unequal. Details are given in Table below:

Table 1

Disparities across the Provinces

Provinces	% of Land area in 1996	% of population in 1996	% of income by poorest 40% in 1990/91	Unemployment % of total labour force in 1996	GDP Share 1995
Central	8.7	13.1	15.8	10.6	11.1
Eastern	14.9	6.9	-	-	3.9
Northern	13.5	7.6	-	-	2.5
North-Central	15.9	5.9	18.1	8.1	6.4
North-Western	12.1	11.7	14.7	8.3	10.3
Sabaragamua	7.7	9.8	15.9	12.2	7.6
Southern	8.5	12.8	15.9	14.8	9.7
Uva	13.0	6.3	17.0	9.0	5.1
Western	**5.6**	**25.8**	**14.5**	**12.1**	**43.3**
Sri Lanka	**100.0**	**100.0**	**14.8**	**11.3**	**100.0**

Note: Data for income distribution and unemployment in North and Eastern Provinces are not available.
Source: Various Reports of Central Bank of Sri Lanka and Department of Census and Statistics, Government of Sri Lanka, Colombo.

The average unemployment is 11.3 per cent of the total labour force. It varies in different provinces and is highest at 14.8 per cent in the southern province. The unemployment is also at variance on the basis of gender (male and female) and sector (urban, rural and estate sectors).[9]

The income disparities have been lessened after the implementation of the Samurdhi (prosperity) Programme. The poorest 40 per cent of households share increased to 15.30 per cent of the income in 1996/97.[10] This is clear improvement at the national level as it was 14.8 per cent in 1990-91 but there is provincial variation as well. The richest 20 per cent still enjoy more than half of the total income in the island. This denotes income concentration in the hands of upper strata of the society.

The figures in Table 1 show that the richest 20 per cent of households had 42.95 per cent of the income during the early 1970s. Its share has increased to 52.30 per cent of the income in 1986-87 and again it has come down to 49.90 per cent of the income in 1996-97. The period 1977-89 generated employment and increased economic growth but the increasing disparities have severely affected the estate sector. The figures indicate that 11.5 per cent of the people in the estate sector received 5.5 per cent of the income whereas the rural sector inhabiting 70 per cent of population received 63 per cent of income as against the urban sector, which inhabited 20 per cent of population and received 31.5 per cent of total income in the island. This shows income distribution in favour of the urban areas. It is evident that unlike in other countries where people in rural sector are the poorest, in Sri Lanka the people in the estate sector are the poorest because in most of the countries urban and rural are the two main sectors whereas in Sri Lanka the estate sector is a distinctive feature. However, in all the countries the urban sector always gained priority and prominence in government policies and, was therefore, better off than the rural sector.[11]

Disparities across households, provinces and even ethnic groups are still in alarming proportion. Despite the poverty alleviation programmes, the income disparities are continuing. Forty per cent of the households are surviving on 15.30 per cent of the total income notwithstanding the bold policy pronouncements in the country. This shows that the island is worse off in terms of income equality. Even the poorest countries like Bangladesh where 48 per cent of the people are still below the poverty line have greater income equality. Forty per cent of the population shares the 17.41 per cent of income as against 15.4 per cent in Sri Lanka, whereas the top 20 per cent of population share 44.87 per cent and 49.90 per cent of the income respectively in Bangladesh and Sri Lanka. This is a clear indication that Bangladesh, while being poorest, has better income equality.[12] Obviously, the position of income disparities is staggered in Sri Lanka while in the poorest South Asian country like Bangladesh the disparities are continuously reducing or static.

Similarly the per capita income is highest at Rs.947 in the Western Province whereas the average per capita income at national level is as low as Rs.708. The intra-provincial disparities are again an important aspect. For instance, the average per capita income in the Ratnapura district of Sabaragamua province is Rs.517 while in Kegalle district of the same province it stood at Rs.650.

Certainly the high per capita income has reduced poverty to a certain extent, as indicated in the Western Provinces where per capita income is highest. But the level of poverty is not so acute despite the regional and provincial variance in the impact of poverty alleviation programmes.[13] It is, therefore, obvious that per capita income at the national level is misleading in terms of widening disparities and inequalities. Such a situation helped in mitigating social tensions to some extent.[14] Moreover, the Western Provinces shares 43.3 per cent of GDP while Northern and Eastern provinces share 2.5 and 3.9 per cent respectively. This might have been the effect of ethnic conflict but in the case of other provinces like Uva, which shares only 5.1 per cent of GDP, the rate of the growth of GDP is also unequal. The rate of growth in the Western Province is 7.2 per cent against the national average of 5.5 per cent. It is a serious income and GDP disparity in the island.

There are also wide disparities in regard to contribution of various sectors in the GDP. The figures indicate that about 58 per cent of the GDP is contributed by the services sector and agriculture and manufacturing sectors each contributed around 20 per cent. The remaining percentage was contributed by mining. This shows that the services sector is growing faster than other sectors of production and thus the island is heading towards imbalanced growth. It should, therefore, concentrate and also have potential for developing the island as a centre of commerce and finance in South Asia like Singapore in South-East Asia.

The Impact of Revolt

Revolts in Sri Lanka are almost controlled by the coercive power of the existing state apparatus though the political settlement process is also continuing. In the case of the JVP the killings of the main leaders during 1988-89 brought it under control while the revolt by Tamil groups has also been weakened by internecine strife between different Tamil groups. However, the LTTE emerged as a strong group and is therefore continuing over a long period of time with little hiccups as and when the political process begins through peace initiatives of various kinds. Ultimately the revolt led by the JVP joined the mainstream democratic constitutional process but the revolt led by the LTTE still forms a separate legal political administrative socio-economic and cultural identity. It is aspiring to institutionalize and consolidate the new political order. Irrespective of the magnitude of the revolt by LTTE, the Sri Lankan society is not in regression.

Should it be called society in regression? It is so if one has theoretical logic and Western experience in mind. If the historical experience and diversified and pluralistic socio-economic set-up which forms the Sri Lankan social reality is taken into account, it is more a transition than a society in regression.

When civil society is extremely impaired, a perceptible decline in economic conditions and state does not have the capability and strength to repair the civil society and sustain the economic growth, then the whole society is on the brink of collapse, and can be called society in regression. These conditions also exhibit the violent civil strife and highly divergent perceptions and views prevalent in the elite stratum of society. Apart from these internal conditions, some external factors also play an important role. The society in regression in Afghanistan is mainly attributed to external factors while in Myanmar it is primarily attributed to internal conditions. Sometimes external factors also save a society from its regression as in the case of Sri Lanka where India played a positive role and halted the drift towards polity in regression.

The patrimonialism is responsible for erosion in the credibility and capacity of the state. The politically committed persons and groups were given favour in the authoritative allocation of resources and services, which were utilized for private gains undermining the wider social interest. Those who are excluded from the patrimonial network are suffering marginalization. Strangely enough, the statutory provision for the benefit of certain sections of the society, often for weaker sections, provisions for equal opportunity, influence of ascriptive traits and patrimonialism all in combination reversed the drift towards the society in regression, at the same time strengthening the transition.

The marked deterioration in the conditions and position of one ethnic group and highly restricted mobility both vertical and horizontal may impair civil society and reduce the credibility of the state. In turn, the impaired society and weak state may also cause deterioration in the conditions of a particular ethnic group and also restrict the mobility. Both the situations have a causal relationship and take the society in regression. Such an extreme does not exist in the Sri Lankan society right at the moment but the prevalent situation may push the society to regression, if some corrective measures are not taken in time. The rise of ethnic upsurge and their assertive perception may intensify the revolt.

The variegated record of performances and achievements of past decisions and policies proved to be of little relief and inflicted some sufferings in particular on the ethnic group in society. In sum, neither polity in regression nor revolt in proliferation but crisis will continue. The existence of revolt is due to exclusion of the ethnic group from the process of change, therefore the inclusion of all ethnic groups both in governing and production processes will certainly reduce the potential of the revolt and mitigate the crisis.

Conclusion

The revolt may be defined as the use of extra-constitutional means as an act against traditionally sanctioned norms of behaviour against laws of the society or act for enforcing own scheme of the things which is legally and normally not sanctioned at a particular point of time. In this way, it is an extreme form of dissatisfaction and disagreement. Revolts in post-colonial Sri Lanka are not isolated events as conventionally believed but a process in the long historical evolution and are therefore larger in scale, size and impact. They have a heavy toll of violence both in the revolt and response to it from the state apparatus. They have grown with strong external accelerators. They are responses to the policies pursued by the state apparatus and thus, certain groups are in complete defiance of the state authorities, in turn inviting very strong response from state authorities to bring them under control through coercive measures. ■

Notes & References

1. Karori Singh; "Wounded Nation Needs Healing: Nationalism and Nationality Movement in Sri Lanka". Paper presented in a Seminar, Nationalism and Nationality Movements in South Asia, 11–13 March, 1999, South Asia Studies Centre, University of Rajasthan.
2. Ibid.
3. Dayan Jayatilleka, *Sri Lanka Travail of Democracy, Unfinished War, Protracted Crisis*, Delhi, 1995.
4. K.M. de Silva, *Separatist Ideology in Sri Lanka: A Historical Appraisal*, International Centre for Ethnic Studies, Kandy, 1994.
5. Sisira Kumar Edirippulige, Ethnic Conflict in Sri Lanka: Obstacles to the Peace Process in Sri Lanka, Ph.D. Thesis, Unpublished, University of Auckland, Auckland, 2000.
6. Ibid.
7. Karori Singh, "Poverty Alleviation in Sri Lanka: Trends and Lessons", Paper submitted at CROP/UNESCO Workshop, November 7–10, 1999, Amman.
8. Ibid.
9. Department of Census and Statistics (1996), *Provincial Profile of Labour Force: Sri Lanka 1996*, Ministry of Finance and Planning, Colombo, p. 16.
10. Central Bank of Sri Lanka (1998), *Economic Progress of Independent Sri Lanka*, Colombo, pp. 39–43.

11. The application of the conventional development theories under the top–down approach merely used the rural sector as a major input to alleviate some socio-economic problems of the country at a national level. This gives only a short-term solution to the problem of the rural poor. Piyadasa Ratnayake, *Towards Self-Reliant Rural Development: A Policy Experiment in Sri Lanka*, Colombo, 1992, p.45. The most important class conflict in the poor countries of the world today is not between labour and capital. Nor is it between foreign and national interest. It is between rural classes and urban classes, so the urban classes have been able to "win" most of the rounds of the struggle with the countryside. Resource allocation within the city and the village as well as between them reflects urban priorities rather than equity or efficiency. The damage has been increased by misguided ideological imports, liberal and Marxian, and by the town's success in bringing off part of the rural elite, thus transferring most of the costs of the process to the rural poor. Michael Liptan, *Why Poor People Stay Poor—A Study of Urban Biases in World Development*, Great Britain, 1977, p. 13.
12. *Bangladesh; Economic Review*, 1997, Ministry of Finance, Dhaka, pp. 77–83.
13. D.M.P.B. Dissanayake, *Capacity Building for Fiscal Devolution*, Status paper on Fiscal Devolution to the Provinces, Chief Secretary, Ratanpura.
14. There seems to be, however, some relationship between the income levels and poverty ratios across provinces. For instance, Western Provinces has a record with the highest per capita income and lowest poverty ratio. Although the poverty ratios of CP and UP are relatively low, their income levels are also rather low; but the relatively high proportion of estate population in these two provinces, which is not covered by the income support schemes, could be one reason for these low figures. For many other provinces, ranks of these two indicators have gained somewhat similar values. W.D. Lakshman, et. al., Regional Economic Development in Sabaragamuwa Province in Relation to the National Macroeconomic Framework, Report by Sabaragamuwa Provincial Council in collaboration with Ratnapura IRDP, University of Colombo, 1998.

Democracy in Nepal: Bumpy Ground, Road Blocks

B.C. Upreti*

Nepal is among the few countries of Asia where the roots of democracy were sown more than half a century back, yet it is striving for a stable democratic order even today. Nepal's transition to a gradual democratic order way back in 1950 was rather quick and unexpected. But the recent history of Nepal bears testimony to the fact that the installation of democracy in the country on a long-term basis is rather an unfinished agenda. The unsuccessful years of democracy over the last one decade and the suspension of democracy during the last two years has raised serious questions regarding the sustainabilitiy of democracy in Nepal. Why is a stable democratic system not possible in Nepal? Where lies the fault? Is there any way out for the establishment of a broad-based democratic order in the country? These are some of the issues relevant in the context of present-day Nepali politics.

Struggle for Democracy: An Unfinished Agenda

In Nepal the quest for democracy was rooted in its struggle for the abrogation of the Rana autocracy. India provided a ground for the exiled Nepalese to plan and launch a movement against the Ranas. The Indian National Movement facilitated political training to the Nepalese[1]. It was obvious that the British model of liberal democracy became an ideal for the Nepalese who were struggling for the abrogation of the Rana rule and establishment of a democratic order in the country. The process of democratization began in Nepal soon after the overthrow of the Rana political system in 1951 when the coalition government consisting of the Nepali Congress and the Ranas came to function.

* Associate Professor, South Asia Studies Centre, University of Rajasthan, Jaipur, India.

The coalition was expected to work for the installation of democracy. However, it was not smooth sailing and the decade of the 1950s was marked by political instability and disorder. The parliamentary system was shortlived and abrogated by King Mahendra in December 1960 to establish his own direct rule[2]. Before proceeding further it would be necessary to understand why democracy could not be sustained in the kingdom during the early period.

Actually, two factors were important in bringing the 1950 revolution to an end. One, the dramatic escape of King Tribhuwan who foresaw restoration of his powers from the royal palace to the Indian Embassy in Kathmandu. Thus, before the movement could take root in the kingdom it reached a sudden end. Two, in the New Delhi Agreement of 1951, because of the treaty it had concluded with the Rana rulers, and also because of her own strategic interests in the Himalayan region, India did not favour total uprooting of the traditional political order. India's apprehensions were that a total uprooting of the traditional order might create political chaos, which would not be in her own interest. Nehru's 'middle way approach' might be justified in the then prevailing conditions, but not from the point of view of the growth of democracy in the kingdom in the long run. The net result was that the 1950 movement was reduced to a mere restoration of power of the monarchy. It did not help in the strengthening of democracy later on.

The Indian Memorandum of 8 December 1950, as well as the February 1951 New Delhi Agreement had emphasized the formation of a Constituent Assembly in order to prepare a new constitution for the kingdom, but it never materialized. Even in 1959 when the new constitution of Nepal was to be prepared, King Mahendra did not accept the demand for the formation of a Constituent Assembly and he himself promulgated the constitution. Thus, a basic provision regarding the promulgation of the constitution through a duly elected Constituent Assembly could never be materialized in the kingdom. This shows that the traditional elite was still assertive; that it did not subscribe to democratic norms and beliefs; and that it was interested in the democratization of the polity only to the extent that was essential in order to fulfil certain commitments on the part of the monarchy.

The political parties which played a leading role in the overthrow of the Rana regime and which were expected to function for the stabilization of the democratic system failed to act in an appropriate direction. On the contrary, the manner in which the party politics carried on, it only paved a way for the emergence of the royal authority. Due to the endless rivalry and scramble for power among major political parties and politicians, the goal of democracy was totally lost.

It naturally paved a way for the re-emergence of the traditional elite under the leadership of monarchy. The old land-owning class and the Ranas found sufficient opportunity to further their sectional interests. They united to defeat the reforms taken up by the Nepali Congress government. The army and the bureaucracy also represented the bulk of the traditional interests of society. It was very difficult to challenge these forces.

It should also be pointed out here that nationalism which took root in Nepal towards the middle of the 1950s was narrowly based. In fact, the traditional elite in its quest for reassertion of political power, found India's special relationship with Nepal a major obstacle. Hence it raised the bogey of anti-Indianism[3]. It soon became a major tool of new Nepali nationalism. The Nepalese ruling elite failed in developing a broad-based nationalism, which would have been supportive of democracy. Thus, the Nepali society lacked those basic premises which were essential for the growth of democracy.

King Mahendra was apathetic to the Western style of democracy[4]. He was of the opinion that the party politics was not suitable to Nepali conditions. He blamed political parties for the creation of disorder in the country and decided to play an active role in politics.[5] He said that party politics had brought about instability in the country.[6] In spite of his personal dislike of the Western democratic systems, King Mahendra could not take steps to immediately uproot the democratic processes in the kingdom. But his ambitions and the lust for power ultimately compelled him to take drastic steps such as the abrogation of the infant parliamentary democracy in December 1960.

After taking over power, King Mahendra moved towards searching for an alternative political order which would establish supremacy of the Monarchy and at the same time fulfil the minimum democratic aspirations of the people of Nepal. With this objective he appointed a 'Constitution Committee' to study the political systems of some of the developing countries, like Pakistan, Indonesia, Egypt, Nigeria and Yugosalvia[7]. These countries had established a political system which claimed to be the 'third world model of democracy'. It would be interesting to note here that in these countries the so-called alternative democratic political order was evolved by the rulers in order to legitimize their own dictatorial authority, such as Ayub Khan in Pakistan, Sukarno in Indonesia and Nasser in Egypt. King Mahendra's intention was clear. He wanted to evolve a democratic cover for his own rule. As a result, the partyless panchayat system was introduced in Nepal in 1962.

The main features of the panchayat system were the "party less" character of the polity, supremacy of the Monarchy and its guidance and control at all levels of the panchayat organizations. In a nutshell, the panchayat system established a highly centralized political order in the country under the leadership of the monarchy. The panchayat system, despite reforms, remained undemocratic and did not fulfil popular aspirations. On the whole it was a tool for the legitimization of the royal authority. Neither was it broad based nor mass oriented. Hence, the panchayat system faced widespread dissatisfaction and opposition since the beginning. The reforms in the panchayat system after 1980 referendum also failed to satisfy the democratic forces.

After 1987 there was a growing realization that changes were not possible in the panchayat system through constitutional means. Therefore, various dissatisfied political parties began to mobilize people for a mass movement against the panchayat system and restoration of democracy. The factors leading to a movement in early 1990 were clearly underlined in a statement of the Nepali Congress President K.P. Bhattarai thus:

> Today a new wave of democracy and freedom is sweeping the world. Despotic and dictatorial regimes have become islands in the ocean of the free world and their days are numbered. This is true of Nepal as well. Even senior leaders of panchayat system are now admitting publicly that the system has achieved nothing. The impact of the deadlock in Indo–Nepal relations has proved how hollow the claims of development made by the panchayat system are.[8]

He further stated that:

> The Nepali Congress remains committed to the goals of full democracy and human rights in Nepal. We have convened this conference to decide on the character and date of a nationwide peaceful movement aimed at the liquidation of the present party less or one party system.[9]

The 1990 democratic movement received nationwide support. However, when the movement was at its peak, King Birendra declared abrogation of the panchayat system and introduction of multi-party democracy in the country. This brought an end to the movement. The king constituted a Constitution Committee to frame a new constitution, which was promulgated in November 1990.

If we look at the two movements of 1950 and 1990 we find that:

1. Both the movements came to a sudden end.
2. The King himself took initiatives for Constitution making instead of constituting the Constitutional Assembly for this purpose.

3. The new arrangements which emerged after the movement ensured the continuation of the traditional political elite.

It can, therefore, be said that the democratic movement failed to bring about the appropriate conditions for the working of democracy and its sustenance from a long-term perspective. Hence, every time there has been assertion by the traditional political elite after a certain period of installation of the democratic political order.

Working of New Democracy: Instability and Disorder

The new democratic order came into operation in 1991. But its functioning has not been smooth and healthy. There are many problems and issues. One of the major problems since democracy came into operation in Nepal has been the shortlived governments. It has led to political instability and questioned the ability of the government to govern the country. The first elected government of the Nepali Congress was formed in May 1991. It was a razor-thin majority government under the leadership of G.P. Koirala. The general election and the process of formation of the government were badly affected by the factionalism within the party. Soon enough the K.P. Bhattarai faction of the party began to criticize the Koirala government. The United Marxist Leninist Party (UML), which was looking for an opportunity to topple the government joined the dissatisfied members of the Bhattarai faction of the Nepali Congress. Before the Koirala government could take concrete steps to implement its reforms programme it began to face several problems. The UML and the Unity Centre opposed the government on several issues. The leadership clashes and intra-party disputes brought party and the government face to face. Koirala was constrained to step down.

In the mid-term elections of November 1994, none of the political parties secured a majority in the House of Representatives. The UML government tried to launch a number of populistic programmes. But the actual objective of the UML government was to strengthen its position among various sectors of society as well as in different bodies of the government. Despite being a minority government, the UML took course to politicization of media, educational institutions, higher positions in the administration and thus invited opposition from NC, RPP and NSP together. The minority government collapsed after nine months. It also became a victim of the oppositional politics and the discontent within the party. Man Mohan Adhikari, the UML PM resigned in mid 1995 and recommended the dissolution of the parliament as Koirala had done in 1994. However, Adhikari's recommendation was rejected in the court and the parliament was revived in September 1995. The Nepali Congress formed the government under the leadership of Sher Bahadur Deuba with the support of the NDP and NSP. This time the Nepali Congress decided to hand over Prime Ministership to the second rank leadership, as there were strong differences between the top leaders of the party. It was then that an era of unsuccessful coalition governments began in Nepal. Sher Bahadur Deuba faced strong opposition from his own party as well as from the UML. Although Deuba was a compromise candidate between the top leadership of the party, he was closer to K.P. Bhattarai. Hence the Koirala group was not happy with the government. The Deuba Government was charged with corruption and inefficiency. The Maoist insurgency had begun by this time and his government was also criticized for being unconcerned about the Maoist problem. The Deuba Government survived a no-confidence motion in March 1996 but had to step down in March 1997.

The UML-NDP and NSP formed another coalition government in March 1997 under the leadership of Lokendra Bahadur Chand of NDP. This coalition could not survive more than six months. It was replaced by another coalition of UML-NDP-NSP under the leadership of Surya Bahadur Thapa of NDP. Interestingly, both Lokendra Bahadur Chand and Surya Bahadur Thapa enjoyed Prime Ministership with only 19 seats in parliament. The Thapa government faced strong opposition from the Nepali Congress and had to quit in April 1998.[10]

The Nepali Congress began to search for possibilities for the formation of a new coalition government. Incidentally, towards the end of 1997, after the local bodies' elections, the UML had split with 40 MPs under the leadership of Bam Deo Gautam and C.P. Mainali to form a new political party called CPN-ML. The Nepali Congress and the ML reached an understanding to form a coalition government. While the NC was in search of a new partner, the ML wanted to enhance its position against the UML. G.P. Koirala became Prime Minister. The understanding was that the Prime Ministership would go to the other coalition partner after six months. In December 1998 Koirala refused to hand over Prime Ministership to the ML. The two partners also developed differences over several other issues. Koirala resigned and fresh elections were declared for May 1999. The NC-ML-NSP formed a national government till the elections were held.

The coalition government was a bitter experience in Nepali politics. It resulted not only in political instability but reduced the prospects of strengthening of democracy in the country. In the 1999 elections the Nepali Congress projected K.P. Bhattarai as the Prime Ministerial candidate. K.P. Bhattarai won the first election of his life and as per internal understanding of the party he became the leader of the parliamentary party. Not much later the

Bhattarai government began to face criticism from its own party cadres. It was charged for ineffectiveness, indifferent attitude towards the Maoist problem, etc. K.P. Bhattarai had to resign in February 2000. Thus, the pressure tactics of the Koirala faction proved to be successful. But the things were not as smooth for Koirala as these had been earlier. Sher Bahadur Deuba also claimed the leadership of parliamentary party. The leadership question had to be resolved through a voting, which went in favour of Koirala who became Prime Minister in March 2000. Koirala's Prime Ministership was marked by a number of developments. His government was charged with widespread corruption. The Maoist problem had aggravated by this time. The Koirala Government could not take concrete steps towards the resolution of the problem. On 1 June 2000 King Birendra and his whole family was assassinated. The Koirala government was accused for being cool on this issue. Koirala was also targeted by the opposition political parties for the above-stated reasons.

Koirala had to resign in July 2001 and Sher Bahadur Deuba took over as Prime Minister. Deuba seemed serious to resolve the Maoist problem but the attempts made by him bore no results. It led to the declaration of the state of emergency in Nepal in November 2001. The army was called into bring the Maoists under control. The emergency was extended in February and May 2002. In May 2002 Deuba resigned and Parliament was dissolved. The fresh elections were to be held in November 2002 on a phased basis. But before that Deuba was removed from the Prime Ministership in October 2002 by King Gyanendra and a new phase of installation of a government by the monarchy began subsequently. It was yet another blow to democracy in Nepal as Parliament was suspended and the monarchy brought in his own man as Prime Minister. However, the instability of the government continued.

Monarchy Overpowers Democracy

In October 2002 Deuba had suggested that due to the Maoist insurgency it was not possible to hold general elections in time. In fact, it was being suggested that the elections could be postponed for some time. But the king did not agree to the Prime Minister's suggestions and dismissed him. After the dismissal of the elected government King Gyanendra nominated Lokendra Bahadur Chand of NDP as Prime Minister with a small cabinet. The larger parties like Nepali Congress and the UML did not join the government. The king himself assumed responsibility to revive the democratic process. However, since then neither were elections held nor was the dissolved parliament revived. The main political parties were also kept out of the mainstream politics. The political parties demanded the revival of the parliament but they failed in making any united efforts towards the reinstallation of democracy in the kingdom.

The monarchy on the other hand has tried to consolidate its authority. During the middle of 2003 the king brought the Maoists to the negotiation table but the parties could not reach any agreement as the Maoists were not prepared to give up their earlier demands and the monarchy was not prepared to accept the same. The monarchy wanted to take the credit for solving the Maoist problem in which it failed. Nevertheless, it succeeded in the marginalisation of political parties. The failure in talks with Maoists lead to the departure of Lokendra Bahadur Chand and Surya Bahadur Thapa became Prime Minister. It is interesting to note that the king relied on the old guards of the panchayat era. Both Chand and Thapa had been the strong leaders of the panchayat era. Because of their pro-panchayat image both Chand and Thapa could not seek support from various political parties. Even their position in their own party was not very strong. Demands were raised in the party in the beginning of 2004 to expel Prime Minister Surya Bahadur Thapa from the party. However, in May 2004 Thapa resigned from the Prime Ministership due to strong pressure from political parties[11].

It is clear that there has been a resurgence of the powers of the monarchy. The political parties failed in providing stability to the government and as a result they opened doors for political assertion by the monarchy. It is significant to note that in a statement in February 2004 King Gyanendra said that the monarchy would not remain a silent spectator to people's suffering. He further held that the days of the monarchy being seen but not heard were gone. The king cannot remain a silent spectator of people's tearful faces. It clearly shows that perhaps in the prevailing political conditions in Nepal the monarchy was looking for an assertive role in politics.

The royal coup of February 2005 not only reversed the democratic process in Nepal but also signified that the traditional political forces are still important and capable of changing the course of politics in Nepal. After the coup the monarchy is trying to consolidate its powers. There is an attempt to activize the panchayat leadership and seek its support. King Gyanendra has also attempted to control the media, democratic leadership and the intelligentsia who have been considered a supporter of democracy. The fact remains that the king has so far not succumbed to the domestic and international pressure to restore democracy. The point is that it would require a strong internal pressure on the king, which is possible through unifications of the democratic forces. Therefore, much would depend on the political parties, their polarization and commitment to democracy. But one has to accept that the Nepali democracy would continue to receive threats from the traditional political elite in the present political set-up of Nepal.

Divided Parties Weaken Democracy

Political parties have been a divided lot in Nepal. The Nepali Congress, which was expected to take the responsibility to give the country a resolute, efficient and progressive government and thus provide a stable footing to democracy, is suffering from factionalism, dissensions and groupism. The party leadership has been divided on several issues. It appears that there has been a conflict of personal ambitions.

The Koirala Government had to quit in mid 1994 due to the opposition of a group of its own party MPs. When Sher Bahadur Deuba became Prime Minister, it was believed that the new leadership would be able to keep the party united. But Deuba too had to face opposition from the Koirala group. The Deuba Government also faced the same kind of internal opposition as earlier. The group politics within the party was again instrumental in the change of leadership of the government in March 2000 and 2001. Thus, it can be said that the Nepali Congress is a highly faction-ridden party and the incumbent governments of the party have to pay heavily for it. Due to strong groupism the Deuba faction got separated from the party in 2003 to form a new party.

It is not the Nepali Congress alone which is faction-ridden. The UML party got separated towards the end of 1997, when its hardcore faction formed the CPN-ML. The Nepal Democratic Party, which at the time of its formation represented the former panchayat and other traditional elite, got divided into Chand and Thapa groups. Nepal Sadbhavana Party has also been suffering from internal dissensions and factionalism.

Apart from intra-party groupism and leadership clashes the inter-party conflicts too have been prominent. The main political parties were opposed to each other on core issues due to their rivalries and politics of power. The political parties lack consensus on national issues. Their attitude and role has been rather opportunistic. The oppositional role of various political parties has been based on their strategies to hold power instead of following any principles.

It can be argued that the political parties have not been able to play their role fairly. They lack inner strength, strong social base, ideological commitment, strong and far-sighted leadership and a clear approach and perspective on national issues. It is true that political parties remained inoperative during the long period of panchayat rule. Hence, their organizational base has been weak but what about their commitment to democracy, ideology and development? In fact, these issues have become insignificant and the political parties seem to be power-oriented only.

Leadership Clashes and Decline of Ideology

A strong leadership is an asset to the growth and institutionalization of democracy because it provides the necessary direction to polity and ensures democratic governance. In Nepal, however, the democratic elite has not been able to provide a national leadership after B.P. Koirala. The top leaders are not acceptable to their own party factions. They have been accepted as party leaders or as Prime Minister only as compromise candidates. In the Nepali Congress the earlier leadership was divided between Ganesh Man Singh, K.P. Bhattarai and G.P. Koirala. After the death of Ganesh Man Singh the two contenders have been K.P. Bhattarai and G.P. Koirala. At the level of second rank leadership as well, there is a strong contest. Communist leadership is also faction-ridden. After the death of Man Mohan Adhikari there are many contenders for party leadership. The Nepal Democratic party is divided on the question of leadership. The leaders of two factions are Lokendra Bahadur Chand and Surya Bahadur Thapa, while the second rank leadership has also been assertive on many occasions.

The various political parties have been striving for power and so are its leaders. As pointed out earlier, parties and leaders remained out of the political scene for a long time. This also resulted in their ineffectiveness and a narrow social base. The democracy has opened avenues for the fulfilment of their political aspirations. While they have not been able to strengthen their organizational and social base, the lust for power has increased. As a result, political leaders and parties have tried to seek power by any means. The coalition between UML and NDP and NC and NDP are examples of such a lust for power and position.

There has also been a sharp erosion of the ideological bases of the political parties in Nepal. This has adversely affected the inculcation of democratic values within the society. Most of the political parties lack a clear-cut programme and even if it is there, they have hardly any time to implement it or to struggle for it. The Nepali Congress, which was known for its ideology of democratic socialism at one time has moved far away from it. The party remained divided between reconciliationists and those who believed in democratic movement. Similarly, the communists were also divided between reconciliationists and revolutionalists. It can be said in the context of most of the political parties that the ideology has taken a back seat and power politics has acquired prominence[12]. It is indeed a serious challenge to all the political parties as to how to strengthen their social and ideological bases.

Corruption

Corruption is yet another factor which has vitiated the political atmosphere in Nepal and created hurdles in the smooth functioning of the government. The various ministers, bureaucrats and important government functionaries including the Prime Minister of the country have been charged with corruption. It is true that corruption is not a new phenomenon in the context of developing societies but in a highly divided and faction-ridden political context corruption becomes a highly politicized issue. In Nepal the issue of corruption has been significant in the sense that it has provided an edge to the conflicting political parties and leaders. The party cadres have even targeted their own leaders for corruption charges and malpractices in politics. The opposition parties have found corruption a powerful issue in the parliament to take the governments of the day to task. Thus, it has been an important factor in contributing to governmental instability and political disorder.

Impact of Maoist Insurgency on Democracy

The failure of the successive governments to effect change in the socio-economic environment and meet minimum needs of the people and its inability in providing a stable political order has led to a situation in which Nepal is facing insurgency organized by the radical communists. These hardcore Maoists have been demanding overthrow of the constitutional monarchy and establishment of people's democracy to which they call Naulo Janbad (new democracy). However, during the initial phase they took part in the parliamentary process. The organisation of the Maoists, the United People's Front (UPF) participated in the 1991 general elections and fought on seventy seats and won nine seats. But gradually the hardcore Maoists began to realize that it was only through a violent movement that a total social change could be possible in the country.

It was during the mid-1990s that the Maoists began to indulge in violent activities against the governmental establishments and the Maoist terrorism became a regular feature after 1996. It seems that the Maoists have taken advantage of infighting of the political parties, weak and instable governments and the inability of the subsequent governments to realize popular needs and aspirations. The Maoist insurgency first erupted in three districts of western development region of Nepal, namely, Rolpa, Rukum and Jajarkot. But gradually it has spread to nearly two-third of the country. It is believed that nearly 8000 people have lost their lives due to the insurgency. Their victims have been party workers, political representatives, businessmen, officials and common men.

The Maoist terrorism has flared up in Nepal in the background of the communist movement, which took root in the country as early as 1948-49[13]. The communists never liked the compromising attitude of the leaders and parties towards the monarchy. They were unhappy with the democratic political parties' reaching an understanding with the royalists and surrendering to the feudalistic forces. They demanded a Constituent Assembly as early as 1951. During the days of panchayat rule in Nepal it was the communists who never stopped their underground activities against the authoritarian forces and thus nurtured some of the areas where they have a strong hold in the context of Maoist insurgency.

The communists joined hands with the Nepali Congress and other democratic forces to ouster the panchayat rule in 1990. But they got frustrated with the functioning of the constitutional monarchy. A Maoist leader stated in an interview thus:

> Our war is aimed at destroying the current regime, which is based on two hundred years old coalition between feudalism and imperialism and to establish a people's republic. During this long period political systems have changed with different name coming into existence but the fundamental structure of the regime remains the same.[14]

It may also be noted here that the Maoist insurgents have gradually expanded their social base. In fact, the one time left-oriented intellectual movement limited to upper caste has now expanded to different caste groups. Even the women have been participating in terrorist activities[15]. It shows that the movement has expanded socially as well as geographically.

It has indeed become a big challenge to the successive governments of Nepal. However, the government has looked upon it as a law and order problem and used force to bring it under control. In May 1999, when K.P. Bhattarai became Prime Minister of Nepal he constituted a committee to resolve the Maoist problem under the leadership of Sher Bahadur Deuba during whose regime the problem had actually flared up. This committee could also not suggest any solution to the problem of insurgency. Various rounds of talks with the Maoists in 2002 and 2003 failed due to the differing perceptions of the two groups.

It can be said that the Maoist problem has to be looked at in the broader perspective of socio-economic problems and the basic causes behind popular discontent. Only then can the problem be resolved. It is true that in a backward and politically fragile country like Nepal, an insurgency is a serious setback. It has caused private and public losses. The country is in a state of uncertainty and the people feel insecure. Hence, the Maoist movement is an unwanted and unfortunate development. More unfortunate is the failure of the government in finding a solution to the problem. But some of the issues raised by the Maoists need serious consideration. The demand for a Constituent Assembly seems to be the core of the whole issue of Maoist insurgency in Nepal. Similarly the question of declaring Nepal a Republican state is important. The demand for a Constituent Assembly in Nepal is as old as the resurgence of democracy. Since then, this issue has been raised on many occasions. Is it not that by conceding the demand of Constituent Assembly the problem of Maoism as well as the problem of democracy in Nepal can be resolved to a large extent? It is for the ruling elite of Nepal to take these considerations into account. It may also be pointed out here that the issues of socio-economic development with which Maoists are also concerned can be taken up only when the political uncertainty is over and a broad-based democratic political order starts operating. Hence, in the present context, resolution of the Maoist problem is a political question. It is too near too far to a solution. There can be no doubt that the present situation may take Nepal to a difficult stage. Nepal is already developing into an anarchic state. The state power has failed in controlling the Maoist insurgency by the use of power. The fear of Maoists is spreading rapidly in the society. Now even the elected members of the local government bodies are constrained to resign due to fear of Maoists. The king's initiatives to resolve the Maoist problem have also failed. It is also a fact that in the present situation unless the Maoist problem is resolved, democracy and political stability cannot be given a strong footing in Nepal. Therefore, the Maoist problem needs urgent attention from all corners of Nepalese society and polity. And some of the issues raised by them need wider consideration and a public debate. It can be said that the Maoist problem has adversely affected the functioning of the governments there by adding to instability, aggravated the law and order situation, weakened the state and opened doors for the militarisation of state as well as encouraged external interference.

It is the political parties who have to take a lead in resolving the present tangle. Fortunately Nepal has political parties, groups and leaders who can be and are in a position to shoulder this responsibility. What is required is that they realize their responsibilities and play a constructive role. It is possible only when all the political parties agree to a one-point programme to re-establish democracy. The political parties alone can resolve the Maoist question and reach an understanding with them on broad political issues. It has to be kept in mind again that the Maoist issue can be resolved only through a political settlement. The parties have to understand that their own future lies with democracy. During all these years political parties have remained confined to wielding of power which has led to leadership clashes, intra- and inter-party conflicts and governmental instability. It is necessary that they concentrate on building their social base because in any struggle for democracy their strength would be their organizational base.

Developmental Issues and Constraints

The developmental issues bear serious challenges to democracy and good governance in Nepal. It is a well-known fact that Nepal is among the least developed countries of the world. For a long time the Nepali rulers followed a policy of controlled modernization. They allowed developmental process only to the extent necessary for their own political survival.

The perpetuation of the traditional political elite also resulted in the continuation of the feudalistic nature of the society. In fact, the land-owning feudal class was not only retained by the politico-administrative structures that emerged in the post-1950 era, it also assumed new roles so as to gain sustenance. The traditional political elite and the feudal class had convergence of interest, hence they supported each other. As a result neither was the political power broad-based and representative nor could there be equitable distribution of economic resources and benefits.

Nepal's perpetual problems have been a weak infrastructure, scarce capital resources, technology and trained manpower. This has affected the developmental process adversely. Nepal's heavy reliance on foreign aid has not been fruit-bearing enough due to the vested interest of the ruling elite and the bureaucratic elite representing the traditional caste-religion-class hierarchy.

Poverty and underdevelopment have been the main characteristics of contemporary Nepali society and economy. There is a large number of people and regions still struggling for basic needs. Poverty, unemployment and inequalities in income distribution is the major challenge for the Nepali ruling elite. With the dawn of democracy in the country it was expected that these problems would be taken care of by the government. However, due to governmental instability and disorder these problems have remained unattended. The people are frustrated with the governments' ignoring their expectations. It may be pointed out here that the poor economic conditions of the larger sections of the society have been one of the major reasons for the rise of Maoist insurgency in Nepal. It is a hard fact that the democratic government has failed in delivering goods to the people and as a result, they lacked feedback from the masses.

Ethno-Regional Issues

Ethnic issues are also becoming significant in Nepal's political dynamics after 1990. The Nepali rulers tried to lay the foundation of a monolithic state in Nepal. Various tribal and non-Hindu communities or groups were brought into the fold of Hinduism. These ethnic groups remained contained so long as the political order was authoritarian. But with decline in democracy there is a resurgence of ethnic identity in Nepal. Various Mangolian communities are asserting their distinct identity and demanding recognition or representation in the politico-administrative and socio-economic structures. They have indeed posed a challenge to the Brahmin–Chettari–Newar domination of Nepali polity and society. The ethnic communities have stressed upon:

1. Equitable representation in politico-administrative structures.
2. Recognition to their ethno-cultural identity.
3. Equitable distribution of economic resources and goods.

The ethnic issue is likely to become a significant factor in Nepali politics. The regional factor has been important in Nepal ever since the beginning of the democratic era. The two geographic regions of Nepal, Hills and the Terai not only represent two distinct geographical identities but also two societies, cultures and economies. The transportation and communication barriers and the perception of the ruling elite kept the two regions isolated from each other for a long time. Since Terai was an underdeveloped region and inhabited in small pockets, only Kathmandu and the Hill region remained the seat of political power. It was obvious that the power was identified with Hill culture and the upper caste people of the Hills. This resulted in the negligence and isolation of the Terai people. The identification of the majority of Terai people with the Indian culture also caused their marginalization. Economic disparities, language, citizenship and representation in the politico-administrative structures are the major issues confronting the people of Terai today.

Apart from the internal dynamics of politics, the ethnic, regional and developmental issues are also important in Nepal. These problems can be resolved amicably only within a broad-based democratic political order. The absence of democratic governance can further complicate these issues. The Maoist insurgency has its roots in the developmental divides within the country. There has also been a growing nexus amongst Maoists, ethnic and regional groups. The negligence of the government in realizing these emerging patterns of social and political alignments may cause serious harm to the country. Nepal can learn from the experiences of the success and failures of the neighbouring countries in dealing with these issues and take measures to resolve them before it is too late.

In essence, it can be said that democracy is at a crossroads in Nepal. There have been political intricacies leading to such a situation. The question of resolution of the Maoist problem and the re-establishment of a democratic political order are important. The two are interrelated to a large extent. It depends to what extent the Nepalese ruling elite realizes this inter-relationship and acts accordingly. Nevertheless, there is an urgent requirement for a positive resolution of the problem, lest the situation becomes further complicated and goes beyond reach. The political parties of the kingdom have greater responsibility and they need to come out of their narrow political interests, biases and ill feelings towards one another. The developmental and ethno-regional issues are equally important and have serious implications for the smooth functioning of democracy. These need to be resolved. ■

Notes & References

1. Kanchan Moy Mozumdar, *Nepal and the Indian National Movement*, Calcutta, 1975.
2. Anirudha Gupta, *Politics in Nepal*, Bombay, 1964; Bhuwan Lal Joshi and Leo E. Rose, *Democratic Innovations in Nepal*, California, 1965.
3. B.C. Upreti, *Uneasy Friends: Readings on Indo–Nepal Reactions*, Delhi, 2001.
4. King Mahendra, *Proclamations, Speeches and Messages*, Vol. 7, HMG, Kathmandu, 1967, p.2.
5. Bhola Chatterjee, *Nepal's Experiment with Democracy*, New Delhi, 1997, pp. 99–100.
6. Mahendra, n.4.
7. Margaret W. Fisher & Leo E. Rose, *Politics of Nepal, Persistence and Change in an Asian Monarchy*, Ithaca, 1970.
8. B.C. Upreti, *Nepali Congress, A Study of Party's Performance in 1991 General Elections*, New Delhi, 1993.
9. Ibid.
10. Dhrub Kumar (ed.), *Domestic Conflict and Crisis of Governability in Nepal*, CNAS, Kathmandu, 2000.
11. *Hindustan Times*, May 8, 2004.

12. Some of the aspects related to democratic values, social roots and ideological bases of political parties have been discussed in Martni Hoftmn et.al., *People, politics and ideology, Democracy and Social change in Nepal,* Mandala, Kathmandu, 1999. Also see Lok Raj Baral (ed.), *Leadership in Nepal,* Delhi, 2001; Lok Raj Baral (ed.), *Nepal, Political Parties and Parliament,* Delhi, 2004.
13. Deepak Thapa, *A Kingdom Under Siege, Nepal's Maoist Insurgency* 1996–2003, Kathmandu, 2003; Arjun Karki and David Seddon (eds.), *The People's War in Nepal,* Delhi, 2003.
14. *The Kathmandu Post,* February 12, 1997.
15. C.K. Tiwari, "A Note on Maoist People's War in Nepal", Part I, *Spotlight,* September 17, 1999, p. 32.

Rise of Islamic Fundamentalism in Pakistan: An International Concern

Surendra Chopra*

The rise of Islamic fundamentalism is an important issue of international concern. The 9/11 events, happenings in Chechnya and fundamentalist activities in various other parts of the world have raised the question of closer examination of this issue.

The roots of Islamic fundamentalism go back to the middle of the eighth century when the concept of *Salaf* (literally ancestor) appeared. *Salaf* referred to the authority of the early generations of the Muslims, more specially the first three generations of the followers of the Prophet. This line of thought was christened *Salafiyya* or Islamic fundamentalism. Sanction for this doctrine was sought in a *Hadis,* which says, "The best generation is mine (i.e., the Prophet's), the next best the following one and the next one the succeeding one".[1] This statement contains the crux as well as the roots of Islamic fundamentalism in so far as the fundamentalists believe that the order established by the Prophet and the Caliphs succeeding him, was the best order. The need of the day, according to apologists of Islamic fundamentalism, is to redesign the present system in all Muslim countries on those lines. They exhort strict observance of the precepts of the *Quran* and the *Hadis* as understood and practised by the *Salaf.*[2] The "basis of Islam and the heart of Muslim belief and thought, lies in its holy scripture the Quran considered by Muslims to be the direct and true word of god, transmitted by the angel Gabriel to Mohammed (in Arabic) while the latter was in a state of divine inspiration akin to trance."[3] In other words, Islamic fundamentalism means going back to the classical age of original beliefs and faith and taking Muslims back to the stage of their purity in the golden era of Islam, such as it

* Former Professor in Political Science, Guru Nanak Dev University, Amritsar.

was in seventh-century Arabia.[4] The apologists of Islamic fundamentalism believe that Islam is an ideology and worship, a home and nationality, a religion and state all at the same time. They do not regard Islam as a factor to be confined to private lives of Muslims alone but a solution to all the ills of society. They consider it a total philosophy affecting every aspect of human activity. According to a distinguished Islamic scholar, Islam is a "revolutionary, systematic theology and movement directed equally against such human failings as immorality, materialism, political and ecclesiastical tyrannies, wherever and when ever such defects are seen to exist".[5] According to another writer, "It is the moral orbit around which human life ought to revolve in order to revive the content of the divine message".[6] In other words it is a faith which binds its members into a fraternity transcending the boundaries of state, language, race, colour and local traditions.[7]

The contemporary Muslim world is witnessing, what at first sight appears to be a revival of Islam and assertion of Islamic fundamentalism. The overthrow of the Shah of Iran, the unchallenged leadership of Aiyatollah Khomeini in Iran and his follower, Zia-ul-Haq's efforts at establishing *Nizam-e-Mustafa* in the 1980s and Talibanization of Afghanistan were considered examples of Islamic solidarity and spiritual unity which are indicative of a new wave of Islam or of Islamic revolution, defeat of Taliban notwithstanding. Some scholars regarded it as a case of Islamic self-assertion or of Islamic resurgence and search for identity.[8] Fundamentalist Islam upholds the Islamic law based on: (a) Holy *Quran*, which is the fountainhead of all teachings of Islam and Islamic jurisprudence (b) *Hadis* (tradition) and (c) the *Sunnah* (custom). The *Shariat* is the codified form of all the three. In addition to this, *Ijthhad* (independent legal decisions based on reasoning in matters pertaining to the Shariat); *Qiyas* (inference), *Ijma* (consensus mainly of *Ulema*, one of the four principles of Jurisprudence) are also considered the bases of Islamic law.

The deteriorating condition of the masses in some Muslim states has prepared a fertile ground for a fillip to the Islamic fundamentalist movement. The poor and the downtrodden, frustrated by the politics of the ruling classes, have often sought refuge in the promise of the fundamentalists who assure them a better life, if not in this world, undoubtedly in the next.[9] Moreover, dismayed by the secularism of both capitalist and communist ideology, Muslims see Islam as an essential element that gives direction to their social aspirations and saves them from the dissociation and immorality they see in the West.[10] It is considered as inherently anti-Western and anti modernist but revolutionary without clearly defined goals.[11] The purpose of these fundamentalists of Islam is to enable Muslims to lead their lives totally according to the will of God or the basic principles of their religion.

Fundamentalism has been defined in many different ways. According to a recent work, Islamic fundamentalism is a vague term, currently in vogue as a catch phrase used to convey the militant ideology of contemporary Islamic movements. It indicates a certain intellectual stance that claims to derive political principles from a timeless divine text.[12] The eminent British theologian James Bara states, "Fundamentalism is a bad word; the people to whom it is applied do not like to be so called. It is often felt to be hostile and opprobrious term, suggesting narrowness, bigotry, obscurantism and sectarianism".[13] Pan-Islamic ideology and movements seem to have been presupposed at various times, a part of all following promises for the achievement of unity and union:

(a) the need for a strong central authority to lead Pan Islam and to impose its ideology generally vested in the Caliph;
(b) the rallying of the entire Muslim world;
(c) obedience of Muslims everywhere to the Caliph;
(d) total solidarity with the cause even at the risk of sacrificing personal or local interests;
(e) readiness for common action—political, economic, even military, establishment of a state comprising all Muslims everywhere.[14]

Islam is considered to function as an integrative force, not only at the national level but also to a certain extent at the international level, by promoting an international organization movement among the Muslim states. Pakistan has practically worked in this direction, be it RCD (now ECO) or Islamic conference. The objective of the former was regional integration while the latter aimed at promotion of Islamic solidarity, safeguarding of Holy places, support of the Palestinian people, elimination of social segregation and colonialism. Additionally it has set up an international Islamic News Agency and an Islamic Bank.[15]

Most believers of Islam are of the view that there is only one Islam; there are, however, many manifestations and interpretations. In the words of a leading scholar the basic division is now between populist fundamentalism and traditional fundamentalism. Both types of Islamic fundamentalists compete to demonstrate their greater commitment to the faith and law. Each tries to discredit the beliefs and practices of the other.[16]

Populist Fundamentalist Islam

The fundamental input for resurgent Islam comes from the grass roots of society. It is a force generated by the mass citizenry referred to as the downtrodden and deprived class of society. It is also called Al-Islam-Al-Habi and directly confronts the various ruling elites in the Muslim world. Al-Salaf[17] movement is the extreme form of populist Islam while Al-Islah[18] (reform) is slightly less dogmatic and Al-Ikhwan[19] (Muslim Brotherhood) groups are even more accommodating.[20]

The followers of Populist Islam share the following characteristics:
(a) a fundamentalist faith in the Quran, the Prophet Mohammed and the Sunna;
(b) a strong opposition to corrupt and oppressive governments;
(c) a commitment to the related principles of human equality and social justice;
(d) a condemnation of external intervention in the West Asian region.[21]

This type of fundamentalism does not exist in Pakistan while it is recognized as a potent force in many West Asian countries.

Traditional fundamentalist Islam is the type of Islamic resurgence, which is sponsored by existing rules and may be characterized by state-sponsored Islamic revivalism and is a selective implementation of the Sharia[22]. The ruling classes implement only those parts of Islamic Sharia which eminently suit their political purposes and the enforcement of punitive measures are meant only for strengthening the position of the ruling elite and provide emotional satisfaction to the masses.[23] Islam was conceived as an instrument to preserve and to strengthen their position and to keep the status quo whenever the ruling classes perceive danger to their regime they shrewdly talk about the *Dawah* (call for faith in Allah). The basic emphasis of this thesis was on the performance of *Salat* (prayer), *Saum* (fasting during the holy month of Ramzan) and *Haj* (performing pilgrimage of the holy places).[24]

These are the obligatory duties for the devotees of Islam. Its emphasis is on social and economic justice, equality and universal brotherhood. It also condemns exploitation and oppression of the other classes. Only those aspects of *Sharia* are enforced by the ruling elite which do not pose any threat to the existing system and the enforcement of punitive measures are meant only for strengthening the position of the ruling elite and provide emotional satisfaction to the masses.[25]

The new phase of Islamic resurgence has been spurred by the following events:
(a) the Arab–Israel war of 1967, the defeat of Arabs and the burning down of Al-Aqusa Mosque in Jerusalem;
(b) greater control by the West Asian states over their oil reserves and the formation of the OPEC;
(c) Overthrow of the Shah of Iran and control of Iranian Revolution by the Shia Muslim clergy;
(d) Talibanization of Afghanistan gave a tremendous boost to the fundamentalists and the rise of Osama Bin Laden and Al-Qaida terrorists;

(e) Zia's claims of introducing Islamic order, Nizam-e-Mustafa in the country;[26]
(f) Western success at destroying Saddam's regime;
(g) disintegration of the Soviet Union and the emergence of six more Muslim states.

The impact of Islamic ideology on Pakistan's foreign policy may be briefly examined to prove the point that Pakistan, right from the day of its birth, made efforts to maintain close links with the Muslim countries of the world. Pakistan took definite steps to promote Muslim unity and proclaimed Pakistan's identification with the cause of Islam in any part of the world. The main purpose of the effort to seek friends in the Muslim world was to seek their support against India as it was involved in a bitter clash over Kashmir with the latter.[27]

After the death of M.A. Jinnah, the Muslim League which had doted on his personal stature began to disintegrate. Thereafter the agro-managerial-military-bureaucratic oligarchy on the one hand and the conservative class of the *Ulema* on the other hand, started strengthening their position in Pakistan. A sharp controversy started in Pakistan concerning the positive content of Pakistan's Islamic ideology and its application in the new state's structure, programme and politics. The debate gave rise to two general ideological directions. One, a traditional Islamic state in which the organic connection of religious and the state was exemplified by the *Shariat*; and two, a modern national state based upon Western codes of law with its secular pre-supposition.

However, Pakistan continued to maintain Islamic fervour in its relations with the countries of the Muslim world. Liaquat described the role of ideology in the foreign policy when he said that Pakistan came into being as a result of the urge of the Muslims of the subcontinent to secure a territory where Islamic ideology could be practised and demonstrated to the world. Since a cardinal feature of this ideology is to make Muslim brotherhood a reality, it was part of her mission to do everything in her power to promote fellowship and cooperation between Muslim countries.[28] Liaquat stressed that our relations with the Muslim world should not only be friendly but brotherly and should be made stronger every day because the mission of Pakistan can achieve its success only when we make other Muslim countries join it.[29] Jinnah had stressed that only by putting on a united front could the Muslim states make their voices be heard in the councils of the world.[30] Liaquat said to visit many Muslim countries like Egypt, Iran and Iraq with the purpose of forging pan-Islamic unity.[31]

But the efforts made by Pakistan for Islamic unity in the early period of independence got only a lukewarm response. A well-known Pakistani writer gives two important instances to prove that the whole move was over-optimistic and amateurism; one, that King Farouq of Egypt ridiculed Pakistan's manoeuvres by saying "don't you know that Islam was born on 14 August 1947?" In November 1951, the Egyptian Foreign Minister Salah Al Din-Pasha told an Indian correspondent in Cairo that Egypt looked to India for moral support in its struggle for national independence. Two, during Nehru's visit to Indonesia in December 1950, Sukarno said publicly, "Nehru politically was his father".[32] Another Pakistani writer has pointed out yet another important incident to prove the point. In November 1951, Turkey demanded the recall of Bashir Ahmad on the ground that he was encouraging religious reactionaries in Turkey.[33]

The rebuff by Muslim leadership led the Pakistani leadership to think afresh. In December 1956, the then Prime Minister of Pakistan, H.S. Suhrawardy ridiculed the concept of Muslim unity, saying that "the Arab World is divided amongst themselves and even if they were united, zero plus is after all equal to zero."[34] The 1956 Constitution, which has significant Islamic provisions, underlined the need for strengthening the bonds of unity among the Muslim world.[35] The Ayub Constitution of 1962 omitted the word 'Islamic' from the name of the state but had certain Islamic provisions which were implemented. The stress on preservation of ideology by Ayub and Yahya Khan was merely a political tactic to stabilize the system and keep the status quo.

As eluded to above, the Arab–Israel conflict of 1967, which resulted in disaster for the Arabs, made the rules of the Muslim world take a fresh look at the problems of the Islamic world. They came round to the view that some solid steps were required to check the trends which threatened the status quo. They underlined the need for pooling their resources and harmonizing their strategies to deal with the common problems. This realization made it possible to hold the first summit of Organization of Islamic Countries (OIC) at Rabat (Morocco). Pakistan was represented by the then President Yahya Khan. The first summit declared the resolve of Muslim states to consult, to gather with a view to promote close cooperation and mutual assistance in the economic, scientific, cultural and spiritual fields.[36] The Muslim world was very helpful to Pakistan after its defeat at India's hands in 1971 and its bifurcation. In the first place, they quickly replaced Bangladesh as a market for Pakistani exports and it continues to do so; secondly, the oil-rich Muslim countries started underwriting Pakistan's economic programmes, thirdly, these countries became a haven for Pakistani skilled as well semi-skilled labour and entrepreneurs.[37] It is interesting to note that Bhutto, who rode the bandwagon of socialism—*roti, kapra* and *makan*—which was characterized as *kufr* by fundamentalists and the *Ulema* warned the Muslims not to vote for him in a *fatwa*, incorporated provisions in the 1973 Constitution which showed the impact of Islamic fundamentalism. As part of the Islamisation process, Bhutto used emotive religious phrases like *Musawat-e-Muhammadi* (the equality of the followers of Mohammed) and Islamic *Musawat* (Islamic equality) as part of his rhetoric to justify and win mass support for his policies.[38]

In external affairs Pakistan tried to use the changed environment to strengthen its political position and close alignment with Muslim countries in economic, social, cultural, political and military affairs. The major concern of his visit to the Muslim states of West Asia which Bhutto visited in January 1972 was to inform those countries about Pakistan's stand on Bangladesh. He succeeded in his mission because many fellow Muslim countries like Iran, Saudi Arabia, Libya, UAE and Jordan extended recognition to Bangladesh only after it was recognized by Pakistan. However, there were some doubts about his policies in the minds of the ruling elite of conservative Muslim states, particularly Saudi Arabia. The Saudi monarch who did not relish Bhutto's friendly overtures towards Col. Gadafi of Libya and Shah of Iran was suspected to have financed the anti-Bhutto campaign, which was carried on in mosques while Bhutto banned the use of loudspeakers in mosques.[39]

It may be pointed out that Bhutto's policies and his tours to a large number of Muslim states without doubt endeared him to the Muslim leadership and masses.[40] A distinguished Pakistani writer has said that there is a number of ways in which the formulation and execution of Pakistani foreign policy was touched by Islamic resurgence and fundamentalism. First, Islam reinforced the national interest; second, Islam bestowed an instant ideology on Pakistan. It helped to nationalize, according to her ears of vacillating, foreign policy orientation by binding a suitable niche for Pakistan in the world's competing ideologies. Third, Pakistani foreign policies capitalized on the economic assets of the oil-rich states. Fourth, Pakistani diplomacy brought the earlier experience with Pakistan's trilaterialism meaning thereby developing cordial relation with three super powers and three major Muslim powers such as Saudi Arabia, Iran and Libya. Finally, the convening of the Second Islamic summit and the election of a Pakistani as chairman of the conference established Pakistan's pre-eminent role in the Muslim world.[41]

Islamic fundamentalism had a fuller play in Zia's regime, which removed Bhutto from power on 5 July, 1977. The Islamization programme of General Zia's government was qualitatively different from that of the previous ones. During his regime concrete steps were taken to demonstrate the beginning of new Islamic order. The steps were:

(a) the advisory council of Islamic ideology was recognized and reinstituted;
(b) Islamic penal reforms were introduced, i.e., the application of classical *Shariah* punishments for crimes of theft, adultery and dacoity;
(c) Fundamentalists were appointed to key government positions that oversaw Pakistan's march towards fundamentalization of state, society, school curriculum and foreign policy.[42]

Zia used Islamic fundamentalism cleverly in order to strengthen Pakistan's relations with the Muslim countries in order to strengthen his domestic position. Immediately after capturing power he visited Iran, Saudi Arabia, the UAE, Kuwait, Turkey, Libya and Jordan to secure political support for his regime as well as to get maximum economic assistance from these states.[43] In another visit to Saudi Arabia in April 1978, Zia got strong support from the Saudi regime. The then crown Prince (now the king of Saudi Arabia) publicly declared that "as long as General Zia-ul-Haq is holding the affairs of Pakistan stability and order will rule in Pakistan".[44] Zia always referred to the Saudi king as the servant of Muslim religious shrines, which the monarch relished.

Zia posed himself a great advocate of *Ummah*. He always used to attach importance to the unity of the Muslim world. While delivering his speech at the first Asian Islamic conference held in Karachi on 6 July 1978, he stated that Pakistan attached great importance to the unity of the Islamic world[45] and he repeated it on 15 April 1979 at the General conference of mayors of Islamic capitals held in Karachi.[46]

The *Saur* Revolution and the Soviet presence in Afghanistan had given a golden opportunity to Zia to strengthen his position. He got tremendous support from the Muslim countries particularly the key ones. Saudi Arabia provided immediate relief of 80 million rupees to Jamaat-e-Islami, a fundamentalist organization to look after the Afghan refugees who had taken shelter in Pakistan.[47] Such support was used to train and arm the anti-leftist regime in Kabul, which ultimately resulted in the establishment of an extremely rightist fundamentalist regime in Kabul, friendly to Islamabad. Pakistan was the creator of the Taliban movement, Osama Bin Laden and the dreaded Al Qaida.

According to a Pakistani writer during the 1980s there was a trend towards the growth of "fundamentalist neo-totalitarian Muslim movements" which is "contrary to the political culture and historical tradition of the Muslim majority". The fundamentalists such as Muslim brotherhood in the Arab world, the various organizations like Jamat-e-Islami in Pakistan, the Sharekat Islam in Indonesia and the Islamic government of post-revolution Iran, seek to restore the past to its idealized form. But none of these movements succeeded in attracting the majority of workers, peasants and intelligentsia.[48]

On the international level Zia availed of a God-sent opportunity to represent the OIC and expressed his views regarding the Soviet military intervention in Afghanistan in the United Nations General Assembly on October 1, 1980.[49] The exit of Zia from the political scene and the emergence of Benazir Bhutto and Nawaz Sharif did have some change in the foreign policy options but the fundamentalists' group was successful in dislodging the liberal Marxist group in Kabul. The influx of Taliban and Al Qaida into Pakistan and clandestine support to these groups by ISI is a serious threat to India's security and a matter of concern to international community. Pakistan's foreign policy is one field in which there is near unanimity in the country but it is at a crossroads at this moment, for many qualitative changes have taken place like the collapse of the Soviet Union, the emergence of six independent states mentioned above, the fall of the Taliban government in Afghanistan, Saudi Arabia, Iran, Turkey, Pakistan rivalry in respect of the favours of these countries and thaw in the Indo–US relations.

These are indigenous environmental inputs as well as clamour for Islamisation by a small but powerful group of fundamentalists, the second important input being the anti-American feeling which has grown tremendously over the years specially after the defeat of the Taliban regime in Afghanistan and finally to have a plus point vis-à-vis India, Islamic polities now have greater credibility than even before in Pakistan because Washington is perceived as aiding India to gain military pre-eminence in the region. The emergence of fundamentalists as an important force after the last elections to the national and provincial legislature is a serious threat to India's security and an important issue of international concern.[50]

CONCLUSION

To sum up, it may be pointed out that the Islamic factor has played a dominant role in the country's affairs. Since the inception of Pakistan its leadership has used this factor one way or the other. Zia played the Islamic card very tactfully to strengthen his domestic position, suppress his political opponents, divert the attention of the masses from the existing problems and their political participation in the administration and on the other, to get maximum political and economic assistance from the conservative Muslim countries. During his regime the fundamentalists sneaked into a position of responsibility, which started ignoring liberals with a vengeance.

What the fundamentalists fail to recognize is the fact that in the modern period the political heroes of the Muslim world, the liberators and founding fathers of contemporary Muslim nations have generally been secular, such as Mustafa Kamal Pasha (Turkey), M.A. Jinnah (Pakistan), Almed Soekarno (Indonesia), Gamal Abdul Nasser (Egypt) and Habib Bourguiba (Tunisia). The liberals in Pakistan seem to be so demoralized that they avoid emphasizing such facts to avoid the wrath of fundamentalists. This phenomenon, it may be emphasized has not grown overnight; a large number of factors, other than the spinelessness of liberals and the ones mentioned above has gone into the rise of fundamentalism. The first significant factor is the decline in the influence of Sufis. The Sufi saints had tremendous impact on the people of Punjab and Sindh, particularly the ruralites. As opposed to the Maulvi, the Sufi saints were unpuritanical in their approach. Urbanization presumably is a factor in the reduction of *Sufi* influence. Secondly, *madrasas* and mosques, which have multiplied during the last thirty years, have also contributed to fundamentalists' regimentalism. Thirdly, the steps taken by Z.A. Bhutto, such as declaring Ahmediyas as non Muslims, banning liquor shops and night clubs and changing the weekly holiday from Sunday to Friday; fourthly, Zia's efforts like raising the social status of Mullahs by giving them stipends and setting up a parallel judiciary consisting of *Maulvis*, *Hudood* Ordinance of 1979 and *Diyats* Ordinance of 1979. Ulemas declared Benazir Bhutto's headship of the government as un-Islamic and she was painted as an agent of the Indo–Jewish lobby. All these factors have shocked the majority liberals, yet gladdened the minority conservative fundamentalists. ■

Notes & References

1. Cited in M.S. Agwani, "Islamic Fundamentalism: Myth and Reality", *Man and Development*, Vol. 11, No. 3, September 1980, p. 86.
2. M.S. Agwani, "Islamic Fundamentalism in India", *Democratic World*, Vol. 16, No. 6, 1987, p. 10.
3. *International Encyclopedia of Social Sciences*, Vol. 8, 1968, p. 204.
4. Rain Zakaria, "What Exactly is Islamic Fundamentalism", *The Statesman*, September 15, 1985.
5. Anthony Hyman, *Muslim Fundamentalism*, The Institute for the Study of Conflict, No. 174, 1985, p. 4.
6. A.A. Kurdi, *The Islamic State: A Study Based on the Islamic Holy Constitution*, London, 1984, p. 3.
7. Manzooruddin Ahmed, "Integration of the Muslim World: Problems and Prospects", *Pakistan Horizon*, Vol. 34, 1981, p. 4.

8. Moin Shakir, "Politics of Islamic Fundamentalism", *Mainstream*, Vol. 8, June 14, 1980.
9. Rain Zakaria, n. 4.
10. Daniel Paes, "No Understanding Islam in Polities", *Middle East Journal*, Vol. 6, No. 2, Winter 1983–84, p. 12.
11. Ali Karaosmanglu, "Islam and Foreign Policy: A Turkish Perspective", *Foreign Policy*, Vol. 12, Nos. 1–2, 1985, p. 64.
12. Youssef M. Chourie, *Islamic Fundamentalism*, London, 1990, p. 9.
13. James Barr, *Fundamentalism*, Philadelphia, 1977, p.2.
14. Jacob N. Landou, *The Politics of Pan Islamism, Ideology and Organisation*, Oxford, 1990, pp. 5–6.
15. *Pakistan's Thrust in the Muslim World: A Study of The RCD* (India As a Factor), New Delhi, 1992.
16. John A. *Islam: Continuity and Change in the Modern World, Boulder*, 1982, pp. 282–291.
17. For details see Yousef H. Chorie, n. 12, pp. 46–63.
18. Ibid., pp. 31–52.
19. Ibid., pp. 46–52, 150–4, 153–4.
20. James A. Bill, "Resurgent Islam in the Persian Gulf", *Foreign Affairs*, Vol. 63, No. 1, 1984, p. 108.
21. Ibid., p. 111.
22. Lucian S. Vandenbroucke, "Why Allahis Zealots? A Study of the Causes of Islamic Fundamentalism in Egypt and Saudi Arabia," *Middle East Review*, Vol. 16, No. 1, Fall 1983.
23. For details see Asgher Ali Engineer, "Why Religious Revivalism Among Muslims", *Mainstream*, Vol. 24, No. 9, November 10, 1985, pp. 43–46.
24. Ibid.
25. Ibid.
26. Hasan N. Gardezi, "Resurgence of Islam: Islamic Ideology and Encounters with Imperialism," Hasan N. Gardezi and Jamail Rashid, eds., *Pakistan the Roots of Dictatorship: The Political Economy of Praetorian State*, London, 1982, p. 353.
27. Surendra Chopra, *UN Mediation in Kashmir: A Study of Power Politics*, Kurukshetra, 1971.
28. *Pakistan News*, Karachi, Febraury 18, 1951, pp. 16–17.
29. M. Rafique Afzal, ed., *Speeches and Statements of Quaidi Millat Liaquat Ali Khan 1941–51*, Lahore, 1967, p. 432; Also See S.M. Burke, *Pakistan's Foreign Policy: An Analysis*, London, 1973.
30. Syed Sharifuddin Pirzada, "Quaid-I-Azam and Islamic Solidarity", *Pakistan Horizon*, Vol. 29, No. 4, 1976, p. 60.

31. "Pakistan's Role in International Affairs", *The Second Year: Pakistan 1948-49*, Karachi, 1949, p.1.
32. S.M. Burke, n. 29, pp. 66–67.
33. Arif Hussein, *Pakistan: Its Ideology and Foreign Policy*, London, 1966, p. 16.
34. Ibid., pp. 143–144.
35. *Constitution of the Islamic Republic of Pakistan*, Article 24.
36. S.S. Pirzada, "Pakistan and the OIC ", *Pakistan Horizon*, Vol. 40, No. 2, 1987, p. 28.
37. Shirin Tahir Kheli, "In Search of an Identity: Islam and Pakistan's Foreign Policy", Diwesha, *Islam in Foreign Policy*, Cambridge, 1968, p. 74.
38. Riaz Hassan, "Islamization: An Analysis of Religious, Political and Social Change in Pakistan", *Middle Eastern Studies*, Vol. 21, July 3, 1985, p. 263.
39. Samuel Baid, "How Islamic is Islamic Resurgence", *IDSA Journal*, Vol. 11, No. 4, 1979, p. 346.
40. Surendra Chopra, *Post-Simla Indo-Pak Relations: From Confrontation to De-escalation*, New Delhi, 1988, pp. 11–30.
41. Shirin Tahir Kheli, n. 37, pp. 72–73.
42. Javid Iqbal, "Islamization in Pakistan", *Journal of South Asian and Middle Eastern Studies*, Vol. 8, No. 3, 1985, pp.35–52.
43. Mehrunisa Ali, "General Mohammed Zia-ul-Haq's Visit to Muslim Countries", *Pakistan Horizon*, Vol. 30, No. 3 and 4, 1977, p. 103.
44. *Dawn*, April 18, 1978.
45. Ibid., July 7, 1978.
46. Ibid., April 16, 1979.
47. Kulwant Kaur, *Pak-Afghan Relations*, New Delhi, 1985.
48. Eqbal Ahmed, "Islam and Polities", Asghar Khan, ed. *Islam, Politics and the State: The Pakistan Experience*, 1985, p. 25.
49. For full text of his speech, United Nations General Assembly A/35/AV 181, October 10, 1980.
50. Surendra Chopra, "Islamic Fundamentalism and Pakistan's Foreign Policy", *India Quarterly*, January–June 1993, pp. 1–36.

Struggle for Democracy in South Asia: Case of Bhutan

Mathew Joseph C.*

South Asia has the unique distinction of a region having different kinds of political systems in coexistence. Among the countries in South Asia, India and Sri Lanka are established democracies. In fact, these countries are the examples of successful democracies in the post-colonial world. Pakistan offers a contrast to this. Bangladesh is now maturing into a functioning democracy. The Maldives have an autocratic system of administration. Nepal and Bhutan are monarchies where the clamour for democracy is strengthening day by day. This paper is an attempt to illustrate the indigenous struggle for democracy in Bhutan, which is one of the very few absolute monarchies in the world.

I

Bhutan is a multi-ethnic and multi-religious country. Mainly three ethnic groups, namely, *Ngalong, Sarchops* and *Lhotshampa* (people of Nepali origin) form around 98 per cent of the country's population.[1] Among these ethnic groups *Ngalongs* are migrants from Tibet who reached Bhutan in the ninth and tenth centuries.[2] They are concentrated in western Bhutan. The ruling elite of the country is largely from this ethnic group. They follow the *Drukpa Kagyupa* version of Mahayana Buddhism and speak *Dzongkha*—the national language of Bhutan.[3] Eastern Bhutan is the habitat of *Sarchops*, who are considered to be the earliest settlers in Bhutan.

The people of Nepali origin are concentrated in the southern part of the country.[4] Most of them came to Bhutan in the latter half of the nineteenth and early twentieth centuries. Though they are a combination of caste groups like

---

* Fellow, Centre for Strategic and Regional Studies, University of Jammu, Jammu.

Bahun, Chhetri, Magar, Gurung, Rai, Limbu, Tamang and *Newar*, a common Nepali culture and language unites them.[5]

The population figures of Bhutan are always under suspicion due to the unreliability of the data provided by the government. According to one source the total population of Bhutan in 2002 was 7,16,423.[6] Out of this the people of Nepali origin formed 25 to 30 per cent,[7] *Ngalongs* 20 per cent and *Sarchops* 37 per cent.[8] But this is contested by the Nepali sources. According to them the people of Nepali origin form between 45 and 50 per cent.[9]

The present Bhutanese state was founded by *Shabdrung* Ngawang Namgyal in the seventeenth century. The theocratic political system, called *Chhoesid*, which he created continued without much of a change and gave way to a hereditary monarchy in 1907.[10] The establishment of the hereditary monarchy resulted in the centralization of political power. The first two kings, Ugyen Wangchuck (1907–26) and Jigme Wangchuck (1926–52) paid great attention to the consolidation of royal authority and the integration of the society.[11] The third king, Jigme Dorji Wangchuck (1952–72) initiated major reforms like the introduction of land ceiling and the abolition of slavery and serfdom. The establishment of the *Tshogdu* (National Assembly) in 1953, the commencement of Five-Year Plans since 1961, the formation of the *Lodoi Tshogde* (Royal Advisory Council) in 1965 and the *Thrimkong Gongma* (High Court) in 1968 were some of the other politico-administrative reforms undertaken by him.[12]

The reforms initiated by King Jigme Dorji Wangchuck and Prime Minister Jigmie Palden Dorji created panic among the traditional elements of the society and led to the latter's assassination on 5 April 1964.[13] Shortly after, some dissident officials staged a failed coup attempt against the king in December 1964.[14] These two incidents and the opposition towards the reforms compelled the king to enter into an alliance with the traditionalists. This has hampered the modernization process on the one hand and on the other alienated the ethnic groups other than *Ngalongs* from the national mainstream.

The king is the central figure in the Bhutanese political system. He has executive and legislative functions of the state. Apart from that, he is the highest court of appeal in the country.[15] So far Bhutan has no written constitution and political parties are not allowed. Bhutan's identity is anchored mainly around two institutions, the *Drukpa Kagyuppa* sect of Buddhism, which is the state religion, and the monarchy. Central and western Bhutan (Paro, Thimphu, Punakha and Tongsa valleys) are considered to be the landscape of the Bhutanese cultural core. The religious-ritual practices of this core landscape are accepted as the national ones. So the language of this area (*Dongkha*), dress patterns, food habits and the nomadic-pastoral economic practices became symbols of Bhutanese identity.[16]

The Nepalis of southern Bhutan, the *Sarchops* of eastern Bhutan and the various indigenous groups in the country are deliberately kept out of this scheme of things. They remain in the periphery of the already mentioned Bhutanese politico-cultural landscape. Any attempt of movement towards the centre of the Bhutanese politico-cultural core by these groups will be resisted.

The Nepali-dominated south and the *Drukpa*-dominated north were cut off from each other till the beginning of the state-sponsored modernization process. The attitude of the Bhutanese authorities towards the demographic and cultural challenges posed by the Nepalis has varied over the decades. Their initial policy was to isolate the Nepali Bhutanese completely from the rest of Bhutanese society by restricting them to southern Bhutan. The migration of Nepalis to Bhutan ended by 1959 with the granting of citizenship rights to the Nepali settlers as per the Nationality Law of Bhutan enacted in 1958 and the subsequent tightening of the borders.[17]

The ethnic groups other than the *Ngalongs* were further alienated from the national mainstream under the present monarch Jigme Singye Wangchuck (1972). The unilateral imposition of the *Drukpa* identity as the authentic Bhutanese identity over other ethnic communities, especially Nepalis precipitated ethnic tensions between the *Ngalong*-dominated state and the Nepalis. It later developed into a struggle for democracy and human rights in Bhutan.

II

Popular movements for the realization of political and economic rights for the people of Nepali origin passed through three different stages: (i) initial struggles, the formation of the Bhutan State Congress (BSC) and its collapse in 1969 (ii) the Nepali resistance movement that started after the census conducted in 1988, based on the Bhutan Citizenship Act of 1985 and the promulgation of *Driglam Nam Za* (code of social etiquette)18 in 1989, and (iii) the forceful eviction of the people of Nepali origin and the struggle for democracy and human rights under the banner of political parties and human rights groups operating in exile.

Political activity by the people of Nepali origin started way back in 1927. In that year the *Mandal* (village headman) of Lamidara village in Chirang, Pashupathi Adhikari protested against the excessive land tax rates. The authorities threw him out of the country and confiscated his land and other belongings.[19] In 1947, J.C. Gurung and S.B. Gurung, two *Mandals* from Dagana, approached the Gurkha League in India for some kind of help in bringing about a political transformation in Bhutan. The leaders of the Gurkha League advised them to mobilize people under the banner of Jai Gurkha Solidarity Front to put forward their demands. But the Bhutan government reacted to it in a hostile manner and expelled the leaders of the Jai Gurkha Solidarity Front from the country.[20]

The Bhutan State Congress (BSC) was formed in 1952 at Patgaon in Assam.[21] The leaders of the BSC were D.B. Gurung, D.B. Chhetri, G.P. Sharma and D.S. Sunwar.[22] Its major demands were the abolition of the feudal system, democratization of the administration, granting civil and political rights for all Bhutanese citizens and maintaining closer ties with India.[23]

The BSC planned a satyagraha, a non-violent mode of protest to mobilize support for its demands. The satyagraha was scheduled for 22 March 1954. On that day the BSC activists assembled for satyagraha at Sarbhang, near the Indian border. Their plan was to peacefully get arrested and fill the jails in Bhutan. But this was not allowed and the authorities opened fire at the protesters. Around 25 people were killed and many were injured in the firing.[24]

After the failure of the first satyagraha, the BSC had tried to organize more satyagrahas but none was successful. The Indian attitude towards the political activities of BSC was also not very sympathetic. As per the request of the Government of Bhutan, the Government of India issued an order to the BSC to stop using the Indian territory as a base for its operations.[25] Later, the BSC shifted its headquarters to Siliguri in West Bengal and kept it alive till 1969. When the king offered amnesty to its leaders on the condition that they would not take part in any kind of political activity, they accepted and returned to Bhutan.[26]

The BSC was purely a Nepali organization. The major reason for the failure of its struggles was its inability to expand its socio-political base among the other ethnic groups in Bhutan. Apart from this the dynastic despotism of Wangchucks, the relative backwardness of the polity and the Indian policy to keep the monarchy intact for political stability in Bhutan were the other reasons for the failure of the BSC activities.

Bhutan was free from any kind of anti-government political activity after the failure of the efforts of the BSC in the 1950s. This tranquility did not last long. In 1964, the Prime Minister (*Lonchen*) Jigmie Palden Dorji was assassinated and a coup attempt followed. There was an abortive attempt to kill the present king at his coronation in 1974. These incidents revealed the underlying tensions within the Bhutanese polity.[27] Apart from these domestic political developments, the integration of Sikkim with India in 1975,[28] the struggle against illegal immigrants in Assam during the late 1970s and early 1980s[29] and the Gorkhaland agitation led by the Gorkha National Liberation Front (GNLF) in Darjeeling Hills for a

Nepali-speaking state in the mid-1980s influenced the thinking of the Bhutanese elite.[30]

The merger of Sikkim with India[31]created panic among the Bhutanese elite. They began to anticipate a situation of being marginalized by Nepalis in their own country. This fear was intensified by the violent assertion of Nepalis in Darjeeling Hills for the creation of a Nepali-speaking state in India.[32] The perceived threat from Nepalis dominated the government policies throughout the period after 1975. The strategies adopted by the All Assam Students' Union (AASU) and the Assam Gana Sangram Parishad (AGSP) during their struggle against illegal immigration into Assam helped the Bhutanese authorities to evolve similar kinds of measures to deal with the problem of the people of Nepali origin in Bhutan.

Measures like Bhutan Citizenship Acts of 1977 and 1985, the Marriage Act of 1980, the decentralization policy of the early 1980s, the Green Belt Proposal, the nation-wide census conducted in 1988 based on the Citizenship Act of 1985 to identify "illegal immigrants" and the incentive scheme for *Drukpa*-Nepali intermarriage clearly illustrate this.

The Bhutan Citizenship Act of 1977 attached citizenship to marriage and ownership of property in Bhutan.[33] This Act was modified into the Bhutan Citizenship Act of 1985. As per this Act, knowledge of Bhutanese history, culture and national language (*Dzongkha*) became the basic requirements for citizenship. It also made people who were not residents of Bhutan on or before 31 December 1958 illegal immigrants.[34]

The Marriage Act of 1980 was designed to strictly control the marriage of Bhutanese citizens to foreigners. According to this, a Bhutanese citizen who marries a non-Bhutanese has to undergo penalties like denial of promotion in the civil services, denial of admission in the foreign ministry and armed forces, denial of agricultural and industrial loans and so on.[35] Since the people of Nepali origin used to marry from across the border, this Act constrained their upward mobility.

The decentralization policy was designed to strengthen grass roots decision making. Instead, it ended up in centralizing political power. Because of the decentralization programme the *Mandals* lost their power and *Dzongdags* (district administrators) became strengthened. In 1985, elections to the post of *Mandal* were scraped and its term of office was reduced from five to three years. *Dzongdags* were given the responsibility to nominate *Mandals* in their respective *Dzongkhags*.[36] Due to these measures Nepalis lost the administrative control of their own villages in southern Bhutan.

The Green Belt Proposal, which had taken shape in 1984 actually aimed at the dislocation of Nepalis in southern Bhutan. It was supposed to be a one-kilometre swathe that would run the Indo–Bhutan border. According to the government, the purpose of the proposed Green Belt was to check erosion, prevention of flooding in India and the creation of a distinct physical border between Bhutan and India. It could not be implemented due to widespread opposition from different quarters. Had it been implemented, around 20–30 per cent of the Nepali population would have been displaced.[37]

The monetary incentive-induced inter-ethnic marriage scheme between the southern and northern Bhutanese was considered a genuine attempt towards national integration.[38] But this has to be viewed in the context of the Marriage Act of 1980. The Marriage Act completely prohibits the marriage between Bhutanese nationals and non-nationals. The inter-ethnic marriage scheme was actually intended to create a new group of people who lack both *Drukpa* and Nepali identities.[39]

The government introduced a new term *Lhotshampa* for the Nepalis in Bhutan in the mid-1980s. The term *Lhotshampa* means southern people.[40] By this the government hoped that it could create a wedge between Bhutanese of Nepali origin and the people of Nepali ethnicity both in Nepal and India. But this was not successful. The ethnic conflict between the *Drukpa*-dominated government and the people of Nepali origin, which started in 1989 was a direct outcome of the promulgation of *Driglam Nam Za* in that year and the census conducted to identify "illegal immigrants" in the previous year.

As per official sources, the influx of Nepali immigrants into southern Bhutan was caused by the easy availability of fertile land.[41] According to the Government of Bhutan the census was conducted in 1988 only to stop the Nepali immigration to Bhutan. Based on the Bhutan Citizenship Act of 1985 people were divided into seven (F1–F7) categories. The F1–F7 categories are:

F1 – Genuine Bhutanese
F2 – Returned Migrants (those who had left Bhutan but returned)
F3 – Drop-out (those not available during the time of census)
F4 – A non-national woman married to a Bhutanese man
F5 – A non-national man married to a Bhutanese woman
F6 – Adoption cases (children legally adopted)
F7 – Non-national (migrants and illegal settlers).[42]

In effect, barring people who belong to category F1 (people with tax receipts of 1958 and who could produce a certificate of origin), F2–F7 regardless of the difference between the categories, were targeted for eviction. Many of the people in the F1 category were also targeted on the pretext that they are either "anti-nationals" or relatives of "anti-nationals".[43] Tek Nath Rizal and B.P. Bhandari, the two Royal Advisory Council members from southern Bhutan, submitted a petition to the king on 9 April 1988 regarding the way the census was conducted. Instead of addressing the petition, the authorities arrested Tek Nath Rizal for treason. He was released after three days. Later, fearing arrest he left for Nepal.[44]

Driglam Nam Za came into effect all over southern Bhutan on 1 May 1989. People of southern Bhutan resisted it in many ways. The main centres of opposition were the educational institutions like the Sherubtse College at Kanglung, the National Institute of Education (NIE) at Samchi and the Royal Polytechnic Institute at Deothang.

The People's Forum for Human Rights, Bhutan (PFHRB) was formed on 7 July 1989 at Kakarivitta in Nepal.[45] Tek Nath Rizal became its chairman. The major demands of the organization were:

1. Right to culture, language and script.
2. Right to freedom of religion.
3. Right to freedom of: (a) expression, (b) press, (c) speech, (d) trade and occupation.
4. Right to equality: (a) before law, (b) proportionate representation, (c) opportunity in public employments, (d) distribution of wealth and development funds.
5. Right to education.
6. Right against exploitations.
7. Unconditional release of all the political prisoners.[46]

The PFHRB functioned as an umbrella organization of all the dissidents belonging to varied political opinions. The activities of PFHRB created panic among the Bhutanese ruling elite. On 17 November 1989, Tek Nath Rizal, Sushil Pokhrel and Jogen Gazmere were extradited to Bhutan with the connivance of the Government of Nepal.[47] After a prolonged trial in Thimphu, Rizal was sentenced to life imprisonment on 16 November 1983 by the *Thrimkong Gongma* (High Court).[48] T.N. Rizal's imprisonment affected the activities for some time. It was reconstituted in January 1990 with Rizal as its Chairman-in-absentia. In May 1990, the Amnesty International adopted T.N. Rizal as a "prisoner of conscience".[49]

The Bhutan People's Party was formed on 2 June 1990 at Garganda Tea Estate in Siliguri, West Bengal.[50] R.K. Budathoki and D.K. Rai were elected as the

President and General Secretary of the Party respectively. As per its manifesto the BPP believes in democracy, a parliamentary system of government, constitutional monarchy and multi-party system.[51] The establishment of the BPP increased the political opposition in Bhutan. The BPP, the PFHRB and the Students' Union of Bhutan (SUB) which was formed in March 1988, together put forth a charter of thirteen demands ranging from the right to basic freedoms to far-reaching transformations in the political system of Bhutan.[52] The BPP organized demonstrations throughout southern Bhutan from 19 September till 25 September 1990. Fresh demonstrations followed in Chirang on 4 October 1990. As per government sources, about 50,000 people were mobilized in these demonstrations.[53] These demonstrations were the biggest expression of political dissent by the Bhutanese of Nepali origin since the satyagraha organized by the BSC in 1954.

The Bhutanese authorities were taken by surprise by the enormity of the mass mobilization in the above-mentioned pro-democracy demonstrations. The government tried to suppress the wave of discontent through various means. A new term, *Ngolops* (anti-nationals or terrorists) was coined to describe the agitators and it became synonymous with anybody who demanded human rights and democracy in Bhutan. Apart from this the king himself along with his entourage has undertaken a nationwide tour and addressed public meetings.

As a reaction to the demonstrations in September-October 1990, the government deployed the Royal Bhutan Army (RBA) throughout southern Bhutan in a big way.[54] The government sources themselves confirm the state of violence in southern Bhutan.[55] The hostile atmosphere created by the Bhutanese authorities led to the exodus of the people of Nepali origin from the country. The people who left Bhutan at first came to India and then moved to eastern Nepal. According to one account, 135,000 Bhutanese of Nepali origin left Bhutan of which around 105,000 people are living in seven refugee camps in Morang and Jhapa districts of eastern Nepal managed by the United Nations High Commissioner for Refugees (UNHCR).[56] The rest of the refugees are scattered throughout India and Nepal.

From September-October 1990 onwards, the struggle for democracy and human rights has been carried out from outside Bhutan. As the pro-democracy movement has grown in strength, the different trends dormant in the movement surfaced. Organizations like the PFHRB, the SUB and the BPP which led the pro-democracy movement initially started distancing themselves from one another. New organizations like the Bhutan National Democratic Party (BNDP), the Bhutan Congress Party (BCP) and the Druk National Congress (DNC) have been formed. The PFHRB itself underwent reorganization and split into three groups, namely, the Human Rights Organization of Bhutan (HUROB) and the two splinter groups of the PFHRB led by S. K. Pradhan and D.P. Kafle respectively.

The BNDP came into being on 7 February 1992 in New Delhi. R.B. Basnet and D.N.S. Dhakal were chosen as the President and General Secretary of the organization.[57] According to the BNDP manifesto, "multi-party parliamentary democracy, the only viable alternative to absolute monarchy, is the need of time for safeguarding the rights and freedom of individuals".[58] The BNDP believes that "the southern problem is a struggle for democracy" and demands for "the establishment of constitutional monarchy in a multi-party democratic set-up, institution of secular constitution and respect for the 1948 UN Declaration for Human Rights in all parts of Bhutan".[59]

The HUROB and AHURA Bhutan (Association of Human Rights Activists, Bhutan) were formed on 7 September 1992[60] and 16 November 1992[61] respectively. The BCP was formed in May 1993 after a split in the BPP.[62] The DNC was formed on 16 June 1994.[63] The DNC is a non-Nepali political party. Rongthong Kunley Dorji, a *Sarchop* from eastern Bhutan, is the chairman of the DNC. According to its manifesto the party stands for "parliamentary democracy" and wants to declare Bhutan a "multi-ethnic, multi-lingual, indivisible, independent and democratic Buddhist constitutional monarchical kingdom".[64]

In 1995 broad coalitions of political parties and human rights groups were formed to strengthen the struggle for democracy. On 22 June 1995, seven organizations that were functioning separately came together to form the Bhutanese Coalition for Democratic Movement (BCDM). Later, more groups were included in BCDM and subsequently rechristened as the BCDM General Assembly.[65] This was followed by the formation of the Appeal Movement Coordinating Council (AMCC). It came into existence on 7 September 1995. It aims at "the restoration of fundamental human rights in Bhutan and the early repatriation of the Bhutanese refugees to their homes and hearths in Bhutan".[66]

As a coalition of political groups the BCDM General Assembly explains the refugee problem in the context of the crisis in Bhutanese polity and expects a comprehensive struggle for the establishment of democracy and human rights. On the contrary, the AMCC tend to view the refugee problem as an issue of human rights violation that can be resolved through a non-violent struggle.

The release of Tek Nath Rizal under tremendous international pressure turned out to be a turning point in the recent history of the Bhutanese pro-democracy movement. Pro-democracy organizations once again regrouped under his leadership to form the Human Rights Council of Bhutan (HRCB) on

13 July 2003.[67] The constituent organizations of the HRCB are: the Association of Human Rights Activists of Bhutan (AHURA Bhutan), Bhutanese Refugees Representative Repatriation Committee (BRRRC), Centre for Protection of Minorities and Against Racism and Discrimination in Bhutan (CEMARD Bhutan), Human Rights Organization of Bhutan (HUROB), People's Forum for Human rights Bhutan (PFHRB), Bhutanese Refugee Women Forum (BRWF) and the Students Union of Bhutan (SUB).[68] The HRCB has a six-point agenda, which is as follows:

- To work for the establishment and realization of human rights in Bhutan.
- To work for the just, fair and early repatriation of Bhutanese refugees to their original homesteads in Bhutan with safety, dignity and honour.
- To promote goodwill and co-operation and foster tolerance, forbearance between and among communities, cultural, linguistic and religious groups for strengthening the multi-ethnic, multi-religious, multi-linguistic and multi-cultural society of Bhutan.
- To promote and propagate the principles and provisions of International Instruments of Human Rights in Bhutan and among the Bhutanese communities.
- To generate international awareness about the violation of human rights of Bhutanese people by the Government and the plight of Bhutanese refugees and mobilize international public opinion and support for the Council's work.
- To initiate local, national, regional and international alliances, establish network and work in close co-operation with organisations, inter-governmental organizations and the United Nations Specialized Agencies for the just, fair and early repatriation of Bhutanese refugees with dignity, honour and safety, to their original homesteads and establishment of human rights in Bhutan.[69]

The radicalisation of politics in Nepal by the Communist Party of Nepal (Maoist) has had its impact on the Bhutanese refugees. The indifference of the Bhutanese government towards the non-violent struggles of the moderates among the refugees for repatriation has led to a great amount of resentment. Due to the futility of the struggles hitherto conducted by the moderates resulted in the formation of the Bhutanese Communist Party (Marxist-Leninist-Maoist) in the early months of 2003.[70] The BCP (MLM) is a member of the Coordination Committee of the Maoist Parties and Organizations of South Asia (CCOMPOSA).[71] The BCP (MLM) has put forth a ten-point charter that is as follows:

1. Bhutan Government must declare sovereign democracy and guarantee people's rights and freedoms.

2. Bhutan Government must repatriate all its citizens with dignity and honour.
3. Bhutan Government must guarantee with acceptance in principle of right to self-determination.
4. Following the principle of "Land for the people", distribute the lands to poor peasants and landless farmers.
5. Bhutan Government must fix the minimum wage of Nu. 150/- per day. Also the emergency fund for forthcoming catastrophe, health insurance and shelter must be guaranteed.
6. Guarantee all fundamental rights of women and equal judgment.
7. Bhutan Government must guarantee cost-free education and employment.
8. Guarantee democratic and employment-oriented education.
9. Do away with all the draconian laws and acts reconstruct new democratic laws and constitution.
10. Guarantee the freedom of speech, press, and freedom to travel within the territory of country.[72]

The radicalization of the Bhutanese refugees will have a serious impact on the political developments of Bhutan, Nepal and the Nepali-dominated areas of India. The politico-economic and cultural marginalization of the people of Nepali origin in Bhutan resulted in the ethnic conflict between them and the *Drukpa*-dominated Bhutanese ruling elite and the consequent movement for democracy and human rights. The pro-democracy movement succeeded in compelling the king to surrender some of his powers to a cabinet in 1998 and initiate a process to draft a constitution for the country.[73]

The ethnic conflict and the consequent movement for democracy and human rights brought about a high degree of politicization among the people of Bhutan cutting across ethnic lines. In contrast to the various contemporary experiences the ethnic assertion of the people of Nepali origin in Bhutan has developed into a movement for the democratization of the Bhutanese polity and society. ■

Notes & References

1. A.C. Sinha, *Bhutan: Ethnic Identity and National Dilemma*, New Delhi, 1991, pp. 22–30.
2. Michael Aris, *Bhutan: The Early History of a Himalayan Kingdom*, New Delhi, 1980, pp. 58–58.
3. D.N.S. Dhakal and Christopher Strawn, *Bhutan: A Movement in Exile*, Jaipur, 1994, p.42.
4. S.D. Muni, "Bhutan in the Throes of Ethnic Conflict," *India International Centre Quarterly*, Vol. 18, No. 1, Spring 1991, p. 146.
5. Dhakal and Strawn, n.3, pp. 43–44. Also see Nari Rustomji, *Bhutan: The Dragon Kingdom in Crisis*, Delhi, 1978, p.7.

6. http://www.bhutannewsonline.com/at_aglance.html, March 12, 2005.
7. King Jigme Singye Wangchuck, in "Conversation: The People Will Decide", *Sunday*, October 28–November 3, 1990, p. 27.
8. From King Jigme Singye Wangchuck's interview with Reuter News Agency in February 1992, cited in *Himal*, Vol. 5, No. 4, July/August 1992, p. 17.
9. Mathew Joseph C., *Ethnic Conflict in Bhutan*, New Delhi, 1999, p. 24.
10. Bikrama Jit Hasrat, *History of Bhutan: Land of the Peaceful Dragon*, Thimphu, 1980, p. 156.
11. A.C. Sinha, "The Bhutanese Experience of State Formation", *Social Science Probings*, New Delhi, Vol. 2, No. 2, June 1985, pp. 216–22.
12. Hasrat, n.10, p. 135. Also see Parmanand, *The Politics of Bhutan: Retrospect and Prospect*, Delhi, 1992, p. 64.
13. Ram Rahul, *Royal Bhutan*, New Delhi, 1983, p. 41.
14. Ibid.
15. Parmanand, n.12, p.51.
16. Sinha, n.1, p. 188.
17. Lok Raj Baral, *Regional Migrations, Ethnicity and Security: The South Asian Case*, New Delhi, 1990, p. 28. Also see Jigmi Y. Thinley, "Bhutan: A Kingdom Besieged" in Ministry of Foreign Affairs, *Bhutan: A Traditional Order and the Forces of Change, Three Views from Bhutan*, Thimphu, 1993, p. 10.
18. *Driglam Nam Za* comprises virtues such as respect for the sovereign, teachers, parents, elders, the institution of marriage and family, civic duties and behaviour that keep together the Bhutanese social fabric. It also stipulates how people should conduct themselves at different occasions and includes a dress code requiring *Gho* to be worn by men and *Kira* by women.
19. Christopher Strawn, *Falling Off the Mountain: A Political History and Analysis of Bhutan, the Bhutanese Refugees and the Movement in Exile* (Unpublished dissertation submitted to the University of Wisconsin), p. 49.
20. Ibid.
21. Leo E. Rose, *The Politics of Bhutan*, Ithaca, 1977, p. 110. Also see Sinha, "The Bhutanese Experience of State Formation", p. 234.
22. Dhakal and Strawn, n.3, p. 136.
23. Rose, n.21, pp. 110–11. Also see, A.C. Sinha, "The Bhutan State Congress: First Political Stirrings", *Hima*, Vol. 5, No.4, July/August 1992, p.20.
24. Dhakal and Strawn, n.3, pp. 139–40.
25. Sinha, n.23, p. 20.
26. Ibid.
27. S.D. Muni, "Bhutan Steps Out", *World Today*, Vol. 40, No. 12, December 1984, p. 517.

28. A.C. Sinha, *Politics of Sikkim: A Sociological Study*, Faridabad, 1975, p. 166.
29. For details about the Assam problem, see Sanjib Baruah, "Immigration, Ethnic Conflict and Political Turmoil—Assam, 1979–1985", *Asian Survey*, Vol. 26, No. 11, November 1986, pp. 118–206 and Alfred T. Darnell and Sunita Parikh, "Religion, Ethnicity and the Role of the State: Explaining Conflict in Assam", *Ethnic and Racial Studies*, Vol. 11, No. 3, July 1988, pp. 263–81.
30. Democratic Youth of Bhutan (DYB), *Our Future in Democratic Bhutan: Eye-opener to the People of Bhutan* (n.p., DYB, n.d.), p.2. Also see John Bray, "Bhutan: The Dilemmas of a Small State", *World Today*, Vol. 49, No. 11, November 1993, p. 215.
31. Nepalis, who were the majority of Sikkim's population, wholeheartedly supported the accession of Sikkim into the Indian Union. For details, see Leo E. Rose, "The Nepali Ethnic Community in the North-East of the Sub-Continent", *Ethnic Studies Report*, Vol. 12, No. 1, January 1994, p. 108.
32. Manorama Kohli, "Ethnic Crisis in Bhutan: Implications", in Ramakant and R.C. Misra (eds.), *Bhutan: State and Polity*, New Delhi, 1996, p. 97.
33. Ministry of Home Affairs, *The Southern Bhutan Problem: Threat to a Nation's Survival*, Thimphu, 1993, pp. 49–54.
34. Ibid., pp. 55–58.
35. People's Forum for Human Rights, Bhutan (PFHRB), *Bhutan: A Compilation of Major Laws and Treaties with India*, Kathmandu, 1995, pp. 18–20.
36. Strawn, n.19, p. 40.
37. Bhakti P. Sharma, *Bhutan: Human Rights and Inhuman Wrongs* (Mimeograph), p.12. Also see Institute for Human Rights, Environment and Development-International (INHURED), *Bhutan: An Iron Path to Democracy*, Kathmandu, 1992, p. 9 and People's Forum for Human Rights, Bhutan (PFHRB), *Bhutan: Forced Evictions and Human Rights*, Kathmandu, 1995, pp. 2–3.
38. Thinley, n.17, p. 18.
39. Joseph C., n.9, p. 138.
40. Thinley, n.17, p. 14.
41. Department of Information, *Anti-National Activities in Southern Bhutan: A Terrorist Movement*, Thimphu, 1991, p. 2.
42. Appeal Movement Coordinating Council (AMCC), *Bhutan: Revocation of Citizenship*, Damak, 1995, p. 4.
43. Sharma, n. 37, p. 13.
44. People's Forum for Human Rights, Bhutan (PFHRB), *Tek Nath Rizal: The Prisoner of Conscience*, Birtamod, PFHRB, n.d., pp. 6-7. Also see Bhakti P. Bhandari, "Hostage in Thimphu", *Himal*, Vol. 7, No. 2, March/April 1994, p. 32.
45. PFHRB, n.44, p. 7.

46. People's Forum for Human Rights, Bhutan (PFHRB), *Bhutan: Cry for Human Rights*, n.p., PFHRB, n.d., p. 10.
47. PFHRB, n. 44, p. 7.
48. *Kuensel*, Thimphu, November 20, 1993. Also see Amnesty International, *Bhutan: Appeal for the Release of Tek Nath Rizal*, London, 1994, p. 1.
49. Amnesty International, *Bhutan: Appeal for the Release of Tek Nath Rizal*, p. 1.
50. Bhutan People's Party (BPP), *Objectives, Manifesto and Ideology*, Sarbhang, 1992, p. 3.
51. Ibid., pp. 3–4.
52. Bhutan Solidarity, "Tyranny in Bhutan: Findings of Journalists" *Team into Allegations of Coercion and National Oppression*, New Delhi, 1995, p. 36.
53. *Kuensel*, December 22, 1990.
54. *Kuensel*, January 12, 1991. Also see David B. Thronson, *Cultural Cleansing: A Distinct National Identity and the Refugees from Southern Bhutan*, Kathmandu, 1993, p. 27.
55. Department of Information, *Anti-National Activities in Southern Bhutan: A Terrorist Movement*, p. 5.
56. Human Rights Council of Bhutan (HRCB), "Position Paper on Bhutanese Refugees and Human Rights Situation in Bhutan", See http://www.bhutannewsonline.com/hrcb_positionpaper.rtf (accessed on March 16, 2005).
57. Dhakal and Strawn, n.3, p. 290.
58. See Bhutan National Democratic Party (BNDP), *Ideology, Manifesto and Organisation Structure*, Thimphu, 1992.
59. Ibid.
60. Human Rights Organisation of Bhutan (HUROB), *Annual Report* 1992, Birtamod, 1992, p. 7.
61. Brochure brought out by the Association of Human Rights Activists, Bhutan, Damak: AHURA Bhutan (n.d.), p. 1.
62. David B. Thronson, *Cultural Cleansing: a Distinct National Identity and the Refugees from Southern Bhutan*, Kathmandu, 1993, p. 16.
63. The Druk National Congress (DNC), *Ideology and Manifesto*, n.p., DNC, n.d., p. 3.
64. Ibid., p. 8.
65. Bhutanese Coalition for Democratic Movement (BCDM) General Assembly, *Bhutanese Coalition for Democratic Movement General Assembly*, n.p: BCDM General Assembly, n.d.
66. Appeal Movement Coordinating Council (AMCC), AMCC *Newsletter*, Damak, Vol. 1, No. 1, November 1995, p. 1.
67. See <http://www.bhutannewsonline.com/hrcb.html>, (accessed on March 21, 2005).
68. Ibid.

69. Ibid.
70. See <http://cpnm.org/new/English/documents/ps_ćcomposa.htm>, (accessed on March 22, 2005).
71. Ibid.
72. The Bhutan Communist Party (Marxist-Leninist-Maoist) press release on May 2, 2003.
73. For details see Mahendra P. Lama, "Experiments with Democracy", *Frontline* (Chennai), Vol. 21, No. 1, January 3–16, 2004, pp. 17–21. Also see Wasbir Hussain, "Bhutan: Racing Towards Democracy", *The Hindu*, January 11, 2003 and Parmanand, "Changes in Bhutan", *The Statesman*, January 15, 2003.

Track Five Diplomacy: Role of Higher Education in Conflict Transformation

Jane E. Schukoske* & Manjri Sewak**

Conflict Transformation is emerging as a field of academic and professional interest in India and the US. The term "conflict transformation" encompasses and goes beyond the more frequently used term "conflict resolution". Conflict resolution is a field that offers various non-violent options and approaches to end violent conflict, including the processes of negotiation, mediation, 'good offices' and facilitation. Conflict transformation entails a further question: how do we build or rebuild relationships and institutions that can support and sustain non-violent social change? The focus as John Paul Lederach, Founding Director of the Conflict Transformation Program at Eastern Mennonite University (EMU), in Harrisonburg, Virginia, USA, suggests, is on "what we are trying to build", not just "what we are trying to end".

Institutions of higher education in India show eagerness to better equip their graduates, teaching staff and members of their communities to contribute to the emerging conflict transformation field. Course offerings, mediation practice opportunities for teaching staff and students, research support, discussion groups and training of community members are key roles these institutions can play. Sharing information on existing efforts can lead to rapid development of teaching models and resources in this field so critical to the region in the 21st century.

USEFI offers Fulbright fellowships to Indian scholars in the field of conflict transformation under both its Junior Research Fellowships and special Conflict Resolution Fellowships offered every other year. The US Fulbright scholars in the field come to the region to facilitate workshops and conduct research.

---

* Executive Director, U.S. Educational Foundation in India.

** Fulbright Scholar (2001) and Research Associate at WISCOMP.

Recognizing Education as a Track

In the last two decades, efforts to resolve violent conflict and to build peace undertaken by civil society outside the structure of government have come to be called "track two diplomacy", in contrast to government-to-government interactions between instructed representatives called "track one diplomacy". Former American diplomat Joseph Montville coined the term "track two diplomacy" in 1981 to refer to the range of informal, non-governmental and unofficial peace initiatives between non-state actors. Track two peace initiatives involve non-governmental, informal and unofficial citizen interaction between individuals/groups in conflict, often with the assistance of a third party. Louise Diamond and John McDonald, co-founders of the Institute for Multi-Track Diplomacy in Washington, D.C., defined track two diplomacy as the realm of professional, non-governmental action attempting to analyze, prevent, resolve and manage international conflicts through non-state actors.[1]

In the late 1980s, there was a growing sense that the designation of track two no longer covered the diversity and depth of civil society initiatives. In this context, Diamond and McDonald designed a nine-track model to highlight the diversity of actors and approaches to peace building in intra- and inter-State conflicts. The notion of multi-track diplomacy is based on the premise that citizens from a variety of backgrounds have certain skills and expertise, which can be used effectively to transform conflict habituated systems. It provides a conceptual framework that reflects the variety of activities that contribute to international peacemaking and peace building.

The nine-track model recognizes the role higher education contributes to conflict transformation. According to this model, "track three" actors comprise the business community, providing financial resources to fund peace-building efforts. "Track four" encompasses a variety of peace and development activities initiated by private citizens. "Track five" is defined as the educational component of the model. It comprises universities that offer education in conflict resolution as well as think tanks that include a variety of research, analysis and study programs. The peace activism field—"track six"—comprises activities associated with issues such as human rights and social and economic justice. Drawing on religion as a resource for peace, "track seven" comprises the various faith-based engagements that bring together individuals/groups torn by violent conflict. "Track eight" consists of the funding community—those organizations and individual philanthropists who engage in peace building by providing financial resources for many of the activities undertaken by the other tracks. "Track nine," the pro-peace media (print, film, video, radio, the arts), is seen as a mirror of society, articulating the voices of all the stakeholders in a conflict.

This paper focuses on track five diplomacy, the role for higher education institutions to play. Traditional fields of study and new roles are discussed in the following sections.

Traditional Fields of Study Relevant to Conflict Transformation

Universities and other institutions of higher education offer in their traditional curricula, courses which contribute to understanding of conflict and to building of skills for analysis and discussion of conflict situations. Political science, history, law, psychology, social work and other social sciences afford opportunities for studying past and present conflicts and analysis of elements. Knowledge and skills from these fields can contribute to the less studied area of resolution of existing violent conflict. A few examples from international relations, law and philosophy are given below.

The field of international relations, emerging from the discipline of Political Science, contributes directly to the development of knowledge of both track one and track two diplomacy. Key areas of study include international politics, international organizations, disarmament studies, diplomatic studies (negotiation and foreign policy), international legal studies, international trade, human rights, gender, ethnicity and ethics. Networks of professors teaching these courses are forming in South Asia.[2]

Within the discipline of law, there are many courses relevant to the field of conflict transformation. International law is a constantly expanding field, addressing not only treaties between states but also customary law and conventions setting internationally agreed norms. Course offerings in the fields of negotiation and alternative dispute resolution for both law students and legal professionals develop skills and analysis relevant for inter-group conflict. Courses are offered on interviewing, negotiation and counselling in most US law schools and in some law faculties in India. They focus on skills of active listening, identifying stated and underlying interests of parties, developing creative solutions and drafting agreements. They often assign *Getting to Yes*[3], a book conveying key principles of The Harvard Negotiation Project: the need to identify parties' multiple interests (beyond those that seemingly form the basis of the dispute), to brainstorm creative options from shared as well as separate interests and to set measurable criteria for the parties to assess their progress as they move forward in implementing an agreement.

Within the field of philosophy, Gandhian thought is the key to these studies. With its focus on the principle of satyagraha, defined as grasping on to principles or "truth force",[4] Gandhian philosophy and praxis offers tools for non-violent conflict resolution.[5] Degrees or diplomas in Gandhian thought and peace science/peace research are offered at several institutions in India.[6]

Within the field of psychology, many seminal theories of conflict resolution have become cornerstones of the developing thought on the multiple levels of sociopolitical conflict intervention. Various academic programmes and journals rooted in the discipline of psychology promote the utilization of psychological theory to analyze the multiple causes of conflicts as well as the possibilities of prevention and intervention. Johan Galtung, considered by some to be the father of peace research, has been pivotal in illuminating the concept of structural violence—the systems of inequity and injustice that are as much inhibitors of peace as direct violence—in framing the development of peace building and conflict transformation activities worldwide.

In reviewing courses in the traditional curriculum to fine-tune them for contemporary conflict resolution needs, educators should also assess the suitability of the teaching methodology. Conflict transformation courses benefit from a "clinical" or practical skills aspect, which requires active participation of learners. Traditional courses have often been taught in a lecture method. Strengthening existing courses relevant to conflict resolution by adopting an interactive learning method can optimize their effectiveness.

Other Roles for Higher Education Institutions: Mediation Practice, Applied Research and Innovative Training in Conflict Transformation Skills

Institutions of higher education have the opportunity to teach their communities about innovations to build and sustain peace processes. These include problem-solving workshops, mediation, consultation to ongoing peace processes, trainings, dialogue groups, networking, private one-to-one diplomacy and message carrying.

Higher education institutions offering conflict transformation programme may provide 'practice' opportunities for professors, staff and students. With proper preparation, members of the academic community may act as practitioners making important interventions in different regions of conflict; significantly impacting the development of theory and research; and also facilitating personal and social change. For example, the EMU Master of Arts Conflict Transformation Program (CPT) positively affects peace processes in different regions of the world. Faculty activists include John Paul Lederach

(Nicaragua, Columbia, Northern Ireland, Tajikistan), Barry Hart (from former Yugoslavia), and Ronald Kraybill (South Africa). This contemporary work greatly enriches classroom discussions because students and professors are able to test theories and models based on their practical experience.

Research and Publication Support for Conflict Transformation Materials

University professors and press aid in the development of materials to support coursework and workshops in this emerging field. A recent example of a book available in India is the publication of *Gandhi's Way: A Handbook of Conflict Resolution* by The Regents of the University of California, in 2002, reprinted by Oxford University Press in 2003[7]. Such publications supplement activist materials, which can be important references for coursework as well as practice.[8] Another opportunity for faculty and practitioner contributions to the field is through academic journals on dispute resolution, such as the *Journal of Peace Studies* published by the International Center for Peace Studies in New Delhi.[9]

Conflict Transformation Curricula: EMU Example

The Conflict Transformation Program (CTP) at Eastern Mennonite University (EMU) specializes in:

- Conflict Analysis
- Conflict Prevention
- Interventions and approaches to conflict transformation (disaster response, humanitarian relief, restorative justice, socio-economic development, trauma counselling and healing, negotiation and facilitation, among others)
- Post-conflict peace building (transitional and restorative justice, healing of fractured relationships, rebuilding structures and institutions).

An important focus of the programme relates to ensuring that short-term interventions (mediation or humanitarian assistance) are informed by the long-term goals of rebuilding human relationships and building institutions and communities that can support sustainable transformation.

The courses offered can be divided into four categories:

1. Personal Transformation: Walking our Talk

   Several Professors emphasize "walking our talk". In other words, they see transformation as beginning with the self and then moving out into families, communities and nations. The belief is that we cannot help people in conflict if we ourselves are caught in hostile and conflicting relationships (intra-personal and inter-personal).

2. Conceptual clarity and theoretical knowledge needed to facilitate a sound analysis of conflict and a comprehensive design for intervention. Courses included in this category:
   - Comparative Approaches to Conflict
   - Introduction to Conflict Transformation
   - Metaphor, Narrative and Worldview Conflicts
   - Violence, Non-violence and Conflict Transformation
   - Identity and Conflict Transformation.
3. Capacity building: skills and techniques for intermediaries
   Since every conflict is different and unique, options for resolution and transformation must also vary, keeping in mind the cultures of a country/region. This suggests that peace builders need to continually expand skills and techniques for use in different contexts. Courses focus on roles for intermediaries and on techniques such as negotiation, mediation, facilitation, active listening and counselling.
4. Trauma Healing and Reconciliation, Restorative Justice, Appreciative Inquiry, Facilitation Approaches and Skills, Conflict Transformation and Education.

Such courses enable students to specialize in a particular area of intervention, given their own professional background and personal interests. For instance, the field of trauma awareness and healing is extremely specialized yet integral to any process of transformation. Some students feel the need to specialize in this area because it directly impacts upon the effectiveness of their interventions in a conflict setting.

Conflict Resolution/Transformation Courses in India

According to the Association of Indian Universities, there is no listing of institutions in India offering conflict-resolution courses, though some law faculties offer courses in international law, negotiation and alternative dispute resolution, and some institutions offer courses in Gandhian thought and peace studies. The authors are collecting information on existing and emerging conflict transformation and peace studies programme and ask readers to inform us of programme not mentioned here. Examples of conflict-resolution courses and programme in India follow.

Malaviya Centre for Peace and Reconciliation (MCPR), an interdisciplinary Centre in the Faculty of Social Sciences at Banaras Hindu University in Varanasi, strives to analyze and contribute to the peaceful resolution of intra- and inter-state conflict, issues of peace building and conflict transformation within and outside Indian borders. The Centre has three main activities: projects, seminars/workshops/symposia, and international collaborations.

One of the oldest academic relationships of the MCPR has been the exchange programme with the Department of Peace and Conflict Research (DPCR), Uppsala University, Sweden. Four students and a number of faculties of the Banaras Hindu University have received Swedish International Development Agency (SIDA) scholarships to pursue Masters' and Advance International Diploma courses in conflict resolution at DPCR.

MCPR has provided academic support to graduate students of the University of Wisconsin, Madison, Wisconsin, US. So far seven students have written their dissertation under the guidance of the MCPR faculty, and a number of students has conducted fieldwork. Over the past few years MCPR has also been extending academic support to the students of the University by offering its facilities and guidance to students as a part of their College Year Program in India. MCPR is in the process of designing a diploma course in Conflict Resolution.

The Department of Politics and Public Administration, University of Madras, in collaboration with the Department of Peace and Development Research (PADRIGU), Göteborg University, Sweden offers a course on peace and conflict resolution to master-level students at the School of Social Sciences, University of Madras. Conceptualized to promote peace studies in India, this long-term research collaboration also has a complementary research component, which analyzes the current teaching and research in peace and conflict resolution within and outside India, and which shall produce a publishable monograph on curriculum guide. Further, a peace studies reader encompassing essays on topics relevant to developing countries in general and India in particular will be produced to help students of peace studies.[10]

Centre for Peace and Conflict Resolution Studies at University of Madras was formed in April 2003 by faculty from the Departments of Politics and Public Administration, International Law, Anthropology, Christian Studies and Islamic Studies. Its objectives, inter alia, are to understand the nature of peace and conflict and study conflict-generating situations, to provide educational and scientific support to peace-building activity with an ethos of cooperation rather than competition, to increase the effective and informed participation of scholars in India regarding peace and conflict resolution studies and development of a peace culture, to create a network of scholars in the field and to offer possible assistance to victims in terms of policies, practices research and international cooperation. Its activities include peace and conflict resolution course development, research, seminars, resource building and skills training. In fall 2003, a Fulbright senior scholar, Barbara Tint, Director, International and Intercultural Conflict Resolution, Portland State University, Portland, Oregon, conducted Mediation training while based at the Centre.

Jain Vishva Bharati Institute (JVBI), granted a Deemed University status in 1990, is "dedicated to cultivate and practice high ideals of 'Anekant' including tolerance and peaceful co-existence for the weal of the mankind." The status was granted for and on the basis of the work done by Jain Vishva Bharati Institute in the field of 'Ahimsa and Anekanta'. Ahimsa means non-violence. Violent mental, emotional, verbal and physical expressions are attempted to be understood and overcome. The concept of Anekanta says truth is multi-dimensional: at the metaphysical level it allows for plurality of thoughts; at the day-to-day level it advocates peaceful co-existence and tolerance. The Institute offers programme for university students, as well as lecture series on Anekanta and short-term programmes for school children on peace studies. Some key programmes follow.

Degree programmes: A two-year Masters course in Non-violence and Peace and a three-year Bachelor's course cover conflict resolution, human rights, peace education and training, peace movement and treaties, environmental ethics and the like. A Masters Programme in Jainology and Comparative Religion is designed to help resolve conflicts arising on the platform of religion. A Masters Programme in Social Work has a fieldwork component in rural surroundings, which focuses on sustainable developmental activities. Over 70 students have worked in 10 villages within a radius of 20 kms of JVBI. Their activities include health camps in the villages, sanitation drives, planting trees, strengthening Anganwadis and work with children who dropped out of the school. Also, rallies have been conducted against *gutkha* chewing, alcoholism and other addictions and to strengthen village institutions and organizations.

Certificate programme in Non-violence: In collaboration with Gandhi Smriti Darshan Samiti, JVBI launched a three-month certificate course in peace and non-violence.

WISCOMP is a project of the Foundation for Universal Responsibility of His Holiness The Dalai Lama. It creates a space to engender an inclusive, conceptual vocabulary in the areas of peace, security and conflict transformation. To this end, it seeks to empower new voices (specifically people 20 to 35 years of age) and promote a more people-oriented and gender-sensitive discourse on matters relating to peace and security. By introducing the study of peace and conflict to a new generation, WISCOMP reaches out to those who will be decision-makers 10 to 20 years from today to equip them with the motivation, the skills and the knowledge to choose dialogue and non-violent engagement over the use of force and violence. WISCOMP provides a unique professional network of women and men in the South Asian region committed to enhance the professional efficacy of women in the areas of international affairs, regional co-operation, multi-track diplomacy, reconciliation and peace processes. WISCOMP organizes Conflict Transformation Workshops designed to introduce the field of conflict transformation to university students and young practitioners and scholars from South Asia. WISCOMP plans to convert its ten-day Workshop into a Summer School, which will offer a certificate course.

Other Conflict-Resolution Resources in South Asia

Peace Studies Program of the Social Scientists' Association, Colombo, Sri Lanka: The Centre for Conflict Resolution, Department of Peace Studies, University of Bradford (England) is collaborating with the Peace Studies Program of the Social Scientists' Association (SSA) of Colombo, Sri Lanka, to offer a Diploma in Conflict Resolution and Peace Preparedness in Sri Lanka. This course aims to provide participants an applied framework for peace preparedness and conflict resolution. A further programme in conflict resolution and security studies is being planned for the police and the military. The SSA, founded in 1977, is a non-profit organization engaged in a wide range of social, educational/training and research activities. The SSA brings together academics, intellectuals and practitioners from a broad spectrum of Sri Lankan society with competencies in Tamil, Sinhala and English.

The Diploma in Peace Preparedness and Conflict Resolution provides a foundation in conflict resolution, humanitarian intervention and peace building within a peace studies' perspective. The modules for the course include: human rights, reconciliation and justice; comparative peace processes; dynamics and analysis of conflict; conflict resolution—theory and practice; gender peace and conflict; culture and conflict resolution; development, peace and conflict and religion and conflict transformation.

The South Asian Forum for Human Rights in Kathmandu, Nepal, runs a six-month course on peace activism and human rights. Although the focus is human rights, the forum does address the fields of conflict transformation and peace building.

Conclusion

Institutions of higher education in South Asia are turning attention to the role education can play in preparing the next generation to address the problems of violent conflicts in the region. Given the foundational tenets of non-violence, mutual understanding and social justice that Gandhi espoused as the trans-formative principles within India's history, it seems a natural evolution that these ideas become the backdrop for academic programs. Higher education in India has both the privilege and responsibility to become a visible and strategic partner in the transformation of conflict and the making of peace. The sharing of preliminary research and anecdotal information on courses offered or planned will help South Asian educators and activists coordinate their efforts to carry out this important work. Formation of networks of conflict transformation/peace studies educators in South Asia could contribute significantly to this effort.

The U.S. Educational Foundation in India (USEFI) administers the Fulbright Conflict Resolution Program, which has supported study of the emerging field of conflict transformation by South Asian scholars,[11] Virginia, USA, under this program. This paper has been revised from a paper presented at the International Conference on Conflict Resolution: Peace and Development at BITS, Pilani, October 28–29, 2003. ■

Notes & References

1. U.S. Educational Foundation in India, ed., *Teaching of International Relations in South Asian Universities*, New Delhi, India, 2003 (a collection of essays prepared for a roundtable discussion by professors of international relations in Bangladesh, India, Nepal, Pakistan and Sri Lanka).
2. Ibid.
3. Fisher, Roger, Ury, William, and Patton, Bruce, *Getting to Yes*, New York, 1991.
4. Juergensmeyer, Mark, *Gandhi's Way: A Handbook of Conflict Resolution*, New Delhi, 2003, at 3 (cited Gandhi, *Young India*, November 5, 1919.)
5. Basic rules of Gandhian conflict resolution have been summarized as follows: (i) Do not avoid confrontation. (ii) Stay open to communication and self-criticism. (iii) Find a resolution and hold fast to it. (iv) Regard your opponent as a potential ally. (v) Make your tactics consistent with the goal. (vi) Be flexible. (vii) Be temperate. (viii) Be proportionate. (ix) Be disciplined. (x) Know when to quit. Gandhi's Way, supra note iii, pp. 63–64.
6. For example, Gandhigram Rural Institute offers a Masters in Gandhian Thought and Peace Science, Gujurat Vidyapith has the Jamnalal Institute of Studies in Non-

Violence, Mahatma Gandhi University in Kottayam has a School of Gandhian Studies and Peace Science, and Madurai-Kamaraj University offers certificates and diplomas in Gandhian Thought. Association of Indian Universities, Universities Handbook, 29th edn., New Delhi, 2002.

7. Mark, n. 4.
8. Mekenkamp, Monique, Van Tongeren, Paul, and Van de Veen, Hans, *Searching for Peace in Central and South Asia*, USA, 2003.
9. http://www.icpsnet.org.
10. Stellan Vinthagen, stellan.vinthagen@padrigu.gu.se can be contacted for more information on this collaborative effort.
11. http://www.fulbright-india.org.

Section II

Indo–Pakistan Relations A Paradigm Shift

Indo-Pak Relations and SAARC: Retrospect and Prospect

A.S. Narang*

According to many observers the 12th Summit of the South Asian Association for Regional Cooperation (SAARC) held in Islamabad in January 2004 has perhaps been the most successful one in the organization's chequered 20-year history. It was so particularly for signing of the South Asia Free Trade Agreement (SAFTA), which was first discussed in 1995, and had been too long in the coming. The experts have always suggested that for South Asian countries it was imperative to significantly accelerate cooperation in the core economic areas. South Asian countries, with more than half of the world's poor, remain mired in an unacceptable level of poverty, human deprivation, population pressure and environmental degradation. At the same time the increased pace of globalization of economic processes, the information revolution, new technological advances and the growth of trade in services and greater movement towards trade liberalization have further exposed countries in the region to the challenges inherent in the present phase of globalization.[1]

In recent decades, countries—developed as well as developing—have been looking at regional economic integration as a means of strengthening their international competitiveness and as an engine of economic growth. The experience of the European Union suggests that the formation of the single European market led to substantial restructuring of industry on a pan-European basis and hence enabled it to exploit the economies of scale, scope and specialization.[2] In the WTO, we find various such regional groups such as EU, ASEAN, MERCOSUR, etc. South Asia is one of the few regions without an effective economic grouping in a world where bilateral and regional trade pacts are proliferating by the year. This is in spite of the fact that

* Professor in Political Science, IGNOU, New Delhi.

South Asian countries have certain inherent advantages in regional cooperation. The group of eminent personalities of South Asia in its report suggests that these countries have the advantage of geographical contiguity and shared economic, social and cultural characteristics, which should serve to reduce the transaction costs. They also have an inherited development infrastructure, even if it has not been upgraded over the years. With its combined population of 1.3 billion, South Asia commands a huge potential market. If these countries are able to sustain the current dynamism in their economies and raise the purchasing power of the large proportion of their populations who live below the poverty line, such a market could grow exponentially to a point where it would be coveted by the rest of the world, and could thereby attract significantly larger flows of foreign capital. The world trading system is in the process of being divided into three mega-groupings centred in Europe, the Americans and the Asia-Pacific. These groupings are designed mainly to bolster the competitive positions of the three regions through expanding the scale of the markets and mobilizing larger resources for research and development. Such groupings are also intended to enhance the bargaining power of the member states in regional and global economic negotiations of a strategic character, which increasingly involve the establishment of new trading regimes and new rules of the game. The immediate implications of such mega-groupings are to enhance discrimination against outside countries, either directly through their preferential arrangements or indirectly due to their policy of deeper integration in areas other than trade.

Those outside these mega-groupings, which include the South Asian countries, are being progressively marginalized in the world economy. Their option is either to join one of these groupings—which is not feasible because they are either not welcome or have to pay on entry fee which they can ill afford—or form groupings of their own to place themselves in a better bargaining position to come to terms with mega groupings. The South Asian countries thus have no alternative but to strengthen their own regional groupings in order to survive within the emerging global system.[3] Also, if one goes by the results of limited experiences with trade liberalization in the region, the conclusion will be that SAFTA will lead to important industrial restructuring. The Indo–Sri Lanka bilateral FTA, for instance, even within a short period of less than three years of implementation, has led to a lot of dynamism in the intra-regional investments. Similarly, the India-Nepal FTA of 1996 spurred some Indian companies to shift production of common consumer goods of everyday use such as toothpaste for the north-Indian market to Nepal. As a result these items emerged as some of the most important items of Nepal's exports to India. Thus, if SAFTA comes into existence, by conservative estimates, it may help in trebling the proportion of intra-regional trade, making it possible to trade directly rather than through third countries, and lead to savings of substantial value for the region.[4]

In the light of the above-mentioned account, observers opine that SAARC has taken the long-awaited first step. If its leaders can carry forward the process of economic cooperation, they will have contributed substantially to improving the climate in region. However, observers also feel that SAARC has a long way to go before it can even think of emulating the EU or even ASEAN. There are many daunting challenges that must be met if the new effort at promoting trade in South Asia is not to fail as well. Let it not be forgotten that this is the third and not the first time that the member-countries of SAARC have laid down a target date for setting up a free trade area. The proposal was first mooted in 1995 and it was envisaged that SAFTA would be achieved by 2005. The SAARC Summit held at Male in 1997, brought forward the date of achieving SAFTA to 2001. If the new effort at promoting SAFTA and other related issues is not to fail, then we have to analyze the reasons for the failures so far in a proper South Asian perspective, the background of the 12th Summit decisions, access the prospectus and suggest necessary steps to maintain the momentum that appears to have been generated.

II

Looking at the South Asian perspective, while it has been generally believed that a regional federation would undoubtedly benefit the member states, the success of creating such a federation has remained on the one hand, at the mercy of the Indo–Pak relations and on the other, the size and geographical location of India in the region. It was because of these that South Asia was a late starter in the movement for regional cooperation. The South Asian countries embarked upon the venture of institutionalized regional cooperation only in 1985 when the SAARC was established. Then for the first eight years of its existence, hardcore economic issues such as trade industry, money and finance were kept outside the scope of cooperation. This situation was somewhat redressed with the adoption in 1993 of the agreement on the SAPTA and its implementation in 1995 with the conclusion of the first round of negotiations for the exchange of trade preferences. But since then achievements over the years have fallen short of aspirations. Consequently SAARC countries have not developed any collective leverage in global economic negotiations nor do they constitute an effective voice in global economic forums. Often this has been due to lack of vision and differences in perceptions of Indian and Pakistan political elites having roots in partition.

As far as Pakistan is concerned the main effect of its creation by the partition of India, as Gyanedra Panday suggests, is that it is a 'minority nation': one that has never quite overcome the belief that it is the 'nation of the Indian Muslims'. Pakistan spokespersons have struggled to define it in more positive and self-contained terms. We start then with something of a paradox, for the concept of a 'minority nation' is an oxymoron, a contradiction in terms. Certainly any visitor to Pakistan and any observer of official Pakistani propaganda, will note the massive doses of anti-Indian rhetoric upon which Pakistan TV, the Pakistani state and Pakistani politics more generally seems to thrive: though one should note straightway that the Indian media and India official renouncements have hardly been short on anti-Pakistani rhetoric, even if India as a much larger and more self-sufficient country perhaps has less need of defining itself against this 'other'.

After the loss of its eastern-wing, which became Bangladesh in 1971, leaving Pakistan as a much smaller and weaker state to the north-west of India, Pakistan could no longer claim even the distinction of being the refuge of the subcontinent's Muslims: both Bangladesh and India have a larger Muslim population. It was in this context, as Aijaz Ahmad and others have noted, that the ruling class launched into a programme of Islamization and a search for an Islamic identity through West Asian connections. This thrust towards a rightwing Islamic politics was also encouraged by the emergence of an oil-rich Saudi Arabia, and by the American-led drive for the containment of communism. Throughout this period, the military–bureaucratic complex in strength, with the military clearly taking the upper hand, the general process of militarization increased and wide sections of the population gained access to arms and to a new religious militancy. The Pakistani regime's aggressive renewal of its long-standing pledge to liberate the Muslim-majority state of Kashmir from Indian control, and its support for what the Indian government describes as cross-border terrorism in that region, must be seen in the context of this changing national and international situation.[5] Thus the Pakistan state has been subscribed by the military and a shrill anti-India tenor has been ingrained into the collective psyche of the nation as a substitute for the chemistry of cohesion that must keep a state government. It is quite clear that more than the problem of Kashmir, it is the attitude and the psyche with which Pakistan projects it. In 1972, after the Bangladesh war, Zulfikar Ali Bhutto publicly vowed to turn his back on India and seek Pakistan's fortune among the Islamic countries to the West.

Another related aspect of partition is that the parts of India which came to Pakistan were primarily feudal dominated. Politics and political decisions therefore came to be feudal controlled. This went to the extent that even those who did not own vast tracts of ancestral land, once in position of power, tended to cultivate a certain feudal style: the Pajero car, the perfectly tailored *salwar kameez* and the manners of chamberlains at a royal court. Thus, business and feudal elites are not quite as segregated as is assumed. Both Benazir Bhutto and Nawaz Shariff fitched their stars to modernization and openness, yet both relied on feudal intrigue to further their policies.[6] Within this perspective Pakistan has also convinced itself that a close economic relationship will work to India's advantage. What better way to cause harm to India than not having these ties? It did not mind the loss of revenue, caused by informal trade, a respectable name for smuggling via Dubai and other places. Over the years, the ruling establishment there, irrespective of its composition and complexion, has worked public opinion so intensely that it reacts sharpely to even a slight show of official moderation. Some time ago a senior official in Islamabad drew attention to a routine point that, under the WTO regime Pakistan had to accord India the most-favoured nation (MFN) status. This led to a shrill chorus of protests, with shrieking headlines in newspapers about a "sell-out" and an "unpardonable departure" from a cherished policy. The Urdu papers translated the MFN in words which when translated into English meant a plea to treat India as a highly likeable country. This was enough to inflame the public sentiment and the poor official was shunted out. His only sin was to draw attention to the stand and norms in international economic dealings. It was forgotten that India had already accorded MFN status to Pakistan, which had to be reciprocated under mandatory dos and don'ts of the WTO.[7]

Independent India arrived on the second stage in the middle of the 20th century with rather different ambitions. The Indian national movement had emerged as one of the most powerful and inspiring struggles of the preceding decades, its remarkable popular support combined with an internationalist perspective that enabled Jawaharlal Nehru to claim in 1939 that the boundaries of the movement lay in China on the east and in Spain in the west. The new nation state quickly laid claim to being a leader of the nonaligned world, bound neither to the capitalist West nor to the Soviet bloc, charting out another path to modernity—an ancient civilization marked by a unique spirit of 'accommodation', now a modern nation state, contributing generously and distinctively to the making of a modern, international community of peace, secularism and democracy. At the same time, in spite of its commitments and rhetoric for non-violence, India, or at least significant sections of its elite, thought in terms of a powerful nation and need for its consolidation and projection as such.

Major General K.M. Cariappa, Deputy Chief of the Indian Army Staff, declared in October 1947; that only a strong army could make India "one of the greatest nations in the world". Durga Das, a young correspondent of the nationalist daily, *The Hindustan Times*, went further, demanding the building of a strong state (through the liquidation of 'enemy pockets') and a strong army of the Nazi model. Nathuram Godse, Gandhi's assassin, put it no less plainly in explaining his hostility to Gandhi: India needed to become a modern nation, "practical, able to retialiate, and... powerful with the armed forces".[8] India, having a grudge against Pakistan as being responsible for partition and with estimations of its own capability, obviously looked down upon Pakistan. India's Pakistan policy, if not always hostile, has been mired in a welter of ambivalence. Even after 55 years and three generations, the two nations are as much, if not more, entrenched in deep-rooted suspicion and mutual dislike. SAARC in many ways had become a hostage to this Indo–Pakistan antagonism, even for matters purely economic. A significant example of this is SAARC'S behaviour vis-à-vis WTO negotiation.

As is well known, the Uruguay Round was a fait accompli. The developing countries not just the South Asian countries, hardly had any time to study the proposals and arrive at decision on the contents. Thus the case for a common South Asian position did not arise. As South Asian countries needed considerable time to study the Uruguay Round Agreement, the need for identifying common interests were set aside during the first and second WTO Ministerial meetings held in Singapore (1996) and Geneva (1998). The politics of the region, pivoted around the Indo-Pakistani nuclear explosions in 1998, also prevented the South Asian countries from discussing a common position for the second Ministerial meeting. By 1999, after the Tenth SAARC Summit in Colombo (July 1998), the tension in the region had considerably eased and the South Asian countries were prepared to put forward a common position for the third WTO Ministerial meeting in Seattle, US. This set the trend for a common position in the subsequent fourth WTO Ministerial meeting in 2001 in Doha, Qatar.[9]

Although a common position was submitted to the unsuccessful WTO Ministerial meeting in Seattle, it got considerably diluted at the time of submission because at the last minute India refused to recognize the new commerce minister of Pakistan and thus was not prepared to sign it at the Ministerial level before submission. Eventually, the document was submitted with the signatures of the commerce secretaries of the seven SAARC countries. Likewise, at the Doha Ministerial meeting, the common position got considerably weakened due to a departure from the common position by two SAARC member countries at the time of submission. Despite the common position of opposing any new Trade Negotiating Rounds until the implementation issues were fully addressed (agreed in New Delhi in August 2001), Pakistan and Sri Lanka stated that they could be flexible on investment and environment issues. It not only weakened the common position, but also called into the credibility of the document.

This brings us to the fundamental issues related to taking a common position by South Asian Nations at the WTO. The first factor is the well-known politics of the region that has spilled over to economic issues such as Pakistan not granting MFN status to India on a number of products. Regional politics has forced some South Asian countries to keep a distance from one another. The second factor is the division of South Asian countries between developing countries (India, Pakistan, and Sri Lanka) and Least Developed Countries (Bangladesh, Nepal, Bhutan and the Maldives). Nepal and Bhutan are yet to become members of the WTO; however, they do have observer status. This division leads to problems in prioritization of issues in which coherence to the stance is absent when taking a common position.[10]

III

It thus becomes clear that notwithstanding the positive developments which have accompanied the end of the Cold War, South Asia has remained susceptible to tensions and conflicts originating from the unique history of the region. Obviously, therefore, the outcome of 12th Summit seems to be historic. But given the close co-relation between the fortunes of SAARC and the state of Indo–Pak relations, the big question therefore is: can India and Pakistan set aside their history of conflict and animosity? Statements, negotiations and euphoria of Islamabad Summit apart, as things stand today there is no clear answer to this question. It is not only that both sides have been down this road several times before, but even the way decisions have been taken and reacted to particularly in Pakistan point towards possibilities both of failure and success.

To begin with, most observers of the South Asian scene believe that more than the realization by leaders of the two countries that peace is an imperative factor that jump-started the process at Islamabad summit was pressure brought on Musharraf and to a lesser extent on the Indian government by the Bush Administration. Pakistan is critically dependent on the US for its economic and military needs and could ill-afford to antagonize Washington. The Bush Administration has been nudging it for several months now to engage with India by creating a conducive atmosphere. New Delhi has been demanding: is this what Musharraf is attempting to do? According to some observers a cursory glance at the 153-word joint press statement issued after the 65-minute meeting between Vajpayee and Musharraf it is enough to show that Islamabad has made serious commitments in return for starting a composite dialogue on all outstanding issues, including Jammu and Kashmir.[11] If that is so, those who know the US behaviour in international politics and in the region can say without any reservations that depending on its own needs it can change its stand in favour of or against any state. Washington has also made it clear that at least at this juncture it considers Islamabad a major nuclear proliferator. Washington also views Pakistan as one of the unstable states in the region. It recognizes that power in the wrong hands in Islamabad is a threat to its interests. Washington fears that after Musharraf it could be the deluge in Pakistan. So it cannot afford Musharraf's coming under too severe pressures at home. But Musharraf after the Islamabad Summit has begun to face serious criticism.

Inside Pakistan, there was sharp criticism in some quarters against what is perceived as a betrayal of Kashmiri interests. There are growing fears that Pakistan might abandon its Kashmir policy altogether. For instance, Musharraf's statement that Pakistan had 'left aside' UN resolutions on Kashmir came as a shock even to many liberals, some of whom commented that Musharraf government had dumped the Kashmiri cause just as the Taliban after 11 September, 2001. As Murlidhar Reddy[12] writes, all those who smell a rat in the deal, to borrow a phrase from President Musharraf, are liberals and progressives. There is a sense of outrage and betrayal in their write-ups. They believe that Musharraf has signed on the dotted line under pressure from the United States. The liberals are worried about the fall-out of the deal on the future of Pakistan. Reddy quotes some of the writings of such commentators. For example, Ayaz Amir, former Foreign Service Officer and columnist wrote: "History has been made," declared a visibly jubilant President General Musharraf after the issuance of the joint Indo–Pak statement on the sidelines of the 12th SAARC Summit. He was right. History has indeed been made, but not perhaps in the sense he seemed to imply.

For what Pakistan has agreed to is to bid a last farewell to jihad in Kashmir: the final curtains drawn on the blood and iron of 15 years of history. Any doubts on this score should disappear with these words from the joint statement of Prime Minister Vajpayee that "in order to take forward and sustain the dialogue process, violence, hostility and terrorism must be prevented". President Musharraf reassured Prime Minister Vajpayee that he would not permit any territory under Pakistan's control to be used to support terrorism. For all the care taken of Pakistani concerns, this could have been a statement drafted in the office of Brajesh Mishra, Vajpayee's National Security Adviser.

For 15 years we defined the uprising in occupied Kashmir as an indigenous freedom struggle. Now a Pakistani ruler has put that struggle squarely in the locker of terrorism. We should forgive the Kashmiris if they feel a bit like the Taliban, whom we once supported and then threw to the wolves. If they utter the dread word "sellout", what do we say?

Historic compromises can be forgiven if you get something in return. What is Pakistan getting? Merely a resumption of a "composite dialogue". No wonder Pakistan's quasi-military government is frantically trying to spread the impression that the mere announcements of talks somehow herald a breakthrough. General Musharraf says he was disappointed after Agra but is now a happy man. If memory serves right, the mood in the Pakistani camp was triumphant after Agra, as if Pakistan by harping on Kashmir had somehow scored a victory over India. Chastened, we now seem grateful for small mercies.

Coming to the all-important question of whether a peaceful relationship with India is good for Pakistan, a thousand times, yes. Was *jihad* in Kashmir a sustainable and sensible policy? A thousand times, no. Then isn't Musharraf on the right course, doing the right thing? He is. "The only thing is he could have embarked on this journey much sooner and with less loss of face for Pakistan".

Kargil took care of all that sharing of vision, peace, stability, progress and prosperity. Then there was a five-year long, painful lull. On 7 January 2004 came the Vajpayee–Musharraf 153-word 'joint statement', in which the two promised 'to carry the process of normalization forward....'

Plenty has changed between Kargil and SAARC in Islamabad. The 'children of *Jihad*' declared a '*jihad*' against the Commander-in-Chief of the Islamic Republic of Pakistan. America is aggressive about peace in the subcontinent like never before. We are dependent on American relief like never before. Colonel Gaddaffi abandoned all his WMD programmes. Teheran accepted all IAEA demands. Saddam was retrieved from a hole.

To be certain, India's economy is one of the best performers on the face of the planet. Poverty in India is declining. Poverty in Pakistan is growing. Time is decisively on India's side. Corporate America is also on India's side. India's military-strategic superiority is growing faster than ever. Pakistan's strategic choices are narrowing by the hour. Vajpayee is strongly placed. India is forming partnerships both with China and Iran. Can Pakistan risk isolation?

At the SAARC gathering, President General Musharraf was asked, 'Now that you are turning your back on 56 years of misgivings, can it be said that friendship with India is part of your strategic doctrine? The General first paused, and then said: 'Of course!'

Is our enemy internal or external? For the past half a century we have been indoctrinating our children and teaching our soldiers that India is our only enemy. Is our President General serious about reversing fifty years of indoctrination?

Is our General priming to win a permanent plaque in the history of peace or impress the Norwegian Nobel Committee (nominations must be post-marked no later than February 1 each year) and share the Nobel Peace Prize (rules permit a division of the prize among a maximum of three laureates)? Only time will tell.

Is our General going to sit alongside President Roosevelt, who won the Nobel Peace Prize for drawing up the 1905 peace Treaty between Russia and Japan,or Anwar Sadat, who negotiated peace between Egypt and Israel, or Mikhail Gorbachev who helped bring the Cold War to an end? Neither a plaque in history nor the Nobel Peace Prize is going to be easy.[13]

Munno Bhai, an intellectual and columnist wrote: "How can an enmity, half a century old, suddenly change into friendship? How can abiding suspicion change into instant trust? Many a rainy season is needed."[14]

The fact that Musharraf deemed it necessary to meet representatives of political parties from Pakistan-occupied Kashmir (POK) and assure them that there was no 'secret deal' with New Delhi on Kashmir was an indication of the extent of misgivings on the issue. Carefully avoiding any reference to UN resolutions on Kashmir, which has been the mainstay of Pakistan's Kashmir policy in the last 54 years, Musharraf told leaders from POK that their wishes would be kept in mind while holding the dialogue with India. In other words, both for critics and supporters of the deal a significant question is: is Pakistan ready to reverse its policies on Kashmir and India that it has been nurturing since its birth in 1947? It is no ordinary question, as the answer would invariably have to touch the very ideological edifice on which Pakistan is built.[15]

On the other side also is the question, how will India take the Kashmir question? India says that Kashmir is not the "core issue" and the issue is more about the problem in Kashmir rather than the problem of Kashmir. It does not recognize Kashmir as a dispute, therefore discussing the loyalty of its accession to the Indian Union does not arise at all. Whereas for Pakistan, the disputed territory of Kashmir is the core issue, two definitions of the problem, which implies that parties are, in fact, looking at two different aspects.[16] In this context, the vital fact is that neither India nor Pakistan will part with what they are holding.

Then there are vested interests that have benefited from the continuous tensions between India and Pakistan, like the weapons dealers, the smugglers and conflict entrepreneurs. Any cutback in the defence budget would invite the wrath of the influential arms dealers and middleman. So will the smugglers allow SAFTA to become a reality? An observer, therefore, points out that many might benefit from friendship between two countries but many benefit from hostility as well. Their interests are spread far and wide and have grown deep roots. All such elements, including the Kashmiri fundamentalists, who are clearly unhappy with the deals, would make every effort to sabotage the peace offensive. It is a fact that whenever some progress is being made on the Indo–Pak front, militancy picks up. It is a question of survival of the fundamentalist elements. They would be without a job if things were to improve. How the leadership and administration, which have been playing into the hands of hawks by pointing fingers at each other, will deal with militancy, is yet to be seen.

Taking note of the above-mentioned background and existing & emerging ground realities, one can agree with a Pakistani columnist and former chief secretary Kunwar Idris, that the India-Pakistan joint statement on the normalization of relations has aroused undue hopes, which need to be tempered with a bracing skepticism. It has also aroused unnecessary fears in some minds, which need to be dispelled. If

President Musharraf's confidence that history has been made is hyperbole, Qazi Husain Ahmad's suspicion of a conspiracy hatched to determine the freedom struggle in Kashmir represents the other phobic extreme. The leaders of the two countries agreeing to start a composite dialogue, which they feel confident would lead to a peaceful settlement of all bilateral issues including Jammu and Kashmir to the satisfaction of both sides neither makes history nor smells of a conspiracy.[17]

If the history of the last 55 years and the resultant mindset in the two countries are hindrances in ways of peace offensives, the changed geo-strategic and global environment do provide optimism. The dynamics of changes in the global and economic environment due to scientific and technological progress have been such that the need for a vibrant and effective regional organization for South Asia has now become imperative. India and Pakistan can ignore this only at the cost of their own peace, progress and stability as also of all member-states of SAARC. The 12th SAARC Summit made it very clear that there is realization by all member-states about necessity for economic cooperation to strengthen their competitive position, both individually and as a group. And for that they are prepared for mutual compromises. For instance, Bangladesh Prime Minister Begum Khaleda Zia said that trade liberalization in the region would lead to a "win-win" situation for all SAARC countries. Although Bangladesh had some objection to SAFTA before the summit began, it was resolved after the concern of the least developed countries in the SAARC region—Bangladesh, Nepal, the Maldives and Bhutan—were adequately addressed by incorporating some special measures such as allowing them to put more goods on their sensitive list and granting an adequate time for a full-fledged free-trade regime.

The WTO negotiations amply demonstrate that when countries forge alliances they can generate synergy and become powerful players. The EU, Cairns Group, and the African bloc can exert powerful influence because countries in these blocks operate together, develop proposals together and support one another during discussions. This is not an impossible task for South Asia in spite of the problems highlighted above. In fact, it is a challenge for South Asia.[18] Thus SAFTA may help in evolving a horizontal specialization across the region to enable the most optimal utilization of the synergies of the member countries for their mutual advantage. Sri Lanka may well emerge as the region's hub for rubber-based industries, Bangladesh for energy-intensive industries and Bhutan, forest-based industries, and so on. The other lesson that comes out of recent experiences of regional economic integration in South Asia, as elsewhere, is that relatively smaller and poorer countries benefit more from RTAD. India–Sri Lanka FTA has brought down the trade surplus of India with the country from 8:6:1 to 4:9:1 in just two years. Regional economic integration will also make member countries, especially the smaller ones, more attractive destinations for third-country investments by obviating the constraint of small domestic market.[19]

Pakistan and other SAARC countries have evidently overcome their fear of being dominated by Indian business and have taken the strategic decision to use trade as a method to improve bilateral relations. Indian exporters control over 70 per cent of the intra-regional shipment. Duty-free goods from India have the potential of wiping out domestic industries in other South Asian countries. The six SAARC countries have a trade deficit of more than $2.2 billion with India. The SAFTA agreement is also evidence that the bigger countries in the region are capable of accommodating the interests of the smaller ones despite fears to the contrary. India and Pakistan both strove to remove one of the last stumbling blocks to SAFTA by agreeing to fast track the lowering of tariffs on imports from the less developed member-states.

Of course, civil society in both countries is tired of the bad blood. A young generation both in India and Pakistan wants to make it good in life and is convinced that the only way to make the economy grow is to ensure peace. There is also a great deal of consensus among political parties for improving relations. When Vajpayee went to Lahore in 1999, the religious parties organized massive protest rallies. This time there was no display of dissent. Even the opposition parties, the Pakistan People's Party Parliamentarians and the Pakistan League-Nawaz, which had boycotted the summit since it was a government affair, made it a point to greet Vajpayee at the dinner hosted by Menon and professed support to his peace initiative.[20] For the first time in the history of SAARC, a Pakistani Premier did not mention the Kashmir dispute. The cross-border terrorism also did not figure in Vajpayee's speech. Pakistani officials say that Musharraf's comments on the Security Council resolutions only reflect the reality on the ground. They say that a plebiscite in divided Kashmir is no longer a feasible proposition, politically as well as logistically. Indian officials, too, say that the bilateral ties would not be derailed even if there are stray terrorist incidents. They said they were convinced that Musharraf comprehended India's concern about terrorism. In short, the blame for terrorist incidents will henceforth not immediately be put on Islamabad and such acts will not be allowed to derail the dialogue process between the two countries.[21]

General Musharraf also appears finally to have realized that as a country that is part of the subcontinent and whose destiny is linked with the Indus-Gangetic area, Pakistan would never be accepted as part of West Asian Islamic states. Long ago, a noted US analyst said that Pakistan's geo-strategic importance arose out of its proximity to the three largest nations of the world—China, India and the USSR—and its commanding the oil sea lanes from the Gulf. But in a unipolar world with no active tension among these three major powers and the US, that geo-strategic location has lost much of its significance. Pakistan's source of financial support, Saudi Arabia, is coming increasingly under US scrutiny.[22] Pakistan thus now realizes that it has more in common with the rest of the subcontinent than West Asia and its future economic growth and political and social advancement depend increasingly on peaceful interaction with other SAARC nations. It has, therefore, also revised its decision not to go ahead with economic ties with India.

All these developments suggest that in spite of 57 years of bad blood and Kargil's setback to the Lahore Process, India and Pakistan can achieve peace and conciliation. Such things do happen in the real world among bitter rivals once they begin addressing the root causes of tensions and insecurity and realize the merits of cooperation. Perhaps such is the situation in South Asia at present. If the leadership of the major countries in the region can set aside their history of conflict and animosity, then SAARC could well 'reinvest' itself as the South Asian equivalent of the European Union. This requires both India and Pakistan to make unilateral concessions for each other as well as for smaller countries in the region to address economic insecurity among them. India, in particular geographically been placed in an unenviable position that also gives it a bad image. This calls for extra efforts by New Delhi to correct any misperception. Lakshman Kadrigamar, the former Foreign Minister of Sri Lanka stated that all other six members of SAARC share affinities of language, ethnicity and territorial contiguity with India, which they do not share with one another. He considered India as the hub and other countries as spokes of a wheel. Many Pakistanis argue that a union on the model of European Union would have been possible if India had not been united into such a giant country.[23] Right or wrong, India has to take note of such apprehensions. In fact, India must shed its obsession with Pakistan and devote more political and diplomatic energies towards tending its relationship with other neighbours. To quote Raj Mohan, in the absence of a consistent political tending of the neighbourhood, India will find itself repeatedly confronting poisonous weeds. At the same time, while India, in the light of its past experience, has to be extremely cautious, it must also take into account the enormous compulsions on Pakistan to break with the past. And for Pakistan, in order to effect a shift in a policy that has been the mainstay of that polity for 57 years, it is essential to prepare the ground for a change in mindsets nurtured and spawned by the state.[24] Let it take the initiative on the Kashmir issue, at least in the near future. Avoiding haste in improving relations and taking cautious steps one by one, they can move towards the desired goals. Yes, to quote President Musharraf, "there are extremists on both sides who may not want peace, take extreme and inflexible positions, who may like to sabotage this process". They have to be dealt with and isolated. Instead those who believe that South Asia is a region that has a core identity need to be supported. What has stopped the region from developing into a major player primarily is Indo–Pak tension. Resolution of this tension would result in the prosperity of the entire region. India and Pakistan therefore have to take the lead. This aspect is gaining ground on both sides and needs to be consolidated. ■

Notes & References

1. South Asian Association for Regional Cooperation (SAARC), *SAARC Vision Beyond the Year 2000*, Delhi, Shipra, 2001, p. 12.
2. Nagesh Kumar, "SAFTA: Trade or Development", *The Hindu*, January 7, 2004.
3. n. 1, pp. 47–48.
4. n. 2.
5. Gyanendra Pandey, "India and Pakistan, 1947–2002", *Economic and Political Weekly*, March 16, 2002, p. 1027.
6. Sagarika Ghose, "Feudal-Modern Mix in Pakistan", *The Times of India*, June 16, 1997.
7. K.K. Katyal, "Dealing with the Neighbourhood", *The Hindu*, November 5, 2002.
8. n. 5, p. 1027.
9. Saman Kelegama and Indra Nath Mukherji, "WTO and South Asia, From Doha to Cancun", *Economic and Political Weekly*, September 13, 2003, p. 3864.
10. Ibid. p. 3865.
11. B. Muralidhar Reddy, "A Deal for Peace", *Frontline*, January 30, 2004, p. 11.
12. ________ ,"Sense of betrayal", *Frontline*, January 30, 2004, p. 10.
13. Ibid., p. 10.
14. Ibid.
15. Ibid.
16. Ashutosh Mishra, "Indo-Pak Peace Efforts", *The Hindu*, September 15, 2000.
17. n. 12, p. 11.
18. n. 9, p. 3865.
19. n. 2.
20. Raj Chenguppa and Indrani Bagchi, "Gambling on Peace", *Frontline*, January 19, 2004, p. 29.
21. John Cherian, "Towards Amity", *Frontline*, January 30, 2004, p. 6.
22. K. Subrahmanyam, "Pakistan's Home Coming", *The Times of India*, January 7, 2004.
23. ________, "Common Cause: South Asia Can Go E.U. Way", *The Times of India*, January 7, 2004.
24. n. 11, p. 12.

Relevance of Mediation for India–Pakistan Peacemaking

P. Sahadevan*

This paper is concerned with the contrasting approaches of India and Pakistan to peacemaking. More specifically, it seeks to analyse India's insistence on bilateral approach and Pakistan's desire for third-party mediation. Will external involvement lead to constructive conflict resolution? What are the gains and costs of mediation? What are the limitations and merits of the bilateral approach? At the outset, some of the basic characteristics of the India–Pakistan conflict and structural constraints in constructive peacemaking are to be explained. The idea is to demonstrate the complexity of the India–Pakistan conflict and consequently the inherent difficulties in conflict resolution.

Characteristics of the Conflict and Peacemaking

Identifiably, there are at least seven notable features of the India–Pakistan conflict. First, there is an interlocking of issues between the two countries in the process of conflict formation.[1] This means that the conflict has not resulted from a single incompatible goal but a variety of competing interests which are linked to each other in a manner that solution or difficulty in resolution of one issue influences the other. As the issues constituting the conflict are composite, a combined solution is considered effective and enduring. The interlocking nature of the conflict can easily increase its intensity and result in its protraction reflecting in incessant violence and intractable peace process. To elucidate, the Kashmir conflict not only has a territorial dimension but also a strong security dimension, which is linked to both countries' search for power and dominance leading to an unending bilateral "prestige dispute".[2] The greater the criticality of

* Associate Professor, South Asian Studies, SIS, Jawaharlal Nehru University, New Delhi.

states' interests at stake in territorial dispute, the stronger their impact on the security competition. Also, cross-border terrorism forms an important subsidiary issue resulting from the conflict over territory.

Interestingly, the India–Pakistan territorial dispute is a multi-pronged affair in the sense that both countries have competed for more than one part of territory at a time. If Kashmir is a dominant issue between them, Siachen and Sir Creek have been subsidiary issues. In a way one territorial dispute is linked to the other, as is evident from the Siachen dispute's linkage with Kashmir. This means that solution to one issue is expected to facilitate resolution of other issues. Differently, at times, lack of agreement on one issue can concomitantly deny solution to others too. This suggests that the conflict-resolution process should entail a composite framework for negotiations. This is what has been adopted for India–Pakistan peacemaking. Such a composite dialogue process has a daunting task of achieving a comprehensive, composite solution. This has been the fundamental challenge of peacemaking in the India–Pakistan conflict.

The second important feature of the conflict is that from the standpoint of both countries, their conflict goal is forcibly linked to their 'national ideology'. Such an internalization of the goal in the national systemic framework and consciousness of the people makes very little scope for compromise by the parties. In this context the incongruent ideological position of India and Pakistan is an important source of conflict formation. Whereas the Indian state has adopted secularism as its mainstream ideology, the Pakistani state asserts itself to be Islamic. As a corollary, Pakistan sees itself as the guardian of Muslims in the whole region and considers the Indian claim of being a secular polity as sham, given the aberrations caused by some religious-oriented political parties. For Pakistan, therefore, Indian nationalism is essentially Hindu nationalism even though Indians and their state assert to the contrary and work for maintaining secular credentials amidst internal pressure for vitiating the basic secular character. Pakistan gives larger religious dimensions to its conflict with India; it is more evident in the Kashmir dispute. India considers the possession of Jammu and Kashmir as an ideological fulfilment of its secular statehood and in a similar vein Pakistan likes to possess the territory to achieve its ideological fulfilment of being an Islamic state. This has given rise to slogans that the J&K (for Pakistan) and POK (for India) are an 'unfinished agenda of partition'. Such antithetical ideological commitments have not only made the Kashmir dispute highly intractable but also extended their influence to the security spheres of their relations to create more competition and conflicts. The argument is that linking the conflict goal to the fulfilment of nationhood tends to create an intractable conflict structure.[3]

The third feature of the India–Pakistan conflict results from the previous one. That is, the conflict has a 'larger political value' since it forms an important factor in politics. There are jingoists on both sides who constrict peace efforts of the central leaders. Out of electoral compulsions and to ensure regime survival, even national leaders with a moderate face cannot genuinely seek peace or concentrate on a peace process. This situation has often marked the Kashmir dispute. There has been a strong tendency on the part of the Pakistani ruling elite (both belonging to the bureaucratic-military and civilian establishments) to effectively use the notion of Indian threats to capture or remain in power. All those generals who wrested power from the democratically elected leaders made India into a scapegoat for their misdeeds and unconstitutional activities. If India's military power and battlefield performance (in 1965 and 1971) have provided the basis for the local political use of regional security issues, Kashmir has been a useful rallying cry and a strong issue of diversion from the daunting task of nation building and maintaining democracy. Similarly, the political forces in India have tried to take a partisan stand on bilateral conflicts and make political use of them. Of course, the difference is that whereas India has been a critical factor in electoral politics in its neighbourhood, none of India's neighbours has had such a distinction in Indian politics. This is because the inter-elite competition in India has had a wider base and larger issues and the informed public opinion could judge foreign policy issues on the basis of their merit and in a proper perspective. Thus, the foreign policy orientation of governments and the inter-state conflicts hold very little value for electoral politics. At the most, the hawkish elements, both from the ruling and opposition parties, criticise the government for being soft towards the neighbours. Resultantly, some of the regimes in India have taken tough postures while others tried to ignore the internal pressures. For instance, in the past, the Jana Sangh always advocated a firm Indian policy to deal with Pakistan; so did some hawkish elements in the Congress during the Lal Bahadur Shastri regime. During the Janata party rule, the Congress was critical of the government's neighbourhood policy of beneficial bilateralism and later the same Congress government was criticised by the right-wing political forces. Until recently, on every occasion, the Bharatiya Janata Party (BJP)-led National Democratic Alliance (NDA) government was targeted by none other than its own ideological allies—Vishwa Hindu Parishad and Rashtriya Swayamsevak Sangh—for what they called the government's failure to contain the Pakistani threat and appeasement policy on Kashmir. These forces can emerge as a stumbling block to any meaningful peace process based on mutual compromise, particularly on the Kashmir dispute.

Fourth, the India–Pakistan conflict is 'manifested' in everyday life. It is known as a 'stable conflict' formation, which is defined in time (spreading over an extended period), space (encompassing the entire region) and consistency (in motives and tactics of the parties).[4] On the contrary, an 'unstable conflict' formation is limited in space (largely bilateral) and time (short period), and inconsistent in its process. The India–Pakistan conflict is stable and its significant indicators are: inter-state war, border tension, cross-border intervention, subversion, crisis, hostile propaganda and belligerent behaviour. Details of all these indicators are well recorded in various studies.[5]

Fifth, CBMs have 'limited real' value for India–Pakistan peacemaking. It is accepted that CBMs themselves are not solutions to international conflicts; instead they merely facilitate solutions by providing a vehicle for a peace process.[6] Since the outbreak of a conflict signifies the breakdown of communication between conflicting states and complete loss of trust in each other, CBMs are those arrangements designed to enhance an "assurance of mind and belief in the trustworthiness of states and the facts they create".[7] Thus, CBMs increase openness and transparency on issues of mutual concern to adversaries; alleviate their fears and anxiety; remove uncertainties and surprises, prevent pre-emptive actions out of miscalculations; reassure each other's intentions in pursuing security measures; enhance predictability in their behaviour and transform a competitive relationship into a co-operative relationship. In short, CBMs are those political principles which help bring about perceptional changes among the adversaries locked in intractable conflicts; they are those mutually agreed rules and norms governing and regulating their behaviour. They are designed for "increasing predictability in international security relations" and "expanding the scope for states to reassure each other about their security policies". They embody the notion of "common concerns which transcend competing interests in international relations" and, therefore, increase "political *demonstration* of good will and common interest".[8] A successful CBM is the one that ultimately makes adversaries redefine their objectives and adopt mutually profitable policies while keeping peace and co-operation in mind.

None of these has happened in India–Pakistan relations even though the list of CBMs has been long.[9] In fact they have under-performed their role. It must be noted that in a complex conflict situation CBMs have a very limited contribution to make as far as peace building and conflict resolution are concerned. Expecting too much of CBMs and exaggerating their importance in the peace process can only bring disappointments. This, however, does not mean that we undervalue the importance of CBMs either. Some of the reasons for their under-performance are: First, there is a problem of commitment. CBMs are seen as a political arrangement that does not entail legal binding or commitment. Thus the contracting parties have selective compliance to CBMs and use them according to their needs. This argument is more relevant to Pakistan. Second, conflict environment in the India-Pakistan case is complex. This undermines the effectiveness of CBMs. Third, when the contracting parties, mostly the weaker ones, perceive CBMs as a peaceful way to dilute their original conflict goal, they seek to undermine the agreed CBMs. Many India–Pakistan CBMs have become redundant or dysfunctional because of this perception held by Pakistan. Fourth, coupled with this is the feeling of one or both parties that CBMs are ways to avoid or postpone finding a solution to their problem. This is more widespread in the minds of Pakistanis. Fifth, destabilizing vicissitudes of domestic politics often curtail the prospects of success of CBMs. This is demonstrated in the India-Pakistan case. CBMs fail because the states of the contracting parties remain suspicious of each other as they refuse to have mutual trust. At the same time, developing a mutual understanding among their peoples is highly undesirable for them. In most cases, non-military CBMs suffer or fail because of this sort of politically motivated fixation.

Sixth, the India–Pakistan conflict has 'entrapped' the people and leaders.[10] The 'entrapment' factor in the conflict needs to be removed for a successful conflict resolution. Entrapment can be seen at two levels. Elite entrapment is related to the extent to which the leaders of both countries have committed their political futures to winning the conflict. General entrapment denotes the feeling of the critical masses in both societies that they have invested so much in terms of men and materials that they cannot give up the fight without actually accomplishing their original goal.

Finally, interruptions mark the India-Pakistan peacemaking efforts. Peace talks have been invariably short and negotiations are unsustainable. Taking a process approach, we can state that India and Pakistan have not developed their 'peace talks into a peace process'. Process entails a series of activities and intense interactions between the adversaries, providing continuity for negotiations, which are sustainable for a long time. A closer look at the history of India–Pakistan peacemaking will reveal that the peace process has not evolved itself to become a strong factor. Both countries engaged themselves in peace process only four times—during 1948–1950 under the UN mediation, during 1962–63 when the two countries conducted a series of ministerial-level bilateral negotiations on Kashmir, and during 1985–92 when talks were held on the Siachen dispute. To this list, we can include the composite dialogue process initiated in 1998, which continues even now despite some intermittent breakdowns in the recent past. None of these peace processes has ameliorated the India–Pakistan conflict. Besides, there were four summits—at Tashkent (1966) mediated by the former Soviet Union, Simla (1972), Lahore (1999) and Agra (2001). Importantly, barring the Tashkent summit, all other summits were bilaterally initiated and conducted. While the first two summits resulted in agreements and the Lahore summit produced a declaration, the Agra summit could not bring both countries together to agree even on a joint declaration.

It is evident that bilateralism has constituted the dominated approach of peacemaking. While it has produced CBMs, agreements and declarations, the core issues threatening peace and friendship have not been resolved. This does not mean that India and Pakistan do not have any a track record of resolving their disputes; the Indus water treaty and the settlement of the Rann of Kutch dispute remain the most telling examples of India–Pakistan conflict resolution.[11] Incidentally, both these settlements were reached with the help of external intermediaries. The World Bank mediated the Indus water treaty and the Rann of Kutch dispute was resolved through arbitration. Bilateralism has its own limits as revealed in the context of the intractable India–Pakistan conflict. But its advantages cannot be discounted. The factors which limit bilateralism are mostly those (discussed above) characterizing the India–Pakistan conflict. Bilateral negotiations have not been able to make the two adversaries change their behaviour (from violence to political), redefine their goal with a view to reaching a compromise solution and commit themselves to a negotiation process. Because the fundamental nature of the problem itself has not been defined and there is no mutual acknowledgement of the existence of the conflict, at least from the Indian side, talks are not structured. They are exploratory at the most and not aimed at working out compromise proposals. Parties have not done the cost-benefit analysis. And, there is no "hurting stalemate" in the conflict process in the sense of evolving a "ripe moment", which is crucial for reaching a settlement.[12] Does this situation augur well for mediation?

Mediation

International mediation is a third-party intermediary activity forming an integral part of a larger bargaining or negotiation process in conflict. A variety of actors or parties (ranging from private individuals to sovereign states of different size and strength and regional and international organisations) undertakes this function. The key to the process of mediation is the third party's objective of changing the behaviour, choice and perception of the adversaries so that a settlement can be reached between them. Although all mediation activities carry the same objective, their varied success in each conflict is determined by the mediator's strategies and the parties' responses. Implicit in this argument is the assumption that mediation is a diverse process involving a broad and versatile range of intermediary strategies. They include facilitation of communication between the adversaries and persuading them to give up their intransigent position in negotiations. A mediator may clarify ambiguous issues, offer suggestions to the adversaries, participate in negotiations and formulate proposals for the consideration of the adversaries. Its third-party position evolves a triangular relationship within the conflict structure, thereby changing the structure of interaction from the level of dyad to triad. With regard to the mediator's qualities, two divergent views are advocated in mediation literature. The traditional view of 'impartiality', which is linked with the mediator's 'disinterest' in the given conflict, has been questioned by the recent assumption that attributes the character of 'partiality' or 'bias', resulting from the mediator's interest in conflict, to its behaviour. Coercion is forbidden in a mediation process, but in practice some mediators use pressure tactics or provide various incentives to the adversaries with a view to changing their behaviour, choice and perception so necessary for reaching a negotiated settlement. In sum, mediation is a peacemaking exercise that should be acceptable to both adversaries; it entails a variety of costs and benefits both for the mediator and the conflict parties.[13]

The issue of mediation has been prominent in India–Pakistan relations since the early 1990s. As stated earlier, India accepted the third-party intermediary role on various occasions in the past. But its aversion to mediation and, at the same time, interest in bilateral negotiations have become strong only after the conclusion of the 1972 Simla Agreement which laid emphasis on the latter approach to peacemaking. This does not mean that Pakistan has stopped crying for an external role in conflict resolution. Neither was India altogether rejected the world community's direct and indirect role in facilitating a peace process and preventing as well as defusing crisis involving both countries. It is widely acknowledged that the Unites States played a significant role in ending the Kargil crisis when the Clinton Administration had exerted pressure on the Nawaz Sharif government to sign a declaration for withdrawal of the Pakistan's army from the occupied Indian territory and end its direct and indirect support to the mercenaries. Another time the US played a significant role in crisis management was in 2002 when India resorted to coercive diplomacy through military mobilization and Pakistan responded in kind by deploying its troops along the India–Pakistan borders. Aimed at preventing a war, the US adopted a strategy that combined political persuasion with discreet coercion.[14] Besides, the US has constantly been persuading both India and Pakistan to engage in negotiations. It is evident that India is not opposed to indirect external role in preventing or managing crisis or facilitating a peace process, but it still has strong reservations about accepting direct third-party mediation presumably for the following reasons:

1. A mediated settlement requires India to make a compromise on its original stated conflict goal. The government fears that this would have serious political implications in the country.
2. Given its dissatisfaction with the third-party mediated settlements in the past, it wants to avoid another imposition of solution by a determined power mediator who alone can make any negotiation process a success.
3. Since the US is considered a potential mediator or a main force behind any mediation process, it is feared that it would not be impartial and a mediated solution would benefit Pakistan more than India. Still the political opinions in India have difficulty in accepting the US as an impartial and honest peace broker.
4. India feels that openly accepting an external role in peacemaking will set a bad foreign policy precedent for international intervention in its internal and interstate conflicts in South Asia. It is felt that this would weaken India's position in the region.
5. India, a dominant party in the conflict, is confident of meeting the challenges from Pakistan. It has developed the required strength and capability to inflict damage and absorb shocks.
6. India thinks that bilateral negotiations with a less powerful country like Pakistan will enable it to create scope and space for greater manoeuverability. It can walk out if the process develops an adverse situation for India. This is not easy, though not impossible, once a mediation process is accepted. It cannot behave in a manner to jeopardize its credibility as a responsible nation.
7. India feels that mediation will come with a cost. Mediator(s) will have their own interests to promote at the cost of the conflict parties while conducting the peace process.

At the same time, why is Pakistan hell-bent on involving an external mediator in the conflict? The following reasons can be advanced:

1. Being a weaker party in the entire conflict with India, Pakistan feels assured of accomplishing its basic conflict goal with the help of a mediator. It expects that involving a friendly country will work to increase its credibility as a party

to the conflict with legitimate grievances. In this context it must be stated that mediation is largely an instrument of the weaker party in any conflict. The powerful adversary always seeks to resist the idea of mediation and reject any external intervention so long as it is strong enough to bear the cost of the conflict.

2. The bilateral approach has proved its inadequacy and inability to work for peace. As far as Pakistan is concerned, this approach is outdated and ineffective in bringing both countries together to agree on a compromise formula of peace.
3. Pakistan thinks that by sticking to the bilateral approach, India does not want to engage in serious political negotiations, which are guaranteed in a mediation process.

Now the question is: will mediation work in the India-Pakistan conflict? Generally it is said that a mediation process becomes successful only if the following conditions exist:[15]

1. The identity and characteristics of the parties are clear.
2. The parties are small powers and not regional contestants.
3. The cultural and ideological differences between the adversaries are narrow.
4. The adversaries had not been engaged in a previous dispute.
5. There exists a "ripe moment", exemplified by a "hurting stalemate" in the conflict.
6. The conflict management efforts of the parties have reached a stalemate.
7. The nature of conflict is related to security.
8. Neither party is prepared to countenance further costs of continuing the conflict.
9. Both parties are prepared to commit themselves to break the stalemate in the peace process.

Unfortunately, most of the conditions listed here do not exist in the India-Pakistan conflict. We should note that a third party will involve in mediation when the perceived benefits outweigh the perceived costs. While extending their good offices to resolve conflict, they expect gains and rewards for their role. Since mediation is a policy instrument, a mediator can pursue some of its interests eventually at the cost of the disputants. Also, there is a question about impartiality and biases.[16] It is empirically proved that not every mediator is impartial. Since not many mediators are disinterested in a given conflict, many are partial. Interested third parties can be leverage mediators and disinterested mediators may not be able to pursue power mediation, which involves persuasion, coercion, deprivation (of resources), gratification (adding resources) and extraction (of promise).[17] Mediation without power may not yield any result in protracted conflicts. At the same time, an agreement reached out of a leverage mediation process by an interested third party may not be based on consensus among the parties.

Despite these difficulties, the importance of mediation is not underrated in the India–Pakistan conflict. It is increasingly being made clear that Pakistan can be forced to adopt a moderate position and commit itself in the task of creating sub-continental peace only under international pressure. Also, its intransigent position pertaining to the conflict goal can be changed only with the help of international forces. Furthermore, the international community can also be useful in underwriting a peace agreement between India and Pakistan.

There are many misconceptions and rigid myopic views on mediation at least in India. It is necessary that the conventional mindset should change. Mediation is not based on a trilateral agreement involving the two parties and the mediator, but results primarily from an understanding among them. It is not a permanent arrangement; parties can walk out of the process if they are not happy with it. Powerful countries like India can prevent a leverage mediator from exerting undue pressure to accept an undesirable framework of solution. The point is that even under a leverage mediation process, India can enjoy a lot of leverage.

It is quite normal and expected that when one approach fails to create peace, the other option should be tried. It need not be pure mediation. It can be another form of third party role. Given the difficulties, constraints and concerns over mediation, it is advisable to have a power-baked facilitation process, at least to start with. The idea is to graduate from the current non-workable approach, which has created an impasse and move forward to have a process which is realistic and less costly. There may be a question as to who will be those facilitator(s). These are not very difficult issues to be resolved once a policy decision to that effect is made. A coalition of facilitators, assigned with a wider task, and not the routine minimal ones, can yield constructive results. In all these endeavours, the United States is the most powerful factor that is inevitably linked to the India–Pakistan peacemaking venture. Of course, involving the world's sole superpower has both advantages and disadvantages and costs and benefits. India should assess them properly before making its own decision. Violence and peace process cannot coexist. For a constructive conflict resolution, Pakistan has to do everything possible to help India in de-escalating, if not ending, violence in Jammu & Kashmir. A peace process based on an 'incremental approach' pursued with prudence, determination and commitment will gradually change the climate of hostility and antagonism—a necessary pre-condition for conflict resolution and sustainable peace between India and Pakistan. In this process, the international role, whatever may be it nature and level, cannot be wished away. ■

Notes & References

1. Interlocking denotes overlapping of conflicts. Kriesberg identifies six ways in which conflicts are interlocked: (i) Serial or nested in time, i.e., "every conflict may be viewed as one in a series of fights between the same adversaries"; (ii) Converging or nested in space, i.e., "separate groups may coalesce as allies against an adversary or coalition of adversaries"; (iii) Superimposed or linking of issues, i.e., "few or many contentious issues may be superimposed on each other"; (iv) Cross-cutting, i.e., "divisions within and across adversaries or among a set of adversaries allying themselves differently on several issues of contention"; (v) Internal i.e., conflicts which are "internal to adversaries" interact with conflict between; and (vi) Concurrent, i.e., one conflicting party is engaged simultaneously in conflicts with other adversaries. Louis Kriesberg, "Interlocking Conflicts in the Middle East", in Louis Kriesberg, ed., *Research in Social Movements, Conflicts and Change,* Vol. 3, Greenwich, Connecticut, 1980, pp.100–102.
2. See Ashok Kapur, "The Changing Dynamics of India-Pakistan Security Relationships in the World Today: The Problem of Conflict Formation and Conflict Resolution", Moonis Ahmad, ed., *Internal and External Dynamics of South Asian Security,* Karachi, 1998, p.17. Also see for details, P. Sahadevan, "Competing Regional Interests, Conflict Formation, and Conflict Management in South Asia", P. Sahadevan, ed., *Conflict and Peacemaking in South Asia,* New Delhi, 2001, pp.19–26.
3. For a theoretical explanation of intractability of conflict, see Louis Kriesberg, et al., eds., *Intractable Conflicts and their Transformation,* Syracuse, 1989.
4. Indicators of stable conflict formation are: limited confidence-building measures, normalisation talks, balancing, intrigues, hostile propaganda, arms race, war and subversion, and crisis. Ashok Kapur with A. Jeyaratnam Wilson, *Foreign Policies of India and Her Neighbours,* London, 1996, p. 36.
5. See Sahadevan, n.2., pp. 33–37. For a comprehensive analysis of the India-Pakistan war and crises, see Sumit Ganguly, *The Origins of War in South Asia: India-Pakistan Conflict Since 1947,* Boulder, 1986; Praveen Swami, *The Kargil War,* New Delhi, 1999; and Kanti P. Bajpai, et al., *Brasstacks and Beyond: Perception and Management of Crisis in South Asia,* New Delhi, 1995.
6. For conceptual studies, see Marie-France Desjardins, *Rethinking Confidence-Building Measures: Obstacles to Agreement and the Risks of Overselling the Process,* Adelphi Paper.307, Oxford, 1996; Johan Jorgen Holst, "Confidence Building Measures: A Conceptual Framework", Survival, Vol. 25, No.1, January–February 1983, pp. 2–15; Michael Krepon, Dominique M. McCoy and Matthew C.J. Rudolph, eds., *A Handbook of Confidence Building Measures for Regional Security,* Handbook No.1, Washington, DC, 1993; Michael Krepon, Jenny S. Drezin and Michael Newbill, eds.,

Declaratory Diplomacy: Rhetorical Initiatives and Confidence Building, Report No.27, Washington, D.C., April 1999.

7. Holst, n.6, p.2.
8. Ibid., p.3.
9. See Michael Krepon and Amit Sevak, eds., *Crisis Prevention, Confidence Building, and Reconciliation in South Asia*, New Delhi, 1996; Sumit Ganguly and Ted Greenwood, eds., *Mending Fences: Confidence and Security Building Measures in South Asia*, Boulder, 1996; Dipankar Banerjee, ed., *CBMs in South Asia: Potential and Possibilities*, Colombo, Regional Centre for Strategic Studies, 2000; Dipankar Banerjee, ed., *Confidence-Building Measures in South Asia*, Colombo, Regional Centre for Strategic Studies, 1999; Maqsudul Hasan Nuri, "CBMs in South Asia: Practice, Problems and Prospects", *Regional Studies*, Vol. 14, No.2, Spring 1996, pp.28–72.
10. For a conceptual explanation of entrapment, see Joel Brockner and Jeffrey Z. Rubin, *Entrapment in Escalating Conflicts: A Social Psychological Analysis*, New York, 1985; and Dean G. Pruitt and Jeffrey Z. Rubin, *Social Conflict: Escalation, Stalemate and Settlement*, New York, 1986, pp.121–5.
11. See R.P. Anand, "The Kutch Award", *India Quarterly*, Vol. 24, No.3, July–September 1968; and Niranjan D. Gulati, *Indus Water Treaty: An Exercise in International Mediation*, Bombay, 1973.
12. For a brilliant pioneering explanation of these concepts, see I. William Zartman, *Ripe for Resolution: Conflict and Intervention in Africa*, New York, 1985.
13. A large body of literature is available on international mediation. See C.R. Mitchell and Keith Webb, eds., *New Approaches to International Mediation*, Westport, 1988; Saadia Touval and I. William Zartman, eds., *International Mediation in Theory and Practice*, Boulder, 1985; Jacob Bercovitch, ed., *Resolving International Conflicts: The Theory and Practice of Mediation*, Boulder, 1996. Oran R. Young, *The Intermediaries: Third Parties in International Crisis*, Princeton, 1967.
14. V.K. Sood and Pravin Sawhney, *Operation Parakram: The War Unfinished*, New Delhi, 2003.
15. Some of the conditions are identified by Jacob Bercovitch, "The Structure and Diversity of Mediation in International Relations", Jacob Bercovitch and Jeffrey Z. Rubin, eds., *Mediation in International Relations: Multiple Approaches to Conflict Management*, London, 1992, pp.1–29.
16. Peter J. Carnevale and Sharon Arad, "Bias and Impartiality in International Mediation", Bercovitch, n.13, pp.39–54.
17. Jacob Bercovitch, n.15, pp.14–21.

Two States in One River Basin System: Conflict to Cooperative Co-Existence

Mohd. Tajuddin* and Muzaffar Ali**

Introduction

The sovereign right of exclusive use of the natural resources within the defined, delimited, demarcated and protected borders of the nation-states by their legitimate governments is absolute. The nation-states have devised ways and means through international law to exploit the natural resources even of those regions on this planet which fall beyond their sovereign control. There are natural resources, particularly surface waters that are trans-national in character. Water flow does not restrict itself to political boundaries and thus could be a cause of conflict between states. Present-day knowledge and technology has expanded the exploitability of the natural resources in a traditional manner and has created new avenues of their utilization. This has increased the value and importance of these resources and has created new areas of conflict between or among the co-sharers of common natural resources, particularly surface waters.

Water covers almost one half of total land surface of the globe.[1] The exploitation of the surface waters has always been a parameter for development. The trans-national courses of flow of some rivers have made things more critical, particularly amongst the countries falling in arid/semi-arid geographical zones in the contemporary period. The demand for water has increased manifold in the developing countries because of high population growth, rapid industrialization and the availability of Green Revolution agricultural technology. This increase in the use of water has resulted in its scarcity. Occurrence of conflict on water issues between states is becoming

* Reader in the Department of Political Science, University of Jammu, Jammu.

** Research Scholar, Department of Political Science, University of Jammu, Jammu.

frequent and, getting directly linked with a variety of socio-economic factors, has become a prominent area of environmental and international conflict.[2]

Considering the present scenario of the water crisis and rising hostile relations among nations, an important question before the political analysts is: would water sharing among countries continue to be peaceful? Water conflict, as history suggests has never been violent.[3] Would the same trend be true in future? This is a challenge before the technocrats dealing with trans-national rivers and the political decision makers of the co-riparian sovereign states of our time. The shared river basins between/among neighbouring states, if handled unconventionally with a futuristic vision may become a catalyst for lessening hostility and if mishandled, may add a new area of conflict, and tension.

Rationality demands that all possible attempts should be made to find ways and means of sharing river waters between/among the co-riparian states, in the spirit of sustainable development rising above uncompromising, parochial and immediate national interests. The trans-national course of flow of a river is natural and pre-historic; the nation-states with their 'sacrosanct' boundaries are nascent infants in the hoary record of formation and disintegration of states from the ancient to modern times in the river basin. Human civilization has survived the man-made ordeals, which became the cause of disintegration of statues located in the river basin at different times in history. The basin has provided a congenial environment for the birth of another succeeding state. It will be the greatest irony of history if man of our times, the inheritor of past knowledge and wisdom, and creator of the contemporary explosion of knowledge dragged the human civilization on this planet to an end as a result of his omissions and commissions.

Through this paper the authors try to understand the water dispute between India and Pakistan over the Indus Basin System and its resolution through the Indus Water Treaty. This treaty is a glowing example of cooperation between the two hostile neighbours which has worked effectively and uninterruptedly even during the 1965 and 1971 Indo-Pak wars. Excepting this the two states have failed till now to settle any of their other important bilateral disputes peacefully. The secure availability of waters of the Indus system is a more vital national interest for both the countries than even Kashmir. Pakistan and India have both survived and developed with one portion of Kashmir, the other portion each remaining with another, but it is doubtful if Pakistan and north-western India would have survived and developed without the peaceful settlement of this problem.

Even in the area of bilateral or sub-regional cooperation, the Indus Water Treaty is the only example of permanently settled river waters dispute in South

Asia. The Ganges Waters Treaty, which India has signed with Bangladesh in 1996 after many temporary agreements is valid for thirty years, after which the signatories might renew it.[4] Nepal, Bhutan, India and Bangladesh have many common rivers which have immense potential for cooperation in the fields of irrigation, electricity generation and inland navigation. The optimum utilization of a trans-national river is possible only through the cooperation of all the riparian states of the river. In the absence of such cooperative projects the riparian states are not only losing the benefits of cooperation but suffering from the calamities of flood and drought due to abundance of water in one season and scarcity in another, keeping the region as one of the poorest zones in the world.

The ruling elites of the regional states are over-conscious of their national sovereignty. They define their respective national interests vis-à-vis their neighbours through conventional wisdom in an urbane, upper class perspective. The nationalist approaches on the trans-national rivers are bereft of the miseries of the masses living in the common river basins. Suspicion and fear in India among the small states of the region and lack of an enlightened and accommodative approach in the Indian leadership on regional issues have worked against the launching of any serious project of regional cooperation, including common river waters. A feeling of South Asian-ness has not emerged despite the institutionalization of regional cooperation in the form of SAARC for twenty years. The Indus Water Treaty was signed twenty-five years before the launching of the SAARC and has worked successfully but has failed to become a model for river waters cooperation for harnessing the common water resources in the region.

The Indus water dispute erupted between India and Pakistan soon after partition in 1948. Its degeneration into a crisis was checked by a temporary water-sharing arrangement between the two states on their own. Formal negotiations under the auspices of the World Bank started in 1952 when their bilateral initiative failed and the world community intervened to avoid its degeneration into a crisis of international implication. The Indus Water Treaty was concluded between the two neighbours in 1960. The treaty is not an idealistic resolution of the Indo–Pak water dispute over Indus rivers system but a realistic permanent solution of the problem. The treaty was negotiated and decided without any consideration of their bilateral disputes on any other issue.

The Indus Basin System

The Indus Basin System of rivers comprises nine rivers. The system is named after the most important river of the system—Indus. Six rivers of the system—Indus, Jhelum, Chenab, Ravi, Sutlej and Beas—are placed in one group because their flows are shared commonly by India and Pakistan. The other three rivers of the system Kabul, Swat and Kurram—are placed in another group because their flows are commonly shared by Afghanistan and Pakistan. Eight out of the total nine rivers of the system are big rivers in their own right with their own tributaries and independent courses of flows. They are treated as tributaries of the Indus because they all culminate directly or indirectly into it, which in turn culminates in the Arabian Sea.

The system in common perception includes only the first group of six rivers because the territory through which they flowed were part of the British Indian empire. The colonial administration understood the importance of the water resources of these six rivers for economic development and exploited them for irrigation with the help of modern technology. The Indus, Jhelum and Chenab are known as Western Rivers of the system because they originate in the western region of Shivalik and Pir Panjal ranges of mountains and their flows work as drainage of the northwestern Himalayas. Ravi, Sutlej and Beas are called Eastern Rivers since they start their course from the territory lying east of these ranges and function as natural drainage of the south-eastern region.[5]

The Indus river is historically and culturally one of the most important rivers of the Indian subcontinent. Its original name given by the Aryans in their language, Sanskrit is Sindhu, meaning ocean. The migrating Aryans who were unfamiliar with the ocean in their mountainous existence till that time when confronted with this mighty river in their march to the plains called it Sindhu because it appeared to them like ocean.[6] The words Hind, Hindu, Hindustan, Hindi have been derived from Sindhu as a result of the association of this river and its basin with Persians during the time of King Darius (561–486 B.C.). The words Indus, India and Indian have their origins in the Greek influence on this territory at the time of Alexander (356–323 B.C.).[7]

The river valley has been the nourisher of one of the oldest civilization of the world which was named after this river when colonial archaeologists excavated its remains in Sind and Punjab in the third decade of the twentieth century. This single archaeological discovery stretched the antiquity and continuity of Indian history in time by three thousand years before Christ. The dilapidated remains of the excavated towns and the artifacts discovered there proved that a highly developed civilization had flourished in the valley of this river. In the opinion of Sir John Marshal, the chief excavator and the acknowledged authority on the Indus Valley Civilization, the remains of the two towns show, 'many millenniums of human endeavour behind it'.[8]

The Indus is a great trans-Himalayan river of South Asia and the fourth longest river in the world having a length of 2880 km. The length of its tributaries is 5600 km. The Indus River rises in south-western Tibet at an altitude of 16,000 ft. (4900m) from the Dinghai-Xizong plateau north of Kailash Mountain. It flows through Laddakh and the Baltistan plateaus of Jammu and Kashmir province of India before it enters the North West Frontier Province of Pakistan. Important places located on its banks are Demchok, Nyoma, Leh, Kumdok, Skardu and Chilas in India, Tarbella and Attock in Pakistan. Its five tributaries from Punjab after meeting with each other join it at Mithankot in Sind province of Pakistan. It passes through Sukkar, Nawabshah and Hyderabad towns to enter the Arabian Sea. Near Thatta it begins a deltaic stage and breaks into distributaries, which reach the Arabian Sea at various points south-east of Karachi.[9]

River Jhelum originates from a spring at Verinag situated in the southeastern part of the valley of Kashmir.[10] The length of the river is 730 km. It forms the de jure boundary between India and Pakistan before it enters into Pakistani Punjab below Mangla in the PoK (Pak occupied Kashmir). The city of Srinagar is located on its bank and Wular Lake is part of its course. It joins the Chenab, another tributary of the Indus at Trimmu.

The Chenab river rises as two streams: Chandra and Bhaga in the north-western Himalayas in the Lahul region of the Indian province of Himachal Pradesh. In its course of 1800 km, it flows through the Jammu region of J&K before it enters into Pakistan near Marla. It is the second important river of the system after the Indus. It submerges in itself the Jhelum and Ravi. Important places on its bank are Kishtwar, Doda, Ramban, Reasi and Akhnoor in India and Gujrat in Pakistan.

The Ravi river rises near the Rohtang Pass in Himachal Pradesh. Ravi is the most seasonal amongst the rivers of Punjab.[11] It enters the plains near Madhopur in Indian Punjab then flows along the boundary between India and Pakistan until it enters Pakistan near Lahore, which is located on its bank. The length of its total course of flow is 725 kms. It joins the Chenab below Trimmu and above Multan. The famous excavated city of Harappa of the Indus Valley Civilization is also located on its bank. The Jhelum, Chenab and Ravi even after their confluence are known as Chenab till they meet the Sutlej at Panjnad.

River Beas is not an international river; it rises and flows fully in India. It takes its birth from Beas Kund near the Rhotang Pass, at the south-eastern end of the Pir-Panchal Range. Its headwaters are closely hemmed in by the Sutlej to the south and east, and Ravi and Chandra—a tributary of Chenab—to the west and north. The Beas is the shortest of the Indus System Rivers, only 470 km long, although the contribution it makes to the system is a very respectable one. It meets the Sutlej at Harike.[12]

The Sutlej is the eastern most river of the Indus system. It rises from Rakas Lake situated in Tibet. It is also connected with Mansarovar Lake. It flows northwest and enters Himachal Pradesh at the Shipki-La Pass. It enters Punjab at Nangal. This course brings it to the inner Shivaliks at Bhakhara, which is a dam site. The rim station of the Sutlej is Ropar (Rupnagar) where it cuts through the last of the foothills and emerges on the plains.[13] It covers a distance of 1440 km before it joins the Chenab at Panjnad. Its flow makes the boundary between India and Pakistan from Ferozepur to Sulemanke.

Development of Modern Irrigation System in the Indus Basin

The Indus Basin consists of three geographical regions: Himalayan region, Sub-Himalayan region and Plains. The Indus Plain is a semi-arid and arid region. No agriculture is sustainable in this fertile plain without artificial irrigation except in a narrow belt near the foot-hills and the river margins where cropping is possible subject to inundation during floods. The flat Indus plains with the perennial rivers flowing through it like the fingers of a hand is ideally suitable for the development of the largest contiguous canal irrigation system. According to some experts no other area in the world has a similar natural advantage for the development of a canal irrigation system. Three pre-requisites for the development of the canal system were: (i) single political control over whole or almost whole Indus Basin (ii) availability of appropriate technology (iii) availability of a large population to construct, maintain and utilize the irrigation system.[14]

The British colonial power had acquired all these conditions by 1850. The colonial administrators conceived the idea of developing the irrigation system to utilize the abundant water of the Indus system for the development of agriculture in the 'Crown Waste Lands' of Punjab to overcome food deficiency of northern India and produce fibres for the textile industry. The construction of the canal system provided a satisfactory solution of the disbanded Sikh army of around 40,000 soldiers.[15] The colonial administration decided to settle these past soldiers as farmers within a small area between the Sutlej and Indus rivers to delimit their potential threat to the empire. The provincial Punjab administration envisaged and executed canal irrigation as a source of revenue also.[16]

The first canal constructed by the Punjab colonial administration was Upper Bari Doab Canal (UBDC), 247 miles in length on River Ravi, which was started in 1849 and completed in 1859.[17] It provided water to about a million acres of land between the Ravi and Beas rivers. The construction of Sirhind Canal on the Sutlej from Ropar was started in 1869 and completed in 1872. This canal improved agriculture in three million acres of land in the Punjab and the neighbouring princely states. The old inundation canals,[18] taking off from the Sutlej, Chenab and Indus were improved, extended and enlarged.

The second phase of canal construction in the Indus Basin was undertaken after the severe north Indian famine of 1878, which caused hundreds and thousands of starvation deaths. The British Indian administration decided in the early 1880s to increase the acreage of cultivable land by developing canal irrigation in the desert and waste land areas of the Indus Basin. The main difference between the first and the second phase of canal construction was in their purposes. The first phase of construction improved the agricultural activities in the settled areas but the second phase converted the government waste lands unfit for settlement and cultivation into fertile lands where canal colonies came up. Lower Sohag and Para Canals from Sutlej, Sidhani Canal from the Ravi were completed in the 1880s. The Lower Chenab and the Lower Jhelum Canals came up in the 1890s.

Impressed by the result of the second phase in terms of economic growth and prosperity, which increased government revenues from different sources the government decided in favour of Integrated Indus System of Canal in the first decade of the twentieth century. The Upper Jhelum Canal, the Upper Chenab Canal and the Lower Bari Doab Canal (LBDC) were interlinked in 1915 under Triple Canal Project (TCP). Two new big irrigation projects proposed after the First World War were: the Sutlej Valley Project (SVP) and the Sukkur Barrage Project (SBP).

The lower riparian Indus Basin region—Sind—at that time part of Bombay province raised objection about the development of canals in the upper riparian region Punjab that adversely affected their right over the river waters. The Indian princely states of Bahawalpur and Bikaner were also affected parties. The SVP and SBP were sanctioned and executed when all the concerned parties—the provinces of Punjab and Bombay, the princely states of Bahalwalpur and Bikaner, Government of India and the Secretary of State in London—approved the projects after multilateral negotiations.[19] Under SVP, four barrages were planned to be constructed on the Sutlej at Ferozepur, Sulemanke, Islam (originally Pallah) and Panjnad. The upper barrages, viz. Ferozepur, Sulemanke and Islam were completed in 1927 and the Panjnad was completed in 1933. Three canals each from the headwork at the upper three barrages and two canals from Panjnad lower barrage headwork were constructed to facilitate agriculture. The SBP comprised a barrage across the Indus at Sukkar in Sind and seven canals taking off above this barrage.

The working of the new canals was not problem-free. The government of India appointed the Anderson Committee in 1935 to find a solution for these problems. In addition, the method of observations of river flows and their record keeping were settled between the provincial governments of Punjab and Sind and the decisions arrived at were institutionalized. For procurement of the relevant data a comprehensive system of discharge stations was set up for regular daily observation of river flow and canal withdrawals at different points on the rivers and the canals. The Anderson Committee presented its unanimous recommendations in 1937, prepared on the basis of full consensus of the affected parties. As per the recommendation of the committee withdrawal was increased in some canals and reduced in others. The supplies to Haveli and Thal canals were arranged according to the recommendation of the committee. The Haveli Canal from Chenab was sanctioned in 1937 and completed in 1939. The Thal Canal from Indus was started after this.[20] Unlike the past canal construction in the Indus Basin, work on these two post-1935 canals could begin only after the analysis of reliable data about the trend of water supplies available in the rivers.

Prior to the Government of India Act 1935 the central government was the final authority on the river waters and any irrigation projects to be developed on any river. Its decision was binding on both the upper and lower riparian provinces. A distinct change came in the mechanism of the resolution of the inter-provincial water dispute after the Act came into effect on 1st April 1937. The Act placed irrigation and electricity under provincial jurisdiction. Every province became empowered to undertake river water development projects on the rivers passing through its territory. The central government could intervene only when another province complained against the proposed project.[21]

Utilising these provisions Punjab undertook investigations of several new irrigation schemes, involving fresh diversions and storages. On the request of Sind made in October 1939, the Government of India appointed the Justice B.N. Rau Commission in September 1941, which submitted its report in July 1942. The recommendations of the commission were not acceptable to either party. It was decided to refer the dispute to His Majesty's government in London. Meanwhile the chief engineers of both the provinces reached an agreement through their informal meetings and prepared a draft of it in September 1945. But they failed to reach any final agreement and in early 1947 the Government of India referred the matter to the Secretary of State for decision. The reference was followed by the partition and decolonisation of India in August 1947 through the Indian Independence Act passed by the British Parliament on 18 July 1947. The partition plan divided the Indus basin between the two sovereign independent nation states—India and Pakistan.[22]

Impact of Partition on the Indus Irrigation System

The partition of the Indian subcontinent and the creation of the two dominions of India and Pakistan in August 1947 led to the division of the Indus Irrigation System that was originally designed as one scheme. It was beyond the scope of the Indian Independence Act to define the pattern of relations between the two states or a principle for the division of the waters of the Indus rivers system. Sir Cyril Radcliff, Chairman of the Punjab Boundary Commission, felt that fixing of boundary in Punjab is 'complicated by the existence of canal systems, so vital to the life of the Punjab but developed only under the conception of a single administration'. He expressed hope in the Boundary Award that 'a solution may be found by agreement between the two states for some joint control of what has hitherto been a valuable common service'.[23]

The Boundary Award placed 21 million acres of land irrigated annually by the Indus canals system in Pakistan and 5 million acres in India. Most of the canals and the canal colonies went to West Punjab. Out of the total population which depended on the waters of the Indus system according to the 1941 Census, 25 million were in Pakistan and 21 million were in India. The partition severed the hydrologic unity of the Indus canals system. The uninterrupted flow of irrigation waters to the fields in West Punjab became dependent on the decision on another sovereign state, India. The decision to develop several million acres of arid but fertile land in India and also in Pakistan which was feasible only through the supply of waters of the Indus rivers system became problematic as a result of the division of sovereignty over the rivers system. At the time of partition the most profitable and technically easier irrigation schemes based on the Indus Rivers system had been executed. Areas distant from the rivers for which storages were essential were yet to be taken. Most of these areas were in India.[24]

The most affected irrigation schemes were the UBDC and Dipalpur Canal. The Indo-Pak boundary line had severed the UBDC at several places, its headwork at Madhopur in East Punjab became part of India and most of the irrigated areas went to Pakistan. The headwork of Dipalpur Canal at Firozpur and about half mile of its length below the headwork became part of Indian Punjab.[25] The barrage at Ferozepur also regulated the water supply from the Sutlej between canals taking off from it and those taking off at Sulemanke and Islam.

The Governor General under Section 9 of the Indian Independence Act, 1947 set up an Arbitral Tribunal on 12th August 1947 to make awards in respect of division of assets and liabilities between the new provinces of East Punjab and West Punjab and any other matter arising directly out of partition and referred to it.[26] The issue of distribution of waters of the Indus Irrigation System was not brought to the Tribunal. At the same time, West Punjab sought assurance of the status quo on the flow of waters in the canals. To avoid the effect of partition on the flow of waters in the canals, the chief engineers of East Punjab and West Punjab signed an agreement on 20 December 1947 which provided among other things that the pre-partition allocation of water in the Indus basin irrigation system would be maintained up to 31 March 1948. This agreement was called the Standstill Agreement.

The idea behind this short-duration agreement was that the two states would negotiate and reach a proper agreement on the distribution of waters of the Indus system before the deadline. West Pakistan did not take any step to negotiate a new agreement with East Punjab till the expiry date of the Standstill Agreement, 31 March 1948. It is difficult to say whether this inaction by Pakistan was deliberate or accidental. In the absence of any agreement, East Punjab discontinued water supplies from Madhopur to the main branch of the UBDC and from Firozpur to Dipalpur Canal. Chaudhry Mohammed Ali, then Secretary General of Pakistan and later Prime Minister termed it as 'Machiavellian duplicity of East Punjab' and 'neglect of duty, complacency, and lack of common prudence of West Punjab', which had disastrous consequences for Pakistan.[27]

As a result of this discontinuation about 5.5 per cent of the sown area in West Pakistan at that time found itself without water at the beginning of the critical *Kharif* crop-sowing phase. The city of Lahore simultaneously was deprived of the main source of municipal water. The supply of electricity from the Mandi hydroelectric scheme was also cut off. By stopping the flows of canal waters from their headworks in Indian Punjab, India utilized its upper riparian status in the absence of any agreement to assert its privilege status and to make Pakistan realize its vulnerability and dependence on India for rivers flowing to Pakistan from India. Government of Pakistan 'in its official publication called the stoppage of waters `in its implication and results...more devastating than an armed attack....'[28]

Bilateral Initiatives to Resolve the Dispute

The government of East Punjab had formally notified to the government of West Punjab the expiry of the Standstill Agreement on 29 March 1948, two days before its actual expiry. In its response the government of West Punjab requested the East Punjab government for extension of the agreement. East Punjab asked West Punjab to send its chief engineer to Simla, its new headquarters on 15 April to negotiate an agreement for the resumption of water supplies. Liaquat Ali Khan, the Prime Minister of Pakistan sent a telegram on 15 April to the Prime Minister of India requesting him 'to take immediate action for restoring water supply'. The two chief engineers concluded two agreements on behalf of the two provincial governments on 18 April, which were 'to take effect after the ratification by the two central governments. One agreement sought to restore water supply from Madhopur to CBDC or UBDC until 30 September, except for some very small channels for practical and administrative reasons. The second agreement, valid till 15 October, was about restoring supply of water from Ferozepur headwork to Dipalpur and other Pakistani canals taking off from the Sutlej at Sulemanke and Islam. The supply of waters at Ferozepur was fixed in proportion to the flow in river Beas and not on the basis of the flow of Sutlej below Ropar. The Sutlej waters were kept reserved for the Bhakra areas in accordance with the original plan of 1920 which had been altered in 1942 for the sake of SVCs, seven out of nine of which canals were in Pakistan. These agreements included provision for payment by Pakistan to India of seigniorage charges,[29] proportionate maintenance cost and interest on proportionate capital.

In another telegram of 24 April the Pakistani Prime Minister requested the Prime Minister of India to fix the 'place and date' for the Inter-Dominion Conference to resolve the issue, which was fixed on 3 May 1948 at New Delhi. On the instruction of Pandit Nehru East Punjab issued orders on 30 April to resume water supply on the basis of the agreement arrived at Simla, subject to any variation which might be made at the Inter-Dominion conference.

At the conference Pakistan raised objection to the payment of seigniorage charges and to the capital cost of the UBDC to be taken for calculation of interest charges. The conference could not reach any agreement. The impasse was broken in a luncheon meeting between Prime Minister Nehru and the Finance Minister of Pakistan and leader of the delegation Ghulam Mohammad. A new agreement was decided in which the two disputed issues were postponed for resolution in the future.

The agreement indirectly recognized the primary right of East Punjab over waters flowing through it into West Pakistan. It also recognized the right of West Punjab to utilize the river waters for its agricultural development. East Punjab gave assurance to West Pakistan that it would not disrupt the flow in the canals of West Punjab suddenly but would gradually diminish the supply to these canals, giving ample time to West Punjab to develop alternative sources.

The Prime Minister of India was authorized to specify an *ad hoc* amount that West Punjab would deposit with the Reserve Bank of India. The undisputed claims of East Punjab would be transferred to it out of this amount and the balance would remain deposited in the Bank representing disputed charges.

Both the parties also agreed to meet again after study of the relevant legal, technical and financial matters. Another notable difference of this agreement from the earlier Simla Agreement was that it did not mention any terminal date for its validity. The Punjab Partition Committee, on the request of West Punjab took note of the new agreement in its meeting on 26 and 27 May 1948. It also stated that the subsequent negotiation on the issue would take place at dominion level. Both the dominion governments hoped that the agreement would provide a basis for a friendly solution of the water dispute.[30]

The Inter-Dominion Agreement was not a solution of the water dispute but it provided a modus vivendi for the supply of waters to West Punjab from the two headworks in East Punjab at Madhopur and Ferozepur. Though Pakistan expressed its dissatisfaction on the terms of the agreement just after one year in 1949 it remained the basis of water supply to Pakistan with few temporary exceptions till a treaty was signed in 1960 to settle the issue.[31] Although Pakistan stopped payment of disputed charges after one year, it continued to deposit the undisputed charges with the Bank.

The agreement could not work smoothly in the environment of post-partition grievances of both the parties against each other and the ongoing war between them in the state of J& K. Complaint and counter-complaint about starting new unauthorized canal projects in their respective territories began just after the signing of the agreement. Pakistan in its telegram to India on 13 June 1949 disputed the proprietary right of India over the common rivers because of its upper riparian status. It called the existing terms of water supply by East Punjab to West Punjab as 'onerous and unsatisfactory'. In a note sent to New Delhi on 16 June 1949 it asked for another Inter-Dominion Conference for the purpose of equitable division of waters and the resolution of 'all disputes incidental to the use of these waters'. The note also hinted that Pakistan might approach the International Court of Justice if the problem were not resolved bilaterally.[32]

The conference took place in early August 1949 but failed to resolve the problem. A bilateral Negotiating Committee was formed which met in March 1950 in Karachi and May 1950 in New Delhi. This committee also failed to reach any agreement. A stalemate situation had emerged on the water dispute issue. While Pakistan was determined to seek adjudication for which India was not ready, India regarded the terms of the 1948 agreement as non-negotiable, which was not acceptable to Pakistan.

Pakistan took the plea that it had signed the agreement under 'duress' so the agreement is legally invalid. India's proposal for a judicial tribunal for the settlement of the dispute could not materialize on the issue of chairman from a neutral country. At last, in September 1951 India agreed to refer only and exclusively the validity of the May 1948 agreement, but not the dispute as a whole to an impartial international authority.

Despite their dispute over the Indus Irrigation System, both countries began their independent plans to develop new uses from the Indus and its tributaries. India decided firmly in December 1949 to construct the Harike Barrage, upstream of Ferozepur at the confluence of Beas and Sutlej. In the late 1950s the plan was revised to incorporate three feeder canals from three head regulators from the barrage: one head regulator for the proposed Ferozepur–Sirhind Canal, another head regulator for the proposed Rajasthan Canal and a third regulator for the proposed Makhu Canal. East Punjab was constructing new distributaries from the UBDC for the settlement of the refugees from West Punjab. Work on Nangal Barrage and Canal which was part of the Bhakhra Nangal Project and had began in 1946, continued undisturbed and was ready by 1952. Government of India reoriented the construction programme to give the highest priority to the construction of the Bhakhra Canal system with the objective to begin irrigation from the canal by June–July1954.[33] This was a grand project, which would increase the use of waters in the Indus basin for irrigation in the Indian portion of the basin three times from the pre-partition period. In its magnitude it was comparable to Indus basin projects undertaken in West Pakistan.

Pakistan also started construction of Bombanwala–Ravi–Bedian–Dipalpur (BRBD) Link to divert the waters of the Chenab to CBDC and Dipalpur Canal to remove dependence on the headworks of these canals in East Punjab. This project was completed in 1958. It also constructed Balloki–Sulemanke (B-S) Link and Marla Ravi (M–R) Link, which were finished in 1954 and 1956 respectively. To ameliorate the negative impact of the development of irrigation projects in the upper region of Indus basin on Sind Pakistan sanctioned a barrage on Indus at Kotri in the lower Sind in 1947. Construction work on the project started in 1950 and it was completed in 1956. It was named the Ghulam Mohammad Barrage to commemorate the Head of Sate of Pakistan. Another project undertaken to ensure the equitable share of Indus waters to Sind was Gudu Project below Mithankot. The work on the project began in 1955 and the barrage was completed in 1962. The old project of a barrage at Tansua across Indus in West Punjab was commenced without objection from Sind in 1952.[34]

Involvement of the World Bank and End of the Impasse

The Indo–Pak water dispute attracted the attention of the international community. To know the nature of the dispute *Collier's* Magazine of the USA sponsored a fact-finding tour of David E. Lilienthal who had served as chairman of the Tennessee Valley Authority (TVA). His work in the authority had created national recognition for him on river development project. He agreed to take the tour and write a series of articles for the magazine for the information of the American people because he was free at that time after resigning as Chairman of the US Atomic Energy Commission. During his visit he met the two Prime Ministers and visited different sites of the river valley development projects in the two countries. He also held wide-ranging discussions on the geo-political aspect of economic development of the Indus valley with the irrigation engineers of the two countries.

After his tour he wrote a series of articles on the situation in the subcontinent. In his article on the Indo-Pak water dispute titled *Another "Korea" in Making,* he viewed the problem as a fall-out of partition. In his 'judgment' the solution of the bilateral dispute lay not in international adjudication on the division of the respective share of the two countries but in the further development of the whole Indus system 'as a unit—designed, built and operated as a unit'. He viewed that a very small proportion of the available waters in the Indus basin was being utilized by both the riparian states. The river system still had enough water resources, which could be developed for the economic prosperity of the basin states. The project must be jointly financed by India and Pakistan. He proposed international involvement in the form of World Bank as a facilitator and financer of the new Indus basin development projects to be undertaken in the two countries.

The future development of the two basin countries was inherent in the utilization of the unused flow of waters of the Indus basin which is larger than the presently used proportion of that 'flow to the Arabian Sea unused'.[35] The essential conditions for resolving the dispute, according to Lilienthal, was that all bilateral political disputes including Kashmir must be detached from this dispute because of the difference of their nature. Its solution should be searched on a functional plane keeping in consideration the hydrology of the river basin and its potential for development.

Eugene R. Black, the then President of the World Bank and a close friend of Lilienthal, was impressed by his views about the solution to the Indo-Pak water dispute. In September 1951, Black formally wrote to the two Prime Ministers in which he offered to lend the good offices of the Bank in 'such directions as might be considered appropriate by the two governments' in the development of the Indus water resources on 'the lines suggested by Lilienthal'.[36] Both the Prime Ministers responded immediately and positively to Black. In his second letter of 8 November 1951, Black proposed a road map for the 'comprehensive long-range plan for the effective utilization of the water resources of the Indus basin in the development of the region'. He asked the two governments to designate their respective engineers for the plan preparation. A World Bank engineer who would not be an arbitrator but would only assist them. This 'Working Party' would be authorized to decide the procedure of their work, the steps to be taken for its completion and a time schedule for the preparation of the plan.[37]

The two leaderships were hesitant to accept the road map of Black without reservation. To discuss the matter personally with the two Prime Ministers to remove their inhibitions Black visited the subcontinent in February 1952. After his visit and correspondence both the parties formally agreed in March 1952 to participate in the meeting of the engineers and appreciated the role of the World Bank as a 'good officer'. The important points of the agreement were: non-disruption of available supply of waters by India to Pakistan, joint preparation of a comprehensive long-term plan for the entire basin with the objective securing most effective utilization of the water resources to enhance substantially the use by the two states at that time.[38]

Mediation of the World Bank: The First Phase

Black inaugurated the first meeting of the Working Party on 6 May 1952 at Washington, which lasted up to 18 June. The Indian Designee at the Working Party was A.N. Khosla, Chairman, Central Water and Power Commission and ex officio Additional Secretary to Government of India in the Ministry of Natural Resources and Scientific Research. A team of technical and legal experts assisted him. The Pakistani Designee was M.A. Hamid, Chief Irrigation Engineer, West Punjab. Unlike the Indian team, which consisted only of the Central government officials, the Pakistani team included concerned officials from each riparian province and region of Pakistan. The World Bank representative at the Working Party was Lieut. General Raymond A. Wheeler, Engineering Adviser to the World Bank, formerly Chief of the Corps of Engineers, U.S. Army.

Despite the over-cautiousness of each team to avoid anything which might affect their earlier stand and the non-compliance of the Lilienthal proposal or the essential principles enunciated by Black for the Working Party, the first meeting ended successfully with agreement on some studies to be taken by each team separately not jointly and to meet next at Karachi in November 1952. In the words of Gulati, who was a member of the Indian delegation, the meeting succeeded because of 'the patient and helpful role' of the World Bank representatives and 'the anxiety of each party not to bear the onus of a break down' of the meeting.[39]

The second meeting could not take place in November because the two parties had made not much progress in the exchange of data and information. The meeting was held in early December 1952 in Karachi in which it was decided to take a field trip by the Working Party of the whole Indus basin to collect relevant data. The party proceeded on the trip from the meeting. The entire field trip included more than 9,000 miles by road, rail and air. The Working Party held its third meeting in late January 1953 in which they could not agree on a common approach to plan for integrated development of the Indus basin. It was decided on the suggestion of the World Bank representative that each designee would prepare a separate comprehensive basin wide-plan.

The two plans were submitted in the next Working Party meeting on 6 October 1953. They differed widely in concept and substance. According to the Indian Plan all the water of Sutlej, Beas and Ravi or the 'Eastern Rivers' would be exclusively utilized by India along with 7 per cent of the water of the Chenab, Jhelum and Indus or the 'Western Rivers'. In other words India would develop Bhakra-Beas-Rajasthan Project and would further make some withdrawals from the Chenab for Ravi via Marhu Tunnel. The Pakistani Plan was confined to the Pakistani territory only. It would have allocated all water excess of the past actual uses of India to the Pakistani portion of the basin. It envisaged exclusive use of all the Western Rivers plus 70 per cent of the waters of the Eastern Rivers.

The two plans visualized the division of the present available waters in the basin in quantitative terms. According to the Indian Plan the total usable waters available in the basin was 119 MAF (Million of Acre Feet) of waters. India should get 29 MAF and Pakistan 90 MAF out of this total volume. In Pakistan's estimation the total volume of available waters was 118 MAF, of which India should receive 15.5 MAF and Pakistan 118 MAF. [40]

From Idealism to Realism: The Second Phase

It became clear from the analysis of these two plans and the process of their negotiation in the Working Party that an ideal plan, which would satisfy all the proposed future needs of both the parties, was not possible because the water supplies and storage potentialities in the basin are inadequate to the needs of the two riparian states. The second hindrance in the development of the basin as a single economic unit was the division of sovereignty. Maximum utilization of a natural resource in an economic and efficient manner is not possible when two sovereigns are involved. No decision regarding the development of the resource can be taken without negotiation and agreement between the two. The two states may have different development policies and unequal resources available for development. They may feel insecure to develop a project whose control would fully or partly be in another territory. This type of economic cooperation is possible only when the two states have full political understanding and mutually conversing security perception, which was not the situation between India and Pakistan.

Division of the water resources in the basin was the only realistic solution. Even division, the only available option, was not easy. Any division must have to take into consideration the existing uses of the water resources between the two riparian states. The countries have divergent perception on the existing use of the water in the basin. India perceived the existing uses only as actual historic withdrawals but Pakistan insisted that in addition to the actual past withdrawals the definition of the existing use must include the withdrawals which were planned before partition, i.e. the Anderson Committee, the Indus Commission and the Sind-Punjab Chief Engineers' Agreement of 1945. Secondly, the Indian plan limited the right of Pakistan only to the Western Rivers whereas Pakistan, in addition to the Western Rivers wanted the continuation of the existing withdrawals from the Eastern Rivers and fresh withdrawals after the development of the proposed sites according to pre-partition plans. In Indian opinion none of the pre-partition plans except the Anderson Committee was binding.[41]

Because of the divergent priorities in the two plans a deadlock emerged in the Working Party, which was obvious in the absence of any preliminary political agreement between India and Pakistan, regarding sharing of the waters, costs of development and operation of an integrated system. The World Bank representatives in the Working Party evolved an alternative proposal on the basis of partition of the rivers of the basin, allocating independent and separate supply to India and Pakistan to resolve the problem. When Black discussed it with Lilienthal he approved it. But realizing the limitation of the authority of the Working Party because of its technical nature he advised Black to send it to the two Prime Ministers 'as the best possible solution under the circumstances' in addition to its presentation to the Working Party. On 5 February the proposal was submitted in the Working Party and simultaneously transmitted to Prime Ministers Nehru and Mohammed Ali who had replaced Nizamuddin.[42]

According to the Bank's Plan the entire flow of the Western Rivers would be exclusively available for the use, benefit and development by Pakistan except for the insignificant volume of Jhelum and Chenab flows presently used in Jammu and Kashmir by India. The entire flow of the Eastern Rivers would be available for the exclusive use, benefit and development of India except for a specified transition period in which India would allow the historic withdrawals by

Pakistan from these rivers according to an agreed schedule. The transition period would be the estimated time required to construct the link canals from the Western Rivers to those Pakistani canals which get their present supply from the Eastern Rivers. It also proposed a temporary cooperative administration for the supervision of the progress in the transitional arrangements. The plan did not propose any joint development project. Each country would construct on its own the development projects located on its territory for its own benefit but India would bear the cost of the link canals to be constructed in Pakistan in proportion to the benefits it would receive after the transition period.[43]

The World Bank involved itself in the water dispute to resolve it on the principle of integrated development of the Indus system in September 1951. It revised its stand from integrated development to partition in February 1954 after taking into consideration the ground realities. According to the World Bank plan, the Eastern Rivers based Pakistani canals would become independent from them after the completion of the transition period. It recognized the right of historic withdrawals of the lower riparian but not necessarily from the same source. It provided 'greatest possible freedom of action' to the two riparian states 'in the operation, maintenance and future development' of their irrigation facilities.[44] The proposal provided a solution of the water dispute without touching upon the Kashmir dispute or the issue of determining the eastern boundary of the Indus basin. The great merit of the plan was the simplicity of its concept and execution. No further agreements or continual consensus on operation of the development projects between the two riparians was necessary. It gave full right over the Eastern Rivers to India after a stipulated time, which was necessary for irrigation development in eastern Punjab and adjoining areas that was not possible without exclusive right on these rivers. Even as lower riparian according to the Pakistan plan would get the exclusive right over the Western Rivers which would be assured by India as the upper riparian by a treaty and by the sanction of the World Bank.

The World Bank's proposal was received with different reactions from the two countries. Indian response was early and overall positive. Pandit Nehru got the World Bank's proposal approved by his cabinet on 11 February,1954. India sent formal approval to the World Bank on 25 March 1954. India had neither accepted the World Bank's proposal 'as the basis of an agreement' nor 'the plan in principle' but only 'the principles of the World Bank's proposals' for working out an agreement. New Delhi expected that the agreement would safeguard the relatively insignificant present and future consumptive use of J&K, the upper riparian of the Western Rivers. Nehru also urged the World Bank in his reply that some ad hoc agreement about the distribution of the Sutlej waters should be reached because the Balloki–Sulemanke Link Canal in Pakistan and the Bhakra Main Canal in India were nearing completion.[45]

Unlike India, Pakistan was delaying its response to the plan because it was not satisfied with the proposals therein. In the perception of Pakistan, the plan did not take care of its interest properly because it took away the historic right of Pakistan over the Eastern Rivers in exchange for granting exclusive right over the Western Rivers. The Western Rivers can only be a substitution for the Eastern Rivers at the most for the existing needs of Pakistan if storage facilities on them are constructed, for which there was no provision in the plan. There was nothing in the plan to cater to the future water requirement of Pakistan.[46] Another reason for the delay was the emerging alliance of Pakistan with the USA in the context of the Cold War. Pakistan wanted to hold out for getting further concession either from India or the World Bank. Pakistan softened its attitude after the Indian announcement on 10 May 1954 that it would open the Bhakra Main Canal in June for the benefit of *kharif* crops. The World Bank received the reply of the Pakistani Prime Minister on 14 May 1954. In its reply Pakistan asked for an improvement in the plan to remove its dissatisfaction with the plan.

India had set 21 June as the deadline for an agreement with Pakistan under which to operate the Bhakra Canal. After passage of the deadline without any such agreement, India got rid of the restrictions she had agreed to in March 1952 for maintaining available supplies to the Pakistani canals. After opening of the Bhakra Canal on 8 July 1954 by India, the Working Party set up in 1949 ceased to function.

The World Bank in its response to the Pakistan's Prime Minister sent a memorandum on 21 May 1954 in which it assured Pakistan 'to bring about adjustments' in the plan which would be 'acceptable to both sides'. After this assurance Pakistan sent a new delegation headed by a career civil servant to Washington in June to negotiate with the World Bank the desired improvement in the plan. As a result of the negotiation held in June and July 1954 the World Bank agreed on a set of 'terms of reference' for the resumption of the negotiation.

The terms of reference recognized the water requirements of Pakistan for the irrigation development projects in Sind in addition to Punjab. It included consideration of the need of storage works in Pakistan and the cost of their construction as an item for consideration in the final plan negotiators. It did not accept Pakistan's demand for hiring of outside consultants by the World Bank to verify the estimation in the plan of the quantity and timing of supplies available from the Western Rivers but it authorized each party to bring its own consultants. Pakistan accepted the principles of the plan after the inclusion of the 'terms of reference' in it. The World Bank received the formal acceptance from the Pakistan's Foreign Minister on 28 July 1954 in which he requested Black 'to make necessary arrangement for the next phase of cooperative efforts....'[47]

The negotiation was resumed in December 1954 in Washington. Vice Chairman W.A.B. Iliff led the World Bank team of mediators; N.D. Gulati who was the second man in the first round of negotiation headed the Indian delegation. Ghulam Mueenuddin, a civil servant was the Pakistani team leader. For arriving at a comprehensive agreement Iliff proposed to work out some common assumption or 'preliminary trial plan' and a transitional arrangement for the continued supply from the Eastern Rivers to Pakistan for the *kharif* crop season of 1955 beginning on 1 April. In the course of negotiation on these issues a second tour of the basin for the benefit of the new members in the World Bank's team was decided in February 1955. As a result of these negotiations Iliff gave both sides a note on the last day of the trip in Srinagar on 18 April. The note titled 'Proposed Transitional Arrangements for the Period April 15 to September 30, 1955' restricted additional irrigation usage in India for maintaining supplies to canals in Pakistan as it was on March 13, 1952. India accepted it and the Indian team leader issued instruction to regulate Indian uses from the Eastern Rivers with effect from 21 April.[48] The agreement was formally signed on 21 June in Washington. After the expiry of this agreement during the course of negotiation for a comprehensive agreement, two more transitional arrangements were signed on the request of Pakistan. The successive arrangements were for *rabi* 1955-56, *kharif* 1956 and rabi 1956-57. These single crop adhoc transitional arrangements continued up to kharif 1959 before the arrival of a comprehensive all time agreement.

Pakistan continued to assert during the negotiation that the Western Rivers without storage facilities would not be able to meet even replacement uses in critical rabi crop-maturing and *kharif* crop-sowing phases. The World Bank finally appointed an independent team to check available supplies from the Western Rivers without storage. The team found the Pakistan's assertion correct. After getting the independent expert opinion the World Bank issued an Aide-Memoire or memorandum on 21 May 1956 recognizing that the flow surplus in the Western Rivers would not be sufficient to meet even the replacement needs in early and late *kharif* season without storage facilities.[49] The memorandum asked the two parties to submit their respective revised plans accommodating the proposals of the World Bank. Both the parties submitted their plans in December 1956.

Pakistan in its new plan asked for storage works and new canals on the Western Rivers. Pakistan's estimated cost of the replacement works of the Eastern Rivers in West Pakistan was $2.3 billion. India in its plan placed the demand of run of the river schemes on the Western Rivers in J&K. Neither of the two parties was in a position to accommodate the World Bank's proposals in its plans. They were dissatisfied with each other's plans. On the one hand, India wanted some concession on the Western Rivers and minimum cost of replacement works while on the other Pakistan wanted some development projects along with the replacement projects to be included in an equitable agreement because it felt that replacement projects alone were insufficient compensation for sacrifice of its right over the Eastern Rivers.

In December 1957 and February 1958, Iliff twice visited the subcontinent for meeting the political leadership of the two countries to make them agreeable to the proper approaches towards the settlement of the water dispute.[50] In this situation of non-converging positions the World Bank convened a joint meeting of both the parties in Rome in May 1958. The World Bank presented 'a new approach' in the meeting, which was based mainly on the waters of the Chenab and Jhelum and a diversion canal from the Indus to Jhelum. The World Bank also informed the two parties that friendly countries would be involved to supplement the financial contribution of India. The `new approach' was not acceptable to either of the parties. They decided to revise their respective plans to make them acceptable for each other.[51]

The next meeting of the delegations was convened in July 1958 at London in which Pakistan submitted its revised less expensive plan which proposed a dam on the Jhelum at Mangla for replacement and a dam on the Indus at Tarbela for development of agriculture in Sind and two trans-Thal link canals for lower Punjab and Bahawalpur. The total cost was estimated at $1.12 billion and tentative construction schedule extended over 15 years. India objected to the cost of such replacement and development works and in turn submitted its alternative plan in November 1958.

In the alternative plan India wanted to use the Chenab waters on sites in Himachal and J&K. India proposed to build a diversion tunnel from the Chenab to a tributary of Ravi at Marhu and another from Chandra tributary of the Chenab to Beas at Palchar and if necessary construction of a storage dam on the Chenab at Dhiangargh. India's plea for its proposed use of the Chenab waters was that it was of no use to Pakistan. The replacement requirements of Pakistan were estimated at 10 million MAF. If Pakistan would authorize India to use Chenab sites it would guarantee through treaty to deliver a total of 5 MAF of waters at Firozpur and

Marla if Dhiangarh storage was built. The other half would come from the three link canals, which Pakistan was constructing. The cost of the Indian projects was much lower than that proposed by Pakistan.[52] The alternative plan of India was not acceptable to Pakistan because it was not ready to be dependent on India for its irrigation needs beyond the transition period. Also in its perception the waters of the new link canals were not replacement but diversion.

Signing of a Treaty: The Third Phase

The only way out of the stalemate was to delink the necessary projects in Pakistan and their cost. India's main objection was not the replacement or development plans in Pakistan but the cost that it would have to bear. With this objective in early 1959 the World Bank began approaching the developed member countries for underwriting an Indus basin settlement scheme. The developed member states of the World Bank were ready to contribute a share for the scheme. Another development, which positively affected the reaching of an agreement, was the leadership change in Pakistan in December 1958. The new President, Mohammed Ayub Khan was interested in arriving an agreement by mutual accommodation. The World Bank prepared a compromise plan in January 1959 according to which India would get unrestricted use of the Eastern Rivers after the transition period and restricted use over the Western Rivers. Moreover, India would have to contribute only a limited amount for the projects undertaken in Pakistan. The World Bank would arrange the remaining amount.

In May 1959 Black came on his second visit to India and Pakistan to persuade their leadership to accept the compromise plan. He succeeded in obtaining an acquiescence on the plan from Nehru on the condition that regardless of the cost of projects in Pakistan, India's contribution would be $175 million and it would get a loan for the Beas dam at Pong site. Nehru also agreed to a ten-year transition period during which India would continue to supply water to Pakistan. He succeeded in convincing Pakistan as well to accept the plan with provision of storage dams on the Jhelum and Indus. The next important task before the World Bank was to arrange finance for the projects in the plan, which he initiated after his return. By August he had persuaded the governments of the USA, Canada, the UK, West Germany, Australia and New Zealand to underwrite the settlement that would advance the cause of peace in the Indus basin at a cost of about one billion dollars.[53] The Bank formed a consortium of 'friendly governments' for this purpose.

In the intensive negotiations held during August-September 1959 in London, several 'heads of agreement' were decided which became the basis of the treaty. India raised objection to the inclusion of a dam at Mangla on Jhelum in the proposed treaty because it was in Pakistan-Occupied-Kashmir (POK). It was decided that in the treaty only a dam on Jhelum would be mentioned not the site. India also insisted on her limited right over the Western Rivers. After discussion on the issue India's right to construct 'run of the river' hydroelectric projects and to store limited quantity of water was agreed to. Considerable progress was made on several aspects of the eventual treaty and many issues were left for the next meeting. After the meeting the Pakistani team stayed in London and prepared the replacement-cum-development plan along with estimated cost and construction schedule. The World Bank asked India to prepare estimates for the Beas dam.

Negotiation resumed in Washington in October 1959 to prepare the first draft of the treaty that became ready after three weeks. The draft was discussed for about a month during which it was added to modified, revised and re-revised until the beginning of December 1959 when the preamble and twelve articles of the treaty were printed as the draft of the treaty.[54] The draft included all 'heads of agreements' earlier agreed upon in London meeting in elaborated form as articles of the treaty. Two more items which could not be settled in the London meeting but got included in the draft after mutual agreement as concepts without exact details were: India's right of storage on the Western Rivers in J&K and Pakistan's right of inspection of the development works on these rivers on a reciprocal basis. Two new items which were decided during the draft negotiation and included in the treaty were: setting up of a permanent Indus Commission to supervise the working of the treaty and ways and means for the resolution of differences and disputes that might arise in the course of implementation of the treaty. The transition period remained ten years with a possible extension by another three years despite Pakistan's insistence for inclusion of provision for the consideration of some emergency situation. The World Bank forwarded the treaty to the two governments for their approval. The negotiation continued to draft the annexures of the treaty.

In January 1960 Pakistan submitted its estimated cost of the replacement-cum-development projects at $936 million, which was very high in the World Bank's perception. It asked Pakistan to revise the estimate downward on a realistic basis. The World Bank calculated its own estimate at $838 million. On 1 March the World Bank made public the pledges by the 'friendly governments'. According to the pledges the total aid to Pakistan and India was $747.20 million. The pledge towards Pakistan was $541.20 million as grant and $150 as loan in total $691.20 million. India was to get a loan of only $56 million. Pakistan was not satisfied with the pledge. The negotiation between the World Bank and Pakistan to settle the amount of aid to the Development Fund, which would be organized for construction projects to be undertaken in Pakistan on the rivers, was very frustrating for its President and Vice President. When all other aspects of the treaty were decided Pakistan temporarily accepted $893.5 million in the Development Fund to facilitate the signing of the treaty. But the issue remained between Pakistan and the World Bank, which was finally decided by a Supplementary Agreement between the two under which the consortium provided an additional $315 million. Commenting on the contributions of the World Bank and the developed countries to Pakistan for the success of the treaty, Michel says that the treaty had been virtually purchased by the 'friendly countries' and the World Bank.[55]

By early March 1960, both the delegations had received their governments' comments on the draft treaty. The negotiation resumed to improve the draft on the expected lines. The delegations were also negotiating the annexures to be included in the treaty to explicitly record the meaning, nature and scope of the terms used in the text of the treaty. The second draft of the treaty along with four agreed upon annexures was prepared in April 1960. Iliff visited the subcontinent in August to settle the issue of India's claim of rupees 144 lakh of seignorage charge from Pakistan according to the terms of May 1948 agreement. Pakistan had stopped the payment of the charges after some time. On Iliff's intervention India agreed to waive 72 lakh of seignorage charge. Pakistan was ready to pay only 62 lakh, which India accepted. The negotiation was resumed on 21 August in Washington to settle the final draft of the treaty, which was decided in the first week of September. The treaty consisted of a preamble, twelve articles and eight annexures. The draft of the treaty was approved on 7 September in a meeting of the cabinet ministers, Government of India. Pakistan approved it on 14 September.

The signing of the treaty on 19 September 1960 in Karachi was a big international event. Prime Minister of India, Jawaharlal Nehru, Pakistani President Mohammed Ayub Khan and the Vice President of the World Bank W.A. B. Iliff signed the treaty. This signature resulted in the formal settlement of a serious water dispute between the two riparian states in a peaceful manner. Apart from the Indus Water Treaty, two other agreements were also signed on the same occasion. One was a multilateral international financial plan to create the Indus Basin Development Fund to finance the proposed irrigation works in Pakistan and the other was about a loan of $90 million by the World Bank to Pakistan. The representatives of Pakistan, the World Bank, the USA, the UK, Australia, New Zealand and Germany signed the development fund agreement.

The importance of the treaty was recognized by the World Bank in its press release of 19 September according to which the signing of the treaty 'marks the end of a critical and long-standing dispute' and opens the way of development of water resources in the Indus basin on which depends the livelihood of some 50 million in India and Pakistan, the two riparian states of the basin.[56] The leaders of India and Pakistan expressed their satisfaction and hope for better relations in future. Ayub Khan said, 'the treaty was an event of great historic significance for the two countries concerned ... for the whole world.'[57] Jawaharlal Nehru said, 'we are going to have many benefits out of this agreement but important than the material advantages are the psychological and emotional benefit.'[58] The psychological and emotional benefits of the treaty lay in the fact that it promised to usher in a new beginning of harmonious relations between India and Pakistan. The international press acclaimed it as proof that even a seemingly insolvable international conflict might be resolved if the parties were sincere to find a solution and there was a neutral mediator to steward the negotiation for a success.

The people of India and Pakistan generally welcomed the treaty. It was considered a great opportunity for the promotion of better bilateral relations. But it was criticized by the extremist elements in both the countries. In the opinion of the Indian extremists New Delhi had surrendered its rivers to Pakistan. The Indian contribution for the replacement works in Pakistan was also perceived as an unfair burden. In Pakistan some resentment was expressed on the loss of the three Eastern Rivers.

The treaty was the result of the sincere desire and effort by both the parties in association with the World Bank to come to a diplomatic solution of the problem. It was the culmination of a complex negotiation process for nine years from 1951 to 1960. The negotiation continued in sessions after breaks at Washington, Rome and London in addition to the capitals and other places in India and Pakistan. Whenever any deadlock emerged and there were many, the World Bank found out a way to resolve it by new ideas or by consulting the political leadership of the two countries at the level of President or Vice President of the World Bank who visited the sub-continent many times during the course of the negotiation. The World Bank worked not only as a facilitator and mediator in the negotiation but also as an organizer of funds for the actualization of the settlement of the water dispute. The credit for the treaty should go to the statesmanship of Nehru and Ayub Khan who saved the negotiation whenever a stalemate emerged and to the well-intended persistence of the World Bank to resolve the twelve-year-old dispute for the advantage of India and Pakistan.[59]

Analysis of the Treaty

The treaty consists of a preamble, twelve articles and eight annexures. The preamble of the treaty expresses the mutual desire of both countries to attain 'the most complete and satisfactory utilization of the waters of the Indus system of rivers'.[60]

Article I explains all the terms that have been used in the text of the treaty and its annexure.[61]

Article II—'Provisions Regarding Eastern Rivers'—states that all the three Eastern Rivers—Ravi, Beas, and Sutlej—would be available for the unrestricted use of India after the transition period i.e from 1 April 1970. Annexure B of the treaty recognizes the right of Pakistan to withdraw water in its territory for irrigation purpose from the tributaries of the Ravi: Basantar, Thein, Tarnah and Ujh beyond the transition period. Annexure- H, which is the last annexure of the treaty, specifies the details of the transitional arrangements that would lapse after the end of this period.

Article III—'Provisions Regarding Western Rivers'—states that waters of the three Western Rivers—Indus, Jhelum and Chenab—would be allowed to flow into Pakistan unrestricted by India. The treaty grants limited right to India over these rivers according to the terms of Annexure C—for domestic use, non-consumptive use and agricultural use. India can also use the waters for hydroelectric power generation according to the terms of Annexure D. Annexure C defines the volume of water which India can withdraw from the Chenab, Indus and Jhelum. Annexure D recognizes India's unlimited right to operate existing plants or complete and operate under-construction plants. India's right to plan and construct new plants on these rivers is limited only to one type—'run-of the river plants'. India also has limited right to have new plants on any channel taking off from these rivers. Annexure E defines the limits on India's right to construct new storage works on the Western Rivers.[62]

Article IV—Provisions Regarding Eastern Rivers and Western Rivers'—asks Pakistan to construct the replacement of the Western Rivers in its territory. It defines the general guidelines for the ongoing uses and new future uses of the river waters by the two parties individually in such a manner that no damage is done to the material interests of the other party.[63]

Article V—'Financial Provisions'—defines that the value of India's contribution to the Indus Basin Development Fund in Pound Sterling is 62,060,000 which it would have to pay in ten equal annual instalments. It also defines the amount which India would get, in case of the extension of the transition period in extraordinary situation, in the first; second and the third years.[64]

Article VI—'Exchange of Data'—defines the different types of data with respect to the flow and utilisation of the river waters which each party would maintain for monthly exchange between them.[65]

Article VII—Future Co-operation—records the intention of the two parties to cooperate by mutual agreement for the optimum development of the rivers in the areas of hydrologic observation stations, meteorological observation stations, drainage works in connection with the drainage works of the other party and undertaking of joint engineering works on the rivers. It also binds every party to supply data regarding any planned engineering works to the other party on request.[66]

Article VIII—'Permanent Indus Commission—provides that both the parties would create a post of Commissioner of Indus Waters and a high-ranking hydrology and water use person would man this post. In normal situations each Commissioner would be the representative of his government for all matters related with the treaty. These two Commissioners would together form the Permanent Indus Commission. The function of the Commission would be to undertake all necessary measures that have been defined in the article for the smooth functioning of the treaty. The Commission would meet regularly at least once in a year, alternatively in India and Pakistan. Each Commissioner would have diplomatic privileges and immunities in the other country.[67]

Article IX—'Settlement of Differences and Disputes'—states that any question regarding the interpretation or application of the treaty or the existence of any fact which might constitute a breach of this treaty would be considered a 'difference'. Annexure F of the treaty deals with the provision to appoint a 'Neutral Expert' to settle a 'difference'. Any Commissioner might refer the difference to a Neutral Expert and if the issue is about financial compensation then by both of them. The decision of the Neutral Expert on matters within his competence would be final and binding. If the expert certifies that the difference or part of it is a 'dispute' then each Commissioner would report about it to its government. The two governments would try to settle the dispute through negotiation. They might enlist the services of one or more mediators acceptable to both of them.

In the case of non-resolution of a dispute by bilateral negotiation or mediation, Annexure G provides for a court of arbitration, which would be established to resolve the dispute. The court would have seven members, two each appointed by each party and three more arbitrators or umpires—one of the three qualified by status and reputation to be chairman of the court of arbitration, one highly qualified engineer and one person well versed in International Law. The award of the court would be final and binding on the parties.

Article X is about 'Emergency Provision', that is a precautionary measure about the completion of the replacement work. After beginning of the work diligently and with reasonable expedition if Pakistan found itself unable to procure materials and equipments necessary for the completion of the replacement work by March 31, 1971 due to some large-scale international hostilities arising out of causes beyond its control it might represent to the World Bank about it any time before March 31, 1965. In this situation the World Bank would notify each party about it and they would enlist the good offices of the World Bank to decide if there was a need for any modification in the treaty and if so the extent of the modification.[68]

Article XI is about 'General Provisions' which limit 'the rights and obligations of each party in relation to the other' with respect only to the use of the waters of the rivers and incidental thereto. The treaty would not affect the claims and positions of each party on any other bilateral issue. The Indus Basin Development Fund Agreement, to which India is not party, would not affect the rights and obligations of the two parties based on the Indus treaty.[69]

Article XII—'Final Provisions'—states the name of the treaty, date of effect, scope of its modification by another treaty between the parties and its continuity until terminated by another treaty between them. At the end, the treaty has the signatures of the Prime Minister of India and President of Pakistan for the rights and obligations of their countries emerging out of the treaty. The last signatory is the Vice President of the World Bank for the purposes specified in Articles V and X and Annexures F, G and H of the treaty.[70]

Working of the Treaty

As per Article VIII of the Indus Water Treaty, both the countries appointed their respective Commissioners for Indus Waters in 1961 with their permanent offices in their respective capitals. Together they constitute the Permanent Indus Commission (PIC). The Commission meets once in a year alternately in India and Pakistan. It submits every year a report of its works in the financial year ending on 31 March to both the governments before first June. The first meeting of the PIC was held in June 1961 in Islamabad followed by another meeting in New Delhi in the same year. In both these meetings the ways and means for implementing the treaty to promote cooperation between the parties in the defined area and to settle promptly any question arising between them were discussed. Each country started development works on the allotted rivers and India maintained uninterrupted flow of the Eastern Rivers to Pakistan as agreed for the transitional period.

The meetings of the PIC, its periodical visits to development sites on the rivers, exchange of data and the supply of waters to Pakistan by India continued as usual according to the provisions of the treaty. Even the 1965 and 1971 wars between the two states did not disrupt the functioning of the treaty.[71] The 'Transitional Arrangements' ended in a cooperative manner on 31 March 1970. Till June 2004, 89 meetings of the PIC had taken place. For ascertaining facts connected with various developmental works on the rivers in the Indus system, the Commission had undertaken 101 periodical inspection visits till March 2004.[72]

In fulfillment of the obligations of the treaty both the countries have exchanged data relating to the development projects on these rivers. As per the provisions of the treaty India has transmitted through telegram flood flows of the rivers Ravi, Sutlej, Beas, Jammu Tawi, Chenab and Jhelum since 1962. In 1974 India started broadcasting the flood flows. In February 1989, the Commissioners of Indus Waters signed an agreement to communicate the flood flows of Ravi and Sutlej to Pakistan on telephone during the period of 1 July to 10 October every year. As a good-will gesture, India had not charged any cost of transmission for this data supply though the treaty provides for it. From the year 2001 India has asked Pakistan to reimburse the cost of transmission, which is under correspondence.[73]

The benefits from the treaty to Pakistan have indeed been real and great. The Indus Basin Development Fund Agreement (IBDFA) became effective after the ratification of the treaty. This provided the required finance to begin replacement-cum-development works in a massive way. The storage reservoir-cum-power plant on Jhelum River at Mangla was started in 1962 and completed in 1967. The construction of Tarbela reservoir-cum-power plant on Indus River began in 1967 and was completed in 1977. The proposed Kalabagh multipurpose dam on Indus River was started but could not be completed due to objection by Sind.[74]

Pakistan constructed three new barrages—Gudu on Indus in upper Sind in 1962, Kabagh on the Indus in West Punjab in 1967, Kotri on the Indus in Lower Sind in 1970. Construction works of eight new link canals were started in the early 1960s and all of them became operational in 1971-72. In addition to these link canals, fifteen new canals have been constructed after the commencement of the treaty.[75] During the transition period, India completed three dams that were in progress when the treaty was being negotiated. Bhakhra Dam on Sutlej was commissioned in November 1963; two dams at Beas and Pong on Beas River were completed in 1973 and 1974 respectively. India began construction of Pondoh Dam on Beas, Nagal and Govind Sagar Dams on Sutlej and Thein Dam on Ravi after the end of the transitional period. All these four dams were completed in the 1980s. Works on two major canals—Sutlej–Yamuna Link Canal and Rajasthan Canal from Sutlej were taken up in the1980s. The Rajasthan Canal has been completed but the link canal could not be completed due to objection by Punjab. The other canals which were completed are the Beas-Sutlej Link Canal, Nangal Canal and Madhupur-Beas Link Canal.[76]

After the completion of these dams and canals India has been utilizing on an average about 30 MAF of water of the Eastern Rivers. With this water an area of 25,62,320 acres of land has been irrigated. The secure availability of water for irrigation in more areas both in Indian and Pakistani Punjab after the treaty to the enterprising farmers of this region made it the ideal place in the sub-continent to use new seeds, fertilizers, tools and techniques recently developed by the agriculture scientists to bring tremendous growth in the production of wheat, cotton, rice and sugarcane. In the pre-treaty year of 1959-60 the growth rate of production of these crops in Pakistan was 3 per cent, which became 38 per cent five years after the signing of the treaty in 1964-65.[77] The phenomenal growth in food production lead to food self sufficiency in India, that is known as the Green Revolution.

The Eastern Rivers have the capacity to generate 11,219 MW hydroelectric power at 60 per cent load factor. Projects with 3,945 MW installed capacity have been completed and projects with 4,144 MW installed capacity are in different stages of construction. India is withdrawing water from the Western Rivers to irrigate an area of 2,70,000 acres in the state of J&K. Despite limitation on India to build conservation storage on these rivers, hydroelectric power plants which can be constructed according to the rules of the treaty have been constructed and commissioned with installed capacity of 1400 MW and plants with installed capacity of 2400 MW are in different stages of construction.[78]

The first dispute on the treaty between the parties emerged in 1972 when India started construction of Salal hydroelectric project on Chenab at Dhiangargh in Udhampur district. Pakistan objected to the design as a violation of the treaty. The matter could not be resolved at the Commissioner's level or Water Secretaries' level up to 1978. During the Janata Party regime in India, the dispute was resolved at the Foreign Ministers' level during February-March 1978. An agreement was signed in April 1978 between the Foreign Minister of India and Advisor to Foreign Affairs of Pakistan at New Delhi. According to the agreement the height of the dam was reduced from 125 metres to 113 metres, which reduced the power production potential from the proposed 690 MW to 800 MW.[79]

New disputes emerged one after another when India took initiative to develop sites for hydroelectric generation on the Western Rivers in J&K, which were objected to by Pakistan on the ground that they were a violation of the treaty. The first of these unresolved disputes is Tullbul Navigation Project or Wullar Barrage Project, which began in 1986.[80] An agreement was reached to resolve this dispute in October 1991 but it could not be signed due to the emergence of another dispute in the form of Kishanganga Hydro Power Project[81] that was started by India in the same year. These two projects are on the Jhelum in Kashmir valley. The third dispute is Baglihar Dam on the Chenab in Doda district of Jammu region, which began in 1999 when India started the construction work.[82] Pakistan has taken this dispute to the World Bank in January 2005, which has appointed a neutral expert for resolving it. Endeavours to settle these disputes through different mechanisms are on without any final solution.

Conclusion

The Indus Basin water dispute is the only important dispute between the two states that has been resolved peacefully. The treaty is not the ideal solution for the dispute, which would have been an integrated joint development of the Indus system but it is definitely the only possible realistic solution. It has not only settled the problem of division of waters of common rivers between the two states but also devised ways and means for maximum utilization of the river water resources for irrigation and hydro power generation in their respective territory without hurting the interest of the other party. The treaty also binds them to cooperate for the common interest of optimum development of the rivers, which they are doing faithfully irrespective of their relation in other areas.

The Indus Water Treaty is working reasonably well unaffected by hostility, wars and proxy war between the two states. It has acquired a reputation internationally as a successful instance of conflict resolution. The role of the international community particularly the World Bank is very important in settling the immediate dispute of water sharing and facilitating the two parties to negotiate a treaty which became a legal document to provide them guidance for the settlement of any future dispute on the common rivers. The World Bank succeeded in bringing the two disputing parties to the negotiating table under its good offices when their bilateral negotiation had failed.

The sincere involvement of the Bank as a neutral third party internationalized the dispute which made each of two parties accommodative, flexible and cooperative to avoid any charge on either of them by the international community for the failure of the negotiation. The Bank stewarded the negotiation with a strong determination to achieve a permanent settlement of the dispute, which was achieved after eight years. Whenever the talk reached a stalemate in the long course it applied its pragmatic and imaginative approach to remove the hurdle. It arranged finance from the developed countries along with its own contribution for the establishment of a fund for undertaking development projects in Pakistan, which were essential for the success of the treaty. The World Bank and the other contributors also signed a separate agreement with Pakistan as a formal expression of their commitments.

The treaty is a permanent arrangement between the two riparian states of the Indus River system to utilize the waters in their own territory. Any party cannot abrogate it alone at any time. The last article of the treaty provides that the treaty can be 'terminated only by a duly ratified treaty concluded for that purpose between the two governments'. It has smoothly and successfully obligated the two hostile neighbours to maintain cooperation in water sharing even while fighting wars. This has happened because the negotiators of the treaty and their respective governments deliberated and reflected over the draft treaty clause by clause in the perspective of all aspects of the common rivers and every probable future situation. The language of the draft treaty was added to, deleted and modified through consensus. But no document prepared with howsoever farsightedness, might be able to fulfil the demands of every future situation. If a situation arises the document has to be reinterpreted or amended in the context of the time to keep it relevant.

The treaty has divided the Indus system between India and Pakistan in the spirit of partition. It is functioning without any problem for the eastern rivers but problems started emerging on western rivers in the 1970s which multiplied by the 1990s. These problems are of common nature. Every problem is an outcome of India's initiatives to construct hydroelectric generation plants on the western rivers in the state of J&K and Pakistan's objection to them as violation of the treaty. Due to the nature of the terrain, cultivation is possible only in limited area in J&K so the need for irrigation is also limited, hence till now no dispute has emerged for irrigation water but the demand for electricity is growing as per economic growth and modernization which is creating pressure for generation of electricity from the available resource, i.e. waters of the western rivers in the topography of the region.

The available waters in the Indus River system are being utilized to the optimum level by both the countries for irrigation purpose but that is not true in utilizing the hydro electric generation capacities of these rivers. The demand for electricity in both the countries of the basin is increasing. A potential big source to meet the demand is the waters of these common rivers that are still under utilized. These rivers can be utilized for this purpose in an optimum way only when they jointly devise some ways for it. The Indus treaty has ample scope for it. This is possible only when the decision makers in the two states think imaginatively and unconventionally to sort out the common problem of electricity deficiency in the Indus valley region and come to an agreement.

Shahid Javed Burki, a former Finance Minister of Pakistan who is a former top World Bank official and a reputed economist has proposed one such idea in a series of articles written in *Dawn* newspaper of Pakistan. For bringing about peace and prosperity in J&K he has proposed along with other things, that a joint generation of hydel power with a common electric grid for use in both parts of J&K and selling of the surplus to northern Pakistan as well as to the other provinces of India.[83] To explore such ideas jointly by both the countries with sincerity and determination and sign another treaty like the Indus Waters Treaty is the need of the hour for the problem-free functioning of the water sharing treaty as well as meeting the common growing demand of power in an easy and economic way. The leadership of India and Pakistan must understand the truth that several states have emerged and vanished in the Indus Basin System but the rivers in the system have been flowing since unrecorded time from the mountain to the Arabian Sea and have provided sustenance to human civilization in their laps. Taking a lesson from history they must develop ways and means in a spirit of cooperative coexistence to ulitilise the resources of the common basin for their newly emerging requirements. ■

Notes & References

1. P.H. Glecik, *The World Water: The Biannual Report on Fresh Water Resources*, Washington D.C., 2002, p. 3.
2. Ibid., p. 7.
3. A. Wolf, "Development of Transboundry Water: Obstacles and Opportunities", *Thematic Review (River Basin)*, Vol.3, 2000, Internet Edition, http://www.themrev.org , p. 1516
4. Muhammad Tajuddin, *Foreign Policy of Bangladesh: Liberation War to Sheikh Hasina*, New Delhi, 2001, p. 189.
5. Aloys Arthur Michel, *The Indus Rivers: A Study of the Effects of Partition*, London, 1967, p. 34.
6. Wheeler Mortimer, *Civilization of Indus Valley and Beyond*, London, 1966, p. 35.
7. For details see, Irfan Habib, ed., *India–Studies in the History of an Idea*, New Delhi, 2005.
8. Jawaharlal Nehru, *The Discovery of India*, New Delhi, 1988, pp.69–72.
9. Philip W. Goetz, *The Encyclopedia Britannica: Micropedia*, (15th edition), Vol. 6, London, 1996, p. 302.

10. Tavleen Singh, *Geography of India*, Bombay, 1965, p. 60.
11. Bahadur Singh, *Geography of Himachal Pradesh*, Shimla, 1980, p. 49.
12. Michel, n.5, p.34.
13. A. Gansser, *Geology of Himalayas*, New York, 1964, p. 112.
14. Michel, n.5, p. 14.
15. Khuswant Singh, *A History of the Sikhs*, Vol. 2, Princeton, 1966, pp. 71–89.
16. H.L.O.Garret, *The Punjab A Hundred Years Ago*, New Delhi, 1985, p. 120.
17. N.D. Gulati, *Indus Waters Treaty: An Exercise in International Mediations*, Bombay, 1973, p.31.
18. The pre-modern eco-friendly canal constructed to divert the surplus flood water of a river during rainy season to the fields to be utilized for winter crop.
19. For detail about these disputes and their resolutions see, N.D. Gulati, *Development of Inter-State Rivers, Law and Practice in India*, New Delhi, 1972.
20. For details about the canal development in the Indus Basin see, Paul W. Paustan, *Canal Irrigation in Punjab*, New York, 1960.
21. B.L. Wadia, *Government and Politics of India*, Jaipur, 1990, p.79.
22. Gulati, n.17, pp. 38–39.
23. According to Leonard Mosley, Radcliff tried to keep the Indus Irrigation System undivided under the joint control of India and Pakistan. He met with his proposal Nehru and Jinnah both of whom refused it. For details see Leonard Mosley, *The Last Days of British Raj*, New York, 1962, p. 190.
24. Taiyong Tan and Gyanesh Kudaisya, *The Aftermath of Partition in South Asia*, London, 2000, pp.78–100.
25. Graham P. Chapman, *The Geopolitics of South Asia*, New York, 2003, pp. 124–127.
26. V.P. Menon, *The Integration of Indian States*, Calcutta, 1956, p. 90.
27. Chaudhry Muhammad Ali, *The Emergence of Pakistan*, New York, 1967, p.319.
28. *The Indus Basin Irrigation Water Dispute*, Government of Pakistan, November 1953, p.1.
29. Seigniorage charge is the royalty for the supply of water from the headworks to the feeder canals. It was paid by the princely state of Bikaner to the British Province of Punjab before partition. East Punjab levied the same charge on West Punjab in these agreements.
30. J.S. Bains, *India's International Disputes: Legal Study*, Bombay, 1962, p.60.
31. Michel, n.5, p. 205.
32. Gulati, n.17, p. 89.
33. Ibid., pp. 84–85.
34. Michel, n.5, pp. 209–217.
35. David E. Lilienthal, 'Another "Korea" in Making?' *Collier's* August 4, 1951, in the Appendix-IV of Gulati, n.17, pp.440–447.

36. Letter dated September 5, 1951, from E.R. Black to the Prime Ministers of India and Pakistan, quoted in Ibid., pp. 95–96.
37. G.T. Kerth Pitman, 'The Role of the World Bank in Enhancing Co-operation and Resolving Conflict, International Water Courses: The Case of the Indus Basin' in M.A. Salman and Lawrence Borson de Chazournes, eds., 'International Water Courses: Enhancing Cooperation and Managing Conflict', *World Bank Technical Paper*, No. 414, Washington, 1972, Internet Edition, http//web.worldbank.org., p.162.
38. F.J. Berber, *Partition and India- Pakistan*, New York, 1963, p.210
39. Gulati, n.17, p.110.
40. 'Proposal by the International Bank Representative for a Plan for the Development and Use of the Indus Basin Waters' Appendix I of the *IBRD Press Release No. 380*, December 10, 1954, February 5, 1954, p. 2 quoted in Michel, n.5, p. 231.
41. Ibid., pp. 230–233.
42. A.K. Biswas, 'Indus Water Treaty: The Negotiations Process', *Water International*, Vol. 17, No. 4, May 1992, Internet edition, http//www.gee-21.org.
43. Michel,n.5, pp. 235–236.
44. Ibid., p.236
45. Gulati, n.17, pp. 145–145.
46. Chowdhary,n.27, pp. 328-329.
47. U.Z. Alam, International Conflict to Water Sharing: Indus Water Treaty Negotiations, unpublished dissertation submitted to the Department of Geography, University of Durham, UK, 1998, pp. 75–80, Internet Edition, http//www.durham.ac.uk.
48. Gulati, Indus Water Treaty, p. 184.
49. Mubashir Hussain, *Hundred Years of P.W.D*, Lahore, 1967, p. 63, quoted in Michel, n.5, pp. 244.
50. Aloys Arthur Michel, *The Indus Rivers: A Study of the Effects of Partition*, London, 1967, pp. 229–30
51. Alam, n.47, p.113.
52. A.N. Khosla, 'Development of the Indus River System: An Engineering Approach', *India Quarterly*, No.14, 1958, pp.249–52 quoted in Michel, n.5, p. 246.
53. Ibid., pp. 247–48.
54. Gulati, n.17, pp. 270–71.
55. Michel, n.5, p. 254
56. *IBRD Press Release*, No.618, quoted in Gulati, n.17, p. 339.
57. *The Dawn*, September 20, 1960, quoted in Ajay Saksena, *India and Pakistan: Their Foreign Policies*, New Delhi, 1987, p. 64.
58. *The Hindu*, September 20, 1960 , Ibid., p. 65.
59. A. Appadorai, *India's Foreign Policy and Relations*, New Delhi, 1985, pp.64–68.

60. 'The Indus Water Treaty 1960', Gulati, n.17, Appendix I, p.376.
61. Ibid., pp.376–78.
62. Ibid., p.380.
63. Ibid., pp. 380–383.
64. Ibid., pp. 383–85.
65. Ibid., p. 385.
66. Ibid., pp. 385–86.
67. Ibid., pp.386–88.
68. Ibid., p.390.
69. Ibid., p. 391.
70. Ibid., pp. 391–92.
71. Roshni Chakraborty and Sadia Nair, 'Indus Water Treaty its Relevance to Indo-Pak Relations', *Pakistan Horizon*, Vol. 55, No.4, October 2002, pp. 59–61.
72. *The Daily News*, March 30, 2004, Internet Edition http: / /www.dailytimes.com.pk.
73. http: / /www.water.int.net.
74. Abdul Farah, 'Kalabagh Dam: Doubts and Concerns', *The News*, February 10, 1993.
75. Nazir Ahmed, *Water Resources of Pakistan*, Lahore, 1993, pp.91-96.
76. http: / / www.mwr.inc.
77. Ahmed, n.75, pp. 110–12.
78. Ibid.
79. For details see, Kanyalil Sureedhar John, *Indo-Pakistan Relations: A Documentary Study*, New Delhi, 1993, pp. 218–219.
80. For details of the project see Bharat Bhushan, 'Tulbul, Sir Creek and Siachen: Competitive Methodologies', *South Asian Journal*, Vol.1, January–March 2005, pp.100–102.
81. *The Hindu*, January 15, 2005.
82. Naundhi Kaur, 'Troubled Waters', *Frontline*, Vol.19, No. 12, June 8–12, 2002, pp.26–27.
83. C. Raja Mohan, 'One for Indo-Pak Road: Free Trade Zone', *The Indian Express*, August 13, 2005.

The Changing Policy of the US in South Asia: Impact on Indo–Pak Relations

K.P. Vijayalakshmi*

US Engagement in South Asia

In March 2003, a Congressional hearing of the Sub-committee on Asia and the Pacific of the House Committee on International Relations started an overview of US policy towards South Asia. The Chairman Jim Leach (R-Iowa) in his opening remarks stated that this was necessary as the "region has sharply risen in prominence" for American policy makers after events of September 11, 2001. Clearly, the US re-engagement with the region heralded a serious debate in the US. At the outset, the Congressman called attention to the fact that the US has forged a new relationship with Pakistan in its campaign against terrorism but not "at the expense of our relations with India". He stated further that in his view there was a historical departure from previous relations with India but the US had "vested interests" in warming relations with Pakistan as well.[1] He also placed the relations with India and Pakistan as "exceptionally important" both as part of US' South Asia calculus and its diasporic content at home. In doing so, he seemed to have signalled the changing perceptions of the US as one of having a dramatic opportunity to address key foreign policy goals towards the region, which earlier had concentrated on nuclear non-proliferation. His remarks came at a time when US diplomacy was widely perceived to have been instrumental in facilitating a peaceful end to a tense Indo–Pak crisis of 2002.[2] As noted by experts and others, from December 2001 until July 2002, Indian and Pakistani forces confronted each other across the international border and along the Line of Control. Concerned about the potential for a conventional conflict that could

* Associate Professor, Center for Canadian, US and Latin American Studies, US division, SIS, JNU, New Delhi.

escalate to the nuclear level, the United States played a proactive role in walking both states back from the brink of war.[3] The re-emergence of the subcontinent on US policy agenda was in many ways indicative of the changing perceptions that characterized American thinking towards the end of the Clinton administration. Some of the main developments that influenced them till then were: the May 1998 nuclear tests by India and Pakistan, the Kargil War and the military coup in Pakistan in October 1999. In addition, the US was concerned about the role of China in the subcontinent and the stability and viability of the state of Pakistan. Clinton's visit in April 2000 must therefore be seen as heralding the US determination to re-engage the region. At the same time, the parallel development of positive perceptions about India involved crafting a policy that brought in prospects for better relations with India.

In November 2000, the Bush Administration continued increased attention to the subcontinent. The hallmark however was the "transformation of US-India relations". It argued that the mainframe of US policy toward the South Asian region rested on improving relations with India. The Presidential references to India as an emerging superpower/regional, major power in the world pushed this approach further. The US repeated that as sister democracies, India and America had vital "overlapping national interests".[4] All these perceptions gathered fresh momentum after the September 11 attack on the US. Measuring US interest with reference to its "War on Terror", US policy began removing certain sanctions and relaxing dual use export controls applicable to India and Pakistan.[5]

Congress and Bush Administration
Altered Perceptions and Changing US approach

In the Congress too winds of change were blowing. For instance, Representative Falmovoega [D-AS.) sought the House Committee on International Affairs to begin reassessment of US policy of mutually assured destruction, policy of nuclear deterrence, third-generation nuclear bombs to a full nuclear war and their impact on South Asia, (with its potential for such a conflict). Gary Ackerman (D-NY) similarly highlighted the administration's waiver of democracy-related sanctions against Pakistan as worthy of re-evaluation. The proliferation issue along with its local support for 'terrorists' by Pakistan made US policy assessment overdue in his view.

The administration witnesses Assistant Secretary Rocca for South Asia and Assistant Secretary Administration, USAID, Wendy Chamberlain brought forth testimony that illustrated how much change had taken place in the US policy approach towards India and Pakistan, within the larger context of South Asia.

The main argument was that the mainframe of the US approach for South Asia was its improved relations with India. According to this view, recognition of India's emergence as a major regional power and its "overlapping vital national interests" with the US, the US re-engaged India. In doing so it kept in view the following: the role of China in the subcontinent, consensus about promoting peace and stability in South Asia, combating international terrorism and preventing the spread of WMD. These were to be the basis of partnership with India. These goals were to be pursued by seeking a partnership with India via a consultative and cooperative approach. In her words:

> Over the past year, we've stepped up consultation on strategic and regional issues and greatly justified cooperation in Science and Technology, defense exchanges, intelligence dialogue and law enforcement...stem the proliferation of mass destruction (SIC) and their means of delivery.

She also stated that other issues, such as climate change, reproduction health, HIV/Aids and human trafficking would find "deepening engagement" by the US. Outlining US goals with regard to Pakistan the following were highlighted: reinforcing Pakistan's commitment to non-proliferation, improving its system of export controls, democracy and development of Pakistan as a stable, moderate Islamic state. Here too, the goals were seen as converging with those of Pakistan. The US approach was to provide debt relief and budgetary support and resources to assist Pakistan's economic development and social sector issues. The testimony emphasized that the key goals of US foreign policy in South Asia, namely, moderation, stability and development, which was challenged by the continuing tension between India and Pakistan over Kashmir. Hence the US approach was to continue de-escalatory efforts, increase communication between Kashmir India and Pakistan and to provide support to the peace process between India and Pakistan. Significantly, the articulation of "ending infiltration into Kashmir" as part of US policy was in line with the goal of deepening improved relations with India. However, serving US' larger interests in South Asia and achieving major goals outlined were linked to the diffusion of the ongoing India–Pakistan tensions on Kashmir and vice versa.

The hearing also brought out the changed approach by the US, for instance, reducing Pakistan's foreign debt and providing teachers' training, improving curricula, encouraging community involvement and supporting literacy programmes were all part of the approach. The US policy was also committed to strengthen political institutions to enable a democratic institutional framework for Pakistan.[6] With India, it related to tech-transfer questions and economic trade barriers along with combating HIV/Aids and counter-terrorism. US leaders' insistence on improvement in New Delhi's human rights record in Kashmir, or to set other preconditions for the US-Indian relationship to improve was acknowledged belatedly by the Clinton Administration officials as counter productive. In fact, it had begun to dawn on them that developing a good working relationship with India should be one of America's top foreign policy priorities. President Clinton's visit to South Asia in March 2000 was an important symbolic step undertaken in pursuit of this vision. However, the logic of easing tensions between India and Pakistan has also simultaneously occupied centre-stage in America's strategy pursued in South Asia. As a key official in the Bush Administration stated:

> Conflict[s] between India and Pakistan are made even more urgent by the global war on terrorism. Secretary State Colin Powell had said that war ... is just not an option in resolving the differences between India and Pakistan—it will only make the situation worse, probably much worse. The only realistic way forward is the path of dialogue and confidence building.

The Secretary also publicly recognized that Kashmir is now on the international agenda. Given the potential cost of a conflict, the international community focused on the need to reduce tension and demobilize. While acknowledging that no one from the outside can impose a settlement, Powell stated that "we must work to help the two sides further de-escalate current tensions and begin to tackle the more fundamental differences between them."[7]

The altered US perception of linking Indo-Pak tensions over Kashmir as vital to its core interests in South Asia has resulted in (a) 'sharp focus on its own role (in a new/modified form) in mediating the conflict between India and Pakistan; (b) on encouraging cooperative structural dialogue between the two and (c) continuation of its role as a crisis manager.

There was also a noticeable change in the US approach towards nuclear non-proliferation. Illustrated officially, it basically involved exercising restraint, minimizing missile test, announcing tests in advancing, bringing to an end to production of fissile material and not building ICBMS or deploying nuclear capable warheads or ballistic missiles and keeping them in separate locations. As the US articulated its policy preference in South Asia, there was increased emphasis on bringing the export control regimes to international standards to prevent leakage of sensitive technologies. Again, the US elucidated it as a part of its policy, which would require close working with India and Pakistan. Finally, the risk of crossing the nuclear threshold due to the existence of high tensions and cold war between India and Pakistan were outlined as a key challenge to the US policy. Therefore, defusing tensions became the dominant aspect of the US approach. In sum, by the end of 2003, the US approach of having close warm ties with both countries to work on the issues outlined above was a change from the "tilted", "hyphenated" or a "Zero-Sum" mentality that had characterized US policy of the past. It was also clear that India was seen as an emerging superpower with interests complementary to that of the US. It was evident that the US would play a proactive role in containing, and managing the Indo-Pak conflict as it impinged on US' agenda for the region.

Congressional resolutions went further. In one instance, the Committee on International Relations (House) unanimously passed an amendment requiring the administration to disclose to the US Congress and to the American people the extent to which Pakistan is fulfilling its promise to clamp down on cross-border terrorism, shutting down terrorists camps in Pakistan-held Kashmir and halting the proliferation of nuclear technology to rogue states and terrorists. There was bipartisan and unanimous support for H.R. 1950. An amendment proposed by Representative Falmovoega, specifically asked the administration to describe Pakistan government's compliance with closing terrorists training camps operating in Pakistan and POK, infiltration across LOC into India by extremists and the cessation of transfer of WMD, including army-associated technologies to any third country or terrorist organization.[8] The impact of these developments on US policy was felt when a leading Indian daily reported that Washington has put in place a process of verification claims made by Pakistan that all militant camps in POK has been wound up by May 31, 2003.

Impact of Changed Perceptions on Policy

Assistant Secretary of State for South Asia Affairs Christina Rocca had stated that South Asia is a region of "remarkable social, economic and technological transformations" situated in the front line of global war on terror. She cautioned, however, that this region still faced the danger of nuclear war. Speaking to the Asia Society at New York on 4 February, 2004, she outlined the different situation and the region's importance to the Bush Administration. In main the US foreign policy was founded on building a network of partnerships based on national interests and shared values to achieve goals of freedom, democracy, development and human dignity. These goals were not incidental to US foreign policy but essential ones.[9] In the same speech, she alluded to the long and complicated relationship with Pakistan, which faced many political and economic challenges. Maintaining that Pakistan remained a key ally in the global war on terrorism, the Secretary said that the US was committed to help Pakistan to improve education, expand economic opportunities and to establish a functioning democracy. Towards this end, the US promised a $3 bn package once in 5 years starting with $600 million assistance in 2004. The primary focus of this assistance was to expand Pakistan's counter-terror cooperation, bolster economic growth and expand social sector programme. Importantly, the Secretary recognized the costs for Pakistan's cooperation in the 'GWT' and to its social fabric. The speech pointedly referred to the long-term commitment of the US to continuing, broadening and deepening its relationship with Pakistan.

The Secretary highlighted economic themes with stress on reciprocity with India calling it a "transformed relationship" with a strategic partner. She pointed to the Indian potential as one of the world's largest economies with which the US primary objective would be to improve bilateral trade relations. She illustrated the ongoing partnership with India in many fields of economy and commerce and other areas with references to the regularity of consultations, meetings and agreements held with New Delhi. In particular, she called attention to "Next Steps in Strategic Partnership" between Washington and New Delhi by referring to the latest agreement in Civilian Nuclear activities, civilian space programme and high technology trade. The dialogue was expanded to cover strategic stability and missile defenses spelling it out in detail, she stated that these areas would be transparent and would threaten no country. Clearly, it was meant to reassure Pakistan and perhaps China. The overall emphasis was on close cooperative partnership between the US and India.

Domestic Views on US Policy Goals

These developments have to be seen, in conjunction with the larger US goal of regional stability in South Asia. The US role in this region after September 11, 2001 has altered in many ways. There is a perceptional change in the US about the situation between India and Pakistan. For instance, the remarks by Secretary Rocca gave credence to the US claims that it was interested in a "triangle of conflict resolution". This triangle as envisaged by Secretary of State Colin Powell would place the US as a facilitator of peace process between India and Pakistan. Further, it was evident that US officials would closely monitor the Indo-Pak talks scheduled for February 16-18, 2004. Clearly the US diplomatic efforts have expanded from the so-called Middle East to South Asia. Yet, the conflicting interests it is pursuing with India and Pakistan has made it guarded about its plans to settle the dispute between India and Pakistan without war. Many analysts believe that US diplomatic pressure, which started with the Kargil conflict, will continue. They perceive that the US hoped that a flurry of visits by top-level administrative officials could result in both countries beginning the process of dialogue on all issues including Kashmir.[10]

Analysts pointed out that while India was being counted as an emerging world power by the US, calming tensions between India and Pakistan was vital as the latter is a critical ally in the war on terror. Despite India's status as a strategic partner who should be dealt with beyond the framework of arms control, US interests have sparked a debate on how much leeway India should be given in its dealings with Pakistan. For instance, Startfor.com, a strategic think tank and threat analysis group, reported that, "Washington's hesitancy and a naming time frame before monsoon begins means that whatever conflict erupts will likely be contained to Kashmir". An editorial in *Far Eastern Economic Review*, however, put the matter simply as "Extending the US led war on terrorism to include militants in Pakistan-controlled Kashmir" would be the best option for the US. Dennis Kux, former diplomat and author of several works on India, the US and Pakistan, also pointed to the limited choice that US faced on Indo-Pak tensions. He pointed out that the US hesitation to tackle the Pakistanis would have a detrimental effect on Indo–US relations.

Within the US, views ranged from the dangers of nuclear flashpoint to separating Kashmir into three parts and encouraging Indo–Pak bilateral talks.[11] Long-term, South Asia experts argued that US must nudge

> a peace process between India and Pakistan, which had as a major component the well-being of the Kashmiri people would remove one of the causes of radical Islamists. This will be difficult to achieve, but it should be one of the primary goals of American policy.[12]

In the American perception, the US has really three options in South Asia from this point onward. The first is the traditional policy, the good old-fashioned simply 'love them and leave them' policy. There seem to be hardly any vital American interests in South Asia, that is, nothing of direct threat to the United States except possibly events that might occur in Pakistan.

Then the Bush Administration began to see India as a rising Asian power and did not see much value in a relationship with Pakistan. So the first option was to pull out. The war on terrorism transformed that perspective and Pakistan became a front line state in the war on terrorism, not only for the war in Afghanistan but important on its own as the evolution of Pakistan or the deterioration of Pakistan into a state which itself was the source of international terror. The second option was to remain engaged with both, but tilting towards India. A third option was to engage India and Pakistan but ignore Kashmir. As long as the US needed Pakistan as an ally in the war against terrorism clearly there would be a military relationship and a political relationship with Islamabad. However, the Bush Administration still perceived India as a major rising Asian state, indeed world power.

At the minimum then, the US was going to have a closer relationship with India, the enhancing of military cooperation and even nuclear cooperation. As the Indian economy continues to grow, the hope that there will be much greater gains in the US-Indian economic ties also guides this approach. For Pakistan there is the promise of significant economic assistance to help rebuild its infrastructure. There has been renewed military assistance to Pakistan as part of the price the Pakistanis want in order to keep their cooperation and keep American forces in Islamabad. Hence the third option was to engage India and Pakistan but ignore Kashmir.

Yet another option was explored. This fourth option was one that was raised periodically and had hitherto been rejected by successive American administrations. This was to add Kashmir to the mix. To attempt to bring India and Pakistan if not to the bargaining table at least to move towards a process by which they can deal with the Kashmir issue in one form or another. These and other views basically dealt with the need, urgency and benefits of US engagement in the Indo-Pakistan peace process. Such a policy was advocated as

> the elements of a process which would allow us to do this are now in place. We do have close relations with both India and Pakistan, closer relations with both than we've had for many decades. There's good reason to expand our relationship with India. It's important that Pakistan be retained, that we retain our relationship with Pakistan. We don't want to see it deteriorate any further as a state. Finally, there's a whole array of Kashmir proposals on the table.[13]

The US policy eventually straddled these approaches in combination. It acknowledged that instituting peace process was eventually beneficial to American interests. Further, emergence of real prospects for peace between the two nuclear rivals could free American focus on the larger War on Terror.[14] As an influential group of former American officials advised, American policy needed to be firmly embedded in impacting Indo-Pak tensions. As they stated,

> Given the dangers inherent in the festering India-Pakistan rivalry, the United States should become more active in trying to help the two nuclear-armed enemies manage their differences, including the Kashmir dispute.[15]

Role of the United States

The US has, after 9/11, considerable influence over both countries. The significant part it played in the crisis of 2001 and 2002 between India and Pakistan has enhanced its role of discreet facilitator. In the words of Colin Powell, "We do not impose ourselves as a mediator. But we do try to use the trust we have established with both sides to urge them toward conciliation by peaceful means". In the US view, it would continue to constructively leverage both sides to facilitate the openness, sustainable conflict resolution between India and Pakistan. In recent months, many analysts and reports have warned that US needs to pay more high-level attention to simmering rivalry between India and Pakistan or face grave crises that could threaten US interests in the region. The report, co-sponsored by the Council on Foreign Relations and Asia Society in New York, has articulated the need for the Bush Administration to place India and Pakistan conflict resolution as part of US foreign policy priorities in the region describing that as "dark shadows" have descended across South Asia. Titled "New Priorities in South Asia: US policy toward India, Pakistan and Afghanistan", the report recommended that in the medium term (i.e. 2004) US needs sustained bilateral ties with all three countries so as to influence regional developments.

The US approach should, however, be based on sustained high-level attention, sensitive diplomacy, a realistic view of what is possible and especially in Pakistan and Afghanistan, with investment of substantial resources. To protect US foreign policy interests in the region, according to the Report, these three relationships have to be improved. Given the "entrenched Islamist Extremism", Pakistan's instability, the report urged the US Congress to speed up the US $3 billion-aid package requested by the President to help Pakistan. However, the report said that two-third of the money should go to the economic and social programmes instead of the fifty-fifty approach preferred by the Bush Administration.

The Indian perception noted the possibility of US not pursuing the war against terrorism in toto or countering nuclear blackmail (of Pakistan) as boosting Jehadis' morale everywhere.[16] Other Indians debated the impact of bilateral initiatives between India and Pakistan on moving forward on the peace dialogue and concluded that the search for a political accommodation with

Pakistan must be vigorously pursued through regular interactions and meetings at the political, bureaucratic and non-governmental levels.[17]

With regard to the US, the Indian criticisms of its double standards regarding the dismantling of infrastructures of terrorism everywhere voiced concern that the US and India would remain as targets of terrorists. What India wanted from the US was succinctly reported in *The Hindu*. In that it was reported that the Indians felt that the possession of nuclear weapons alone did not necessarily threaten a nuclear war. Poor governance, political instability at home and undue external dependence could also encourage use of nuclear arms.[18] In essence, the Indian keenness to use the US to leverage the Pakistani leadership by the issue of terrorism was reflective of the new perceptions that characterize its relations with the US. While maintaining India's opposition to any formal third-party mediation in Indo–Pak tensions, a subtle alteration has taken place. India had successfully placed the central issue of peace in the region as the major factor in US policy towards South Asia. Further, as the US engagement in South Asia is likely to be long term, Indian interests in containing Pakistan are interlinked to the global war on terror.

Conclusion

While the issue of Kashmir continues to be regarded as a "flash point" and "sensitive" by US policy-makers and other analysts in any recurrence of Indo-Pak conflict, US perceptions on South Asia have changed. From being a black spot on the radar screen of the US, it has become a vital area. As Senator Lugar (R-Ind), then chairman of the powerful Senate Committee on Foreign Relations put it:

> Stability in the South Asian region was vital to US interests both because an India-Pakistan conflict could escalate into a nuclear war and because of the potential nexus between terrorism and weapons of mass destruction.

He advocated a continued US diplomatic role in ending hostilities between Pakistan and India, as he believed that continued conflict would provide a breeding ground for the recruitment of extremists and terrorists.

Thus, the perceptions that influence US policy towards India and Pakistan and South Asia include averting nuclear exchange, containing and eliminating terrorists' threats, bringing India–Pakistan to the negotiating table, using new relationships with both on different angles without negatively impacting either, maintaining a proactive US diplomacy to monitor progress on peace negotiations and providing economic and strategic assistance to both through different initiatives. The US interests are now being perceived as both long term and short term. In the short term, the US approach towards Pakistan has been related to the following interests: (a) cooperation on terrorism as a key ally (b) issues of non-proliferation (c) stability in Afghanistan (d) opening the dialogue with India, and (e) working with the Pakistan state as it is.

In the long term, US interests include: (a) democratization of Pakistan (b) Assistance in social sector (c) halting economic decline (d) enhancing Pakistan as a moderate Islamic state (e) changing the internal dynamics of Pakistan society.

For India the US interests are larger and broader. In the short term, they include:

(a) strategic cooperation in dual-use technologies
(b) nuclear safety measures and non-proliferation
(c) dialogue with Pakistan
(d) monitoring the peace initiative
(e) political and diplomatic engagement at all levels for economic and political goals
(f) crisis prevention and management of conflict between India and Pakistan by assurances of audit and verification of Pakistan's claims on camps in POK.

The long-term interests include:

(a) harmonizing foreign policy goals with Indian American community desires
(b) anti-terrorism and counter terrorism
(c) intelligence sharing and cooperation of law enforcement
(d) civil, nuclear and space collaboration
(e) scientific and medical research
(f) tapping India's market potential
(g) balancing China.

This list is neither exhaustive nor placed in order of priorities. Yet, it gives some idea of the core US interests in the region with impact on India-Pakistan conflict. It also explains the US approach towards the two in a policy context. The wide influence of Asia Society Report can be estimated by the Assistant Secretary Rocca's speech on 4 February 2004. Specifically praising the report, she stated that official US policy was in effect consistent with the recommendations and insights given by the authors. More significantly, the US policy approach has initiated, as per the Secretary's remarks, a long-term commitment of the US in South Asia. It also clearly indicates US perceptions regarding the challenges and policy options in the region, particularly with India and Pakistan. Thus, the US seems committed to a long-term proactive role in managing the India-Pakistan conflict. While the global war on terror is top priority with Pakistan, it is clear that US perception of urgent changes needed within Pakistan has led to the proposed 3 billion aid package initiative.

With India, the convergence of interests is bringing the US closer. In the words of the Chief Policy Advisor for South Asia, Jonah Blank, to the Senate Foreign Relations Committee, "China, Pakistan and Counter Terrorism" are the three most important concerns driving US-Indian "strategic convergence of interest." In the deliberations at a CSIS panel on "Bridging US-India: A Defense Perspective", observers (including Secretary Rocca and Julie MacDonald) maintained that the US would essentially play a stabilizing role while giving military assistance to either India or Pakistan. In particular, the US concern that China does not become a "non-status-quo power" or try to "radically alter" the balance of power in Asia would remain at the back of US policy options.[19]

US perceptions and policy approach towards South Asia as a whole and Indo-Pak conflict in particular have changed since 9/11. While Pakistan has become a key ally in the war against terrorism, the inherent complexities of managing a long-term relationship with it has engaged US policy makers. This has evolved the US policy towards managing three dimensions: domestic change, border conflicts with India and Afghanistan, nuclear proliferation. With India, the US convergence of interests on China, Pakistan and counter terrorism have prioritized defense and technology sales.

Challenges for US Policy

The repercussions of 11 September attacks has upset the regional agenda for US policy. A main effort to strengthen its ties with India stated during Clinton Administration and continued by its successor, had been the centre-piece of US regional policy. But after 9/11 Afghanistan has become the eye of the storm and Pakistan a key ally (Sri Lanka awaits). The renewed attention to Pakistan will have lasting consequences. The underlying interests of US approach to India to broaden the policy framework continues but increased importance of encouraging the peace process in Kashmir has strained it considerably.

The US military actions in Afghanistan have triggered reaction within Pakistan and keeping General Musharaff's government stable has inhibited the goal of rebuilding political institutions within Pakistan. The US agenda of regional security, peace and stability is constrained by proliferation disclosures of Pakistan's scientist A.Q. Khan's activities. So will India, Pakistan and US face, divergent goals in the coming future? For India, the goal of minimizing US relationship with Pakistan is considerably weakened as the US moves away from zero-sum mentality of its past relations. For Pakistan, centralizing the Kashmir dispute has taken a back seat given the enormous pressure on its government to survive domestically and face threat of international inspections of nuclear facilities. For both, the centrality of nuclear risk reduction and peaceful settlement of Kashmir issue has been the obvious choice to minimize domestic turbulence within. For the US, pursuing a multi-layered, complex, regional security agenda dictates a long-term, proactive role in the region. Relations with both India and Pakistan need to be sustained with India as a star player. While promoting peace in Kashmir is different from its anti-terrorism campaign, the two are linked. Finally, the US challenge is to face the reality that as long as Kashmir issue festers, it will feed India-Pakistan hostility and create a potential breeding ground for fresh terrorists.

Given these realities, the role of the US will not be confined to that of a facilitator or crisis manager. Unfolding evidence in the last few months points to the fact that the US has to balance its proliferation objectives in the region with new partners. With the new agreement it has signed with India on July 18, 2005, the US has clearly chosen India to be the balancer on Asia. At the present time, it looks as if the Congressional road may be stormy. Indian domestic political logjams may also stall convergence with the US on proliferation issues, particularly with Iran. However, with regard to the Indo-Pakistan peace process the US remains the third party despite bilateral initiatives by the two. In the coming years, it is difficult to see an end to the US role for both India and Pakistan have yet to find a lasting peace on Kashmir. To be emphasized here is the fact that such an approach was quite different from the previous initiatives. For instance, Washington's over-emphasis on the proliferation issue illustrated the tendency of US policymakers to treat India as a potential adversary rather than a friend. ■

Notes & References

1. U.S. House of Representatives, Committee on International Relations, Subcommittee on Asia and the Pacific., Hearings, "The United States and South Asia: Challenges and opportunities for American Interest." 107th Congress, 1st session, Washington USGPO, March 2003. See also United States Congress, House Committee on International Relations. Subcommittee on the Middle East and South Asia, Hearings; "The Current Crisis in South Asia", 107 Congress, second session, Washington : U.S.G.P.O June 6, 2002.
2. Several media reports have detailed analysis of this aspect. Some worth perusal are: Vaiju Naravane, 'French jets patrolled Indo-Pak. coastline', *The Hindu* Online, in:

http://www.thehindu.com/2002/07/04/stories/2002070407221200.htm, "Musharraf, India & the US—The betrayal of Kashmir—Analysis" in *Pak Tribune Discussion Forum*, February 7, 2004 and Randeep Ramesh "The rhetoric of war" May 29, 2002 in http://www.guardian.co.uk/comment/story/0,3604,723900,00.html

3. Samina Ahmed Workshop Report of Pugwash Meeting No. 280, Pugwash Workshop, titled "Avoiding an India-Pakistan Nuclear Confrontation" held in Lahore, Pakistan, March 11–12, 2003.
4. Amos Perlmutter, "Toward a US-India strategic kinship", *The Washington Times*, December 9, 2000 in www.washtimes.com, see also, Victor M. Gobarev, "India as a World Power: Changing Washington's Myopic Policy", *Cato Policy Analysis*, No. 381, September 11, 2000 for a detailed analysis on change in American thinking.
5. President Waives Sanctions on India, Pakistan, September 22, 2001 Presidential Determination No. 2001–28 which stated the following: Pursuant to section 9001 (b) of the Department of Defense Appropriations Act, 2000 (Public Law 106–79), I hereby determine and certify to the Congress that the application to India and Pakistan of the sanctions and prohibitions contained in subparagraphs (B), (C), and (G) of section 102(b)(2) of the Arms Export Control Act would not be in the national security interests of the United States. Furthermore, pursuant to section 9001(a) of the Department of Defense Appropriations Act, 2000 (Public Law 106–79), I hereby waive, with respect to India and Pakistan, to the extent not already waived, the application of any sanction contained in section 101 or 102 of the Arms Export Control Act, section 2(b)(4) of the Export Import Bank Act of 1945, and section 620E(e) of the Foreign Assistance Act of 1961, as amended.
6. Information related to this aspect is available on USAID website. In an overview the agency stated, "USAID reopened its mission in Pakistan in 2002 to demonstrate its commitment to Pakistan, tangibly improve the lives of the poor in Pakistan and build support for Pakistan's decision to join the international war on terrorism. Pakistan's stability is critical to U.S. foreign policy interests. Thirty-eight per cent of the population lives below the poverty line, making programs to increase their incomes a priority. USAID has focused its program directly on the most pressing needs: economic growth, education, health and governance" URL: http://www.usaid.gov/locations/asia_near_east/countries/pakistan/ On India the mission was "India has the potential to be a catalyst for economic growth and development in an unstable region. However, poverty, rapid population growth, pockets of weak governance and health issues challenge the country. The world's largest democracy, it is also a key US ally in the war on terrorism", http://www.usaid.gov/locations/asia_near_east/countries/india.
7. Asst. Sec. of State for South Asian Affairs, Christina Rocca, Testimony to the Subcommittee in Asia and Pacific of the House Committee on International Relations,

March 2003. See also, Christina Rocca, Assistant Secretary of State for South Asian Affairs; Strobe Talbott and Nayan Chanda, "Prospects for Peace in South Asia" US Institute for Peace, Washington, D.C. September 5, 2002.

8. May 2003, US House Committee on International Relations, Amendment to Resolution 1950.CQ Record *The Times of India*, June 1, 2003.
9. "US Sees Enormous Delays, Dazzling Opportunity in South Asia", US Embassy, Public Affairs Dept., New Delhi, February 5, 2004.
10. Lee Feinstein, David Clad, James Dunn, Lewis Albright, A New Equation: US Policy toward India and Pakistan after September 11 [Carnegie Endowment for Peace, Carnegie Paper No. 27] May 2002. The report argued that "It is also a test for Washington and whether it can leverage its new position to address core concerns, including the dispute over Kashmir, Pakistan's crisis of governance, and the evolving nuclear and missile rivalry in the region."
11. See Discussion in the *Washington Post* with managing editor to see the range of views; "Will Kashmir Go Nuclear?" With Steve Coll Washington Post Managing Editor, Tuesday, June 4, 2002.
12. Stephen Philip Cohen, "The United States and South Asia: Core Interests and Policies and their Impact on Regional Countries", Presented to the *Conference on Major Powers and South Asia*, August 11–13, 2003, the Institute for Regional Studies, Islamabad, Pakistan.
13. "What Role Does the United States Have in the India-Pakistan Crisis?" A Brookings Press Briefing, June 11, 2002. See also Michael Krepon "From Confrontation to Cooperation", Henry Stimson Center, Washington D.C. URL: http://www.stimson.org /pub.cfm?ID=197&print=yes.
14. Such thinking was perhaps behind the Kargil intervention by the US. See, Bruce Riedel, "American Diplomacy and the 1999 Kargil Summit at Blair House", Policy Paper Series 2002,Center for the Advanced Study of India-University of Pennsylvania.
15. New Priorities in South Asia: US Policy Toward India, Pakistan, and Afghanistan, Chairmen's Report of an Independent Task Force, Co-sponsored by the Council on Foreign Relations and the Asia Society, November, 2003.
16 Robert Nolan "Monsoon Season: The U.S. South Asia" in Foreign Policy Association, *Global Views*, February 2004, online edition. URL:http://www.fpa.org/newsletter_info2583/newsletter_info_sub_list.htm?section=Monsoon+Season%3A++The+U.S.+and+South+Asia.
17. B. Raman, "India's Foreign Policy Malaise", *Asia Times*, Online, April 30, 2003.
18. Atul Aneja, "India, US Define New Security Agenda", in *The Hindu* Online, April 10, 2001.
19. Anthony Kawa, "Convergence of Interests leading to Closer US-India Security Ties", US Department of State, International Information Program, December 15, 2003.

Track-Two Diplomacy in Indo–Pak Relations: Problems and Prospects

Happymon Jacob*

Introduction

Track-two diplomacy in South Asia addressing bilateral issues can survive only if it becomes part of the larger civil society movement in India. Unless and until peace activism and track-two diplomacy radically broaden their constituency by way of co-opting more issues, groups and people and also by letting go, at least in part, of the traditional issues like Kashmir, security-related issues and address issues such as water pollution, water scarcity, women's issues, labour issues, education, etc. track-two diplomacy in South Asia will die a premature death. There are many claims, counter-claims and vital stakes involved in important issues like Kashmir, which the present actors and organizations involved in track-two diplomacy are not in a position to address from a larger civil society perspective, and thus, they, to a larger extent, are unlikely to bring radical focus shift in these issues and questions.

The primary focus of this paper is to analyze the present state of track-two initiatives between India and Pakistan. In order to throw light on the present state of the same, the paper looks at what ails the track-two initiatives between India and Pakistan and how these initiatives can be given a new lease of life.

What is track-two diplomacy?

Joseph Montville defines track-two diplomacy as "unofficial, informal interaction between members of adversary groups or nations which aims to develop strategies, influence public opinion, and organize human and material resources in ways that might help resolve their conflict."[1] Others have argued that "track two diplomacy is not a substitute for track one official diplomacy but is a supplemental or parallel

---

* Lecturer, Centre for Strategic and Regional Studies, University of Jammu, Jammu.

operation. It seeks solutions which might satisfy the basic political, security, and esteem needs of the parties to a particular dispute."[2]

Dr. Louse Diamond and Ambassador John McDonald, in their widely-read book *Multi-track Diplomacy: A Systems Approach to Peace* elaborate various tracks of track-two diplomacy.[3] They have listed nine tracks of diplomacy in their book. However, as the purpose of this paper is not to get into terminological hair-splitting, it is not intended to look for definitions of the term 'track-two'. We would adopt a general understanding of the term 'track-two diplomacy': track-two initiatives will include all those non-governmental means, methods and efforts of conflict resolution which will constructively engage people on both sides of the border in order to peacefully solve conflicts between states.

Track-two diplomacy in Indo–Pak relations

This paper does not look at the history of track-two diplomacy between India and Pakistan, therefore it is not necessary to spend considerable space on this issue. There are various accounts in cold print detailing the history and the historical milestones in this regard. One of the important works in this regard has been by Navnita Chadha Behera, Paul M. Evans and Gowher Rizvi, titled "Beyond Boundaries: A Report on the State of Non-official Dialogues on Peace, Security and Cooperation in South Asia".[4]

Why track-two diplomacy?

One of the main reasons usually enunciated in support of track-two diplomacy is that it helps demolish deeply entrenched enemy images, which have been given to people about 'enemy countries'.[5] Indeed, these images cannot be addressed and demolished by track-one processes and mainstream official dialogues, hence the importance of track-two diplomacy. One could cite many examples from the recent years of Indo-Pak relations. We hear many Indian leaders, students, and others saying after a visit to Pakistan, "Oh, they are just like us". While this may sound too simplistic a statement to be given a great deal of importance, such statements, however, do reveal the fact that many among India's educated elite do have such 'enemy' notions about Pakistan and its citizens. Consider also the fact that not many get a chance to travel to Pakistan and those who actually get a chance are mostly from the educated elite. If so, the understanding of ordinary Indians about Pakistan would not be any better.

Second, track-two diplomacy helps prepare the larger societies, ruling elites and the civil society for accepting the strong and often painful decisions, which the governments of conflicting countries may eventually take. Often enough, the larger constituencies including the civil societies may not be in a position to accept strong decisions of the government in favour of peace. In such a context, track-two diplomacy prepares the societies at large for accepting strong decisions. While it is easy to change public opinion, it does take time. Moreover, this role of preparing the public cannot be done by the governments, as it is often not easy for them to go back on their own long-held views. This is where track-two diplomacy with strong roots in the larger civil society can play a big role.

Third, it helps governments to test political waters before major policy decisions are made: apart from preparing the larger civil society for strong decisions, the governments in question can also do a 'test run' of important decisions among analysts, political parties, media and the ruling elite. The famous suggestion of Niaz Naik to R.K. Mishra on behalf of the Pakistani's establishment to consider the *Chenab* formula to solve the Kashmir problem is a case in point.[6] This aspect assumes importance given the fact that democratic governments need to know the views of the public without actually owning up the positives and negatives of a particular decision/proposal.

What ails track-two diplomacy between India and Pakistan?

There is no lack of track-two initiatives between India and Pakistan. What is lacking, regrettably, is any worthy success. The following may be considered to be some of the reasons for the depressed state of track-two diplomacy between India and Pakistan.

A cursory glance over the many track-two initiatives that we have had over these years would confirm that most participants, apart from some exceptions in the recent years, are the 'usual suspects', namely, retired bureaucrats, or professional peace-lovers. Many tend to have their own set notions and ideas about Indo-Pak relations and peace building, and, moreover, they also have a fixed constituency, which in no way is broad. It is interesting to listen to track-two activists saying to one another, 'look, the world is so small' meaning that they keep coming face to face all the time in such meetings.

Track-two diplomacy suffers from extreme elitism. Most issues discussed in track-two diplomacy come across as 'elitist' to most common people. The track-two activists never discuss water pollution or labour problems or such other mundane issues.[7] Indeed, while discussing such mundane issues may not solve the outstanding issues between India and Pakistan, it does, nonetheless, help create a peace constituency.

Most often, with some exceptions in the recent years in the second rung track-two participants, track-two meetings do not have any participation from the younger generation. It is often a myth to think that the 'third generation' in India and Pakistan perceives the ongoing conflicts with less hawkishness than the older generation. Thus the attempts to either not include the younger generation or to take them for granted are imprudent and often counter-productive. However, scholars have also argued that third-generation views on Indo-Pak conflict may be less hawkish. Stephen Cohen, for instance, has argued:

> A third generation is now emerging...the third generation does not have a sense of responsibility for the gloomy history. Their competence and their interest in the things that matter—above all a fresh approach to economic issues, plus the collapse of many institutions dominated by a generation in the past—will bring them to power sooner rather than later. More than any other development in the region, this new group of regional leaders will make it possible for a change to occur.[8]

Either way, it is unwise to keep the third generation out of such dialogues as the exclusion of the younger generation makes the discourse in those forums remain typical and non-creative.

One of the tangible results of peace between India and Pakistan would be a phenomenal increase in trade and commerce between the two countries. In 2001-2002, India's total export trade was $44 billion; whereas its total export to Pakistan was only $204 million.[9] And this gap exists not because both the countries do not have anything to trade. Consider the following facts:

- Pakistan's annual demand for tyres is 1 million; it produces only 200,000 tyres. India is the best option to fill the deficit with affordably priced tyres; however, an import duty of 46 per cent drives the price of Indian tyres through the roof.[10]
- Zinetac, a patent medicine for acidity, sells in India at Rs. 7.20 for 10 tablets; it retails in Pakistan for between Rs. 80 and Rs. 150.[11]

Trade restrictions in both the countries have seen to it that no trade worth its name takes place, with the result that illegal trade thrives between the countries. This leads to revenue loss for both the countries and more cost for consumers. The Federation of Indian Chambers of Commerce and Industry estimates that given a conducive climate, Indo–Pak trade can be anything between $3 billion to $4 billion.[12]

Despite all this, in most of the track-two engagements, trading communities are completely absent. While increased trade can be the single-most important reason for better bilateral cooperation, this unfortunately is the least focused issue. Perhaps the governments of both India and Pakistan are better off at this as business leaders often accompany the official delegations during official bilateral visits.[13]

There is a clear lack of a 'peace constituency' in both the countries. There are no real beneficiaries of peace in both the countries. Peace activists on both sides tend to be 'professional peace lovers'. While it is necessary to have the intellectual and ideological backbone to peace building that they seem to provide, it appears that the fruits, if any, of their advocacy and activism have not really percolated to the grass roots level. On the other hand, there are many beneficiaries of the status quo. Conflict or enmity has become the normal state of affairs and the status quo suits everyone who has a stake in it. Unfortunately, most decision makers seem to have a stake in it. It is aptly said about the Pakistani's military that it may not be in its best interests to have peace between India and Pakistan. Of late, however, experts have expressed opinions contrary to this argument.[14]

Track-two diplomacy so far has acutely failed to tap the vast network of social movements at the grass roots level that may be made use of in order to broaden the peace constituency. A large chunk of civil society is not prepared to address hard issues which ail Indo-Pak relations, and initiate radical policy shifts. That is because there is a divergence between what the civil society engages in and what crusaders of track-two diplomacy do.

Right-wing political ideologies acquiring power in both countries, to a great extent have led to a domestic situation where anything that is said or done different from the national mainstream position will be considered to be anti-national.[15] In such circumstances, individuals and organizations, but for the committed ones with great missionary zeal, are likely to develop cold feet towards track-two initiatives in the longer run. Indeed, with the National Democratic Alliance (NDA) coming to office in the Indian parliamentary elections, the peace process and other track-two initiatives seem to have gained a new lease of life.[16]

Bureaucracies in both India and Pakistan are unyieldingly resolute to such an extent that they totally shut themselves to most non-official initiatives. As a result, they are not used to taking anything unofficial seriously, often contributing to the eventual failure of track-two initiatives and gains wrought by them. This has partly, consciously or otherwise, got to do with the nature of the state in South Asia, especially in Pakistan and India. As these states and their nationhood are still at the early stages of development, they show extreme reluctance to non-official engagements fearing that they may one day challenge the authority of the state.

Media in Pakistan and India, both English and vernacular, are no liberators. Most of the time it is the media in both the countries, which zealously spoil the peace initiatives in the region including track-two ones.[17] What I mean here is a lack of atypical reporting on Indo-Pak relations or peace initiatives, official or otherwise. This is essentially a structural problem in the sense that most reporters depend heavily on information provided by the government, which can be denied to them if they happen to annoy the government as the government is not under any legal obligation to part with information thanks to legal measures like the 'Official Secrets Act'.[18]

The post-retirement change of religion may have occurred for many ex-bureaucrats due to the longing to be in the limelight by playing the game of the day—'peace building'—without changing the roles they are used to—'war-planning'. The habit of war-planning make them bring peace on a war footing which has its own characteristics of haste and exclusiveness contributing to the eventual alienation of the larger constituencies and consequent failure of peace initiatives. In addition, many often look upon bureaucrats and their track-two initiatives, owing to the above-mentioned factors, with suspicion.

There is a lack of an urge for peace within the minds of the general public. One damaging myth that prevails in the minds of many peace and track-two activists in the region is that people in general want to have peace between India and Pakistan. If that is true, how did Narendra Modi win the elections in Gujarat on an anti-Pakistan platform?[19] The argument, however, is not about the innate good and evil in human beings from a philosophical point of view. On the contrary, the point made is about the circumstances that most people in the region live in.

What should be done to improve track-two initiatives in the region?

First of all, there should be more interaction among parliamentarians of the two countries. They should be made part of the track-two delegations. The importance of involving parliamentarians arises due to two reasons: (i) the opposition members of Parliament can persuade the government to take certain measures even if they would not do it themselves when they are in power; and (ii) a change of heart in the house of Parliament can do wonders even if the general public is unaware of it. The assumption here is that politics and politicians of the region have greatly contributed to the peace-less state of affairs of the region. Therefore, they can do a lot in reversing the situation.

Second, there should be exchanges between academic and research institutions between the two countries. At present such contacts are very sparse. Many a time, such delegations are denied visas. To cite another example, it is even difficult to transfer books published by reputed publishers like the Oxford University Press from one country to the other. It is necessary to have exchange of ideas between the two countries because it can put an end to spreading wrong historical facts in the minds of the people. It is also necessary to maintain constant interaction amongst researchers, teachers, analysts, students and so on as these very people will at some point of time be doing the analysis which will be consumed by millions of Indians and

Pakistanis and even contributing to making decisions affecting millions of people.

Third, funding for these initiatives should be made more local. It is often possible to see threads attached to funding which comes from outside the region for conducting track-two initiatives. Local funding also allows people from a cross-section of the ideological spectrum to be at ease in participating in the initiatives. It does not always gladden all South Asians to learn that the funding of what they are engaging in is from the US, as many of them do believe that the US has an agenda in the region's politics.

Fourth, outside parties in track-two initiatives should be kept to a minimum. The single-most important reason as to why it is necessary to keep the third parties out of the track-two is because one of the parties in the conflict, i.e., India, has opposed such moves as it is against internationalizing the conflict. Moreover, often there is a tendency by many non-party mediators or participants to suggest solutions to solving the problems between India and Pakistan without the required expertise to contextualize their solutions. This does more harm than good.

Fifth, there should be more media representation in track-two initiatives including both English and vernacular. In general, people go by the notion that media in India and Pakistan do have uniform views within their own countries. This is certainly not true. In fact, it is a misnomer to think that the South Indian press thinks the way the North Indian press does. There are different schools of thought within the Indian media even on the key question of Kashmir. Thus it is of great importance to involve the media from a wide range of languages in the track-two initiatives. They should not only come from Islamabad and New Delhi.

Sixth, issues should be broadened to include non-elitist and non-conflict issues.[20] If people talk about serious issues, there is every likelihood that the discussion too would get serious where there would be so many stakes involved which they will find difficult to part with. During personal conversations with women track-two activists this author was told that during track-two negotiations, they tend to agree on everything but when it comes to the question of Kashmir, many of them would also start verbally fighting with each other. Thus it is necessary to include such issues in the talk-able list of issues, which may be of mutual interest to common people and the larger civil society.

Traders should be part of track-two initiatives. As mentioned earlier in this paper, while there is a lot of potential for trade between the two countries, most of the trade between India and Pakistan takes place either illegally or through third countries. From a liberal internationalist perspective, increased trade can cater to the bettering of bilateral relations. Unfortunately, traders seem to have no role in the track-two negotiations.

The chief and proclaimed aim of track-two initiatives should not be to solve issues. Many peace activists seem to think that peace is a tangible outcome, which is there to be reached; they often forget that it is not an outcome but a condition. Thus if one starts track-two negotiations with the assumption that the exercise should end in a solution to the problem, he/she may as well not be able to go beyond the status quo. What is probably necessary is to understand that it is the process of peace making that is of vital importance and not the solution. After all, political leaders can sit in closed rooms and make solutions but unless and until this gets entrenched in the minds of the people there can be no peace.

There should be track-two initiatives across sections—amongst hawks, doves and the like.[21] It is not necessary to have peace negotiations between peace lovers as dialogue of the converted will not achieve much; what is necessary is to have talks between conflicting parties—not peaceful parties—to have peace. Professional peace lovers have to be replaced by parties and people in conflict.

Conclusion

This paper has made four major arguments: (i) track-two initiatives are necessary tools for enhancing peace between India and Pakistan; (ii) there are at least 11 reasons why it is difficult to sustain track-two initiatives between India and Pakistan, and; (iii) certain critical measures have to be adopted to make the ongoing track-two initiatives healthier. Unlike how it happens in many track-two initiatives in many other theatres of conflict in places like Europe, the nature of track-two initiatives between India and Pakistan is different in the sense that there is an acute lack of participation from the larger non-Islamabad—New Delhi-based civil society; (iv) The key argument of this paper is that track-two diplomacy in South Asia can survive only if it becomes part of the civil society movement in India as well as Pakistan. ■

Notes & References

1. Joseph V. Montville, "The Arrow and the Olive Branch: A Case for Track Two Diplomacy,". in John W. McDonald and Diane B. Bendahmane, eds., Conflict *Resolution: Track Two Diplomacy*, Washington, 1995, p.9.
2. Aqil S. Shah, Non-Official Dialogue between India and Pakistan: Prospects and Problems, Research of the Program in Arms Control, Disarmament, and International Security University of Illinois at Urbana-Champaign August 1997, http://www.acdis.uiuc.edu/homepage_docs/pubs_docs/PDF_Files/AqilOP.pdf.
3. Louse Diamond and Ambassador John McDonald, *Multi-track Diplomacy: A Systems Approach to Peace*, Connecticut, 1996.

4. For a detailed history of track-two diplomacy between India and Pakistan see: (i) the seminal work done by Navnita Chadha Behera, Paul M. Evans and Gowher Rizvi, *Beyond Boundaries: A Report on the State of Non-official Dialogues on Peace, Security and Cooperation in South Asia*, 1997. This book not only presents a detailed inventory of the track-two (non-official) initiatives in the region along with the organizations, which conduct them but also looks at the achievements of these processes, constraints and obstacles, and ways and means to overcome them. While this paper has adopted some of the arguments used in the book, it intends to discuss some more insights. While this book has made an exhaustive listing of the non-official dialogues in the region till 1997, additional initiatives in this regard after 1997 have been minimal with the notable exception of the famous R.K. Mishra Niaz Naik parleys and the increased meetings between parliamentarians. An article by Behera titled "Need to expand track-two diplomacy" published in July 2003 in the *Asia Times* website gives some new insights about the current state of track-two diplomacy. (ii) Track-Two Diplomacy in South Asia, Sandeep Waslekar, ACDIS Occasional Paper, 1995. (iii) Non-Official Dialogue between India and Pakistan: Prospectus and Problems, Aqil S. Shah, ACDIS Occasional Paper, 1997.
5. "Several myths in my mind about Pakistan are demolished" is what Ram Vilas Paswan an Indian political leader said after his first ever visit to Pakistan as part of a track-two initiative. *The Hindu Business line*, August 31, 2003.
6. For example, Moonis Ahmer of the University of Karachi says that, "the foreign office of Pakistan and the Ministry of External Affairs of India may have their constraints in breaking deadlock in Indo-Pak relations. Same is true with the military and political leadership of the two countries". The point often made by South Asian scholars is that there is a limit to the Indian and Pakistani bureaucracies as far as solving conflicts are concerned.
7. Sagarika Ghosh in *The Indian Express* says the 'People to people contact is simply not reaching out to real people'. *The Indian Express*, July 4, 2003.
8. Stephen P. Cohen, "Every Fifth Person: The Origins of War and Conditions for Peace in South Asia". Forthcoming. Cited in Non-Official Dialogue Between India and Pakistan: Prospects and Problems, Aqil S. Shah ACDIS paper.
9. Sheela Bhatt, "The Indo-Pak Trade Equation". http://www.rediff.com/money/2003/jun/19spec2.htm.
10. Ibid.
11. Ibid.
12. Ibid.
13. During the visit of Prime Minister Shaukat Aziz to India in November 2004 he was accompanied by a 60-member delegation including 15 business representatives. See

for details, "Indian businessmen to push trade issues with Shaukat", *Pakistan Observer*, November 24, 2004.

14. Pakistani writers such as Ayesha Siddiqa-Agha and Ejaz Haider have, of late, been arguing on this line. These opinions were expressed in their personal communication with the author.
15. See for example *The Indian Express* article by Beena Sarwar, "The People's Initiative", June 21, 2000. She writes, "Right-wing, ultra-nationalist and communal forces in both India and Pakistan have threatened and harassed peace activists, pillorying them as 'traitors', 'anti-nationalists' and 'enemy agents'."
16. The Kathmandu meeting of the Pugwash Conferences has been hailed as a successful track-two initiative. The meeting would not have been possible but for the explicit permissions from the governments of both India and Pakistan. For details on the meeting see, http://www.pugwash.org/reports/rc/sa/SAS2004-media.htm.
17. There have been exceptions to this too. During the 2003 visit of Laloo Prasad Yadav to Pakistan the independent television networks of Pakistan covered his 'peace-talks'.
18. Under the Official Secrets Act (OSA), the Government is empowered to restrict publication of sensitive stories. The Government also, at times, interprets this Act to suppress criticism of its policies. There have been instances where newsmagazines and newspapers have been charged with cases. Legal action through the Customs department and the Central Investigation Bureau against *Outlook* and *Tehelka* respectively are cases in point.
19. Most newspapers during the 2003-Gujarat elections had reported that Narendra Modi was raising the Pakistan bogey to win the elections in the state. Ershad Mahmud quoted Modi in *Al-Jazeerah* on July 2, 2003 ("BJP's Domestic Agenda, Kashmir and Pakistan") "If the Congress wins in Gujarat they will burst firecrackers in Pakistan and if the BJP wins, the entire India will celebrate Diwali", and further commented that "the statement by the sitting chief minister speaks volumes of Pakistan being made a factor in India's internal politics by its own hard-liners."
20. Ishaq Khan Khakwani, a Pakistani MP and a member of the Pakistan-India Friendship Forum says that countries should concentrate on issues like eradication of poverty, improvement of living standards etc. www.southasiamonotor.org, June 16, 2003.
21. A case in point is the much-publicised visit of Maulana Fazlur Rahman's visit to India. Pakistani newspaper *Dawn*; August 12, 2003, wrote in the editorial "... Maulana Fazlur Rahman's recent visit to India, for which he was both anointed and criticized, was seen as setting a new precedent for Indo-Pak contacts at the informally political, and not simply the official, level".

Genesis of Indo—Pak Dialogue on Sidelines of SAARC 2004

Harmeet Singh*

For more than half a century, the two major powers of South Asia, India and Pakistan have been at loggerheads with each other. Having fought three wars in the past, in addition to a number of border skirmishes, their mutual hostility is almost well pronounced. Their recently acquired nuclear-power status adds to their lethal dimensions. Due to this gloomy scenario, the stakes involving peace in South Asia are fairly high. It is therefore imperative that they engage each other to sort out their differences. While there has been a number of efforts for dialogue in the past, the track-record of conflict-resolution has not been impressive. For India, the most important issue is cross-border terrorism, while Pakistan wants to focus on Kashmir, which it says is the core issue. At the SAARC summit in January 2004, the two neighbours seemed serious in their negotiations. Whereas Prime Minister Vajpayee was looking forward to a foreign policy achievement before the next general election in India, President Pervez Musharraf perhaps has now realized that the horrid nature of terrorism spares no one including himself. Hence peace is a dividend in itself. The working hypothesis of this paper is that a congenial atmosphere now exists for India to strike a political deal with Pakistan. This paper is divided into three parts. The first part discusses India-Pakistan dispute in the historical perspective. Part Two highlights the easing of tension between India and Pakistan after Prime Minister A.B. Vajpayee launched his famous "Peace Initiative" in Kashmir in April 2003. The process culminated in the signing of Joint Press Statement during SAARC 2004 between the two countries. An appraisal of the situation arising out of these negotiations is also made here. The last part contains the suggestions.

* Senior Lecturer, Department of Political Science, Guru Nanak Dev University, Amritsar.

I

Background

Ever since Pakistan sent raiders into Kashmir in October 1947, the relationship between India and Pakistan has remained strained. Notwithstanding the efforts made to resolve the dispute bilaterally since 1947, there has not been much progress made on the contentious issues. The important exceptions in this context are the Indus Water Treaty, which was signed under the auspices of World Bank in September 1960 and the Simla Agreement of 1972 which excluded Kashmir from its agenda, but demarcated a new ceasefire line called Line of Control (LoC). Following Pandit Jawahar Lal Nehru's assurances to the United Nations, Expert Committees were approved for holding of plebiscite in Kashmir in August 1953, but agreement could not be reached in the follow-on correspondence[1]. Kuldip Nayar argued that the reason for reluctance on part of India to go ahead with the process of plebiscite in Kashmir lay primarily in Pakistan's decision to join American-sponsored alliances in the early 1950s[2].

The 1971 Indo-Pakistan war over the issue of Bangladesh crippled Pakistan's capacity at least for the time being to challenge India's military dominance in the South Asian region. The status of India was further enhanced following its Peaceful Nuclear Explosion (PNE) in 1974. During the late 1970s, though determined to pursue its nuclear programme, Pakistan was beset with domestic compulsions. In the first place, Zulfikar Ali Bhutto's ruling Pakistan People's Party (PPP) was ousted from office and martial law was imposed by General Zia-ul-Haq. Then came the serious uprising in Baluchistan in which even the Baluchs from neighbouring Iran were involved. Finally, Pakistan's relationship with the United States deteriorated to an unprecedented level with the imposition of Symington Amendment and burning down of the American Embassy in Islamabad. All this occurred while India basked in the sunshine emanating due to its leadership of Non Aligned Movement (NAM), and its alliance with the Soviet Union intact. To India, it seemed that Pakistan, which had provoked at least three wars against it in the past had been now rightly cut to size, and that the LoC had become for all practical purposes a de facto international border.

But this was a gross mistake in assessment: Pakistan was just about to get involved in what may be described as its biggest adventure in history. With the Soviet Union militarily intervening in Afghanistan and Carter and Reagan Administrations seeking Pakistan's help in countering the Soviet advance in South Asia, Islamabad began to make plans gigantic enough to convert itself into a military power to reckon with. Not only did Pakistan receive military equipment and economic aid on a vast scale from the United States, its influence with the Mujahideens operating in Afghanistan against the Soviets began to increase. Pakistan's massive operations as a conduit in Afghanistan for transferring US military equipment into *Jehadi* hands on an unprecedented scale gave it the quid pro quo of having control over the weapons supplied. Confident of itself during the 1980s Pakistan supported in a covert manner the militancy in Indian Punjab with arms. And from 1989 onwards, it also directed its attention towards Kashmir for purposes of abetting and aiding an insurgency there against the Indian state. Its role in the Kashmir valley was more overt and lethal as was manifested by its anti-India propaganda, and sending of Pan-Islamic radicals there who had nothing else to do after the Soviet troops evacuated Afghanistan.

Perhaps the Indian government's ill-conceived policies in Kashmir since 1953 resulted in the alienation of the Kashmiri population in the 1980s. But this situation also provided Pakistan an opportunity which no government in Islamabad "could let slip by". Thus Islamabad launched its 'great game' in the Kashmir valley against the background of dissolution of the Soviet Union and development of clandestine nuclear capabilities by both India and Pakistan[3].

Against this scenario, the Foreign Secretary-level talks, which had commenced since 1990 did not make much impact[4]. And by 1994, when these talks were in the seventh round, the situation between the two countries became so grim that not only were the talks suspended in January, even the consulates at Bombay and Karachi were closed down. The next three years proved to be equally gloomy as Pakistan continued to pump primarily non-Kashmiri Pan-Islamic militants and terrorists into the Valley. And the Indian government resorted to use of force for the suppression of a separatist movement with insurgent overtones [5].

In 1993, Gowher Rizvi stated that despite escalation of violence in Kashmir, the relations between India and Pakistan had remained largely intact. He added:

> It is now clear that the Kashmir 'Intifada' is not the work of Pakistan inspired agitators (which is not to deny Pakistan's involvement in supplying weapons or providing sanctuaries from where militants carry out their operations). It is a genuine mass uprising resulting from socio-economic neglect and more importantly from a commitment among the youth to secure an autonomous Kashmir, independent of both India and Pakistan[6].

Rizvi went on to criticize the Indian government for treating the Kashmir crisis as only a law and order problem. And he compared insurgency in Kashmir with Muslim uprisings in the Soviet Union and West Bank (Israel) and with the rebellion of Kurds in Iraq, all of which he said have the aim of "overthrowing the existing order". He predicted that these "popular revolutions", like the Baltic states of the erstwhile Soviet Union, would not stop short of independence[7].

His arguments can be contested on three counts. First, if only the third option is the aim of Kashmir insurgency, what interest does Pakistan have in it? Second, why is there no insurgency for the third option within the Pakistan occupied Kashmir (POK)? Third, while the Indian government through its Election Commission may permit holding of free and fair elections for constitution of the Legislative Assembly and provincial government in J&K, such an option is not available to the people with whom Gowher compares Kashmiris. The fact remains that Pakistan cannot deny its role in the abetment of militancy in Kashmir for the sake of what may be described as cynically bleeding India white through a low-cost proxy war.

Pakistan's conduct in Kashmir conforms squarely to the ideology of sectarianism based on a two-nation theory on which it has thrived for so long and through which it has tried to indoctrinate its elite and masses. Describing India as an expansionist power in South Asia and maligning India's secular credentials have been the two major planks of its attitude towards its eastern neighbour. India's expansionist design was substantiated by President Ayub Khan in his statement that:

> The Indian leaders have often stated that their true border extends from the Hindu Kush Mountains to the Mekong River, that is to say wherever the influence of Hinduism has existed in the past. Their earlier friendly overtures to China were based on the hope that there would be an understanding between them and China over their respective spheres of influence in Asia, and that China would recognize and endorse India's claim[8].

It seems that Ayub Khan through the aforesaid statement is gloating over certain issues, which are part of his conjectural analysis. In this context, the first issue is to portray India as an instrument of Hindu expansionism even in the days of Nehru. Second, the 1962 Sino-Indian war paved the way for Sino-Pakistan nexus. And third, he tried to justify Pakistan's role in becoming an adjunct to the foreign policy of the United States as the surest guarantee against any future expansionist designs of India.

Even, the Pakistanis did not spare the election of Zakir Hussain as President of India. The ridicule they poured on this occasion sometimes went to the extent of idiocy. In this regard Abdul Majid argued that:

> It is already apparent that India will try to reap heavy dividends in propaganda from *Shri* Zakir Hussain's election, which has been claimed and already hailed in interested quarters as a victory for Indian secularism.... It may be utilized to step up a diplomatic front against Pakistan, denounced before the world as theocratic and totalitarian. With a Muslim in occupation of the country's highest elective office, the truth of the accusation that Muslims are denied equality and opportunity in India may be challenged sadistically at home and vociferously abroad.... A Muslim in the seat of the Mughals may be made to yield a common bond with Muslim countries, particularly Arab, to isolate Pakistan[9].

Sangat Singh points out the two subterfuges which are often resorted to by Pakistan vis-à-vis India. One is that the common past is deliberately distorted and two, the present is mutilated. He goes on to say that the Kashmir issue is part of Pakistan's hate-campaign against India. He stated that for Pakistan, Kashmir is not merely a struggle for territory. It is more aptly a struggle for ideology[10].

Coming back to the 1990s, it was in 1997 that contacts between India and Pakistan were resumed in the wake of the 'Gujral Doctrine'. I.K. Gujral's keen interest and Nawaz Sharif's personal business interests with India could have created the congenial environment for reconciliation between India and Pakistan. Thus talks between the two countries were resumed at three levels: first, foreign secretary level in New Delhi; second, foreign minister level during Non Aligned Movement (NAM) conference in New Delhi; and third, Prime Minister level during May 12–14, 1997 at SAARC Summit in Male. On July 26, 1997, Prime Minister Gujral went to the extent to say that he was ready to negotiate with anyone including the militants. The next day he corrected himself by imposing the condition that the militants should lay down arms before the negotiations with them begin. But these offers of talks were hard for the Pakistan military to digest. In August 1997, serious artillery exchanges between Indian and Pakistani military took place all along the LoC[11]. Hence Foreign Secretary-level talks during June 19–23, 1997 in Islamabad and during September 15–18, 1997 could not produce much beyond some pious pledges[12]. Nawaz Sharif and I.K. Gujral met at the United Nations General Assembly on September 23, 1997 where the former proposed a "no war pact" subject to the condition that Kashmir dispute be settled. There was also an understanding to reduce tension along the LoC. But due to the lame-duck status of Gujral, nothing much was expected. Discussions could produce a consensus only for the establishment of a hotline[13].

March 1998 saw Atal Bihari Vajpayee as Prime Minister of India and in May of that year, the two countries detonated their nuclear devices. This brought the interest of foreign powers especially the United States back to South Asia. The 1999 Lahore Declaration was essentially an assurance to the international community at large about the nuclear situation being under control in the subcontinent. It was followed by Pakistan's abortive adventure in Kargil. But even as Pakistan's fiasco in Kargil became part of history, Jaswant Singh, the Indian External Affairs Minister refused to accept that Lahore Declaration had become a dead letter. He described the Kargil conflict as an aberration, which could not be allowed to alter the goals India had set at Lahore[14]. But the Agra Summit in July 2001 proved to be equally futile and when an attack on the Indian Parliament occurred on December 13, 2001, the relationship between the two nations was brought to the lowest ebb with curtailment of diplomatic mission staff, snapping of rail, road and air links and Vajpayee's refusal to talk to Musharraf at the Kathmandu SAARC conference in 2002. This situation remained until Prime Minister Vajpayee launched his famous peace initiative in Srinagar during April 18–19, 2003.

II

Genesis

After the armed attack on Indian Parliament on December 13, 2001, the diplomatic relations between India and Pakistan were snapped. On January 12, 2002 the Pakistan President and Army Chief, General Parvez Musharraf appeared on Pakistan television and gave an assurance to India that Pakistan's territory would not be allowed to be used by the Jehadis for their violent campaign against India. Notwithstanding the past track record of betrayals on the part of Pakistan the Indian government chose to believe Musharraf's words[15]. But Pakistan's duplicity and deceit was soon evident in its deeds. As time passed and terrorist acts multiplied, India complained. Pakistan's dictator's reaction was his advocacy of "offensive defence" which was in fact a step ahead of the mutual deterrence of armed forces of the two countries facing each other eye-ball to eye-ball on the border in the aftermath of December 13, 2001. And on May 27, 2003 in a televised address to his nation, Pervez Musharraf blamed India for not protecting the

Scheduled Castes and Muslims from atrocities of Hindu-fundamentalists and his Information Minister, Sheikh Rashid Ahmed followed suit in accusing New Delhi of piling up stocks of weapons of mass destruction including biological and chemical weapons and oppressing its minorities including Muslims, Sikhs and Christians [16].

Pakistan's dictator was making full use of his country's services to the United States in Afghanistan and in Iraq where Washington was at that moment involved in pre-emptive military action. In retaliation, the Indian Foreign Minister, Yashwant Sinha said that if the weapons of mass destruction, the denial of democratic structures and export of terrorism were the criteria of pre-emptive military action, then Pakistan deserved it more than Iraq[17].

The comments of the Indian Foreign Minister invited ire of the Americans who asked the Indians not to draw parallels between Pakistan and Iraq. Instead India was urged by the Americans to restrain itself from using the US-led pre-emptive war against Iraq as a pretext for an attack on Pakistan. Colin Powell made it glaringly clear that once the situation settles in Iraq, he will turn his attention to South Asia. He also sent his Deputy Secretary of State, Richard Armitage to initiate peace-moves between India and Pakistan. The message was loud and clear that if the two neighbours in South Asia could not have peace based on negotiations and mutual understanding, then a "guided peace" would be imposed upon them. With the American military muscle having been flexed good enough in Afghanistan and Iraq, it was wise on the part of Prime Minister Vajpayee to set in motion the peace initiative during April 18–19, 2003 from Srinagar where a duly elected government under Chief Minister Mufti Mohammad Sayeed was already speaking about the "healing touch"[18].

Peace Initiative of PM Vajpayee

Prime Minister Vajpayee decided to visit Srinagar on the occasion of Naoroz (the Kashmiri New Year) during April 18–19, 2003 and launch a fresh peace initiative by offering negotiations with both Pakistan and All Parties Hurriyat Conference (APHC). His only condition was that violence be totally removed from Jammu and Kashmir by putting an end to Cross Border Terrorism (CBT). While addressing a gathering of 30,000 in Srinagar, he made it clear that he was ready to discuss all "internal and external" issues with one and all, and to solve these, provided peace returned to the people of Kashmir. He asserted that the play of death and destruction has to be stopped to let Kashmir be a garden where birds would sing again[19].

During his visit, the Prime Minister could not ignore one real issue, i.e. the economic package of Rs. 6,000 crore asked for by the Federation of Chambers of Indian Industry in Kashmir (FCIIK). Vajpayee also reiterated his peace initiative and emphasized the point that its outcome would depend on Pakistan's response. He did go on to say that both internally and externally, a new situation had emerged. Internally what contributed to the new scenario was the fact that through a free and fair Assembly election in Jammu and Kashmir, a new coalition had come to power. And on the external front, the US involvement in Iraq had altered the world situation. He asserted that his peace initiative in April 2003 had added new dimensions to Indo-Pak diplomacy despite earlier setbacks in Lahore and Agra. He said that he was deliberately not making a mention of the Nandimarg massacre of Kashmiri Pandits in order to avoid vitiating of the atmosphere. But he cautioned, "Infiltration is going on. Many armed militants are waiting across the border to cross over to this side". He emphasized that no meaningful dialogue with Pakistan was possible without elimination of cross-border terrorism. He said that he was hopeful that peace would ultimately triumph and he would be able to walk in the streets of Srinagar with confidence[20]. In order to drive his point home, PM Vajpayee asserted, "If Pakistan announced tomorrow that cross border terrorism has stopped and it has destroyed all training camps, I am willing to send a senior Foreign Ministry Official to Islamabad to finalise the agenda the same day"[21]. While vehemently vouching for peace in Kashmir, Vajpayee chose to keep his fingers crossed and he advocated that Chief Minister should apply the "healing touch" carefully so that wounds may not deepen and he emphasised that whereas N.N. Vohra, the Indian government's interlocutor in Kashmir, was ready to talk to anyone, he would not invite any group including the Hurriyat for the talks.

Chief Minister Mufti Mohammad Sayeed hailed PM Vajpayee's visit to Kashmir in April 2003 and his peace initiative by describing it as "historic". He stated that it was for the first time that any prime minister had not only made a serious attempt to address the Kashmir issue from the soil of the Valley itself, but also extended a hand of friendship to Pakistan. About the APHC, CM Sayeed said that so great was the impact of Vajpayee's visit in Kashmir that the Hurriyat called off its strike on the second day[22]. On its part, the Pakistan leadership, including Prime Minister Zaffar Ullah Jamali, Foreign Minister, Khurshid Mehmood Kasuri, and Information Minister Sheikh Rashid Ahmad, reciprocated the sentiments of PM Vajpayee's peace initiative[23].

Sumit Chakravarty argued that American hegemonic designs in the Arab world as demonstrated by the US military intervention in secular Iraq should serve as a warning to the peace-loving people in India and Pakistan. It is in this context that he vindicated PM Vajpayee's peace initiative[24].

Confidence-Building Measures

On October 22, 2003 Vajpayee endorsed yet another two-pronged peace proposal. One was the twelve-point peace package offered to Pakistan which included restoration of cricket and other sporting events, a bus service between Srinagar and Muzaffrabad in Kashmir and between Khokhrahar (Rajasthan) and Munnabo (Sindh), re-establishing air-links and upgrading the strength of respective High Commissions in New Delhi and Islamabad. The other plank consisted of an initiative to hold talks with the Hurriyat Conference which Foreign Minister Yashwant Sinha described as "our internal process and which has nothing to do with relations with Pakistan". He also made it clear that N.N. Vohra would remain the central government's interlocutor. However, the Indian government, in a major policy move announced on October 22, 2003 said that the Deputy Prime Minister, L.K. Advani, would hold talks with Maulana Abbas Ansari, Chairman of the breakaway group of the Hurriyat Conference. This decision to hold talks with the Hurriyat Conference came six weeks after that conglomeration of twenty-five parties was split into two amalgamations. One amalgamation was headed by the fire-brand pro-Pakistan leader, Syed Ali Shah Geelani, and the other by the more moderate Maulana Ansari[25].

On its part, the Pakistan government expressed its disappointment on the fact that the peace proposals did not include the agenda for holding talks on Kashmir. At the same time a Pakistan Foreign Office spokesman said that Islamabad had taken note of PM Vajpayee's fresh offer of peace initiatives, but he added: "We hope that India will reconsider its position on the resumption of the composite talks as some of the proposals made by India are integral to the composite dialogue process".

The leading Indian journalist H.K. Dua stated that:

> ...the Indian peace package is bound to be welcomed by people on both sides of the divide.... The rationale behind the Indian initiative is that greater people-to-people contact will slowly dissolve the deep-seated distrust and hatred that over the years have caused tensions and periodic wars and much destruction....It will be a mistake on the part of President Musharraf and others in his military establishment to think that India has once again come out with a peace package because of a feeling of weakness[26].

Sayeed Naqvi proposed that Sindhis as a community especially the Hindus among them, could act as a bridge between India and Pakistan[27]. Meanwhile, the Hurriyat, especially the amalgam led by Maulana Abbas Ansari, and which also included Mirwaiz Umar Farooq and Fazal Haq Qureishi began its own programme of preparatory measures aimed at the holding of negotiations with the government of India. Incidentally, Fazal Haq Qureishi was Hizbul Mujahideen's interlocutor in its negotiations with New Delhi during the Hizbul ceasefire in 2000. The Hurriyat stressed on a "mass contact" programme in order to elicit public opinion for the forthcoming negotiations. Three parties, the JKLF, Jamat-e-Islami and the People's League refused to participate in talks with New Delhi. The Hurriyat amalgam interested in talks described the government offer as "positive" and replied that it would respond to it by November 27, 2003, i.e. after Id [28].

At the other end, the Deputy Prime Minister of India Lal Krishan Advani reiterated his government's policy with respect to negotiations with Pakistan. Our stance is the same that Pakistan has to stop infiltration, destroy the terrorist infrastructure and build a congenial atmosphere before any talks can begin[29]. He also asked the US to help India in the extradition of the underworld don, Dawood Ibrahim from Karachi. Ibrahim had been declared a terrorist by the US itself. About talks with the Hurriyat, Advani said that if the Indian government could negotiate with Nagas and Bodos, it could also negotiate with Hurriyat. The agenda of talks he said would be decentralization of power, provided the unity and integrity of India was not compromised[30].

Mirwaiz Umar Farooq, speaking in response to Advani's comments asserted two points. One, he said that the Hurriyat was neither interested in decentralization of power, nor in the chief ministership of Jammu and Kashmir. Two, he emphasized that Kashmir's vexed problem could not be solved without involving Pakistan in tripartite talks[31]

In response to the Indian peace initiative, the Pakistan officials speaking to *Dawn* said that after a careful review, Islamabad would give the response within a week. Islamabad described Indian peace proposals as having been "recycled". It nevertheless promised a "robust and constructive reply"; while India stressed on fixing of dates for talks[32]. In the meantime, certain expatriate Kashmiri organizations such as International Kashmir Alliance (IKA), All Parties, National Alliance and JKLF leader Shahbir Chaudhri called upon both the Hurriyat and Pakistan to respond to the Indian offer in a positive manner[33].

Mani Shankar Aiyar, a Congress stalwart, while giving his support to the twelve peace proposals of PM Vajpayee, emphasized that without the thirteenth, i.e. talks with Pakistan, nothing would be achieved. He lamented the fact that after Vajpayee Government's attempt to hold negotiations with Hizbul Mujahideen in 2000 proved abortive, no serious effort had been made towards an internal dialogue. He also highlighted his stance that without addressing the cause of terrorism, the malady cannot be redressed. With reference to India asking the US help for the extradition of Dawood Ibrahim, he contended that asking the Americans to pull India's Pakistani chestnuts out of the fire would not help[34]. Writing in the columns of *India Today* entitled "Killing with kindness", Indrani Bagchi supported the Indian government's peace initiative which it said was aimed at promoting the "people-to-people" contact in order to sideline the Pakistan's military establishment in the eyes of her own people[35].

Finally, Pakistan gave its general approval of the peace proposals *but with a rider*. Its Foreign Secretary, Riaz Khokhar asserted that real peace could be achieved only by resolving the Kashmir problem which he described as a "cancerous and poisonous" issue poised between the two states. The Indian External Affairs Ministry's reaction was one of "amusement" at the Pakistan's response[36]. With the peace proposals gaining momentum, terrorism in Kashmir intensified. It is not for the first time that this has happened. Whenever there was a thaw in the Indo-Pak relations, there was sudden increase in terrorist violence[37].

On October 30, 2003 the US Assistant Secretary of State, Christina Rocca, called upon Pakistan to make more efforts at containing and curbing terrorism against India in Kashmir: "The Government of Pakistan has taken many steps to curb infiltration but we are asking it to redouble its efforts". She described Pakistan's cooperation with the United States in anti-terrorism operations since 9/11 as excellent. She also underlined Indo-US cooperation, which reflects the closer relations that the US seeks with India[38].

New Delhi regarded Pakistan's response to India's peace proposals with mixed feelings. While Pakistan's offer of re-establishing air-links was appreciated by India, Islamabad's insistence that travel between Muzaffrabad and Srinagar be conditioned on possession of a UN passport was criticized. Similarly a no-response on part of Pakistan between Mumbai-Karachi, and Khokhrahar-Munnabo came in for condemnation[39]. Justice (Retd.) Rajinder Sachar wrote that the initiative regarding travel link between Muzaffrabad and Srinagar is the boldest. He said it is an offer to the people of POK to travel to the Indian side of Kashmir and see for themselves the conditions therein. He went on to say that Pakistan's rider of a UN passport for the travelers was meant to stall this process because the Pakistan's military regime is afraid of the goodwill generated by people-to-people contacts. Justice Sachar corroborated his statement by referring to the fact that ever since the offer of peace initiative had been made, the *Jehadi* militancy in J&K had been upgraded. He also pointed out that the Hurriyat conference lacks political vision in demanding at the outset that the talks be tripartite by inclusion of Pakistan. Justice Sachar ended his write-up with a plea that the LoC be converted into an international border[40].

On October 30, 2003, India rejected outright all Confidence Building Measures (CBMs) floated by Pakistan, which were directly related with the Kashmir issue. These Kashmir-related CBMs were actually three in number. The first was in the context of 100 scholarships to be granted to Kashmiri children. The second spoke about the humanitarian measures for aged Kashmiris. And the third was in the context of Kashmiri widows and rape-victims of the Indian security forces in Kashmir. The Indian government's arguments were that the scholarships offered by Pakistan were sectarian in nature and contrary to the Indian practice of no-discrimination between a Punjabi, a Baluch or a Sindhi while giving similar sops to the Pakistanis. Again it was Pakistan which was putting curbs on people-to-people contacts in Kashmir. And finally, it emphasized that if Pakistan really sympathized with Kashmiri widows, and other targets of violence, it should put an end to its patronage of cross-border terrorism in Kashmir[41].

Pakistan's substantial offers to India finally came on November 23, 2003 in what was described as a "unilateral ceasefire" on the part of Pakistan. It was the Id offer of Prime Minister Jamali of Pakistan to India. New Delhi reciprocated by asking Pakistan to extend the ceasefire to Siachin, which the latter accepted heartily. Prior to this occurrence, on August 12, 2003, Pakistan had spoken of a ceasefire along the LoC, but had subjected it to the condition that India reduce its armed strength in the Kashmir valley and put an end to the atrocities there.

In a televised address, Prime Minister of Pakistan declared on November 23, 2003 that its armed forces would observe a unilateral ceasefire from Id-ul-fitr. Pakistan related its announcement of ceasefire with the forthcoming SAARC Summit in January 2004:

> Pakistan is interested to live in peace with India and is waiting for the participation of PM Vajpayee in the Summit...with strong political commitment, India and Pakistan could change the atmosphere of confrontation...such steps should be taken which can help restore mutual confidence, so we can find new ways for a peaceful and just solution of the Kashmir issue[42].

India responded positively but cautiously to Pakistan's ceasefire proposal of November 23, 2003. Pakistan's Foreign Minister, Khurshid Mehmood Kasuri described India's response as a step forward[43]. Islamabad also showed signs of moving forward on the peace proposals offered by New Delhi on October 22, 2003. While remaining silent on the issue of UN documents for Muzzafrabad-Srinagar route, Pakistan showed its eagerness for the ferry service between Mumbai and Karachi, as well as for the bus service between Khokhrahar and Munnabo. It also endorsed the Indian proposal of allowing senior citizens above 65 years of age to cross the Wagah border on foot. And Pakistan also proposed a bus service between Amritsar and Lahore[44].

The ceasefire along the LoC came into effect on November 26, 2003. This was the first comprehensive ceasefire between India and Pakistan ever since militancy began in 1989, notwithstanding Vajpayee's limited Ramzan ceasefire offer in 2000 during his negotiations with a section of the Hizbul Mujahideen. The ceasefire had covered the 778 km-long LoC, 150 km-long AGPL and 198-km international border between India and Pakistan. Even as India agreed to holding of a dialogue with Pakistan, it stressed that cross-border terrorism must end first[45]. The Indian External Affairs Minister received a call from his American counterpart appreciating the Indo-Pak rapprochement process. The US Secretary of State hoped that soon cross-border terrorism would end, thus facilitating India's dealing with terrorists within its territory[46].

Even as Salim Hashmi, the Hizbul Mujahideen spokesman in Muzaffrabad, PoK said, "This ceasefire will not make any difference to Mujahideen activity", the Indian Defence Minister, George Fernandes expressed his optimism that the ceasefire may pave the way to the final solution of Kashmir conflict. The Pakistan's PM, Jamali, at an Id function, expressed hope that Prime Minister Vajpayee would attend SAARC – 2004 and hold discussions with the Pakistan's leadership[47].

There were reports of guns remaining silent on the LoC, the AGPL and the International borders during the first day. Sweets were exchanged between the Indian BSF and Pak Rangers and the traders were hopeful of business opportunities in the future[48]. While truce held between the armed forces of the two countries, there was no respite from militant violence as unidentified terrorists hurled a grenade at a BSF picket near Amirkadal Bridge in Lal Chowk, Srinagar, killing one person and injuring 12 others. Pakistan Foreign Ministry spokesman, however, described the ceasefire agreement as a "good beginning" and he said that Pakistan was optimistic about it[49].

The United States on its part denied that it was trying to play the role of a "manager" in South Asia. The State Department spokesperson, Richard Boucher said:

> ...we are not inserting ourselves as some kind of mediator; that the relationship we have with Pakistan, the relationship US has with India is not triangular one, I think is the phrase Secretary Colin Powell always uses....We have relationships with two governments, two countries. Each of the relationship is important to us. Hence we want to encourage them to deal with each other on the issues that are of concern. That's why we've always stressed dialogue between the two countries themselves as the best route to address issues that are of concern to them including Kashmir[50].

Pakistan's Prime Minister Zafarullah Khan Jamali expressed joy at Prime Minister Vajpayee's remarks that the latter would be glad to meet him at SAARC-2004. And what could be described as music to both Indian and American ears, PM Jamali spoke about Pakistan government's decision to ban seven more outfits of the ultras in Pakistan[51].

Just as Pakistan's relationship with India was improving due to the CBMs of October 2003, the ceasefire of November 26, 2003, was holding and Musharraf's whip was cracking against the *Jehadi* groups inside Pakistan, attempts were made on the life of Pakistan's President on December 14, 2003 and again on December 25, 2003. Perhaps the reasons which motivated the terrorist groups to target General Musharraf were that apart from his support of the United States' actions in Afghanistan and Iraq, the General had in an interview to the *Reuters* mentioned that the UN resolutions on Kashmir could be "left aside". General Musharraf had made similar gestures during the Agra Summit of July 2001, but it was perhaps for the first time that he had boldly spoken in a tone that had long been considered taboo in Pakistan[52].

Although Foreign Minister Khurshid Mehmood Kasuri and Prime Minister Zafarullah Khan Jamali had tried to dilute Musharraf's interview, he was nevertheless drubbed by the hardliners as a traitor. But the very fact that Musharraf had dared to take a bold stand spoke volumes about his confidence and also about the fact that the militants had begun to lose ground in Pakistan[53].

General Musharraf has not been consistent in the past. For example, on December 23, 2003 he described Prime Minister Vajpayee's statement on cross-border terrorism as regrettable[54] and the next day he called for a composite dialogue with India, which would also include Kashmir . And on December 30, 2003 the General stoutly dismissed the allegation that he was ready for a "sell-out" on Kashmir. He staunchly denied that there could be a rollback on Pakistan's nuclear or missile programmes[55].

On his part, Prime Minister Vajpayee called upon Pakistan to change its perspective on Kashmir. He emphasised that it is an aberration on the part of Islamabad to describe a Muslim majority area within India as belonging to Pakistan. He said that unless Islamabad mends its way on this count, no meaningful dialogue with Pakistan might be possible. He also rejected the idea of conversion of LoC into a permanent international border[56]. At the same time however, in his interview with *Dawn*, Prime Minister Vajpayee seemed to be strongly in favour of peace with Pakistan. He said he might not get another chance, as age was not on his side. And he gave four reasons why peace in the Indian subcontinent was a must: First, it was the will of the majority. Two, it was in accordance with the imperatives of globalisation. Three, it was in the national interest of both India and Pakistan in the post-Cold War world. And finally, for how long could India and Pakistan pose a threat to global peace[57]?

Prime Minister Vajpayee's most dramatic gesture towards Pakistan did not come till December 12, 2003, when he suggested :

> As we develop greater economic stakes in each other we can put aside mistrust and dispel unwarranted suspicions. Once we reach that stage, we would not be far from mutual security, cooperation, open borders and even a single currency[58].

While Pakistan Foreign Office spokesman, Masood Khan described Prime Minister Vajpyaee's concept of "open borders" and "single currency" as unrealistic, Vajpayee's proposals were supported by Pakistan's former Prime Minster, Benazir Bhutto who said that Indo-Pak rapprochement must follow the track of Sino–Indian negotiations on the border dispute. But she said that Indo–Pak dialogue would fructify only after Pakistan reverts to democracy, because democracies do not go to war against each other[59].

On the Eve of SAARC 2004

As the SAARC 2004 Summit approached, anxiety about Kashmir in Indian minds gained momentum. Kuldip Nayar wrote that the Kashmiris, who constitute 98 per cent of the population in the Kashmir vale, if given a choice would not join either Pakistan or India. In this context, he said that plebiscite in Kashmir is neither feasible nor desirable today. Nayar further said that the plebiscite had not been mentioned in the Simla Agreement of 1972[60].

However, the Pakistan Foreign Office spokesman, Masood Khan said as late as December 29, 2003 that there was very little likelihood of the Kashmir dispute being debated or discussed in the SAARC 2004 forum. He further said that though the SAARC charter may permit discussion of the Kashmir dispute, the tradition of SAARC countries is that they avoid discussion of contentious bilateral issues during summits[61].

Thus at SAARC 2004, there were at least two issues which could directly influence relations between India and Pakistan. One was whether Pakistan should or should not raise a bilateral issue such as Kashmir at the conference venue. Two, whether Pakistan could give India a comprehensive guarantee that its territory would not be used to perpetrate terrorism against India. There was a third issue which could also contribute to the warmth between the two neighbours, but it could do it only *indirectly* and as part of multilateral diplomacy. This was the signing of South Asian Free Trade Agreement (SAFTA). While pressure by the United States could directly influence the first two, the third was essentially an intra-SAARC affair.

On New Year's eve, India reiterated Vajpayee's offers of a bus service between Muzaffrabad and Srinagar, and between Khokhrahar (Rajasthan) and Munnabo (Sindh) and the proposal of raising the number of diplomatic mission staff from 55 to 75. The Hurriyat conference and the JKLF chief, Yasin Malik expressed good wishes for the conference. Yashwant Sinha also received good wishes from both the British and the French Foreign Ministers[62]. At the same time, the Foreign Secretaries of India and Pakistan in Islamabad tried to reach a consensus on the definition of terrorism, and on a draft-treaty for free trade in South Asia.

SAARC 2004 Sidelines

Prime Minister Vajpayee landed in Pakistan in the afternoon of January 3, 2004 and appeared optimistic about negotiations with Pakistan over Kashmir, which he described as a complex issue[63].

While Zafarullah Khan Jamali in his address to the conference described Prime Minister Vajpayee as "a visionary, a poet, a prolific writer, an able politician and a true leader", he also spoke about the grim situation:

> It is a stark reality of political differences and disputes that has held back prospects of real economic cooperation in South Asia... greater economic integration is inextricably linked to the creation of requisite political climate of peace and stability[64].

In his speech Prime Minister Vajpayee spoke of the mutual suspicions and petty rivalries that have continued to haunt the region, making peace impossible. At the same time he offered to contribute $100 million for a regional poverty alleviation programme. This money, he said, would be spent in the region but not in India. In fact he assured the conference that India was in a position to support those countries in the South Asian region, which had fallen behind. Neither did Vajpayee utter "cross border terrorism" nor did Jamali refer to the Kashmir dispute. Instead Prime Minister Vajpayee paid courtesy calls both on Prime Minister Jamali and President Pervez Musharraf of Pakistan[65].

Prime Minister Vajpayee's meeting with General Musharraf on the sidelines of SAARC 2004 resulted in the signing of the Joint Press Statement, which was issued on January 6, 2004 by India and Pakistan. The issues involved were: one, Confidence Building Measures (CBMs) on both sides; two, initiation and progress of a composite dialogue; and three, Pakistan's commitment to not allowing its territory to be used for terrorism[66]. Thus at long last India was able to extract from Pakistan's military rulers a pledge for promotion of CBMs, and a commitment that they would not allow Pakistan's territory to be used for perpetrating terrorism against India.

An Appraisal

The hallmark of the negotiations on the sidelines of SAARC 2004 was the change in approach. Until 1999 India's approach had been to address less contentious issues such as Sir Creek, Wullar Barrage, Siachin, etc. at the first instance; during 1999–2001 it was trade and Kashmir on equal footing; but at the SAARC 2004 sidelines it was trade, economy and travel which came first. No doubt, a composite dialogue over Kashmir was promised, but this was subject to the condition that Pakistan would have no truck with *Jehadis*. Moreover, it was recognized that Indo-Pak negotiations and rapprochement are symbiotic[67].

Pakistan has admitted that in the past its territory had been used to perpetrate terrorism against India and it pledged that it would not let this happen in the future. Taking this to be true, a number of political objectives such as an extradition treaty, de-escalation along LoC, and troop-reduction in J&K can be negotiated in the future[68]. Thus General Musharraf's statement that, "history has been made", may not be far from being absolutely correct. But one wonders what would remain of it after the General steps down from his post of Chief of the Army Staff (COAS) of Pakistan[69].

Till 1971, the United States had a definite tilt towards Pakistan, which was gradually eroded in the late 1970s. Then the 1980s again saw the US and

Pakistan together. However, the 1990s began with the US and Pakistan drifting apart, but the American attitude towards India was still not very positive. In fact, the first six years of the Clinton administration were marked by hostility towards India. It was India's responsible behaviour in nuclear matters, plus its consistent stand that there could be no rollback in its nukes that finally convinced Clinton of New Delhi's creditability. At the same time, Pakistan's support of Taliban, its misadventure in Kargil and the publication of CIA's Report entitled "Global Trends 2015", which portrayed Pakistan as a dysfunctional state, lowered Islamabad's image in the eyes of the Americans. During the administration of Bush Jr., the publication of a report of Joint Task Force sponsored by the US Council on Foreign Relations and Asia Society further exposed Pakistan's misdeeds with regard to terrorism. As a result, the Bush Administration stopped supply of sophisticated arms such as F-16s to Pakistan. At the same time, the United States showed greater interest in trade in the Indian Ocean region with India as an anchor[70]. The Bush Administration promised a $3 billion aid package to Pakistan subject to the condition that it would cooperate with the United States in "war on terrorism" and improve its relations with India[71].

In addition to the US interests and guarantees, there are other reasons why the Indian leadership is optimistic about Pakistan's positive attitude towards India in the future. After attempts on Musharraf's life, there seems to be genuine concern in Pakistan over terrorism. Then there is embarrassment over the nuclear proliferation scandal. The Peace Initiative in Kashmir on the part of Vajpayee and the October 22, 2003 CBMs floated by New Delhi were reciprocated by Pakistan through a ceasefire announcement in November 2003. But probably the most important factors sponsoring peace in South Asia are the economic ones. During the 1950s 50 per cent of Pakistan's exports were to India and 32 per cent of its imports were from India. Today, on both counts the figures are less than 1 per cent. Moreover a peaceful border between the two nations can reduce their military spending to the tune of 20–30 per cent. The increase in business contacts, reduction of nuclear risks, negotiations with Hurriyat, reduction in armaments and force deployment and relaxation of atmosphere in Indian Kashmir is in the interest of the people on both sides of the border[72]. In addition to the above-cited factors, Indo-Pakistan rapprochement can facilitate and even advance SAPTA and SAFTA among SAARC countries.

At least two Pakistani journalists of repute, M.B. Naqvi and Ejaz Haider are of the considered opinion that the time is ripe for India to have a deal with Pakistan. One tends to agree with M.B. Naqvi when he says that this is a historic opportunity for India, as Pakistan's society is split right through the middle, with right calling for rapprochement with India "a sell-out" and the left-liberals describing it as a "positive" development[73]. Ejaz Haider too speaks of Pakistani society being divided among those who are secular and for whom the state comes first, and those who stand for an orthodox Islamic state and for whom the Muslim Umaha is primary and Pakistan secondary[74].

The most knotty problem is that of Kashmir. Robert Wirsing has suggested three plans with which to begin the resolution of that dispute. Plan One is about the third option in Kashmir; Plan Two about India relinquishing its claims to POK; and Plan Three about de-militarisation of Siachin[75]. But the practical solution requires insight, sagacity, mutual adjustments, and preferably recognition of LoC as a permanent international border.

III

In the context of Indo–Pak negotiations on the sidelines of SAARC 2004, three questions are raised and subsequently answered in this part.

Research Questions

1. Is General Pervez Musharraf, the saboteur of the Agra Summit and author of Kargil conflict, serious this time?
2. If the General is serious this time, why is he serious?
3. If we can trust him for his word, what can we ask him during the forthcoming composite dialogue on Kashmir?

Hypothesis

1. Yes, there is reason to believe that General Musharraf is serious this time, at least for the time being and there is good enough time on India's side to do business with him.
2. As about the reasons for the seriousness on General Musharraf's part, there is a number of factors which are responsible. There may not be a genuine change of heart on Musharraf's part or on the part of those who take decisions in Pakistan, but a number of pressures is simultaneously working on the Pakistan's leadership at this time:
   (a) The first and foremost is the pressure of the United States. The US wants Pakistan's soldiers for suppressing insurrection in Afghanistan (to do that Pakistan's eastern borders with India must be secure and quiet. It is for this reason that the United States has made its $3 billion economic package subject to two riders. One is that Pakistan must help in curbing

terrorism and the second is that it must improve its relations with India[76].

(b) The second factor that indirectly pressurizes Pakistan for a rapprochement with India is the Jehadi factor. The *Jehadis* accuse Musharraf of a sell-out to the United States on the issue of Afghanistan. The anti-US *Jehadis* are hell-bent to eliminate Musharraf, as is evident by the two attempts made on his life. Hence Musharraf has to choose between the US and the *Jehadis*. After what happened in Afghanistan and Iraq, Musharraf has not much of a choice (his calculations favour the United States. Incidentally the Jehadis are anti-India too. But if Musharraf is to suppress the *Jehadis* for the sake of America, he cannot support them in the case of India. Hence Musharraf's commitment of not allowing Pakistan's territory to be used by terrorists seems to be genuine.

(c) The third factor seems to be that General Musharraf is in quest of legitimacy for his regime. A deal with India may bring applause at home and perks from the United States. It would also include his legitimization by India, which may pave the way for legitimization in the whole South Asia, the British Commonwealth and the United Nations.

(d) The fourth factor is the economy of Pakistan. In 1985 Pakistan's per capita GDP was 6.5 per cent higher than that of India. Today it is 23 per cent lower than that of India. Added to these figures are the facts related to population. While India's birth rate is 1.7 per cent and decreasing, Pakistan's birth rate is 2.8 per cent and increasing[77]. One great opportunity for Pakistan to improve its economy is through economic cooperation in South Asia and that is not possible without India's help.

(e) The fifth factor is the embarrassment which Pakistan had to suffer due to leakage of information about its connection with Libya, Iran and North Korea in the case of nuclear proliferation. Pakistan knows that India can exploit the situation to its advantage. Hence rapprochement with India can contribute a lot of damage control.

(f) The sixth and the last factor is that the Joint Press Statement issued by Pakistan and India during SAARC 2004 is the first agreement that India has signed with any military government of Pakistan and the Pakistan military is the most stable and the utmost important factor in Pakistan's politics. The Lahore Declaration (1999) was signed by a civilian government in Pakistan but rejected by its military and the net outcome was the Kargil conflict. But any agreement to which the Pakistan's military is party, has chances of being durable. There may not be a genuine change of heart of the Pakistani rulers vis-à-vis India; but the events which are taking place in the Islamic world (around Pakistan, i.e. in Afghanistan Iraq, Iran, Libya and Indonesia) have forced it to see its relationship with India in a different perspective. The pressures on Pakistan are good enough to make it stick to the commitments it makes with India, at least for now.

3. Concerning the question as to what we must ask Musharraf to do, these suggestions are proposed though not exactly in the same order of preference:
   (a) Through a step-by-step approach, India can ask Pakistan for signing of an extradition treaty. New Delhi must convince Islamabad that not only is this treaty in the interest of both the countries, it will also ensure that Pakistan is not dubbed as a rogue state in the future.
   (b) Notwithstanding the 1994 resolution of Indian Parliament demanding annexation of Pakistan-occupied Kashmir (PoK) to India, the latter should ask the former to hold free and fair elections in POK.
   (c) The next step should be negotiations between the elected representatives of the Indian Kashmir and those of PoK. These talks may become the basis of making the border between PoK and Indian Kashmir truly porous. With ceasefire along the entire Indo-Pak border being in place, the whole international border between India and Pakistan could become a soft border. But the process must begin with Kashmir.
   (d) Regarding Hurriyat, India has been insisting that negotiation with that amalgam is India's internal matter. Hence there can be no question about Pakistan's negotiating with Hurriyat. At the same time, India must impress upon Hurriyat to contest an election in Indian Kashmir like any other political party and of course, Hurriyat's elected leadership in Kashmir can negotiate with its Pakistan counterpart as envisaged in the preceding para 3(c).
   (e) Coming to the composite dialogue between India and Pakistan on Kashmir, the question of plebiscite must be ruled out. No sovereign state today allows that option to its people. Pakistan for example would not allow it in the case of NWFP and the United States in the 1840s chose to face a civil war rather than allow its southern states to secede. Moreover, plebiscite in Kashmir can make all minorities within India suspect and invite a majority backlash against them. Kuldip Nayar says that Pandit Nehru gave up the option of plebiscite in Kashmir when Pakistan joined

US-led military alliances in the 1950s which resulted in the intrusion of American power in South Asia. The Pakistan's Prime Minister, Mir Zafarullah Khan Jamali now speaks about the two-nation theory having become redundant in the present context. In an interview with Mohammad Shehzad of *Frontline* on January 29, 2004, the following dialogue did take place:

Shehzad: Is the two-nation theory still valid? If so, then to which nation do the Muslims of India belong and what is the status of non-Muslims of Pakistan?
Jamali: I think the two-nation theory has become a one-nation theory. It was over half a century ago. And whichever nation is there, that is there today[78].

The message is loud and clear that Pakistan is not ready to shoulder any responsibility towards the Muslims of India. Jamali in the same interview, however, considers Kashmiri Muslims as a different category. But he must understand that all Muslims in India today are Indians, including the ones in Kashmir. This would squarely conform to his idea of a one-nation theory of today as it exists in reality.

All that Pakistan can hope for during negotiations with India is minor adjustment along the Indo–Pak border in Kashmir, which may in due course of time become a permanent demilitarized zone. The LoC is *for all practical purposes*, and must ultimately become, a permanent border between India and Pakistan.

(f) The hate-campaign against India on the issue of Kashmir unleashed by Pakistan on its television and other electronic and print media must cease immediately.

Conclusion

While the experience which India had in the past with Pakistan in political matters is not very assuring, there are reasons to believe that Pakistan needs India's help today. There may not be a genuine change of heart on the part of Pakistan's leadership in its attitude towards India, there are nevertheless two factors which may compel it to act in a positive manner. One is that the United States at the moment wants Pakistan to behave responsibly. Although it is true that the United States' track record in this case is that it has cared for nothing in the past except its own interests in South Asia, the fact nevertheless remains that today those interests coincide with the interests of India. The other reason is the poor condition of Pakistan's economy, which may impel it to mend its ways. Therefore, India must seize the initiative to prove to one and all that peace is in itself a dividend, provided it is not at the cost of the self-respect of any nation. ■

Notes & References

1. Robert G. Wirsing, "India–Pakistan Relations and the Problem of Kashmir", Malik, Hafeez, ed., *Pakistan: Founders' Aspirations and Today's Realities*, Karachi, 2001, pp. 415–416.
2. Kuldip Nayar, "Indo–Pak: Breaking the Ice", *The Indian Express*, December 30, 2003.
3. Thomas P. Thronton, "A Long Way to Lahore: India and Pakistan Negotiate", Baxter, Craig and Kennedy, Charles H., eds., *Pakistan-2000*, Karachi, 2000, pp. 63–64.
4. Robert G. Wirsing, n. 1.
5. Thomas P. Thronton, n. 3.
6. Gowher Rizvi, *South Asia in a Changing International Order*, New Delhi, 1993, p. 80.
7. Ibid., pp. 80–81.
8. Ayub Khan cited in Sangat Singh, *Pakistan's Foreign Policy—An Appraisal*, New York, 1970, p. 45.
9. Abdul Majid cited in Ibid, p. 51.
10. Sangat Singh, n. 8, pp. 51–53.
11. Robert G. Wirsing, n. 1, pp. 416–17.
12. Thomas P. Thronton, n. 3, p. 416.
13. Robert G. Wirsing, n. 1, pp. 71–72.
14. Thomas P. Thronton, n. 3, p. 79.
15. Sukumar Murlidharan, " A Surprise Offer", *Frontline*, 20 (3), May 10–23, 2003, p. 17 and also see Raj Chengappa, and Bagchi, Indrani, "Rocky Road to Peace", *India Today*, Vol. 28, No. 19, May 12, 2003, p. 46.
16. Ibid., pp. 17–18.
17. Ibid.
18. Ibid.
19. *The Indian Express*, April 19, 2003.
20. *The Sunday Tribune*, April 20, 2003.
21. *The Indian Express*, April 20, 2003.
22. *The Indian Express*, April 21, 2003.
23. n. 20.
24. Sumit Chakravarty, "Real Lessons of Bushfire II for South Asia", *Mainstream*", Vol. 41, No. 19, April 26, 2003, pp. 2–3.
25. *The Indian Express*, October 23, 2003.
26. *The Tribune*, October 24, 2003.

27. *The Indian Express*, October 24, 2003.
28. Ibid.
29. *The Indian Express*, October 25, 2003.
30. Ibid.
31. Ibid.
32. *The Tribune*, October 28, 2003.
33. Ibid, October 27, 2003.
34. *The Indian Express*, October 28, 2003.
35. *India Today*, October 28–November 3, 2003, p. 54.
36. *The Tribune*, October 30, 2003.
37. Ibid.
38. *The Indian Express*, October 31, 2003.
39. Ibid.
40. Rajinder Sachar, "J&K: Indian Initiative and Pakistan's Response", *Mainstream*, Vol. 41, No. 52, December 13, 2003, pp. 6–9.
41. *The Tribune*, October 31, 2003.
42. *The Tribune*, November 24, 2003.
43. *The Indian Express*, November 25, 2003.
44. Ibid.
45. *The Indian Express*, November 26, 2003.
46. *The Tribune*, November 26, 2003.
47. *The Indian Express*, November 27, 2003.
48. *The Tribune*, November 27, 2003.
49. *The Indian Express*, November 28, 2003.
50. *The Tribune*, November 28, 2003.
51. *The Tribune*, November 30, 2003.
52. Murlidhar B. Reddy, "India and Pakistan: Turning over a new leaf", *Frontline*, Vol. 21 No. 1, January 3–16, 2004, p. 120.
53. Ibid., pp. 120–121.
54. *The Tribune*, December 24, 2003.
55. *The Indian Express*, December 31, 2003.
56. *The Tribune*, January 2, 2004.
57. *The Tribune*, January 3, 2004.
58. *The Tribune*, December 13, 2003.
59. *The Tribune*, December 14, 2003.
60. *The Indian Express*, December 30, 2003.
61. *The Tribune*, December 30, 2003.
62. *The Indian Express*, January 1, 2004.

63. *The Indian Express*, January 3, 2004.
64. *The Indian Express*, January 5, 2004.
65. Ibid.
66. *The Indian Express*, January 6, 2004.
67. Radha Kumar, "Indo–Pak Peace on Right Tracks: Don't Derail it Now", *The Indian Express*, January 10, 2004.
68. V. Sudarshan, "Summit Conquered", *Outlook*, Vol. 44 No. 2, January 13–19, 2004, pp. 36–37.
69. Murlidhar B. Reddy, "A Deal for Peace", *Frontline*, Vol. 21 No. 2, January 17–30, 2004, pp. 8–12.
70. G. Parthasarthy, "American Tilt Towards India-Pakistan Seen as a Problem Child", *The Tribune*, December 18, 2003.
71. Praful Bidwai, "Towards a Breakthrough", *Frontline*, Vol. 21 No. 2, January 17–30, 2004, p. 128.
72. Ibid, pp.128–129.
73. M.B. Naqvi, "Inherent Potential of Pakistani Move—India should Seize the Historic Opportunity", *The Tribune*, January 17, 2004.
74. Ejaz Haider, "Battle for Pakistan", *The Indian Express*, December 31, 2003.
75. Wirsing, Robert G., *India, Pakistan and the Kashmir Dispute*, Delhi, 1995, pp. 261–263.
76. Praful Bidwai, n. 71, pp. 128–129.
77. Fareed Zakaria, "Indo–Pak Thaw: The Global Effect", *The Indian Express*, January 15, 2004.
78. *Frontline*, February 28–March 12, 2004, p. 33.

Section III
Security in South Asia: Need for Rethinking

South Asian Security: India–Pakistan Factor

K.S. Sidhu*

The shift of power equation from the military to the economic seems to be gradually recognized in the South Asian region, almost solely among regions where co-operation is minimal, where the major states, India and Pakistan, have sought to opt for mutual CBMs and adopt the course of dialogue with a spirit of mutual accommodation and compromise at the 12th SAARC Summit meeting held at Islamabad. Four major factors have been referred to in the background as motivators for peace and reconciliation; overwhelming positive popular sentiments, imperative compulsions created by globalization for faster economic development, resolving common problems within and outside the region and refusal to be a source of threat to regional and world peace and, as such, a prospective laboratory for new experiments in conflict resolution[1]. The power position in South Asia has largely been determined by the intrusions from external forces with a motivation provided by internal factors. The lack of a viable political mechanism has not only given rise to instabilities and inter-state conflicts but has also served as linkages between the internal strifes or conflicts and interferences or interventions[2]. Dissonance as a source of security threat in the South Asian region has been projected by Professor Phadnis in the following words:

> Alongside the pressures and pulls of the international security system, the dynamics of the South Asian states system have also evolved their security parameters—highlighting the flashpoint of their threat perceptions. Colonial legacies, divergent state systems, uneven tenor of development and multi-ethnic

* Professor, Deptt. of Defence and Strategic Studies, Punjabi University, Patiala, Punjab.

structure of these states have evolved in a manner as to lead to a state of turmoil and flux in the region characterized by significant divergence of the threat perception of power elite of these states. The asymmetrical power structure in South Asia, the Indo-centric character of the region coupled with disharmony of political systems partly account for this development.[3]

The establishment of cordial and friendly relations between them has been motivated by the realization of the truth generated by their history of unremitting suspicions and hostile relations for over 50 years, as it would pave the way for resolution of bilateral issues. The course of action being proposed relates to the creation of a favourable condition for political, economic and social intercourse. However, the military power continues to be deeply and intimately linked with national security at the cost of their social and economic needs.

South Asian history has been marked by episodes of communal violence, more particularly the "Hindu-Muslim carnage" on a massive scale in the 20th century[4]. Like any other region of the Third World, the South Asian region too was moulded by the process of colonial and imperial rule. The colonial metropolis, while granting independence to the South Asian region, did not completely sever its umbilical cord. It continued to preserve and nurse its basic economic and strategic stakes in the region. The gradual demise of colonialism and the arrival of self-rule introduced a new era of competition with specific ingredients of bloodshed as the partition led to the trans-migration of nearly fifteen million people across the hastily drawn borders[5]. In this wrenching process, approximately 500,000 people were killed[6]. Contrary to the deeply engraved Indian political culture as enshrined and expressed by Kautilya's '*Arthasastra*' which evidently recognized the value, significance and necessity to grasp the elements of '*realpolitik*' such as war, imperialism, military and economic aggrandizement, mistrust, balance of power and geo-politics as the basis of statecraft, the post-independence policy posture of India, propagated and executed by '*Nehruism*', ignored them to adopt the contradictory policies of non-alignment, peace and disarmament[7].

Motivated by the drive to accumulate power at the expense of each other, both India and Pakistan are known to be deriving strength from their respective inherent Hindu and Islamic beliefs, autocratic and democratic values. While India strives to reduce the extra-regional influences and challenges to its power equation, as it perceives South Asia's natural balance of power to be the one which is lopsided in its favour whereas Pakistan seems to work to reduce the imbalance through alliances and aid efforts to internationalize the bilateral issues related to national power and security. A profound strategic dissonance is clearly evident in the security postures of India and Pakistan.

Their foreign policies are firmly rooted in the strategic concerns against each other. Both have been locked in a state of mutual distrust over the last more than fifty years. The existence of each has contradicted the basis of creation of the other. The claim of India providing an environment of co-existence for all religious minorities without any interference from the government, naturally contradicts Pakistan's claim of a homeland for the Muslims of the sub-continent. At the same time, the very existence of Pakistan contradicts India's vision of secularism, due to the devious reluctance of a large number of Muslims to live within the territorial boundaries of India.

The only thing that they have perpetuated as common since 1947 is mutual antagonism.Their mutual disputes and responses continue to be firmly fixed. The reasons for this conclusion seem to be obvious in the light of the dependence on war as a means to settle disputes, whether in the form of conventional war, limited war, proxy war, low intensity conflict and nuclear war and so on. They have negated the recently developed distinct but interrelated phenomenon which envisaged a shift from conflict for destruction to co-operation for development and convergence of ideologies and broader interests of the developed states leading to the end of the balance of power politics.

In the world of tomorrows, Huntington's hypothesis concerning the fundamental source of conflict would, rather than the ideological or economic, be likely to be based on cultural factors, making "the clash of civilizations" to be the dominating factor in global politics[8]. However, this may not fit into the South Asian regional dimensions of the future pattern of conflict where the basic needs, as the reason of conflict, would continue to be economic, if not ideological. It would be a conflict between those sharing a common heritage, civilization, values and history.

The concept of security in the South Asian region is undergoing rapid changes from the traditional to the modern, from the military to the development oriented. No doubt, the concept of peace, security and co-operation in South Asia cannot be structured within a vacuum and without taking into consideration the international security system, yet scholars and experts of different shades have tried to conceive and project their respective views on the issue, with particular reference to the South Asian region in terms of the concept, viability and scope from the intra, internal and inter-state issues, problems and solutions. Imtiaz Ahmad has summed up the criticism of the conventional approach to security in South Asia from four major directions, viz.,

(a) the majoritarian approach has proved to be counter-productive as it has inspired the growth of minorities and sub-national forces;
(b) unrestricted and protracted use of violence as a means to establish peace has bounced back as a means to check or pre-empt violence leading to an unmanageable social disorder;
(c) the heavy dependence on the insecurities theory for all types of response has lead to intra-state conflicts which further added to insecurities more firmly; and
(d) last, but too early to be concluded so, the futility of nuclearisation of South Asia[9].

This criticism, squarely, is the outcome of the mode of governance and the mode of development adopted and practised by these two prominent states of South Asia. The early 1990s witnessed a decline in the frequency of bilateral military conflicts and an increase in the number of domestic conflicts and civil wars[10]. Since the roots of security problems in South Asia are indigenous, the threat perceptions are sufficiently diverse to preclude a common approach.[11] The region has been an area of turbulence on account of the focus on economic reforms, political instability, democratization, regional conflict and co-operation. The bipolar structure breeding insecurity due to proximity is giving way to India emerging as a stronger power in the broader Asian security complex.

The pattern of regional security is shaped by the twin factors of distribution of power and historical relations of amity and enmity[12]. Despite their common colonial legacy, both have been ruling the people against their will, at least so far as peace and security in the South Asian region is concerned. Rather than concentrating on their internal domestic stability and development and on the state-building perception rather than the nation-building perception, they have been resorting to arms build-up including nuclear arms, primarily because India assesses the threat to security from external forces whereas Pakistan foresees India as a hegemonic power in South Asia. It is interesting to note that in this calculation of security neither of the two appreciates the cross-border nature of their respective internal interests; however, the realist demand of national security seeks to put social and economic insecurity in their domestic parameters.

The India–Pak relationship seems to be based, primarily, on a self-contradictory perception of balance of power, which may not be rational due to the inequality of the two states in terms of size, resources, threats and achievements. Besides territorial disputes, ideological differences and differing perceptions of regional dynamics, a paradoxical approach towards the roots of conflict about the very partition of British India has been indicated by the fact that Pakistan considered it (partition) as "necessary and inevitable... but incomplete (without the incorporation of Kashmir), while India regarded partition as un-necessary and tragic, but fundamentally complete".[13] Buzan and Rizvi have comprehended the India-Pakistan rivalry in the framework of what they have called the "security complex",[14] thereby referring to a sub-system of the international community of states, which, for reasons of security, geography, history and culture, are linked together in a more or less direct manner to the extent that their security problems cannot be realistically considered apart from each other. Their security, as such, depends on interdependence of rivalry rather than on the interdependence of the shared interests.

Similarly, P.R. Chari has tried to inscribe a three-feature-based, unique security system, based on the nature of conflict, within the international security system:

1. First, the tensions and instabilities that have marked relations between India and Pakistan since their birth overhangs this region.
2. Second, India dominates the region in political and strategic terms as perceived by the other smaller countries of South Asia.
3. Third, globalisation and liberalization, which are the new mantras of the post-cold war age, do possess discreet security implications, which have not yet been fully understood. This has led to a consequent dissatisfaction with the capacity of governments to satisfy their expectations, which encourages dissent and militancy and can be fomented by inimical powers[15].

Moreover, the very basis of the phenomenon of balance of power, as developed during 19th-century Europe, is not in tune with the traditional Indian culture, which envisages the use of power as a last resort for defence and has not been perceived in terms of offensive strategic formulation. Determined by military insecurity and perceived power differential, the policies and programmes of India and Pakistan for security are based on distorted politico-military concerns. The roots of conflict in South Asia may be classified into two broad categories:

1. legacies of colonial rule and
2. post-Independence strategies and processes of nation and state-building[16].

The challenges to the security of South Asia cannot be perceived in isolation but in the framework of traditional and the contemporary realities. The dilemma of South Asian states in the context of changed global political positioning faces paradoxical situations primarily because they are neither ready to take advantage of the changed international situation, nor ready to challenge the changes. Consequently, the South Asian states remain indecisive and conflict-prone. On the contrary, their inter-state and intra-state conflicts become more unmanageable. The region, today, is facing not only intra and inter-state feuds but a large variety of inherent ethnic, linguistic, religious and other parochial problems related to the process of nation-building despite, more or less, withdrawal of external forces and pressures from the region. Added to this, the region has been facing, from its very inception, constant influence from the extra-regional forces, in one form or the other.

Instead of building an anti-colonial pressure, the communal forces within the region have indulged themselves in a protracted intra-conflictual programme. These communal forces have a trans-border disposition which helped them to connive for their sustenance and growth. The state as a system of governance has failed to create any workable conflict-reducing and confidence-building mechanism in South Asia with particular reference to India and Pakistan. Both have their own reasons and justifications for not doing so, maybe India is apprehensive of losing its status and advantage accrues to it as a result of its stronger position and Pakistan, for fear of losing the undependable economic and military aid from its Western and Muslim friends. Their views are also justified so as to project the Indian pre-eminence in South Asia as a natural outcome of its relative size and superior resources and, conversely, Pakistan feeling that Indian supremacy in South Asia is detrimental to Pakistan's security. How long can they avoid the much-needed regional economic co-operation as an essential part of the ensuing global economy, especially when Pakistan, with a weakened economy that is highly dependent on external aid and investment, is on the verge of defaulting on loan payments[17]? Rather than examining the problems and objectives in a geo-strategic and geo-economic vacuum, the relevance and impacts of developments in the geographic proximity have also to be considered to finalize the approach to grasp the impact of the strategic issues, particularly the prolonged ethnic conflict in Afghanistan, the financial upheaval in eastern Asian states, growing energy crisis, regional nuclear environment with the support of ballistic missile capability, the existence of the world's largest narcotic-producing areas within the immediate vicinity of the region and the unabated strategic uncertainties with particular reference to China, Central Asia and a host of other factors have a direct bearing on India's security in the context of Pakistan.

Above all, the asymmetrical position of the South Asian states in the paradox of a common cultural and civilizational backdrop makes them strive for mutual contradictions in envy of each other for identity, the most serious of which is between India and Pakistan. Unless seen in these parameters, Indian security formulation, in an isolated South Asian region is likely to give the impression of being hegemonic rather than compulsive. In this kaleidoscopic situation, the stability, integrity and prosperity of the South Asian states are of paramount significance for India.

After the collapse of the Soviet Union, the bipolar structure of Cold War has accentuated the emergence of a polycentric world based on the leading role of an expanding constellation of centres of power with a shift from Euro-centred to Asia-centred, a change which the world community did not embrace but which managed as a linear evolution of the ultimate system of nation-states. There appears to be a failure to recognize the entry into the space age and the information age as part of the process of comprehensive and comfortable stability, a silent and apparently a peaceful war. It has been estimated that five out of the seven largest economies will be in Asia by the middle of next decade, i.e., Japan, China, India, Korea and Indonesia inhabited by over 40 per cent of the world's population thereby making Asia as the centre of gravity of the international systems. This feature makes the competition and co-operation concurrent in the Asian region.

The governance of security parameters in the north-western parts of India has to keep in mind the geo-strategic compulsions of India, Pakistan and the United States. India–US differences in strategic perceptions and policies, especially regarding the proliferation issue, as also their trade relationship have a direct bearing on the future of South Asian peace, stability and development. India has to be guided in this context by the fact that both India and Pakistan have moved up to the declared status of nuclear weapon states, both justifying it in their own way. As a result of this, despite having fought three major wars since 1947, both countries have refrained from doing so for more than 30 years. No doubt the earlier conflicts were limited in scope and magnitude by choice but the future wars are expected to be limited by compulsion, imposed by the existence of nuclear weapons.

Pakistan seems to be guided by the principal options of pursuing a strategy of domestic military expansion in a clandestine manner; encouraging and abetting insurgent and terrorist activities in India; strengthening its ties with China; attempting to recover Kashmir by all means and measures. Having unsuccessfully pursued its quest for national identity as an Islamic state, its readiness in foreign affairs, to rely significantly on external powers for economic, political and military assistance[18], Pakistan continues to depend on support from Islamic states. Its strategies, based on strategic depth, strategic defiance and 'strategic vision' would continue to direct its nuclear weapons acquisition policies and programmes and will continue to motivate self-assumptions with regard to threat of Indian hegemonic designs.

The developments in Afghanistan and Central Asia tend to establish that the deteriorating economic and geo-political compulsions make Pakistan a vulnerable state. The frequency of ethno-sectarian tensions having increased in an unprecedented manner, the peace and security conditions are likely to further deteriorate beyond Pakistan's control. Having found regular conflict unsuccessful due to the artificially induced strength gained through extra-regional support, the strategy of Pakistan shifted to that of irregular proxy warfare. The former Prime Minister of Pakistan has publicly acknowledged, that a joint politico-military decision was taken in 1989. The view was that low-intensity operations help to focus attention on Kashmir[19] that Pakistan used terrorism as an instrument of state policy and confirmed what has been generally known but never admitted by Pakistan. There is no denying the fact that the India-Pakistan relations will continue to be strained till the Kashmir issue is resolved and the conflict will continue till Pakistan maintains its support to various guerrilla groups fighting in Kashmir[20]. With the passage of time, the issue has become so complicated that neither India nor Pakistan can afford to assert their respective interpretations. India's restraint prevented eruption of a major war but it could not check the transnational militant activities. In Punjab alone the extensive use of small arms resulted in 21,476 deaths during March 1981 to April 1993 including 3810 of militants. Similarly, 2,424 Klashnikov assault rifles were captured between 1988 and 1992 at the India-Pak border in Punjab. More than 45,640 people were apprehended while illegally crossing the border betwen 1989 and 1992 and another 969 were killed in efforts of infiltration. Of these incidents of violence, 97 per cent were in Gurdaspur, Amritsar and Ferozepur districts.

The post-Independence period rightly proceeded with an emphasis on industrialization and technological transformation; the essential ingredients of developmental strategy, so as to build the military might of the country. Rather than being guided by pragmatism, India's pacifist approach, behaviour and history, envisaged an idealistic view of international relations, the Indian leadership paid scant attention to the relationship between force and diplomacy, and to the development of institutions engaged in the study and long-term planning of foreign policy and strategic goals[21]. On the contrary, Pakistan's offensive strategy has indicated success in its results by which it has not only retained the occupied territory but has been engineering demographic changes in Kashmir, making India's bigger size, status and resources irrelevant and ineffective.

India's passivity is evidently exhibited in the complacent approach towards its national security, which has resulted in the form of Kargil crisis. It may be a matter of satisfaction, temporary though it may appear to be, that the crisis between India and Pakistan has not transformed itself into a war despite the biggest deployment with high alert of armed forces on the border, perhaps due to mutual restraint caused by their nuclearisation which could lead to unprecedented losses to both as also due to the international pressures and their depleted economic resources. But the very fact that the differences between them have not been resolved so far and the precedent suggests that a measure of military threat helped to deliver Indian diplomatic objectives[22] and also restrain Pakistan who, otherwise, could have acted naively.

The fundamental issue attracting attention is that the weaker Pakistan gets more irritated and revengeful. In the post-Cold War period of globalization and liberalization, how long would India and Pakistan continue with their deep-rooted, fixed objectives and policies? In a world where economic strength is overtaking military strength, India and Pakistan have greater reasons for Regional Economic Cooperation to find 'markets' and 'foreign investment'.

Scholars of International Relations have expressed different views and possibilities of co-operation among the nation-states, however, the determining factors, more or less, are self-interests. The egoistic actors, operating in an anarchic self-help environment, the state co-operation is rare and unexpected, therefore, unlikely to be durable or permanent[23]. Whenever and wherever the co-operation is on a regular basis, it is bound to be durable and persistent. Robert Keohane has delineated two kinds of the concept of reciprocity as the foundation of co-operation, namely: specific and diffuse, referring to the situations in which specific partners exchange items of equivalent value in a strictly limited sequence. If any obligations exist, they are clearly specified in terms of rights and duties of particular actors[24]. Based on the essentials of contingency and equivalence, they are expected to be more flexible concerning the sequencing of reciprocal actions[25] and their co-operation automatically ceases when expected reactions or reciprocation cease[26]. Other dimensions of reciprocity are contingency and equivalence, which offer exchange of roughly equivalent values in which the actions of each party are contingent on prior actions of the others in such a way that good is returned for good and bad for bad[27]. Similarly, the diffuse reciprocity is based on the importance of norms, obligations and trust wherein both the parties "contribute one's share, or behave well towards others", not because of ensuring rewards from specific actors, but in the interest of continuing satisfactory overall results for the group of which one is a part, as a whole[28]. The creation of a societal mechanism encourages the fulfillment of obligations by the states as partners of this mechanism.

The lack of mutual rapport, an essential ingredient for regional co-operation, which emanates from shared feelings of security threat among the elites of the South Asian states, further sharpens the strategic cleavages so as to deepen the impediments in an assured security of the South Asian region.

Partha S. Ghosh has suggested three major models for the study of international relations in the South Asian context:

1. The subordinate system views regionalism primarily as part of the global super power-influenced system, in the case of intra-regional relations in terms of super powers' relations with individual countries of the region as also in terms of the inter-state relations within the region in relation to the super powers.
2. The model of economic integration representing the nature of economic problems, faced by the countries is identical, which necessitates mutual co-operation because the region, in terms of land and topography, represents one geographical unit.
3. The model of 'Regional Organization' aims at solving developmental problems through co-operation at various levels.[29]

In the absence of a successful SAARC, the multi-polar dimension of international relationship is likely to harm the interests of both India and Pakistan due to their independent and isolated decisions about their respective security. As a result, the scope of mutual *rapprochement* is almost non-existent either at the bilateral or at the third-party level. In fact, stability, integrity and prosperity are much more essential for both India and Pakistan in their own interest and in the interest of South Asian security. Pakistan as a failed state would harm India as much as it would harm Pakistan, irrespective of the fact whether it fails due to its domestic factors or because of the threats to its borders.

The realization of South Asian security hinges prominently on the security posture adopted and exhibited by India and Pakistan. There still exist three major reasons for pessimism. First, India and Pakistan have not resolved their differences, which remain vast. Second, both of them continue to maintain a high level of military mobilization, which acts as a comparatively expensive and possibly dangerous state of affairs. Third, the wild card continues to dominate their thinking. No doubt, most of the militant organizations have fallen in line behind General Musharraf but the radical tail retains the capacity to strike at the Indian targets[30]. Therefore, the perspective of security has to be deeply and thoroughly thrashed out, understood and propagated for its success. There may not be any other option without normalizing of their relationship. The South Asian region is expected to continue to suffer till these two countries realize that they have a strong interest in avoiding war, unintended escalation and conflictual stance[31].

Security in the present and future context is to be determined by shedding misconceptions, undertaking a sustained dialogue and adopting Mutually Assured Peace (MAP) and not Mutually Assured Destruction (MAD) policies and programmes. The acquisition of nuclear weapons' potential is expected to generate interaction, if not co-operation. The very fact that despite the largest ever mobilization of troops, war did not take place between them shows that both the states have perhaps been trying to manage peace if not establish it.

By setting aside their history of conflict and animosity, both India and Pakistan have to address themselves to the issues of modernisation to join the global mainstream, keeping the issues of terrorism, Kashmir and, above all, mutual hatred and insecurities to the minimum level, if not eliminate them. They have to "stop being held hostage to Kashmir dispute"[32] and learn lessons from the European Union states, promote reconciliation and co-operation in a manner acceptable to both, at least to the extent of forming a South Asian confederation without compromising their respective sovereign status.

Faced with the problem of their respective identities, the states of the South Asian region have inherited under-developed and asymmetrically developed social structures. Realizing that the problem of nation-building being a complex and contradictory, these states have not yet been able to emerge out of their dogmatic commitments[33]. The states and the people of the South Asian region have been conditioned with the realist vision of security, where confrontation and conflict have been regarded as the inevitable characterization. The South Asian security system has been regarded as an insecurity system, and the trade-offs for each regional government involve minimizing, not maximizing security[34]. No doubt, against such a background and given the deep strategic divide that characterized the region, it was considered to be quite premature, for a long period of time after the withdrawal of colonial forces from the South Asian region, to aspire for a consensus over the question of regional security. Consequently, a paradigm based on co-operative arrangement could not even be thought of for more than five decades "in spite of the enormous interdependence of South Asia as a single geo-economic entity throughout its history[35]. The proposal of continuous direct bilateral dialogue to resolve many problems short of Kashmir may lead them to a better understanding for establishing peace, stability and security in South Asia through a joint strategy to eliminate common problems. They speak the same language and understand each other perfectly, including the nuances of each other, a facility which has been exploited by them in the past to outmanoeuvre each other. India's strategy concerning security is reflected in the non-offensive nature of its defence policy and posture, which includes the innovative replication of the Ashokan tradition within the fold of the organization of the Kautilyan tradition. Ashoka believed in alternative non-military approach to peace, but he never slackened his military preparedness. Rather he maintained a powerful army to face any eventuality, but never used it to threaten others[36].

Pakistan has to start thinking and acting as a part of South Asia, rather than assuming the leadership of the Islamic world and also not being used as a "counter-weight to India's growing military capabilities"[37] so as to seek solidarity and support from the West Asian or the Central Asian states without comprehending the fact that Pakistan's "destiny is linked with the Indo-Genetic Region"[38]. Its geo-strategic proximity to China, India and Russia highlights its significance for others and not for itself as it unsuccessfully tried to build its military machine and not its developmental infrastructure, peace and stability. The real potential of the new Confidence and Security Building Measures (CSBMs) will be put to the ultimate test when critical issues will be discussed between India and Pakistan in future parleys as also the reply to the most relevant question in relation to the South Asian security as to whether violence and the threat of violence can ever be eliminated from India-Pakistan relations. ■

Notes & References

1. *The Indian Express*, January 3, 2004.
2. Rasul B. Rais, "South Asia and the Global System: Continuity and Change", Shelton U. Kodikara, ed., *External Compulsions of South Asian Politics*, New Delhi, 1993, p. 22.
3. Urmila Phadnis, "Security Environment in South Asia in the 1990s", *Foreign and Defence Policies for India in the 1990s*, Proceedings of a Seminar, No.13, New Delhi, 1990, p.35.
4. Devin T. Hagerty, *The Consequences of Nuclear Proliferation*, London, 1998, p.64.
5. Robinson Francis, ed., *The Cambridge Encyclopedia of India, Pakistan, Bangladesh, Sri Lanka, Nepal, Bhutan and Maldives*, Cambridge, 1989, p.59.
6. Boxer Craig et.al, *Government and Politics in South Asia*, Boulder, 1991, p. 37.

7. Y.K. Malik and Ashok Kapur, eds., *India and United States in a Changing World*, New Delhi, 2002, p.15.
8. S.P. Huntington, "The Clash of Civilizations", *Foreign Affairs*, Summer, 1993, p. 22.
9. Imtiaz Ahmad, "Security Issues in South Asia", N.C. Behera ed., *State, People and Security*, New Delhi, 2002, pp. 91–116.
10. Justus Richter and Christian Warner, *Regional Security, Ethnicity and Governance*, New Delhi, 1998, p.12.
11. Pervaiz Iqbal Cheema, "Security in South Asia: An Approach", Shelton U. Kodikara, n. 2, p. 42.
12. Barry Buzan, "South Asia Moving towards Transformation : Emergence of India as a Great Power", *International Studies*, Vol. 39, No.1, 2002, p.2.
13. Ashley Tellis, *Stability in South Asia*, Santa Monica, 1997, p.8.
14. Barry Buzan and Gowher Rizvi, eds., *South Asian Insecurity and the Great Powers*, London, 1986.
15. P.R. Chari, "South Asian Security; A Conceptual Approach", Dipankar Banerjee, ed., *Security in South Asia*, New Delhi, 2000, pp.19–21.
16. S.D. Muni, "South Asia", Mohammed Ayub, ed., *Conflict and Intervention in the Third World*, New Delhi, 1980, p.39.
17. Milind Thakar, "Coping with Insecurity: the Pakistani Variable in Indo-US Relations", Gary K. Bertsch, et. al., eds., *Engaging India*, New York, 1999, p.224.
18. Richard J. Kozicki, "The Changed World of South Asia: Afghanistan, Pakistan India after September 11", *Asia-Pacific Perspectives*, Vol.2, No. 2, 2002, p. 2.
19. *The Hindustan Times*, December 14, 2003.
20. Sumit Ganguly, "Putting South Asia Back Together Again," *Current History*, December 2001, p. 413.
21. Y.K Malik and Ashok Kapur, "Indian and America : Engaging Each Other in a Changing World", V.K. Malik and Ashok Kapur, eds., India and United States in a Changing World, New Delhi, 2002, p. 16.
22. Alexander Evans, "India-Pakistan, and the Prospect of War", *Current History*, April 2002, p.165.
23. For details see Kenneth Waltz, *Theory of International Politics*, Reading, M.A., Addison-Wesley, 1979.
24. Robert Keohane, "Reciprocity in International Relations," *International Organization*, Vol.40, Winter, 1986, p.4.
25. Ibid.
26. Peter Blau, *Exchange and Power in Social Life*, New York, 1964, p.6.
27. Robert Keohane, n. 24, p. 8.
28. Ibid, p. 20.

29. Partha S. Ghosh, *Cooperation and Conflict in South Asia,* New Delhi, 1995, pp. 7–8.
30. Alexander Evans, n. 22, p. 165.
31. Michael Krepon, "A Time of Trouble, a Time of Need", Michael Krepon and Amit Savak, eds., *Crisis Prevention, Confidence Building and Reconciliation in South Asia,* New Delhi, 1996, p. 8.
32. Karan Singh, "Snap Out of It," *The Hindustan Times,* December 23, 2003.
33. A.K.M. Abdus Sabur, "South Asian Security in the Post-Cold War Era", Iftekharuzzaman, ed., *South Asia's Security: Primacy of Internal Dimension,* New Delhi, 1995, pp. 6–7.
34. Stephan P. Cohen, "Security Issues in South Asia", *Asian Survey,* Vol.15, No. 3, March 1975, p. 214.
35. Dipankar Banerjee, "Approach to Comprehensive and Co-operative Security", Dipankar Banerjee, ed., *Security in South Asia,* New Delhi, 2000, pp. 298–299.
36. Rajpal Budhania, *India's National Security Dilemma: Pakistan Factor and India's Policy Response,* New Delhi, 2001, p. 288.
37. Amitabh Mattoo, "Shadow of the Dragon: Indo-US Relations and China", Bertsch. Gary. et.al, eds., *Engaging India,* New York, 1999, p.220.
38. K. Subramanium, "Pakistan's Homecoming," *The Times of India,* January 3, 2004.

Foreign Power Involvement and Regional Security in South Asia:

A Roadmap to Peace, Development and Balance of Power System

Bishnu Hari Nepal*

Introduction

South Asia has had deep wounds of alien rule. It damaged the ethno-cultural, socio-economic, politico-strategic, natural heritage and human value system of this region. The hangover of the unstable, insecured, violent and volatile cold war on South Asia still persists. The United Nations Military Observers Group on India and Pakistan (UNMOGIP) totally failed in the process of peacemaking, peacekeeping, peace building and preventive diplomacy. India being the superpower of the region, all the wars in the subcontinent remained Indo-centric, which obviously tends to be so in the future. NAM and SAARC also failed to stop wars and war-related violence in South Asia. Ameliorating the fate of the one-fourth population of the world that continues to suffer from impure drinking water, hunger, disease and shelter has been the greatest of all challenges in South Asia.

Post-9/11 impact, particularly Afghanistan war, changed the strategic map of South Asia. Three nuclear giants from the developing world—India, Pakistan and China—had no spillover effect on the wars, on the contrary, Pakistan had to provide her soil and sky to attack her next-door neighbour. Wars in Iraq and former Yugoslavia were bitter lessons to South Asia. The US invasion in the former and NATO hegemony in the latter challenged the UN and its charter, especially Article 7.2 and Article 51 in both cases. Side by side, the significant changes developing in the Indo-US relations after 9/11 are remarkable. But India should not forget world history—that the character of the unipolarity has remained mostly unpredictable. On this ground, the threat

* Former Royal Nepalese Ambassador to Japan.

to peace and foreign power involvement in South Asia is ever consistent. That strongly applies to the Kashmir dispute between India and Pakistan. Due to India's firm stand recognizing the issue as purely a bilateral phenomenon, the road to this region for the West has been zigzag. The United States conferred the status of "Major Non-NATO Ally" on Pakistan during the visit of Colin Powell on March 18, 2004[1].

Border disputes between India and China and border unrest between India and Nepal have been unresolved. This includes the crucial issue of the Indian military installations in Kaalapaani since the 1960s. Kaalapaani has been strongly claimed by Nepal as her territory. Nepal also regards that the open border pillars neglecting the "das-gajaa or no man's land" between Nepal and India, have been shifted to Nepal in 61 places.

Water sharing between India and Bangladesh as well as between India and Nepal has been another hot zone of conflict in the South Asian region. The Indian claim that Nepal had given a nod to the Mahalisagar dam construction project has been refuted by Nepal[2]. Similarly, the refugee crisis between Pakistan and Afghanistan, Nepal and Bhutan, China and Nepal, China and India, and the concern of nearly 800,000 refugees yet to be returned to Sri Lanka are major fields of constraints. It is estimated that nearly 4-5 million refugees are yet to be returned to Afghanistan. Some 200,000 Tibetan refugees are living in Nepal and more than 300,000 Tibetans are living in India and neighbouring countries.

The number of Bhutanese refugees in Nepal for more than a decade is more than 112,000. The problem for Nepal is that UNHCR has already warned Nepal and Bhutan that it is going to wash its hands off the problems by the end of 2005 or maximum six months further in 2006. UNHCR is keen to hand over the problem to the donor agencies to be handled directly by them. For instance, there are some 42,000 refugee-students in eastern Nepal studying in Classes 1-8 alone.[3] So far, they have been supported by UNHCR. Bhutanese refugees disclosed that the Indian police loading them in trucks brought them up to the Nepalese border. Later on they were not allowed to use the Indian soil to go back to their country.[4]

In the post-Cold War era, the intra-state conflicts like Maoist crisis in Nepal, LTTE independence insurgency in Sri Lanka, secessionist unrest or separatism among certain Indian states, ethnic extremism and leakages of nuclear technology from Pakistan's scientists in Pakistan, radicalism in Bangladesh, crisis created by greenhouse-effect in the Maldives, etc. remain a further threat to peace, security and development in the region. It is likely that any time it could invite further foreign infiltration in the form of direct military interventions. Buying and selling of arms of any form, volume and category and supplying of arms to the adjoining countries are supposed to be inspiring conflict situations in the region. Similarly, financial support in the name of foreign aid and foreign direct investment and supporting the concerned insurgents from behind the screen have been normal practices.

The other side of the coin, i.e. the indirect support from the state level on this ground is very crucial and dangerous because it is boosting heinous terrorism in the region. Finding explosives in the residences of Pakistan's diplomats several times in Kathmandu has created another havoc in Nepal and India, which have already suffered cases of even hijacking of Indian Airlines flights to the wide circulation of fake Indian and Nepalese currencies in the underground markets.

Need Assessment

In the post-Cold War era, South Asia needs a new approach with a far-sighted vision in the decision-making mechanism for the maintenance of sustainable peace, cooperation, security and balance of power system. It appeals to the leaders for a big thaw in the field of domestic and foreign policy concerns. It appeals to the people of South Asia for cultural harmony against stratification and an integrated economic diplomacy in its favour contrary to globalization. It specially addresses the leaders and the political scientists of the region and argues that now the time is ripe to get South Asia and the vicinity united. It is for peace, security, development and balance of power system in the region.

Background of Conflicts and Problem Identification

The greatest glory of South Asia is the Himalayas. Even though it is the youngest mountain system of the world in the eyes of modern science, as addressed by the national geography, it is recognized as "Sarwajeevo Himalaya. Sarwarakshyo Himalaya. Sarwaratno Himalaya. Sarwaramyo Himalaya"—the source of all life, protector of all, source of all jewels and most beautiful of all beauties.[5] It is argued that South Asia is so rich in natural heritage, how can the inhabitants of this region suffer from poverty in the 21st century? This region geographically protects the world, why does it need foreign intervention for its protection?

The Indus Valley Civilization provided deep-rooted footprints to the culture of South Asia and also the way of life to the world.[6] For instance, the history of Hinduism began in India about 1500 B.C. The earliest literary source for the history of Hinduism is the *Rigveda,* the hymns of which were chiefly composed during the last two or three centuries of the second millennium

B.C. So deep-rooted and ancient is the culture of this region, then why does it need to adopt an alien culture today? In post-Cold War perspectives, South Asia and its vicinity has given birth to three nuclear powers: India, Pakistan and China, representing the developing world[7], but why does South Asia need to import more arms from the West and make the rich countries richer and its poor people poorer? Why has South Asia alway remained unstable, insecure, violent and volatile during post-colonial era and with a continuum even during the post-Cold War era? Is it religion that had and has divided and created conflicts in South Asia or is it something else? In the true sense, the answer is "not religion", because all religions—Hinduism, Buddhism, Islam, Christianity, Sikhism, Judaism, Perfect Liberty Kyodan, Bahai—in theory, stand for "peace" not for "war"[8].

The major factor responsible for the conflicts in South is the "political culture of ill-intent", left as "remnant" by the "foreign power involvement/colonialism" in the region, and basically, not what we call the "culture", originated on its soil, has turned South Asia into a conflict zone. The latter is only superficial but the former is the root cause. In this amalgamation, more than 116 countries of the world declared Nepal a Zone of Peace[9]. But today's Nepal, for instance, has been slowly turned into a war zone. The question thus arises: what brought South Asia into conflict? Why is the poverty-affected zone of the region deemed more violent than the privileged ones? Is this the result of borrowing and implementing a faulty planning system by the developing world in general and South Asia in particular? Does this not alarm the need of a new millennium approach in terms of foreign policy framing, trade and balance of power system for regional security as a whole? While studying external power influence and regional security in South Asia, it is important that the convergent and divergent paradigms together with the evolutions of the Indo-centric trends be studied. The submission is unavoidable because India being the superpower of the region, without it history is incomplete. The instances are:

1. Indo-Pakistan conflict 1948/1949 created the establishment of the UNMOGIP in January 1949, which is still functional. Unfortunately, it is a telling case of a failed instance of the UN effort and it proves that the UN is really a paper tiger looking for a better and effective preventive diplomacy[10].
2. The fleeing of the Dalai Lama from Tibet to India, in 1959 created conflict psychology between India and China. On the question of Tibet, different viewpoints persisted between India and China.[11] The questions of Tibet and Sikkim to some extent were normalized only by Premier Vajpayee's visit to Beijing.

3. The Sino-Indian war of 1962 and border dispute between the two countries[12] created a bitter and permanent fissure between the two largest populations of the world belonging to the adjacent geography and economically the same world.
4. The India-Pakistan conflict, 1965, increased hostility between the two countries.
5. The Indo-Pak war, 1971, creation of Bangladesh, entry of China into the Security Council, UN and Twenty-Year-Indo-Soviet-Friendship Treaty brought about the climax of the Cold War in South Asia [13].
6. India demonstrating nuclear capability in 1974 encouraged Pakistan to go nuclear[14].
7. The merger of Sikkim with India in 1975 created terror and fear of identity crisis in the smaller countries of the region.
8. US Support of 4 billion USD to Pakistan in the beginning of the 1980s added more fuel to the fear and fury to India, not with understanding that the cold war could end Afghanistan and the world at large in a couple of years.
9. Operation IPKF in Sri Lanka by Rajiv-Jayawadhane Agreement of July 27, 1987 showed the dual role of India regarding LTTE. India had to pay a heavy price for it.
10. Economic blockade by India to Nepal in the late 1980s, in a sense, put pressure on late King Birendra to re-establish democracy in Nepal in 1990, which was seized by late King Mahendra in 1960 and again has been recaptured by the present King Gyanendra since October 4, 2002.
11. India's second Pokhran Nuclear Test and immediate entry of Pakistan to the nuclear world[15] showed the extreme of nuclear race between two SAARC giants. The world knows that a large section of the people of these countries does not even get pure drinking water. In Musharraf's words in Davos, while visiting Switzerland, his country suffers from "political disputes, poverty and illiteracy". In retrospect, neglecting the basic infrastructure at the home front, the Indo-Pak war broke out in beautiful Kargil, while Musharraf was the C-in-C of Pakistan. Operation Vijaya in the post-Cold War-era was still not a happy end in terms of sustainable peace in the region. Leakage of nuclear technology has added another havoc recently.
12. The preparation of a final war between India and Pakistan in 2002, especially after the violent attack on the Indian Parliament, on December 13, 2001, threatened not only South Asia, but the whole globe. Although India's stand not to be the first country to use nuclear weapons already existed, yet the fear of the West and the rest of the world that it could enter the next nuclear warfare

after August 6, 1945 in Hiroshima and August 9, 1945 in Nagasaki, prevailed.

13. The brutal regime of the Talibans and its nexus with South Asia became a very serious security threat to the Indian subcontinent. The strategic map of South Asia in this regard totally changed by the direct intervention of the US and its allies in Afghanistan[16]. On the above grounds, foreign powers pretend to look for the cause and effect of the violation of human rights and political developments in the region, but the real motive, based on their national interests, perhaps is to imply their spheres of influence in the politics and economy in South Asia. This has been the continuum of the ill-intent based on bipolarity during the Cold War era and global-intent of uni-polarity vs. multi-polarity trend during the post-Cold War era.

Violence, Terrorism and Regional Security

Post-war South Asia has been prey to wars, violence and terrorism frequently. The detrimental effects are applied to socio-economic, ethno-cultural, political and natural heritage perspectives.[17] The post-9/11 scale of violence and terror has given a different dimension. Khatri points out that the latest military balance from International Institute for Strategic Studies lists at least 18 'selected non-state armed groups' in South Asia alone. Out of this number, three are in Bangladesh, eight in India, five in India/Pakistan, and one each in Nepal and Sri Lanka with total strength considered to be less than 39,000 for all of South Asia[18]. But many of the insurgents categorically deny the charge tagged as terrorist groups and the figure mentioned could not be devoid of argument. For, it is many folds higher than 39,000 as mentioned.

The types of technology used for violence are particularly significant after 9/11. Brian Martin's[19] categorization is as follows:

1. Nuclear Weapons: are caused from fission or fusion with fields, of blast, heat and radiation. This factor has been directly related to violence-prone South Asia, because Pakistan's father of the Nuclear Bomb, Abdul Qadeer Khan admitted that he transferred nuclear technology to Iran, Libya and North Korea.[20] Dramatically, on February 5, 2004, in a press conference Musharraf pardoned 'Dr. Nuke' for his 'mistake' declaring him a 'national hero'. On this occasion, he also categorically denied revealing the relevant documents to the world and inspection-permission to the IAEA or UN authorities.[21] On the other hand, among the charged recipients, North Korea strongly condemned the sensational news that this country received the nuke-technology from Khan. This added more confusion in the process. Anyhow, South Asia came into focus of the world power again. British Foreign Secretary Jack Straw

rushed to New Delhi and in a joint press conference on the issue, the Indian Foreign Minister, Yashwant Sinha reacted that it appeared that things would not stop here because it is not merely an internal matter of Pakistan but one which concerns the international community[22]. Former US Security Advisor Brent Snowcroft's remarks in India that in the past 30 years, "Pakistan has been in a state in desperate search of security any way they thought they could find it" and Josse adds and queries, "that, as all know, has greatly to do with the India/USSR-aided creation of Bangladesh out of Pakistan's erstwhile eastern wing. Would other nuclear-capable states have done otherwise?" He further argues why the suppliers, scientists and engineers of the chain of black marketers from Germany, Holland, France and Switzerland have not been brought together with Khan's list.[23] Another type of WMD is chemical weapons. Recently, the historic indictment of Japan of death penalty against the terrorist monk has been brought out in Tokyo. Chemical weapons, thus, are a serious threat to humanity.

2. Biological weapons are disease organisms such as anthrax, that cause illness or death in humans. The dimension of the risk from terrorism has been heightened. Therefore, it is pragmatic that more and more awareness campaigns against the deadly weapons be realized. Many people know about the conventional weapons used for violence, like rifles and explosives. But Martin's list of the technology of repression for mass awareness is very interesting and useful: electro-shock-devices, leg-shackles, trauma-inducing drugs, guillotines, plastic bullets, chemical irritants, night vision cameras, automatic vehicle tracking systems, telephone-tapping equipment and human identity recognition systems. Non-lethal weapons include electrical stunners, infrasound beams to cause disorientation and chemical sprays, etc.[24] The summary of this part is that combating violence and terrorism today needs more sophisticated technical know-how, advanced knowledge of the concerned field and integrated approach in general. On January 9, 2004, Global Information Network, New York, reported that underlying the preparations is a major change in Pakistan's 'mindsets' and much of the establishment there has realized that the costs of running a militant operation from Afghanistan to Kashmir have been extremely onerous for Pakistan. The report further states that extremists have penetrated key institutions of the state in Pakistan. The most lethal indications of their power were assassination attempts on Musharraf on 14 and 25 December 2003. These highlighted the grave internal danger from extremist Islam[25].

Recent US Interests in South Asia

On 29 January 2004 Senator Richard Lugar, Indiana Republican, who chairs the powerful policymaking Senate Foreign Relations Committee said that, it is more important than ever that the US sustain active engagement in South Asia to encourage continuation of this positive momentum. By positive momentum he meant the meetings of Indo-Pak leaders utilizing the occasion of the 12th SAARC Summit in Islamabad. Lugar also disclosed very important information regarding Indo-Pak confrontations and US interests. In his words, "We have seen opportunities for peace squandered in South Asia in recent years. To ensure success, it is crucial that both parties prevent extremists from disturbing the process. Stability in this troubled region is vital to US national interests, both because Indo–Pakistan conflict could escalate into nuclear war and because of the potential nexus between terrorism and weapons of mass destruction." He further disclosed that "the US diplomacy in South Asia has already paid off by helping to avert a possible nuclear war in 2002. India and Pakistan have taken positive steps since that time, including resumption of transport links, restoration of diplomatic ties, and implementation of ceasefire along the Line of Control".[26] It is really a remarkable disclosure, contrary to the Indian stand, that she does not appreciate any foreign involvement regarding bilateral issues between India and Pakistan, particularly on the Kashmir issue. According to Lugar's statement, two vital submissions are made further. The first that President Musharraf is willing to give up Pakistan's traditional claim of plebiscite in Kashmir and the second that Prime Minister Vajpayee has conceded for open dialogue on the issue[27]. Christina B. Rocca, US Assistant Secretary for South Asian Affairs appreciates Colin Powell's terminology of 'triangle of conflict resolution' referring to India, Pakistan and the USA[28]. Vajpayee's term natural partnership and the United State's Next Step in Strategic Partnership (NSSP) clearly indicate that the improved relations between India and USA, in US eyes are purely strategic. The Powell Triangle cannot impose the 'mediator-role' understandably due to strong resentment from the Indian side. But Lugar, Rocca and Powell have all categorically claimed that they have been able to stop nuclear confrontation between the two SAARC giants in 2002. Joint US military exercises with India and military training supports from the UK and US to Nepal again bear a strategic meaning to the USA. Reaching the Unreachable Peace Through Production (P-P) is the natural effect of trade. Two nations who traffic with each other become reciprocally dependent: for if one has interest in buying, the other has interest in selling; and thus their union is founded on mutual necessities. The Earth Summit in 1992 called for a shift from talk to action. What sustainable development means a shift from growth to sustainability?[29] What is then 'sustainable peace' sought by South Asia? Leaders of the region have to reconsider their traditional thinking. It is even further to neo-modernity or post-modern theory. This could be, therefore, termed as New Millennium Theory. It addresses a painstaking effort, farsighted vision and landmark determination. The Millennium Declaration by the UN is not enough to solve the problems of South Asia. Why does South Asia need outside powers to stop war between India and Pakistan? Why did the UN fail? South Asians need to solve their problems by themselves but honestly[30]. Many regard 'peace' as the state of absence of war. Tolstoy regarded it as internal pursuit. Modern critics such as Thomas G. Weiss, Brian Urqhuart, Daisaku Ikeda, R. Rikhey, Wiseman, Jarat Chopra, Dennis C. Jen, Steven Rafner, Robert Siekmann, Sridath Ramphal, etc. almost all follow the same path. Johan Galtung's 'After Violence: 3R's: Reconstruction, Reconciliation, Resolution[31] also is getting traditional because it does not emphatically address the production and distribution pattern in the first 'R' Reconstruction and so many components of peace processes are missing. For 'Reaching the Unreachable' or 'New Millennium Theory', a 'big thaw in foreign policy concerns' is necessary. In the 'multi-polarity vs. uni-polarity' picture of the world, this is applicable in pair-groupings[32]. Before the pair-groupings, let's observe the proximity of the hypothesis of P-P. Simon W. Polachek and John Robst who have said that educating hostility and promoting cooperation are leading to peace. Attempts to diminish hostility and bring about cooperation between two countries are often initiated by third-party nations. The problem is that peace imposed by others may be innately unstable, especially if the underlying differences originally separating the countries remain. For this reason, it seems that a more viable peace is one that exists naturally, without the need for outside intervention[33]. This beautiful definition is applicable to South Asian perspectives. But the problem is that it is based more on bilateralism. That is why hypothesis-I of the 'reaching the unreachable' "P-P" is more pragmatic because it addresses the multi-polar world. Confidence Through Cooperation (C-C) includes voluntary unifications, formation of alliances, cultural or scientific agreements and verbal expressions of support. Much time has been invested seeking CBMs (Confidence Building Measures) and many books have been written on it. To exemplify MID (Military Interstate Dispute) data includes a broader range of conflict than COW (Correlates of War), but excludes minor forms of conflict. Polachek and Robst admit that none of these data deals with cooperation between countries. They further say that the UN General Assembly's voting behaviour need not reflect actual conflict between countries and often deals with a sub-set of possible country interactions[34]. Political and economic factors affect the conflict and CBM. They exemplify that 'tariffs' increase 'conflict', 'foreign aid reduces the actor's conflict vented toward the foreign aid provider', on 'contiguity', many argue that contiguous countries are more conflict-prone, thus 'distance deters conflict' and they find that the 'economic size of the country' is also a determinant factor because by virtue of its economic size a small country has no real influence on the international prices whereas a large country can affect the international price through its volume of trade[35]. Similarly, Ho-won Jeong's 'theories of conflict' include 'paradigms on social conflict', the roots leading to Max Weber, Karl Marx and Sigmund Freud, 'sources of aggression', 'relative deprivation and basic needs', 'social exchange', 'functionalism and social systems' which include polity, economy and culture; 'class conflict'; 'discourse and domination', in which in the post-modern world, the social world is divided into a multitude of communities, cultural traditions and knowledge; 'structure of authority', 'functions of conflict' and 'implications for conflict resolutions[36]. In broader perspectives, in addition to Jeong's concept it is important that we must not allow ourselves to fall captive to perceived differences. The time has now come that we must be the masters of language and ensure that it always serves the interest of the humanity.[37] For Nelson Mandela, the theme stands that you don't make peace by talking to your friends; you have to make peace with your enemies.[38] Thus, hypothesis-II of "reaching the unreachable"– 'C-C' deserves better validity covering CBMs in the socio-economic, ethno-cultural, political and natural heritage systems in South Asian perspectives.

Disarmament Through Detente (D-D). At the beginning of the new millennium, the world had around 30,000 nuclear weapons. This is more than enough to end life on earth, as we know it. The commitments made at the 2000 Review Conference hold out the hope—if meaningfully implemented—that we could eradicate this greatest of man-made threats to our future. The direct cost of implementing the START-I and INF treaties to the United States has been put at US$ 31.00 billion. The cost of clean up, although there is no really safe way to dispose of the highly toxic remnants of nuclear bombs, would add another US$ 365 billion. Russian costs would be comparable. Up to 2001, the US was spending $30 billion per year to maintain its stocks. A Brookings Institute study in 1998 put the overall cost of the US nuclear weapons programme since 1940 at over $5.5 trillion[39]. More than 500 million small arms and light weapons are in circulation around the world—one for about every 12 people. They were the weapons of choice in 46 out of 49 major conflicts since 1990, causing four million deaths, which comprised about 90 per cent civilians, out of which 80 per cent were women and children.[40] The Carnegie Commission on Preventing Deadly Conflict described strategies for prevention as falling into two categories: operational prevention, which refers to measures applicable in the face of immediate crisis, and structural prevention, which consists of measures to ensure that crises do not arise in the first place or, if they do, that they do not recur[41]. Understandably, full disarmament is unreachable. If South Asia and the world are united, the earth can be made free from nuclear, biological, chemical and other forms of WMD. The route to the destination is D-D, in which the meaning of détente in today's context needs to be redefined. Reaching the unreachable hypothesis-III is expected to be the pragmatic tool to be applied by the world leaders.

Resolution Through Reconciliation (R-R) Conflict includes wars and other military acts as well as verbal expressions that display hostility. In terms of economic conflicts, particularly in South Asian perspectives at the present juncture, trade could be hypothesized to reduce conflict and increase cooperation[42] and trade of commodities. During the SAARC Summit in Islamabad Indian media disclosed that the volume of trade between India and Pakistan is nearly of IC Rs.1,000 crore per annum and after resumption of talks, it could reach Rs.3,000 crore. Vajpayee's open border and free trade proposal is very adventurous in comparison to the EU position, and certainly 'one step forward' to reconciliation. Fruitful results are still expected from the February 2004 talks between New Delhi and Islamabad. It must be admitted that unresolved issues on border points, water resources, treaties, transit points, refugee crisis and so on need 'R-R' hypothesis-IV of the 'reaching the unreachable'. The positive symptom to this hypothesis is the statement in Islamabad that India and Pakistan announced an ambitious 'roadmap' for talks and meetings aimed at a peaceful settlement of all bilateral issues, including Kashmir[43]. Meanwhile, "Pakistan Today" said that it was not averse to the idea of having a 'no war pact' with India[44]. This would further support the author's hypothesis-IV: R-R. Eyes are focused on the August 2004 meeting between the Indian Foreign Minister Yashwant Sinha and Pakistan's Foreign Minister Khurshed Mehmud Kasuri, which could contribute further to the support of R-R hypothesis under reaching the unreachable security Through Solidarity (S-S). Nepal, for example, may be said to be following a kind of

Himalayan balance of power policy vis-à-vis its giant neighbours, India and communist China.[45] Robert L. Rothstein concluded that the relationship between rich and poor is never likely to be without tension and conflict. The needs of the poor are too great and the sense of exploitation too salient to expect that demands upon the rich will rapidly diminish or that satisfaction with whatever the rich are willing to offer will rapidly increase[46]. The sensitivities of the Third World need to be respected regarding the humanitarian intervention as well.[47]

Solidarity is the only weapon to counter uni-polarity. This is the basic thrust of the S-S hypothesis. History is demanding a neo-post-modern theory, i.e. 'reaching the unreachable model' or to name it a 'new millennium theory' combining all hypotheses P-P, C-C, D-D, R-R and S-S, after post-modern theory in the new millennium. The new millennium is the millennium of multi-polarity. The author, therefore, suggests that the developing world be united instead of disintegrated and be friendly instead of being hostile. Many correlates can be observed and calculated under S-S hypothesis-V of the 'reaching the unreachable model'. Under S-S hypothesis, a very ambitious Model for Europe and Asia in general and South Asia in particular, has been suggested. It is ambitious because it seeks a total change in the mindsets of the world leaders of this region. It looks for a totally new and farsighted vision. It does not believe in the established facts demonstrated by the Cold War Era bipolar world, neither is it satisfied with the current uni-polar trend of the balance of power system. Therefore, it is neo-post-modern and it is the outcome of the new millennium, therefore, it is valedictory to be termed as the new millennium theory. It is projected for the millennium because it helps stand peaceful, developed and secure in the new millennium. The common enemy of the region in the new millennium, not been able to be overcome so far, is poverty. The P-P hypothesis, therefore, it is understood, could be the strongest weapon to eradicate poverty from the region in just 20-30 years. The justifications are that this region now has the technology, human resource, the largest market of the world and largest manufacturer of the world. India possesses 16 crore hectares, the second largest arable land of the world which is followed by Russia, 12.6 crore hectares and China, 12.4 crore hectares after the USA with 17 crore hectares on the top.[48] Japan is dominating the world in electro-mechanic and auto industries. China and India alone possess the world's one-third populations demographically. If they join hands, in crystal clear words, Asia does not need to kneel before Europe or America. But for this, security of bigger and smaller nations is prima facie. For security, solidarity is obligatory. This is derived from a common formula of 12 steaks breaking together and breaking separately. The S-S hypothesis, therefore, suggests to decision makers that the nations around need to come together and stand together. It is based on optimism. It is empirical. It is pragmatic. It seeks to work for security. Minor border disputes cannot be the bar for the major task of solidarity. There is no problem on earth, which has no solution. It is now time for working together. Let the nations of South Asia really be united. If they unite, half of the tension of the world will be reduced. The author, under the S-S hypothesis, suggests the establishment of the EDA—Euro-Asian Defense Alliance. The EDA can be formed from selected SAARC members and from the particular countries of Asia and Europe. The Founder Members at the first ring are suggested to be Russia, Pakistan, India, China and North Korea, if the latter becomes nuclear. Otherwise, North Korea can join EDA in the second ring with Japan, South Korea, Malaysia, Indonesia, Thailand, France, Germany and CIS States like Belarus and Ukraine. The third ring can be formed with other remaining interested powers of the region. Since NATO is ever consistent with uni-polar command and the Warsaw Pact is no more existent, it is thought that with the existence of EDA the balance of power system of the world will be strengthened. It will also help strengthen peace and security in South Asia. This could be the strongest weapon to resolve the 57 year-old problems of conflict, cooperation and balance of power system in South Asia. With EDA, the conflict-and-poverty-prone-zone can breathe safely. ■

Notes & References

1. *The Kathmandu Post*, March 19, 2004.
2. *The Himalayan Times*, March 17, 2004.
3. *Kantipur*, February 28, 2004.
4. *The Kathmandu Post*, February 26, 2004.
5. Yogi Narahari Nath, *Aitihaasik Sikharini Yaatraa*, Mrigasthali, 2049 V.S.
6. *The New Encyclopedia Britannica*, 1998, p. 2.
7. Pervez Hoodbhoy, “The Nuclear Noose Around Pakistan's Neck”, *Washington Post*, February 1, 2004.
8. Linda Groff and Paul Smoker, “Religion and Peace, Inner-Outer Dimensions”, *Encyclopedia of Violence, Peace and Conflict*, Vol.3, New York, 1999, p. 5.
9. Bishnu Hari Nepal, “Centuries Old Ties”, *The Japan Times*, Tokyo, December 26, 1995.
10. Bishnu Hari Nepal, *UN Peacekeeping During Post-Cold War Era: Third World Perspectives*, Varanasi, 2003, p. 64 and also see Goodrich, Leland M. and Simons,

Anne Patricia, *The UN and Maintenance of International Peace and Security*, Washington D.C., 1955, p. 8.

11. T.S. Murthy, *Paths of Peace: Studies on Sino-Indian Border Dispute*, New Delhi, 1983, p. 9.
12. Ibid., p. 10.
13. Ramesh Adhikari, *South and South East Asia*, Kathmandu, 2003, p. 11.
14. Bishnu Hari Nepal, "Three Days After Second Pokhran Test", bhnf@ wlink.com.np
15. Stephen J. Cimbala, "Nuclear Weapons Policies", n. 8, p.14.
16. Bishnu Hari Nepal, "Taalibaan ke baaremen samyukta raastra League se sabak le", *Aaj*, March 16, 2001, p.16.
17. Ibid., p. 17.
18. Sridhar Khatri, 2003, "Introduction", Sridhar K. Khatri and Gerr W. Kuck, eds., *Terrorism in South Asia*, Delhi, 2003, p. 18.
19. Martin, Brian, "Technology, Violence and Peace", n. 8, p. 19.
20. *The Himalayan Times*, February 3, 2004, p. 20.
21. *The Kathmandu Post*, February 6, 2004, p. 22.
22. See Josse, cited in, *The Kathmandu Post*, February 11, 2004, p.4.
23. Ibid., p. 25.
24. Martin, Brian, n. 19, p. 26.
25. *Global Information Network*, New York, January 9, 2004, p.2.
26. www.rediffmail.com/news/2004/jan/28aziz.htm.
27. Ibid.
28. Christina B. Rocca, "Why South Asia Matters", *The Kathmandu Post*, February 12, 2004, p.5.
29. Wouter Van Dieren, *Taking Nature Into Account Toward a Sustainable National Income: A Report to the Club of Rome*, Copernicus, New York, 1995, p. 31.
30. Bishnu Hari Nepal, n. 16, p. 32.
31. Johan Galtung, *Coping with Visible and Invisible Effects of War and Violence*, Kathmandu, 2002, p. 34.
32. Bishnu Hari Nepal, "Big Thaw in Foreign Policy Concerns", *The Kathmandu Post*, May 13, 2003, p.5.
33. W. Polachek Solomon and John Robst, "Trade, Conflict, and Cooperation Among Nations", n. 8, pp. 559–561.
34. Ibid., pp. 561–562.
35. Ibid., pp. 567–568.
36. Ibid., pp. 516–517.
37. Daisaku Ikeda, *Peace Through Dialogue: A Time to Talk*, Tokyo, 2000, p.21.
38. Peter Harris and Ben Reilly, *Democracy and Deep-rooted Conflict: Options for Negotiators*, IDEA, Stockholm, 1999.

39. Bhaskar Menon, *Disarmament*, United Nations, New York, 2001.
40. *Small Arms: UN Conference Report on the Illicit Trade in Small Arms and Light Weapons in all its Aspects*, July 9–20, 2001.
41. Annan, Kofi, *Prevention of Armed Conflict: Report of the General Secretary*, United Nations, New York, 2002.
42. W. Polachek Solomon and John Robst, n. 33.
43. *The Times of India*, February 19, 2004.
44. *The Statesman*, February 19, 2004.
45. Norman D. Palmer, and Howard C. Perkins, *International Relations*, Calcutta, 1976.
46. Robert L. Rothstein, *The Weak in the World of the Strong*, New York, 1977, p. 4.
47. Bishnu Hari Nepal, "Road to Peace: Reforming the UN and Peacekeeping II", *People's Review*, Vol. 13, No. 28, February 12–18, 2004, p. 4.
48. *Dainik Jaagaran*, November 22, 2003, p. 52.

Impact of Afghanistan Crisis on South Asia

Surinder K. Shukla*

Geo-strategically, Afghanistan forms a part of the extended neighbourhood of South Asia. Housing within its fold a major chunk of the world population, South Asia is a geographic expanse covering several states, namely, India, Pakistan, Nepal, Bangladesh and Sri Lanka. India enjoys a pre-eminent position in the world and more particularly in the South Asian region. This claim is based on the following indicators:

- India is the world's second most populous state.
- It has the fourth-largest army.
- It is the fourth-largest economy (in 2000 in terms of purchasing power parity).
- It is the eighth-largest industrial economy.
- It has the world's second largest pool of scientists and engineers after the USA.
- It has a middle class double the size that of Japan.

In the past, these raw indicators have been extremely critical in deciding the rank of states. Since economic reforms began in 1991, the Indian economy has grown at an annual average of 5 to 7 per cent, placing India among the world's better-performing economies. Consequently, India has certain responsibilities by virtue of being a predominant state of the region. These include the role of building fences as also being a facilitator in building cooperation, as discussed at the end of this paper.

South Asia, because of its size and location needs to follow two sets of strategy—continental strategy and maritime strategy. While pursuing the

* Reader in Political Science, DCS, Panjab University, Chandigarh.

former, South Asia has to deal with Afghanistan, which has been recognized as a 'cradle of civilizations' for a long time. Modern geo-politicians see this situation not as 'spaces of places'—ranging from local to national and to global—but as 'spaces of flows' which challenge the conventional understandings of a geographical scale and compel foreign policy, military and commercial establishments to reorient themselves. Moreover, the quest for energy security is reflected in seeking partnerships for gaining energy resources from the region.

The post-colonial states of Asia and more particularly India, like the rest of the world were focused on the dominant political values embedded in the philosophy of constitutionalism. Constitutionalism hinges on a two-fold relationship—one between government and citizens and the other deals with relationship between one authority and another within the governmental structure. Inroads in these relationships were fostered by the existence of the following main threads:

- patron–client relationship between masses and elite (later masses began to question this relationship)
- nation within nation concept, i.e. 'sons of soil tons of toil' theory
- basic conflict of 'we' and 'they'
- unity and diversity in India.

The Indian political system is based on the philosophy of pluralism and laws in this regard are enshrined in its constitution. Initially, the task of reconciliation between pluralism and nationalism was relatively simple because the citizens were fresh and their fervour of nationalism was very strong. But as post-colonialism settled down, ethnicity, religion, culture, caste and gender have become major issues not only in the politics of India but in the politics of other colonial states as well.

During the system transformation the insecurities which the masses faced were manifold. They included problems of poverty, unmet human needs, high aspirations, inequality and the social consequences of economic, environmental and political crises. The state and nation came into conflict several times in the post-colonial South Asia. The classic cases in point are the problem of Punjab, Jammu and Kashmir and Gujarat.

As the Asian politics settled down, transnational conflicts began to emerge, thereby weakening the process of nation building. The ethnic identity uprising in Sri Lanka, the spurts of ethnic identity crisis in India and the ethnic identity kept under the lid in Pakistan by military pressure indicate a commonality in the region. The conflictual situations are a threat to the development of state and nation irrespective of the fact whether they are a democracy, a semi-democracy, a true democracy, guided democracy, whatever form.

Seeing States Afresh

The political and economic identities of states are under strain. The broad contract between citizen and state is being tested. Questions of security are central. The nuclear era marked the first crack in the security shield and the developing realities of the increasingly global economy have penetrated it further. As a sequel, the states need to view this afresh and consequently the role of security system needs to be reviewed.

Gillian Youngs (1999) has posed three conceptual challenges for the future of state, which need to be mentioned here. First, the most difficult challenge is to remove the state-centric blinkers. This is important because the states as dynamic social entities are subject to transnational forces of change that need to be understood both internally and externally. Second, it is necessary to break down the superficial paradigmatic barriers that have inhibited critical thinking in international relations and global political economy. Third, this should be used as a basis for negotiating the relevant multidisciplinary insights awaiting attention in respect of global relations. In combating the last two challenges, Youngs suggests that the achievements of gender critiques have been identified as the most profound in addressing power, inequality and globalisation in new ways that demonstrate multiple sensitivities of time and space.

Intra-Regional and Extra-Regional Factors

The role of the State is being challenged, as its control diminishes over the flow of information technology, arms, migrants, etc. across its borders. How well a country is governed will decide how it will face up to the forces generated from outside. States with a good and stable system of governance will gain from the changing world while those with an ineffective system will lose out and become breeding grounds for fundamentalism, terrorism, conflict and instability. Generally, democracies will fare better in the long run. Religion too will play an important role in shaping the future world.

While the linkages between internal and external security are evident, the growing inter-linkages between terrorism, narcotics and insurgency have added multiple dimensions to our security matrix. The dynamics of new alliances among nations and 'coalitions' with a completely new basis for cooperation also have significant implications for national security.

Dramatic changes are taking place in our neighbourhood as a result of 'war against terrorism'. From Afghanistan to Nepal and from the Central Asian Republics to Sri Lanka, there has been a sea change in the attitude of hosting foreign military forces and to developing close contacts with the armed forces of foreign countries. This has long-term implications for the region as a whole and for India in particular. National security concerns everyone. At one time the issues of defence of the country and its people were the sole responsibility of the government. Today, threats can touch the common man directly. Terrorism has touched lives of ordinary people and it also undermines the country's integrity and cohesiveness in a subtle manner.

The concept of security is undergoing a change. Threats emerge not only from across the borders but also from within the country. Further internal change in the society as a result of technological changes, population growth, poverty, economic instability, unemployment, widespread urbanisation, environmental degradation, energy and resource depletion can destabilise a country and can become a source of threat to national security. Fractured political mandates, bad governance and corruption can complicate the situation. Nation's currency is also vulnerable. Proxy wars, low intensity conflicts, infiltration across the border, small-arms proliferation, drug trafficking, terrorism and militancy are threats to national security.

Afghanistan has been in a state of turbulence till very recent times. In fact, the last three decades saw the people of Afghanistan helplessly watch their government grappling, perhaps ineffectively, with terrorism.

Demography

Perched across the Hindukush like a leaf and geographically landlocked with ingress and egress hemmed in, transnational activity became the only outlet for Afghanistan. For an Afghan, the trade of perishable goods and movement of nomadic tribes across the borders made the concept of transnational activity a very routine one. The task was, of course, facilitated by the numerous passes that dot the entire length of the Hindukush Mountains.

Afghanistan is a peculiar country. Shrouded in mystery, Afghanistan remained lonely, underdeveloped and landlocked, but not impregnable for the large part of the twentieth century. During this period Afghanistan's internal politics underwent a series of changes. The complexity of Afghanistan manifests itself in the social fragmentation of society, which is compounded by geographic isolation, parochial loyalties, limited objectives and a virtual lack of infrastructure that cannot meet the demands of a modern state. Owen

Lattimore has described Afghanistan as 'the Pivot of Asia'. Strategically located, Afghanistan may be described geographically as sixty-five per cent mountainous, twenty per cent desert and only ten to twelve per cent plain. Height declines abruptly from 20,000 ft to 500 ft in less than 700 miles. The windswept Hindukush Mountains astride Afghanistan cause a drainage that takes the bulk of the water out of the country. The inhospitable geography coupled with socially fragmented society and underdevelopment led to a series of political changes. Unable to keep pace with the modernizing developments, the polity faced severe opposition within the country. This led to the mass exodus of *Mujaheddin* into Pakistan and Iran. Unhappy with the results offered by *Mujaheddins* and their infightings, newer configurations emerged in the form of the rigid and fundamentalist Taliban. The struggle between the leadership of a fragmented society, warlords and the government got exacerbated by the easy availability of money that came from the neighbouring oil money, sale of opium that is grown in this part of the world and also the ammunition. Trans-boundary movement of opium, oil money and ammunition became a live ground for terrorist activities of a large proportion, eventually requiring trans-boundary intervention in a US-led coalition against terrorism.

A sparse population, the estimates of which vary, inhabits Afghanistan. Reasons for variation in the estimates are not far to seek. The terrain renders access and communication difficult, if not hazardous. The administrative system in the country is not only inadequately staffed, it suffers from quite a few limitations of different kinds—a sizable chunk of the people are nomadic; and even those with fixed abode, particularly in non-urban settlements, are hidebound to archaic traditions. As a result, the population is assumed at 17.88 milion according to one source; according to another it is 17.08 million, another source puts it at 19.3 million and some give the figures at 25 million. Half of this population, i.e. women were forced by the Taliban to disappear from public view. Density of population per square kilometre is 30 according to one source and 23.9 according to another. Between two and three million people are estimated to be nomadic and semi-nomadic, forever on the move in search of fresh postures for their livestock. Nearly 15 per cent of the population lives in cities and 3.8 per cent in towns. All these statistics have undergone a drastic change as a result of social and political upheaval that Afghanistan has seen in the last four decades.

Together with the physical fragmentation of the country, a fact of crucial importance is the ethnic divisions in the population. Pakhtuns or Pathans are the largest in number–55 per cent and are politically dominant. Tajiks are the next largest ethnic group and comprise 33 per cent of the population. Tajiks speak Dari (a variant of Persian) and are successful in commerce and finance. Both groups are mainly nomadic and both spill over the frontiers of Afghanistan—the Tajiks into the former Soviet Union and the Pathans into Pakistan. Other groups include Uzbeks, Turkomans, Kirghis, Baluchis and Hazaras. Islam is the only force of cohesion among the various ethnic groups. Ninety nine per cent of the people (Pathans, most Tajiks, Uzbeks and Turkomans) are Sunni. Tajiks living in the mountains and Hazaras are Shias. This heterogeneity of the Afghan people is further complicated by their non-literacy. Clearly, thus, Afghan society is divided into the bulk of non-literates and a rather small segment of those who have had modern education abroad. It is this dichotomy that distances the small urban-based 'elite' from the bulk of the Afghan people scattered in the stark non-urban environs of Afghanistan.

- Roughly 1/5 of the 25 million population is staying as refugees outside the country.
- At home millions are homeless.
- Potable water is scarce.
- Three years of drought has ruined agriculture. Dams and irrigation systems including HAVA Helmand and Argandhab Valley Authority have been destroyed.
- Most of the livestock and seeds to plant new crops have been eaten.
- Most schools have been closed for years.
- The last generation of Afghanistan has been decimated with thousands either dead or long since fled Afghanistan.
- Out of three Afghan children one is an orphan; half the children suffer from malnutrition. Estimates indicate that one among five children won't live to see his fifth birthday.
- Approximately 21,000 mines are known to be laid including in the agricultural farms which can be detonated only by 2010 and that too if funds are available. UNDP, World Bank, Asian Development Bank and the Afghan themselves see the urgency of providing an early peace dividend to the people.
- First priority is security, not the multilateral peacekeeping end, but very much personal security in the neighbourhood. They want a police that works.
- Next in line is the resumption of basic services and salaries.
- The challenge is manifold—political, economic and social.

- Afghanistan with weak governments and a socially fragmented society with powerful warlords and gun-toting water lords became an ideal ground manifested with terrorist activities. Easy accessibility of weapons, both country-made and sophisticated and money from heroin trade made Afghanistan a haven for terrorist activities with a potential of dissemination of terrorism to other parts of the world.
- Water lords have held people to ransom with command over meagre water resources.
- A working class has to spring up.

A middle clan has to stabilise for intellectual movement, to raise questions, to demand explanations. The project is unprecedented and the task is daunting. The demography has naturally impacted on Afghanistan's relations with its neighbours. The people of Afghanistan, helpless at the hands of the *Mujaheddin*, Taliban and warlords have no say in the formulation of the policies of their country.

Impact of Demography: Relations with India

India shares a border with Afghanistan only juridically speaking. For India, however, the Central Asia is of abiding interest. In this context, the following key factors are likely to govern the relations between Afghanistan and India. Frontier Gandhi had played an important role in our national struggle for freedom.

Global trends predict that by 2015 India's population would grow from 1 billion to 1.2 billion and at the same time India and China will see dramatic increase in energy consumption. It is also projected that by 2015 only 1/10 of Persian Gulf oil will be directed to Western markets, three quarters will go to Asia. Therefore, Afghanistan and Central Asia become important for India's policymakers.

Indian cannot absolve itself from its responsibility towards Afghanistan with whom she has shared friendship over a long period of time. The destruction of Afghanistan, the stand-off between India and Pakistan can be traced back, step by step, to the compounding of misjudgments by the USSR, USA, India and Pakistan. Jagat S. Mehta (2002) calls this misjudgment a 'march of folly' into Afghanistan. All these countries are "now inclined to selective amnesia"[1] about their own share of guilt at the tragic developments which eventually culminated in many catastrophes including Kargil and 9/11. For example, it is seldom recalled that the Islamic fundamentalists were trained and inducted by the CIA; the Talibans were recruited by Pakistan and India betrayed the Pathans by abstaining from condemning the invasion. With foresight and sensitivity, these could have been avoided. At least Indian policy-makers could have acted differently especially because the foreign policy of India had taken a new direction from globalism to regionalism.

From Globalism to Regionalism—India

If the Simla Agreement (1972) marks a clear shift in India's foreign policy priority from globalism to regionalism, then Afghanistan should have received much more attention at the hands of India's foreign policy makers than it actually did. Globalism continued to be important for India but regionalism had acquired a much larger place in India's foreign policy pre-occupations. After the emergence of Bangladesh (1971) with Indian help, the power configuration in the sub-continent had altered decisively. John P. Lewis in 'Consequences of Giantism – The Case of India' (*World Politics*; 1991) used the term 'giantism' and argues that it is this factor which engendered considerable fear and mistrust among the neighbouring countries. Indian analyst Sunanda K. Dutta-Ray refers to this phenomenon as an Indian version of the Monroe Doctrine[2].

Afghanistan and China

Beijing, for its part, seeks to prevent the dissemination of Islamic extremism particularly because the Islamic threat hangs over the predominantly Muslim region of Sinkiang. Since the early 1990s Sinkiang has witnessed a series of explosions, assassinations and other terrorist acts by Uighur separatists. The Chinese leaders cannot, therefore, fail to be concerned about the activities of Islamic militants in the areas bordering Sinkiang (including Afghanistan). The penetration of Islamic extremists, weapons, explosives and religious teachings from neighbouring Pakistan and Afghanistan into Sinkiang, has given a fillip to Uighur movement and encouraged its demands for the secession of Sinkiang from China.

Boris Rumer in his study on Central Asia mentions that in the year of conflicts in Kosovo, East Timor, Dagestan, Chechnya, Kashgar (one of the two largest cities in Sinkiang) serves as a powerful reminder that China is also vulnerable to the forces of ethnic fragmentation that have atomized other, once seemingly impregnable, authoritarian states.[3] The Sinkiang situation lends credibility to the media reports that Beijing is pressurizing Pakistan to suspend its support for the Taliban in Afghanistan. According to these reports, China has categorically opposed Pakistan pro-Islamic foreign policy and also not supported Pakistan in its foray in Kashmir. China regards Pakistan as a key element in its strategy to block the activity of Islamic fundamentalists, and fear that the Talibans are serving Islamabad as main base for dissemination of aggressive Islam into Central Asia and Sinkiang.

Afghanistan and Central Asia

The Russian and Central Asian press refer to the pan-Islamic grand design, which lies behind the simultaneous assault of Muslim radical along a broad front stretching from Afghanistan to Chechnya. They refer to a unified strategy and coordination of activities by Islamic militants in both Central Asia and Chechnya, all of whom are directed and financed by a single centre. Vadimir Putin (1999) referred to the plan of Muslim radicals to construct 'an enormous pseudo-Muslim state from the Caspian to the Black Sea'. The 'single centre' is personified in Osama Bin Laden.

Both Afghanistan and Pakistan are seen as a 'twilight zone' due to their involvement in Islamic fundamentalism, narcotics and drug trafficking. President Islam Karimov of Uzbekistan has directly accused (1998) Pakistan and Afghanistan and certain political forces in Tajikistan of providing military assistance to Uzbek radicals acting under the banner of Islam. In the fall of 1998 it was revealed that Kyrgyztan was being used as a conduit for the transfer of weapons to Afghanistan[4]. Further, 65 per cent of the opium from Afghanistan reaches Europe after crossing the territories of states in Central Asia.

A gas pipeline 1270–1464 kilometres long from Turkmenistan–Afghanistan–Pakistan with a possible extension to New Delhi evokes much interest for several states. Japan is interested in creating several alternative routes for the export of hydrocarbons from Central Asia. This would enable Japan to reduce its critical dependence on any single route. Japan's position is shared by the European Union, which officially supports the construction of oil and natural gas pipelines through the territory of any country in the region.

New geo-economic formations are emerging in Central Asia and have a clear impact on neighbouring Afghanistan. American oil and energy corporations have become pioneers in the creation of new alliances of interests and they have been active in Central Asia, Iran, Iraq, Afghanistan, China, Russia and so forth. The new geo-economic formations have interested other global states besides the USA. The economic leaders of the Asia-Pacific region have formed mutually complementary schemes to open up Central Asia.

Japan is the principal creditor; China plays the role of leading trading partner of the region and South Korea acts as investor. With efforts through export-import flows, credits, development aid and investments, countries like China, Japan and Korea are drawing the five Central Asian states (especially Kyrgystan,

Kazakhistan and Uzbekistan) into a general system of division of labour. The system of division of labour is taking place under the conditions of globalisation and within the paradigm of competition and cooperation.

Bogged by ethnic conflicts and internecine fights of warlords, Afghanistan finds itself far backward in the fast emerging geo-economic scenario of Central Asia. Afghanistan has to wake up fast if it does not want to miss the revolution occurring in developmental process of this century. *Loya Jirgah*, the Grand Assembly, the time-honoured tradition of Afghanistan conducted recently is an indication that Afghanistan is beginning to move in the right direction.

A New Beginning

A new beginning was marked when the people of Afghanistan adopted a new constitution at the Loya Jirgah. The endorsement of the constitution is in itself an achievement since ethnic divisions and attitudinal differences among the delegates brought the deliberations to the verge of collapse on at least a couple of occasions. Although those differences have not been resolved, adoption of the Constitution signifies that the Afghans are preparing to live by a democratic order. The new dispensation is under pressure from within and without. The warlords who wield power in different parts of Afghanistan will have to continue to make compromises if the new order is to survive the threat from the remnants of Talibans and other forces, which are opposing the constitution. President Hamid Karzai, who had insisted that his office should be powerful so as to ensure unity of the country, softened his stand during the course of the *Jirgah*. He accepted parliamentary supervision over senior appointments and over some spheres of policy making.

The compromise augurs well for the future of Afghanistan. However, the Constitution has certain inbuilt fragilities that will have to be addressed over time. The fault lies in the provisions that seek to balance conflicting demands of democracy and religion. The constitution does not enshrine *Shariah* as the source of law but it does prohibit legislation that is repugnant to Islam. With the largest number of maimed people in the world, with women pushed back by centuries by the Taliban rule, Afghanistan has much to do. A preliminary glance at the recent history of Afghanistan demonstrates that the result of combining industrial and information revolutions in a short period of time has thrown the population of this country into a whirlwind of change.

During the turbulent 1970s and 1980s, Afghanistan's relations with its neighbours underwent many vicissitudes. There is a need to comprehend, analyse and reflect on Afghanistan and its relations with its neighbours. In the understanding of Afghanistan's relations, certain aspects of the Afghanistan characteristic need to be taken cognizance of.

1. Firstly, whether it was the British or the Soviets, both failed to either completely subjugate or indoctrinate the Afghans.
2. Secondly, opposition to the Soviet-sponsored regime led to armed insurrection in all the provinces by fiercely traditional Muslim rebel tribes' men called *Mujaheddin*. Both these characteristics show that Afghans are a people whose spirit is indomitable.

The flight of thousands of refugees to Pakistan and Iran brought about destabilisation in the entire region. This trend was to continue till 2001. Afghanistan became a further quagmire after the Cold War ended and Soviet Union collapsed. By then Afghanistan had become the centre of trade of heroin, easy accessibility of both country-made weapons and oil money.

Things had begun to change in the mid 1960s after the formation of political parties: Khalq (people) and Parcham (flag) both pro-Soviet and a smaller faction, Shula-e-Javed (eternal flame) with pro-Beijing leaning. In the 1970s, a new class emerged which was western educated, and endowed with technological skills, which pressed for smooth absorption into the slowly modernising Afghanistan. It seems the aim of the government of Afghanistan was to become stable economically, administratively, socially and perhaps politically. Daud cashed in the newly emerging awakened elite and joined hands with Parcham with a promise of share in powers. After coming to power, Daud offered pittance of power, which was refused by Parcham and it re-united with Khalq to become PDPA (People's Democratic Party of Afghanistan).

With the coming of Daud, the constitutional period of Afghanistan came to an end. He created a dictatorship dominated by him and his close associates, jailed his critics and disapproved of dissent and arrested PDPA leaders. The situation culminated in a bloody coup called Saur Revolution on 27 April 1978 thereby marking a highlight in Afghanistan's internal politics.

As a result, PDPA came to power with Marxist leader Nur Muhammad Taraki as President and was marked by infighting of Khalq and Parcham factions, thereby embarking on an unstable and turbulent period, bearing the forebodings of the future. Hafizullah Amin overthrew Nur Mohammad Taraki and tried to bring about stability by introducing a series of land reform measures, including reducing of rural debts. Redistribution of lands was announced. But the programme failed due to widespread opposition by armed insurrection in the province leading to the flight of thousands of refugees (*Mujaheddin*) slowly into Pakistan, particularly into the provinces of

Baluchistan and North West Frontier Province (NWFP). This led to further economic dislocation. The number of refugees was swelled by the outflow of:

- Nationalist groups,
- Disillusioned members of Khalq and Parcham, and
- Bureaucrats and people who had suffered repressive acts of the Afghanistan Government.

Originally the Afghan refugees were welcomed in Pakistan because they became the basis for attracting foreign aid, but soon they became a nightmare for Pakistan. Many refugees developed links with local chieftains for lucrative trade in drugs and arms.

At this juncture three *mujaheddin* groups could be identified:

- One operating from within Afghanistan
- Another operating from Pakistan, and
- Those operating from Iran.

The *mujaheddin* were, therefore not a unified force. Seven larger factions were identified. Among them were the ones led by Ahmad Shah Masud known as Gulbuddin Hekmatyar and Yunis Khalis. Amin's repressive policies abetted factionalism within Khalq and Parcham culminating in Soviet entry in December 1979. This event marks the turning point not only for Afghanistan but for the entire region. The Soviet entry of 1979 had the potential of a complete realignment of relations among the countries of South Asia, China and great powers.

Amin was overthrown, executed and replaced by Babrak Karmal. Several attempts were made by both the United Nations and rulers of Afghanistan to sort out the problem but all efforts failed due to one reason or the other. In an attempt to solve the Afghan *mujaheddin* tangle, the UN conducted Geneva Talks under the leadership of Deigo Cordovez and proximity talks were held but not much headway was made. In 1986 Babrak Karmal was removed and Najibullah was installed. As Najibullah was supported by the Soviets he became a natural suspect in the US perception.

Najibullah made an amnesty offer to *mujaheddin*, which was rejected either due to lack of credibility or the fear of reprisals on return to Afghanistan. Around this time, the Soviet Union was in deep trouble at home and wanted to withdraw from Afghanistan. Consequently, Afghanistan found itself confronted with two major problems: first, the withdrawal of Soviet troops and resultant power vacuum and second, the question of return of *mujaheddin* .

Further, the departure of Soviet troops involved related questions like:

- Soviet aid and armed assistance would come to a halt.

- Fate of Kabul government.
- Shape of the future government of Afghanistan.
- Nature of withdrawal.

These issues were discussed under the aegis of Geneva Talks where the Soviet Union suggested a withdrawal in phases from individual regions beginning with the south in a 4-year period. Pakistan wanted withdrawal within 4 months. Consequently, the timetable for withdrawal of troops evaded solution. In 1987, a National Reconstruction Plan was launched with an aim to attract businessmen, doctors and others, back to Afghanistan by providing job offers and exempting them from income tax. About 80,000 accepted the offer and 10,000 promised to give up insurgency.

During the period 1987-88, Jane's Manual has recorded that US arms deliveries to *mujaheddins* were valued at £630 million. With so many arms pumped in, the *mujaheddins* continued to remain a powerful fragmented force and the situation remained volatile in Afghanistan. William Maley in his book *Fundamentalism Reborn? Afghanistan and the Taliban*, has referred to the failure of UN missions one after the other since 1992 and the reasons he cites are: after the Soviet withdrawal, the UN envoys overlooked important players of the Afghanistan conflict[5]. The transitional government that replaced Najibullah regime was set up without consultation of the *mujaheddin* commanders who were the centre of power inside Afghanistan. The task of UN envoys became even more difficult after the fall of the Soviet Union. Jagat S. Mehta in *The March of Folly in Afghanistan* has argued that rational alternatives were rejected due to misperceptions of the USSR, USA, India and Pakistan. This led to militarisation of the subcontinent and the assembling by CIA of Islamic fundamentalism in Pakistan. Pakistan recruited the Talibans and helped them to overrun Afghanistan and impose a medieval religious polity. India stood marginalized in the scenario.

Talibanisation

After the fall of Rabbani came the Taliban-politico–religious force that ruled area 80 per cent area of Afghanistan from 1992 to 1996. To many, Taliban was to be translated as 'Fundamentalism Re-born' only much later, because originally Talibans used the disenchantment against the existing *mujaheddin* for coming to power. Two features of the Taliban which received attention in the beginning were: the Pakistani link of the Talibans, and their Islamic ideology. Nothing untoward was seen about these features, because Afghanistan had been a Muslim majority state and Pakhtuns, the majority ethnic community had ruled the country through the ups and downs of history. Therefore, Talibans became a military force, which enabled them to sweep the country at a lightening speed. Afghanistan's neighbour Pakistan played a vital role in grooming the Talibans in the *madrassas* located in the NWFP area. Talibans' victory in Kandahar was followed by their victories in the rest of Afghanistan including the capital Kabul. In this task, Pakistan supplied the Talibans with the logistics of war and the necessary military planning and training. In these new developments, Pakistani's generals saw an opportunity to create what they perceived as 'strategic depth' for their country, which they otherwise lacked. Besides this, former Khalq party's military personnel among the Talibans played important role. After 1992 when the Cold War ended, the US had no effective policy towards Afghanistan. It merely followed Pakistan in their policies towards the militia force and hoped that the Taliban would

- Ban narcotics, including poppy growing and heroin refinement.
- Restore security for construction of oil pipeline from Central Asia to Pakistan.
- Contain Iran and Russia.
- Eliminate terrorist groups operating within Afghanistan.

The discordant voice against Taliban came from Iran who along with the minority groups likes Tajiks, Hazaras and Uzbeks perceived the entry of Talibans as an attempt to reintroduce Pakhtun hegemony in Afghanistan thereby undermining the plural character of Afghanistan. The Taliban imposed a very narrow interpretation of the *Shariat* and originally this was seen as an attempt to bring about a semblance of order and peace in the country to facilitate closer units with Central Asia. But slowly the process of Talibanisation showed its harsher side. In Afghanistan, secularism, which is the proud boast of democracies, was regarded as hearsay and agnosticism even of philosophers, an offence, which carried death penalty. Music became an affront and thousand-year-old statues were not considered as gifts of ancient civilizations but as objects of hatred that needed to be destroyed by dynamite.

Talibans condemned the women to live in a life long concealment. The girls were banned from schools by edicts of holy men. Here one of the most sinister nightmares of Orwell's 1984, 'the 'thought police' is street presence[6]. It is also called the religious police, it can boot you out of your house if you are found reading a book when you should be praying, or to a place of public flogging for the crime of not keeping a beard. The Taliban tried to gain credibility but it got recognition from only three states, viz. Pakistan, UAE and Saudi Arabia. Its fundamentalism including closure of schools, position of women and even issues like growing a beard alienated the Taliban government, both domestically and internationally. Their support to the Saudi billionaire Osama Bin Laden was the last straw in the camel's back, especially when his connection was revealed with the September 11, 2001 attack on the World Trade Center and Pentagon, the economic and military bastions of the USA. The presence of Saudi dissident Osama Bin Laden in Afghanistan was initially an embarrassment to Afghanistan. But when pressure for his extradition increased, the Taliban leadership refused extradition. It, however, announced that Laden would not be allowed to use Afghan soil to target other countries.

During the six-year Taliban rule in Afghanistan, Pakistan's support to the Taliban was loud and clear. Pakistan supported the terrorist rule in Afghanistan. Taliban or the students of Islam or *Jehadis* promoted a strict Islamic code of conduct in Afghanistan. Pakistan played an important role. It was the first country to recognise the Taliban government in Afghanistan. The Taliban factor had an important impact on Pakistan's foreign policy. Pakistan being an Islamic country fully supported the cause of militant Taliban organisation. Pakistan also gave military training support to the Talibans besides providing funds. There are still many training camps in Pakistan which provide military know-how to the youth from Afghanistan and Kashmir youth in the name of *Jihad* or holy war. Pakistan's compulsions were that being an Islamic state it began to impart religious education in the *madrassas* in NWFP, area, which was housing the refugees. Slowly over the time, these *madrassas* became the ground for promoting terrorist activities in the neighbouring areas. In Pakistan-occupied Kashmir (PoK) alone, it has been reported that there are 80 camps[7].

However Pakistan's pre-occupation with Afghanistan and support to Taliban billionaire Osama Bin Laden underwent a volte-face after the 11 September attack on WTC towers and Pentagon—the economic and military strongholds of the USA. After the new and changed situation, the Pakistan government began to assist the US-led coalition by providing military bases in Pakistan with an aim to overthrow the Taliban government in Afghanistan. While Taliban was consolidating its grip on Afghanistan with the help of Saudi money and Pakistani arms, India needed to re-think its strategy and in this respect, it may be mentioned here that Indian diplomacy failed. Consequently, India found itself increasingly marginalized in the Afghan affairs.

Threat to demolish Bamiyan Buddhas and its final destruction in March 2001 turned out to be an early warning of the events that were to follow in September 2001. This event thereby throws light on a series of unanswered questions and raises several issues: Did the Taliban carry out their threat because they were not being heard at international level and they wanted to attract world attention? Were they laying the foundation for the deadly events that were to unfold on 11 September, 2001?

- Despite the threats of Taliban leader Mullah Mohammad Omar to demolish the statues, a hope lingered that some last moment consultations would actually save the statues from destruction.
- Pre-Islamic past of Afghanistan was given a severe blow.
- Frustration of Talibans was exposed. Perhaps the frustration had reached a point of helplessness forcing the Talibans to resort to such means of destruction.
- Act of terrorism had deprived Afghanistan of its cultural heritage—a past it was proud of.
- UNESCO and countries like India and Sri Lanka had offered to buy the statues—all offers had failed.
- Why was the offer rejected?
- Was the amount offered low?
- Did the Talibans suffer a genuine grouse and felt further affronted by the offer?
- Was it the result of segregating Afghanistan both economically and physically?
- Could it be traced back to the Osama Bin Laden issue?

The Taliban's Islamic militia blew up the Bamiyan Buddhas and scores of other pre-Islamic figures throughout the country in line with a decree issued in February 2001 from the Supreme Leader Mullah Mohammad Omar. Designed to stop idolatry, the desolation went ahead despite repeated pleas from Muslim and Buddhist countries as well as the UN, the European Union (EU), the Organisation of the Islamic Congress and major museums of the world. Top Islamic scholars from Egypt also failed to convince the Taliban that the edict had no foundation in Islam. Director General of UNESCO, Koichiro Matsuura commented that 'while this crime was being committed, people all over the world raised their voices in protest.[8] Neither the unprecedented scope of international mobilization nor the widespread opposition to their decision expressed by the highest religious authorities of Islam was to be heeded.[9]

The puritanical militia, recognized only by Pakistan, Saudi Arabia and the United Arab Emirates, said it was 'shameful' to have huge statues in an Islamic country and they were 'proud' to tear them down. Mohammad Bashir, an educated Afghan lashed out at the ruling Taliban Islamic militia for the 'brutal' demolition of two ancient Buddha sculptures[10]. The destruction of Buddha, created between the second and fifth centuries A.D. was an irreparable loss to the ancient history of Afghanistan, once a meeting ground on the Silk Road between Asia and Europe. The destruction of ancient Bamiyan Buddha's statues, referred to as 'cultural crime' have brought into focus the need for safeguarding world heritage and for promoting cultural pluralism, inter-cultural and inter-religious dialogue.

Although Afghanistan played a central role in the development of many ancient civilizations, in recent years it has become marginalized in world affairs because of the Afghan government's inability to participate in the global economy. Afghanistan traditional society, its people and culture have remained resistant to change and some analysts refer to this as counter-globalization. Unfortunately the term counter-globalization is considered as synonymous with anti-global. But if we examine Afghan cultural and economic institutions and practices it is revealed that Afghans have actually been operating outside rather than against globalization. This is best illustrated by the *Hawallah* system, which operates in Afghanistan. An understanding of the ideological underpinning and operations of *Hawallah* system in Afghanistan is crucial in determining the chances of success of current and long-term economic development programmes in Afghanistan. This can help identify necessary changes in foreign policies of nations seeking to implement a developmental model in Afghanistan especially in dealing with the closed nature of that system.

Policies Needed

1. Multi-ethnic people-to-people contacts.
2. Opposition to Jehadis' terrorism spawned by fundamentalist forces.
3. Political and diplomatic support to Tajikistan, Uzbekistan, Kyrgystan and North Alliance.
4. The complementary role played by military diplomacy to serve India's national interests and for peace and stability in the region.

The situation in Afghanistan can at best be described as uncertain.[11] Afghan warlords remain strong, active and independent. They have the private police and armies loyal to them. Their capacity to pay and purchase loyalty from their followers depends upon drug trade, which continues unabated. Only a de-weaponisation programme, which is yet to start, will reduce the authority and autonomy of warlords. India's External Affairs Minister Yashwant Sinha's visit to Kabul in August 2002 to Herat and Mazar-i-Sharif in August 2002 served several purposes:

- India's commitment to Hamid Karzai government in its quest for peace and stability in Afghanistan.

- Active participation in Afghanistan's reconstruction activities.
- Consolidation of our people-to-people contacts.
- Help to repair ethnic cleavages that have emerged in Afghan society in recent years.

India is already playing an important role in the reconstruction of Afghanistan, besides a financial assistance of $21.5 million and a $100 million credit.

The restoration of stability in Afghanistan is a matter of urgent necessity. With Taliban and Al-Qaida elements still active in the field the central government must have the ability to enforce order all over the country. However, a confrontation between central government and regional warlords is dangerous especially because the former *mujaheddin* commanders claim that they are entitled to retain control over different regions and ethnic groups because they have defended their respective bases against the Soviets and the Talibans. Afghanistan has to sort out the issue of decentralization of powers. In this respect Afghanistan can learn from India's federal structure. Afghanistan can learn as well as be an example for various issues in the neighbouring region, which share same culture and ethos.

The changed conditions in the northwestern parts of the subcontinent provide an opportunity for re-thinking many of the traditional premises of enduring rivalry between India and Pakistan in Afghanistan. India and Pakistan have viewed each other warily in Afghanistan since the partition in 1947. Besides, Pakistan has been uncomfortable with the active diplomatic presence of India in Afghanistan since the ouster of Talibans. Pakistan has seen Afghanistan as constituting its strategic depth. Accordingly, one aim of Pakistan foreign policy has been to install a regime in Afghanistan which is politically close to Islamabad. Its objective could not be fulfilled as a result of unprecedented internationalization of Afghanistan's security after the ouster of Talibans' regime. There might be sections of Pakistan army, which still hope for the better, once the US attention is no longer in Kabul. This, however, does not seem to be a possibility in the near future.

India cannot wish Pakistan away in Afghanistan. The geopolitical reality of a long and uncontrolled border between the two nations will always provide political opportunities for Pakistan. The emphasis on short-term interests and a sense of rivalry has forced New Delhi and Islamabad to undercut each other in Kabul. However, a changed scenario requires rethinking on the part of both India and Pakistan. It is in the interest of both India and Pakistan to promote a stable, independent, politically moderate and modernizing Afghanistan. Further the long-term regional economic interests of both India and Pakistan demand that they cooperate in Afghanistan. Both New Delhi and Islamabad are already involved in many projects such as road building in Afghanistan. India and Pakistan could jointly work out a trade and transit treaty with Afghanistan. Such an arrangement would benefit all three and link the subcontinent with Central Asia. The possibility of a meeting ground[12] in Afghanistan seems to be round the corner.

Conclusion

It can be concluded that India should have had an edge over other countries by knowing and understanding the region in far better terms such as cultural, religious, lingual connectivity. India's immediate engagement with Pakistan left much to be done. Hence, India's focus was neither Afghanistan nor Central Asia. India needs to take a pragmatic view and to adopt a cooperative attitude in order to march ahead on its path of searching for a major power status, which it deserves. If India neglects the Afghan issue any further it will lead to two fallouts. One, distancing from people of Afghanistan, who are already unhappy with Indian shortsightedness of supporting Soviet entry into Afghanistan and can damage India's interest in Central Asia. Two, India will continue to suffer from the spillover effect of terrorism through Pakistan in its state of Jammu and Kashmir. Pakistan is a key link and the ground seems to be ready for cooperation perhaps on the lines of the European Union. ■

Notes & References

1. Jagat S. Mehta, *The March of Folly in Afghanistan*, 1978-2001, New Delhi, 2002, p. 11.
2. *International Herald Tribune*, April 12, 1989.
3. Boris Rumer, ed., *Central Asia and the New Global Economy*, New Delhi, 2003, p. 27.
4. Zhukov, Stanislav, "Basic Problems of Market Transition in Central Asia", n. 3, p. 83.
5. William Maley, *Fundamentalism Reborn? Afghanistan and the Taliban*, New York, 1998.
6. Manohar Malgonkar, "A Land stalked by the Thought Police", *The Tribune*, October 7, 2001, p. 8.
7. *Hindustan Times*, July 19, 2002, p. 1.
8. Koichiro Matsuura, "International Seminar on Bamiyan: Challenge to World Heritage", New Delhi, September 17–18, 2001.
9. Ibid.
10. *Hindustan Times*, 14 March 2001.
11. Pain Adam, "Afghanistan, A Failed State?", *Economic and Political Weekly*, Vol. 36, No. 44, p. 4179, August 2002.
12. C. Raja Mohan, "A Meeting Ground in Afghanistan", *The Hindu*, September 23, 2004, p. 10.

Energy Scenario in South Asia: A Case Study of India's Energy Policy

Mohd. Monir Alam*

Energy has become an essential component for sustaining and enlarging modern economic development of a nation. In the context of South Asia, since economic and population growth have resulted in a rapid increase in energy demand, all countries have been forced to diversify different sources to meet a domestic requirements of growing demand of energy.[1] In fact, when much of the South Asian countries achieved independence from British colonial rule, the socio-political and economic conditions throughout the region stood at relatively similar levels. While these countries still demonstrate many important similarities, significant variations have emerged on the issue of endowment of natural energy resources. Of course, the varying degrees of energy profiles in South Asia are particularly intriguing, considering the similar historical and geographical backgrounds shared by these countries. But notwithstanding the differences in natural energy endowments of different nations, the institutional and historical similarities suggest that there is more space for cooperation between these countries.

All South Asian countries which are dependent on imported fuels from the Gulf region realized the importance of energy security issues with the onset of the Arab oil embargo in 1973 when prices of crude oil jumped from $2 per barrel to more than $10. Thus, after the oil shocks of the 1970s and subsequent disruptions in the supply of hydrocarbon fuels from the Gulf region, South Asian countries have focused on demand management, investment in energy-saving technologies and alternative sources of energy to ensure uninterrupted supply of hydrocarbons fuels. Still, they are not in a position to meet growing domestic energy demand.

* Fellow, Centre for Strategic and Regional Studies, University of Jammu, Jammu.

Moreover, increasing dependence on imported oil and gas, rising future demand of hydrocarbon fuels, frequent price hike of crude oil in the international market, political instability in the Gulf region, etc. all have together posed pressing challenges for South Asia to undertake and reformulate comprehensive energy security strategy in this new millennium. In order to reduce dependency over imported energy fuels, the countries of South Asia are looking towards diversifying traditional energy supply sources by expanding the use of indigenous energy resources; promoting additional foreign investment for energy infrastructure development; improving energy efficiency; reforming and privatizing energy sectors and promoting and expanding regional energy trade and investment.[2]

This paper focuses on the energy scenario in South Asia. After analyzing the energy security profile of the entire region, it concentrates upon India's growing energy demand and different mechanisms adopted by the government to ensure its future energy security.

South Asia—Status of Present Energy Mix

As already stated, high economic growth rate and increasing population in South Asia have resulted in a rapid increase in overall energy demand. The region's energy demand increased from 72 million metric ton of oil equivalent (MMTOE) in 1971 to 315 MMTOE by 1997, registering an annual growth rate of 6% during the period.[3] Figure 1 shows growth of primary energy supply and increasing demand in South Asia.

Figure 1: Growth in primary energy demand in South Asia

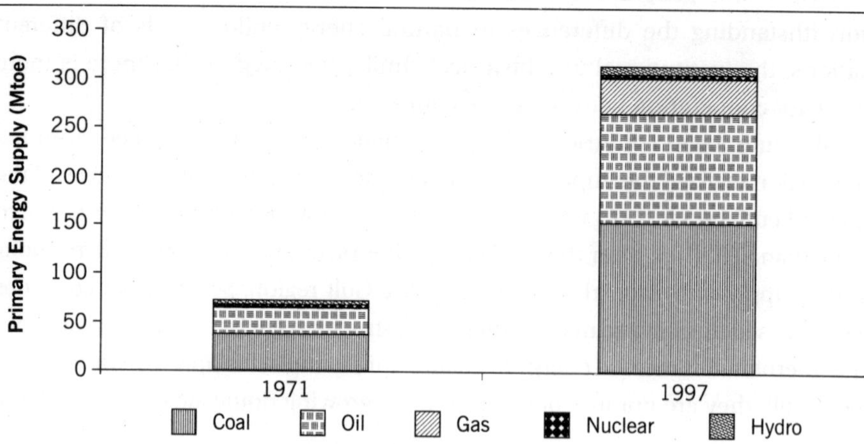

Source : *World Energy Outlook, 2000.*

According to the Energy Information Administration (EIA) reports, South Asia's primary commercial energy consumption in 2001 accounted for approximately 3.8 per cent of world commercial energy consumption, up from 2.8 per cent in 1991.[4] However, despite rapid growth in energy demand, South Asia continues to average among the lowest levels of per capita energy consumption in the world, but among the highest in terms of energy consumption per unit of Gross Domestic Product (GDP). Discounting 'non-commercial' sources of energy, South Asia's commercial energy mix in 2001 was 49 per cent coal, 35 per cent petroleum, 12 per cent natural gas, 3 per cent hydroelectricity and 1 per cent nuclear. Thus, the region's energy mix is dominated by coal, while the share of oil is close to the world average, but the share of natural gas is well below the world average of 23 per cent.[5] (Figure 2 shows the primary energy mix in South Asia).

However, there are significant variations of primary energy mix within the region. Bangladesh's energy mix, for instance, is dominated by natural gas (66 per cent in 2001), while India relies heavily on coal (51 per cent). Sri Lanka and the Maldives are overwhelmingly dependent on petroleum (83 per cent and 100 per cent, respectively); Pakistan is diversified among petroleum (43 per cent), natural gas (41per cent) and hydroelectricity (12 per cent).[6] Finally, the Himalayan countries of Nepal and Bhutan have the highest shares of hydroelectric power in their energy consumption mix. (Figure 3 shows energy consumption in South Asia). In recent years, natural gas identified as the fuel of the 21st century, has been growing in importance as a source of energy in India, especially for use in power generation, fertilizer and petrochemical production.

Figure 2: Primary Energy Mix in South Asia

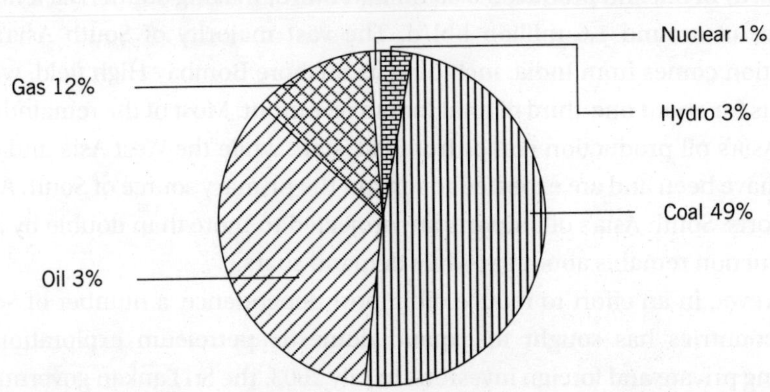

Source: *World Energy Outlook, 2003.*

Figure 3. Energy Consumption in South Asian Countries, 2001

	Commercial Energy Consumption *						
	Total (Quadrillion Btu	Petroleum	Natural Gas	Coal	Nuclear	Hydroelectric	Other**
Bangladesh	0.57	31%	66%	1%	0%	2%	0%
Bhutan	0.02	13%	0%	7%	0%	80%	0%
India	13.99	32%	7%	51%	2%	5%	0%
Maldives	0.01	100%	0%	0%	0%	0%	0%
Nepal	0.06	55%	0%	15%	0%	31%	1%
Pakistan	1.83	43%	41%	5%	1%	12%	0%
Sri Lanka	0.19	83%	0%	0%	0%	17%	0%
Total	**16.67**	**34%**	**12%**	**46%**	**1%**	**6%**	**0.3%**

- It does not include such "non-commercial" energy sources as animal waste, wood, and other biomass, which account for more than half of South Asia's total final energy consumption.
- Other includes consumption of wind electric power for India and net imports of electricity for India and Nepal.

Source: Energy Information Administration, International Energy Database, October 2004.

As far as hydrocarbon resource, especially oil availability in the region is concerned, South Asia contains only 5.8 billion barrels of oil, around 0.5 per cent of the world supply. In 2001, the region consumed around 2.4 million barrels per day (bbl/d) of oil, and produced 0.80 million bbl/d, making South Asia a net oil importer of around 1.6 million bbl/d. The vast majority of South Asia's oil production comes from India, including its offshore Bombay High field, which accounts for about one-third of total Indian oil output. Most of the remainder of South Asia's oil production comes from Pakistan, while the West Asia and Gulf region have been and are expected to remain the primary source of South Asian oil imports. South Asia's oil imports are projected to more than double by 2020 as production remains about flat while demand soars.[7]

However, in an effort to reduce oil import dependence, a number of South Asian countries has sought to expand domestic petroleum exploration by attracting private and foreign investors. In July 2003, the Sri Lankan government approved the 'Petroleum Resources Act', which allows for private and foreign investment in its offshore oil and gas fields. At the same time, Pakistan executed its first 'Production Sharing Agreements' with exploration companies based in France, Malaysia and Austria. Similarly, India has also implemented its 1997 New Exploration Licensing Policy (NELP) to increase foreign involvement in exploration.

In fact, growing demand for transportation fuels and increased industrial power demand have been major factors behind the growth in South Asian oil consumption. Between 1990 and 2000, South Asian oil consumption—led by India—grew by about 75 per cent, and EIA's International Energy Outlook 2003 projects India's oil consumption will grow another 33 per cent by 2010, reaching 2.8 million bbl/d (up from 2.1 million bbl/d in 2000). In Sri Lanka, where oil is the dominant source of energy, oil consumption roughly doubled between 1991 and 2000. Sri Lanka imports all of its crude oil, which is used largely for electricity generation and transportation and has a refining capacity of 50,000 bbl/d. In recent years, Sri Lanka has further increased oil imports in an effort to diversify away from over reliance on hydroelectricity.[8]

In case of natural gas, the fuel of the 21st century, at the end of 2004 South Asia's proven natural gas reserves were estimated at 63.9 trillion cubic feet (Tcf), or about 1 per cent of the world total, with potentially larger resources suspected. India's and Pakistan's reserves are roughly equal in size at 27 Tcf, while the only other South Asian country with reserves, Bangladesh, contains approximately 11 Tcf. Currently, there is much speculation about the actual level of Bangladeshi reserves, with foreign energy companies such as Shell and Unocal believing that the country's reserves may be higher than the official figure. The US Geological Survey recently estimated that Bangladesh contains an additional 32.1 Tcf in "undiscovered reserves".[9] If the higher estimates prove to be correct, Bangladesh could at some point become a major gas producer as well as supplier to the vast potential market in neighbouring India.

Currently, all natural gas production in South Asia is consumed domestically. Moreover, it is playing an important part in supplying new power plants in the region, plus as a means of diversifying away from expensive oil imports. As a result, use of natural gas has increased rapidly in South Asia, growing about 72 per cent between 1991 and 2000. In 2001, the region produced and consumed around 1.98 Tcf of natural gas. Around 42 per cent of this was accounted for by Pakistan, 40 per cent by India and the remaining 18 per cent by Bangladesh.[10] Indian consumption of natural gas has risen faster than any other fuel. Now it accounts for around 6 per cent of the country's energy demand. From nearly 0.8 Tcf in 2000, Indian gas demand is projected in the International Energy Outlook 2003 to reach 1.3 Tcf in 2005 and 1.8 Tcf in 2010, a significant and rapid increase.[11] Increased use of natural gas in power generation will account for most of the increase, as the Indian government is encouraging the construction of gas-fired electric power plants in coastal areas where they can be easily supplied with LNG by sea. Like India, Pakistan plans to make gas the "fuel of choice" for future electric power generation projects, a move that will necessitate a sharp rise in production and imports of natural gas. Meanwhile, natural gas is already Bangladesh's primary source of commercial energy.

Thus, current domestic consumption of natural gas and the long-term projections of its rapidly increasing demand in South Asia will require both significant increases in production as well as imports. But even with expanded production, increased consumption of natural gas in South Asia is constrained by the region's non-cooperation as well as inadequate domestic infrastructure. Gas imports require construction of infrastructure—either cross-border pipelines or liquefied natural gas (LNG) facilities. However, a number of such infrastructure onshore and offshore projects has been proposed in South Asia with varying degrees of success. In that direction, Iran–Pakistan–India Gas Pipeline; involving Pakistan with the Dolphin Project—a scheme to supply gas from Qatar's North Dome gas field to the United Arab Emirates and Oman; Turkmenistan–Afghanistan–Pakistan Gas Pipeline; and Bangladesh–India–Myanmar–Sri Lanka–Thailand–Economic Cooperation (BIMST-EC); an effort for a gas pipeline from Thailand to India, are some of the proposals which might help in solving future energy crisis in South Asia.

India's Energy Policy

India ranks sixth in the world in terms of energy consumption, accounting for 3.5 per cent of world's primary energy (commercially traded fuels only) consumption.[12] Hydrocarbon energy constitutes 41 per cent of Indian commercial energy consumption. After a major oil discovery in Mumbai High in 1974, India had a good balance of self-dependence to the extent of about 70 per cent, which slowly declined to less than 30 per cent. At present, India has a high oil import dependency of around 69 per cent with around 67 per cent of crude imports from the Gulf region which consumes a large chunk of foreign exchange reserves and puts enormous pressure on balance of payment.[13] Currently, since the price of crude oil has already touched $70 per barrel in the international market, India is forced to spend huge foreign exchange to meet the domestic energy demand.

In the case of crude oil, its consumption was 107.27 million metric tonnes of oil equivalent (MMTOE) in 2002–2003, out of which 32 million metric tonnes were met through indigenous domestic sources while remaining 78 million metric tonnes came from imports.[14] Moreover, consumption of oil has grown at a rate of 4.6 per cent in India during the last decade and is expected to increase at the rate of 6 per cent in another two decades, which is much higher in comparison to most of the countries of Asia Pacific.[15] Thus, the demand for crude oil and petroleum products is expected to grow to 173 million metric tones in 2006-2007, 190 MMTOE in 2012 and 364 MMTOE in 2025 of which 85 per cent of consumption would met from imports.[16] According to the Ministry of Petroleum and Gas, the demand of gas in the financial year 2002-2003 amounted to 81.3 million standard cubic meters per day (MSCMD). According to the forecast of "India's Energy Hydrocarbon Vision-2025" gas which is going to replace oil in future, its consumption will grow significantly, rising to 231 MSCMD in 2006-07, 313 MSCMD in 2011-12, and 391 MSCMD in 2024-25 respectively.[17]

Since India is trying to achieve anticipated economic growth of 7–8 per cent in another two decades, this pace of economic development will project India among the top four consumers of energy just behind the United States, China and Japan and ahead of countries like France and United Kingdom. However, to meet the future demand of hydrocarbon resources, the recent decisions of the Union Cabinet while authorising the Ministry of Petroleum and Natural Gas to start negotiations with Pakistan, Iran, Bangladesh and Myanmar on various proposed gas pipelines projects indicates India's future energy security concerns. Current available energy sources, both oil and gas in these regions can be an important source for ensuring the future energy security of India.

Present Strategies to tackle Oil and Gas Crisis

Currently, to meet the growing domestic energy demand, India is trying to achieve energy security with intense domestic exploration; acquiring overseas hydrocarbon assets and restructuring of state-run oil firms. Earlier, to enhance domestic crude production, the Government of India, under the Chairmanship of Finance Minister, had set the following foreign policy objectives of the new Energy Policy in "Hydro-carbon Vision 2025" document, which was instituted in February 1999:

(a) Mobilisation of investment from the private sector including the foreign companies for the domestic sector on attractive fiscal terms;
(b) 100 per cent exploration coverage of Indian sedimentary basins by 2025;
(c) Expansion and diversification of foreign sources of oil and gas supplies;
(d) Ensuring the existing supplies by consolidating energy ties.[18]

However, to limit its dependence on huge oil and gas imports, government has already adopted an aggressive policy to expeditiously explore the sedimentary basins within India's economic zone and also to acquire equity of oil and gas abroad. In this regard, government has already pursued the "New Exploration Licensing Policy".

NELP is an attempt to limit India's dependence on oil and gas imports. This policy permits foreign oil consortiums in exploration of oil and gas which was only restricted to Indian state-owned firms. After launching of the New Exploration Licensing Policy from round I-V, Indian government has offered more than 90 exploration blocks, out of which 52 blocks have been offered to the Oil and Natural Gas Company (ONGC) and rest to private firms along with foreign energy consortiums. Annually, an investment of about US $500 million is taking place in exploration of sedimentary basin areas. Along with Indian Oil Companies, many foreign Oil Consortiums are engaged in the exploration process. For example: Niko Resources of Canada, Cairn Energy and British Hardy Oil of United Kingdom, Gazporam of Russia, Mosbacher Energy of United States and Geopetrol of France are drilling sedimentary basins in different parts of India.[19]

A positive result of NELP has already started pouring in. Reliance Industries along with Niko Resources of Canada have already discovered the country's biggest natural gas reserves in the Krishna–Godavari Basin estimated to have about 10–14 Tcf of gas. After full operation of this project, India can get about 30 million cubic meters gas per day which can add 50 per cent in the present gas supply.[20] Excellent prospects so far are indicated for Krishna–Godavari Basin, Mahanadi Delta, and even around the Andaman and Nicobar Islands. ONGC, Gazporam and Gas Authority of India Limited (GAIL) are further exploring Krishna-Godavari Basin and British Gas is developing Panna-Mukta field. Moreover, the recent discovery by Cairn Energy in Barmer (Rajasthan) and by ONGC at Vasai on the West Coast could be described as stepping stones towards oil security of the country.

India's Overseas Energy Strategies

While there is no declared policy stipulation pertaining to India's overseas energy policies, steps taken by the government of India indicate that there has been a forward thrust of a resolute kind in India's overseas energy policy. Thus, while intensive efforts continue to find oil and gas within Indian economic zone, an annual investment of about US $ one billion is planned for acquiring equity oil abroad. Till now, already more than $5 billion investment has been made in

Russia, Sudan, Myanmar, Kazakhstan and Vietnam on acquisition of properties. This is aimed at oil security and protection against volatility in oil prices.

Indian companies primarily ONGC Videsh Limited (OVL) are engaged in buying stakes and joint ventures in the overseas oil and gas development activities. The countries that are high on OVL's procurement plan include Russia, Libya, Vietnam, Iran, Kazakhstan, Syria, Iraq, Myanmar, Indonesia and Sri Lanka. The OVL plans to invest $3 billion abroad during the Tenth-Five Year Plan. Its first project abroad, which has started production, is in Vietnam. In Vietnam, estimated gas production capacity is 3 billion cubic meters per year, of which OVL's share will be 45 per cent. OVL has acquired 20 per cent stake in Sakhalin project in Russia in 2001, which would add about 5 million tonnes annually of oil from 2005 and 8 million cubic meter of gas per day from 2008.[21] This project is the biggest OVL investment abroad. Indian consortiums consist of OVL, Indian Oil Corporation and Oil India Limited is engaged in Farsi Block in Iran. Yangon—a consortium from Myanmar, DAEWOO from South Korea and ONGC and GAIL have discovered Myanmar's biggest offshore gas field around 4.7 Tcf to 5.8 Tcf, is extremely encouraging.[22] GAIL is currently conducting a techno-economic study for three alternatives to evacuate the gas from Myanmar: (a) Onshore pipeline through north-eastern Indian region; (b) offshore pipeline across Bay of Bengal; (c) and LNG import possibilities.

Apart from these joint ventures in the overseas oil and gas development activities, OVL and United States-based exploration firm IPR are engaged in Syria. OVL and National Oil Company of Turkey TBAO are exploring two blocks in Libya. OVL and Talisman Energy Inc. of Canada are engaged in exploration process in the Muglad basin of Greater Nile Project in Sudan. Apart from joint ventures in drilling and exploration process, OVL has also established contract partnership with BP Amaco, China National Petroleum Corporation, DAEWOO International Corporation and Korea Gas Corporation of South Korea, EXXON Mobil, RN Astra and SMNG of Russia, SODECO of Japan, STATOIL of Norway and Petro Oil of Vietnam in various exploration projects abroad. The logic behind ONGC-OVL investment in foreign oil fields and leaving many domestic oil blocks for private and foreign companies is to ensure uninterrupted supply of oil and gas from external sources while engaging them in strategic and technical alliance.

However, the complexities involved in pipeline locale, India have already taken steps towards supply of gas through chain of tankers. India has already signed a 25-year contract with Rasgas Company of Qatar and Iran for supply of 7 million metric tones of crude gas. The natural gas is thus converted into liquid form and shipped in these specialised vessels to Dahej terminals in Gujarat.[23] India has also decided to set up 15 million tonnes of strategic crude reserves to meet emergency consumption needs on the lines of the United States and Japan.[24]

Alternative Ways of Energy

Apart from domestic and overseas extensive search for hydrocarbon resources, Government of India is also looking for some alternatives to reduce the dependency on oil and gas. India has already taken initiatives to develop "Coal Bed Methane" (CBM) and "Underground Coal Gasification" (UCG) production. By this, India has joined the select club of CBM countries along with the USA, UK, Australia and China.[25] ONGC is also doing a pilot research and development programme for the extraction of gas hydrates from the ocean floor. India and Russia are together developing the technology for deep-sea mining of gas hydrates.

The Government of India is also doing extensive research to get "Ethanol Blended Petrol", a renewable source of energy extracted from molasses, which is a by-product of sugar industry and available throughout the country. In the first phase, 5 per cent ethanol blended petrol has been a success in the 8 states of Uttar Pradesh, Punjab, Haryana, Maharashtra, Gujarat, Goa, Andhra Pradesh and Karnataka and three union territories of Chandigarh, Dadra and Nagar Haveli and Daman and Diu. The second phase which has already begun from January 1, 2004 with Uttaranchal, Madhya Pradesh, Tamil Nadu and Pondichery. In the third phase 10 per cent blending of ethanol with petrol would be initiated all over the country. But important achievement has taken place on "Bio-Diesel". Various central institutes have identified around 100 such plants, which can be used as a substitute of diesel. The seed of jatropa plant are more effective in this regard. Cultivation over 2000 hectares land every year, particularly either side of railway tracks is taking place. Indian Railways is experimenting with the economy-friendly bio-diesel fuel to run the passenger trains. The successful trial of super fast passenger train was conducted on December 31, 2002 when Delhi–Amritsar Shatabdi Express used five per cent of bio-diesel as fuel. The Indian Railways plans to use 10 per cent mixture with the conventional diesel and later it would go up 15 per cent as per accepted global norms.

India has also signed an international project in Washington in November 2003 "the International Partnership on Hydrogen Economy" to develop hydrogen fuel. Apart from India, the USA and European Community, 14 other countries are participating in it. The Planning Commission had constituted four groups to study different areas like production, storage and distribution, application and safety aspects related to hydrogen energy. The Group has already submitted the reports and the Planning Commission is likely to draw a road map for the country. However, with a view to reduce dependency on fossil fuels, there is need to produce hydrogen from renewable sources like biomass, solar energy, etc. Recently, the US government has shown its interest to cooperate India in the field of hydrogen fuel.[26] Growth of hydrogen as an independent energy source will be an important factor in future energy supplies. Vehicles can run by fuel cell technique. Moreover, to ensure security of oil trade routes India and United States have already started military cooperation in the Indian Ocean zone. India has also deployed its tri-services Far Eastern Command in the Andaman and Nicobar Islands to promote stability in the strategically important Bay of Bengal area particularly security of narrow passage going through Strait of Malacca. These strategic steps will ensure smooth supply of oil and gas from Vietnam, Indonesia and Myanmar in future.

Conclusion

In the context of South Asia, economic development and population growth have resulted in remarkable energy demand in this new millennium. Keeping this in view, the growing domestic hydrocarbon demands, to ensure supply stability and reduce price volatility, South Asian countries have already taken various initiatives like regional cooperation, intense domestic exploration, acquiring over seas hydrocarbon assets, restructuring of state-run oil firms and doing vigorous research for other alternatives. Still, these countries have to formulate a long-term future strategy. There are divergent advantages for South Asian countries to cooperate in the energy sector. Though they together possess vast stores of energy endowments, they still continue to be characterised by insufficient quality of energy infrastructure, distribution and inaccessible and costly energy availability. As a result, these countries have remained largely energy importers and increasingly faced a serious energy shortfall. At present, all South Asian countries are dependent upon West Asia and the Gulf region to meet the domestic energy demand. But the recent dynamics of change in the geo-strategic environment in the Gulf region has its direct repercussions on South Asia's future energy security.

In the case of India, since both President A.P.J. Abdul Kalam and Prime Minister Manmohan Singh, in their address to the nation on the eve of Independence Day 2005, referred extensively to the question of India's securing adequate energy supplies, energy security has become very essential for India. However, to meet the growing demand of energy, India has to diversify its hydrocarbon resources. Given their resource base, the Gulf and the Central Asian-Caspian region may provide a substantial amount of the projected increasing production, which may largely help to meet India's energy demand.

Iran as a gateway to both regions can play a pivotal role in the transportation of natural resources for South Asian energy market. At the same time, we can't deny Pakistan's geo-strategic location for the uninterrupted supply of hydrocarbon resources. India is already looking for gas from Myanmar through Bangladesh and substantial progress has already been made in that direction. Thus, all these proposed pipelines—Iran–Pakistan–India, the Trans–Afghan Gas Pipeline and Myanmar–Bangladesh–India Gas Pipeline—may be vehicles for the uninterrupted supply of oil and gas for not only India's domestic consumption but for entire South Asia.[27]

But this would definitely require a whole new outlook and initiative in the multi-lateral strategic dialogue in South Asia in general and between Iran, Pakistan, and India in particular. Moreover, in order to see the light of reality for all these proposed pipelines, greater confidence-building measures between India, Bangladesh and Pakistan are required. Nobody can deny Pakistan's significant geo-strategic location in the transportation of hydrocarbon resources both from Iran and Central Asian-Caspian region. At the same time, Pakistan has to provide necessary infrastructure for the safe passage of pipeline and also ensure India not to create any sorts of hurdles by blocking pipeline during conflict-building scenario. ■

Notes & References

1. This paper focuses only on commercial source of energy, hydrocarbon energy. It does not include other components of non-commercial source of energy.
2. In the post-cold war period, apart from energy security, other kinds of non-traditional sources of insecurity like environmental degradation caused by global warming and deforestation, the impact of globalization, cross-border migration, HIV/AIDS, terrorism, etc. have assumed great importance which represent fuller dimensions of threats to regional security in South Asia.
3. Energy Information Administration statistics include only 'commercial' energy sources, and not animal waste, wood, or other biomass, which accounts for more than half of the South Asia region's total final energy consumption.
4. South Asia Regional Country Analysis Brief, available at http://www.eia.doe.gov/emeu/cabs/sasia.html.
5. For details, see TERI Report No. 2000EM22 "Energy Security Concerns and Response Strategies for South Asia", available at http://www.terina.org/prog.
6. http://www.eia.doe.gov/emeu/cabs/sasia.html.
7. http://www.eia.doe.gov/emeu/cabs/sasia.html.
8. http://www.eia.doe.gov/emeu/cabs/sasia.html.

9. http://www.eia.doe.gov/emeu/cabs/sasia.html.
10. Ibid.
11. Ibid.
12. For details, see Energy Information Administration, International Energy Database, October 2004, available at http://www.odci.gov/cia/publications. Also see, Javed Ahmad Khan, *India and West Asia: Energy Markets in the Liberalisation Era*, New Delhi, 1999, pp. 181–84.
13. *The Hindu*, January 8, 2004.
14. The Ministry of Petroleum & Natural Gas, Government of India.
15. *Business Standard*, November 12, 2003.
16. These figures are based upon "Report on India's Hydrocarbon Vision 2025" Annexure-IV, published by Government of India, February 25, 2000.
17. See "Report on India's Hydrocarbon Vision 2025".
18. For further details, see Girijesh Pant, "India's Energy Security: The Gulf Factor", Gulf Studies Programme Occasional Paper, Jawaharlal Nehru University, New Delhi, GSP 2002/2.
19. For details, see Surjeet Singh Panwar "India's Quest for Energy Security: Policy Options Against Hydrocarbon Dependence on West Asia" paper presented at National Seminar on "India's Energy Security and Gulf", February 19–20, 2004, at Jawaharlal Nehru University, New Delhi.
20. B.K. Chaturvedi, Secretary, Ministry of Petroleum and Natural Gas, Government of India, "Domestic Resourcing of Energy, Gulf and Future of Global Energy II" paper presented at National Seminar on "India's Energy Security and Gulf" February 19–20, 2004, at Jawaharlal Nehru University, New Delhi.
21. India's Giant Stride for Overseas Oil & Gas Supply, Government of India, Ministry of Petroleum & Natural Gas, 2002. Also see *The Hindu*, December 27, 2002.
22. *The Financial Express* (New Delhi), November 11, 2003.
23. Sushma Ramachandaran, "Imperatives of Efficient Gas Use", *The Hindu*, February 14, 2004.
24. *The Times of India*, 8 January 2004; *The Hindu*, January 22, 2004.
25. A Great Leap Forward in Search of Coal Bed Methane (CBM), Government of India, Ministry of Petroleum & Gas, 2003.
26. For details, see *The Hindu*, September 2, 2005.
27. For details, see Atul Aneja "India and Iran: A Time for Reflection" *The Hindu*, August 25, 2005; M.R. Srinivasan, "Energy Security and the Search for New Option" *The Hindu*, September 2, 2005.

Proliferation of Small Arms and Light Weapons in South Asia: Impact on Human Security

Kulwant Kaur*

Small arms have been a source of constant threat to peace and security throughout the world. Proliferation of Small Arms and Light Weapons (SALW) is responsible to a great extent for the growing cult of violence and conflicts in the world. The easy availability of these weapons not only increases the incidence of conflicts but also enhances the lethality and duration of violence. The human security is more threatened by proliferation of small arms and light weapons than even by the threat of nuclear war.[1] It is an admitted fact that since Second World War the highest number of casualties occurred due to the use of small weapons. In the post-Cold War era, more conflicts around the world are intra-state rather than inter-state, which are fought with SALW. The growing menace of terrorism in the 21st century is also the result of easy and widespread availability of small arms. According to some estimates more than 80 per cent of the people killed in war since the 1990s have been civilians, almost all of whom died from small arms or light weapons. In an era in which the risk of nuclear war has relatively receded because of Mutual Assured Destruction (MAD), greater focus should be placed on the weapons that are actually killing people. The traditional arms control and disarmament frameworks and state-centric and national security perspectives failed to address the threats to security caused by small arms and light weapons. In the debate on nuclear and conventional arms control, most of the countries have ignored the menace of illegal trafficking in SALW. However, in view of the harmful effects of proliferation of SALW, there is more awareness in the various communities and governments.

---

* Professor, Department of Political Science, University of Jammu, Jammu.

In South Asia, this problem has assumed a very serious dimension because of the ongoing intra-state and inter-state conflicts. In this paper, the issue of small arms and light weapons, their production, causes of proliferation and impact have been discussed besides suggesting a few measures to control this menace.

Meaning and Definitions of Small Arms & Light Weapons (SALW)

Although there is no universally accepted definition of these weapons, a report by a UN panel of experts in 1997 has defined these in the following words:

> Light weapon is a generic term which is used to cover a range of weapons portable by man, animal or machine—from revolvers and machine guns to anti-tanks and anti-aircraft missile systems. Small arms are a subset of the category of light weapons, which includes only those weapons that can be fired, maintained and transported by a person.[2]

Broadly, small arms and light weapons could include anything from knives to portable mortars and anti-aircraft missiles. Small arms are weapons for use by individuals and light weapons are those that require a crew or team to operate, while still being portable by vehicles. Small arms include mainly pistols, rifles and carbines, sub-machine gun, assault rifles, light machine gun, etc. Besides the above, the light weapons include heavy machine guns, grenades launchers, portable anti-aircraft guns, portable anti-tank guns, recoilless rifles and portable launchers of anti-aircraft missile systems and mortars of calibres of less than 100mm.

Production and Proliferation

According to the Small Arms Survey (2002), there are estimated to be 639 million small arms and light weapons currently in circulation around the world.[3] Out of

Table 1: Distribution of Known Global Arms

Ownership group	Numbers held	Percentage of total
State-owned: combined total	259,600,000	40.6
Armed forces	(241,600,000)	(37.8)
Police forces	(18,000,00)	(2.8)
Civilian possession	370,300,000	59.2
Rebel groups	1,000,000	0.2
TOTAL	**638,900,000**	**100**

Small Arms Survey, 2002 as cited in Jim Coe and Henry Smith, Action Against Small Arms (Oxfam GB and Saferworld, 2003), p. 6.

these, 40.6 per cent are owned by states i.e. by the security forces. Interestingly, civilian possession accounts for 59.2 per cent and rebel groups own 0.2 per cent of these weapons only, contrary to the general belief.[4]

In addition to the existing small arms and light weapons, new small arms are being manufactured, sold, transferred and transported every day. There are more than 1,000 companies involved in the production of small arms in the world and at least 98 countries produce or have the capacity to produce small arms and light weapons. But out of these, only 13 countries dominate the global market for small arms. The United States, China and Russia are top three producers in the list. The 90 per cent proliferation of small arms is being done by five Permanent Members [P-5] of the United Nations Security Council. The total value of global small arms production in 2000 was at least $7.4 billion.[5] With the volume of annual production of such weapons, global stocks are almost certainly increasing. Moreover, these weapons are cheap and re-usable, and therefore remain in circulation for a long period of time.

South Asia has remained one of the major theatres of conflict in the post-colonial era. There are reports that the spread of small arms and light weapons in South Asia has reached a saturation point, particularly in the context of the Afghan crisis.[6] Both the superpowers defused more than $10 billion arms in Afghanistan. The Afghan war against the Soviet Union was long and the withdrawal of Soviet troops followed the civil war among the various factions of Afghan tribal society. The political developments of more than two decades in Afghanistan contributed directly as well as indirectly to the spread of weapons in that country and its neighbourhood. Because of the US Afghan policy and the pre-conditions set by Islamabad, most of the arms supplies were covert, illegal and illicit. It encouraged what has been termed as Kalashnikov or AK-47 rifle culture. Moreover, it helped to create 'grey-market' which means weapons are diverted from the original destinations during the transfer stage.[7] Chris Smith from London has revealed that how the CIA pipeline to Afghanistan had leaked leading to the diversion of almost 70% of weapons and ammunition meant for Afghan guerrillas. Though funded by the Americans, most of these arms were purchased from China. It is reported that a good portion of these weapons found their way to Kashmir.[8] In 'Darra bazaar' located in the North West frontier, various types of sophisticated weapons are available. This area including other tribal areas is considered to be one of the largest private arms producing and trading areas of South Asia.[9] In fact, the Darra Adam Khel is one of the oldest arms bazaars in the subcontinent. It is one of the most lethal home shopping bazaars with cash payable on delivery almost anywhere in Pakistan. Explosives and narcotics are commonly available in the same shops and can be had even on barter. In fact, the entire area on Pak-Afghan borders is still doing a heavy trade in arms, including missiles originating in the USA and Kalashnikovs made under license in China and Egypt. According to some estimates, Pakistan has somewhere 7 to 12 million, Afghanistan has more than 10 million and India has 2 to 4 million small arms beyond the state control, i.e. unlicensed, illegal and illegitimate. Large numbers of small arms and light weapons are also available in Sri Lanka, Nepal, Bhutan and Bangladesh.

Causes of Proliferation in South Asia

South Asia is one of the most heterogenous regions of the world. It is characterised with ethnic, linguistic, religious and cultural diversities. The seven states are asymmetric as far as their size, resources, demography, economic and military capabilities are concerned. Moreover, their political systems and ideological perceptions are different. The colonial legacy has left a number of ethnic, territorial and border disputes, which have become more complicated because of Cold War politics, hostile regional environment and internal dynamics of politics. Religious extremism, fundamentalism, regional and economic disparities, caste, linguistic and ideological divide, corruption and misgovernance, poverty, unemployment and overpopulation mark the whole region. In this complex South Asian setting, the infusion of small arms and light weapons has rendered the intra and inter-state conflicts more violent. The observations of the UN Secretary General are very much appropriate in the South Asian context:

> While not by themselves [small arms] causing the conflicts in which they are used, the proliferation of small arms and light weapons affects the intensity and duration of violence and encourages militancy rather than a peaceful resolution of unsettled differences. Perhaps most grievously, we see a vicious circle in which insecurity leads to a higher demand for weapons, which itself breed still greater insecurity.[10]

One of the significant factors contributing to illicit arms proliferation in South Asia has been the number of political and social conflicts. In fact, different sections of dissatisfied population, particularly ethnic and minority groups, almost in all the South Asian countries, have been asking for more autonomy. Inability of the post-colonial states to address the problems of these groups and accommodate their demands led to insurgency and secessionist movements in these states. Kashmir and Tamil separatist movements in India and Sri Lanka, earlier the Bangladesh liberation movement in Pakistan, the Chittagong Hill Tracts issue in Bangladesh are only a few glaring examples. In Jammu and Kashmir alone, there are more than dozens of militant groups, almost all possessing modern sophisticated arms ranging from grenades to AK-47. It is widely accepted by both Western and non-Western experts that the Inter Services Intelligence (ISI) and the arms bazaars in North West Frontier Province (NWFP) are the main sources of their weapons. Further, the close linkage between arms traders and insurgents and separatists groups complicates the political and social conflicts in South Asia. It has been rightly pointed out that the availability of SALW has militarised societal discontent and empowered the Non State Actors and groups.[11] Outside aid to these groups of arms, ammunitions and even training has continued even in the post-Cold War era. In fact, the nature of insurgencies and guerrilla warfare in South Asia has become intense as a result of proliferation of small arms and light weapons. The political demand of various groups for a separate and independent homeland with accompanied violence could have never sustained for so long, had there been no proliferation of these arms on such a massive scale. The easy availability of the weapons has made the resolution of these conflicts virtually impossible. Thus, the political and social conflicts based on class, caste, religion and language so common in South Asia have contributed to the proliferation of these weapons.

Two, socio-economic backwardness, poverty and unemployment in all the South Asian countries[12] contributed to the production and proliferation of small arms. Failure of post-colonial states to provide social and economic justice after more than half a century of their independence aggravated the social discontentment.[13] The growing frustration, increasing feeling of deprivation and alienation among the youth particularly have led some of them to enter the world of crime. With the help of small arms, they can demonstrate their muscle power and overcome their incapabilities and feeling of helplessness. Moreover, the motive of profit and easy money encourages the proliferation of these arms.

Three, there is a close linkage between arms and politics in South Asia. The possession of small arms by politicians is a growing problem across the sub-continent. It may be to intimidate opponents and voters or to protect themselves. In modern times, political crime is increasing throughout the world, but more so in South Asian countries. Politicians support and even engage themselves in criminal offences in order to achieve political gains and take revenge from their political opponents. Political motive is in fact, a major reason for small arms procurement in South Asia.[14] Lack of political legitimacy, conduct of frequent elections and instability in most of the South Asian countries also contribute indirectly to the proliferation of small arms.

Four, South Asia is at the crossroads of the famous drug trafficking routes such as the Golden Triangle and Golden Crescent.[15] The drug dealers need protection to move the bulk of the contraband items from one place to another and thus build up their own army with lots of sophisticated small arms, It resulted in a nexus among arms producers/ dealers and drug traffickers. Such a development has not only led to arms proliferation but also encouraged terrorism in South Asia.

Last but not the least, the revolution in technology has contributed to the proliferation of small arms and light weapons. With the improvement of technology and the availability of sophisticated production machines and also with the improvement in technical know-how, the quality of small arms and light weapons has improved to a great degree. The nature and size of these weapons make them easy to transport and difficult to track. Consequently, these can be maintained easily in circulation for a long time. The large number of producers, spread over almost in more than 90 countries, makes the availability of these weapons almost uninterrupted and without much restrictions and control.

Impact of Small Arms and Light Weapons

The availability of small arms and light weapons has undoubtedly intensified the internal conflicts, increased the intensity and duration of violence and enhanced the sense of insecurity. SALW create fear-psychosis, terror and situation of chaos on the basis of a well-known proverb "kill one and frighten ten thousand". It has been rightly observed by Bina Lakshmi Nepram that the human cost of the proliferation of small arms is enormous. It destroys cultures and lives, it exacerbates and intensifies conflicts. It kills and injures.[16]

The debates in the post-Cold War period have travelled two parallel tracks for security policy – inter-state and 'societal' or 'human'.[17] The risk that inter-state war will break out because of light weapons proliferation is virtually nil and the resources devoted to these arms, compared to major weapons, are minimum. To reduce a risk of war at this level, 'cooperative security' models are suggested.[18] In the modern context, however, the most serious threat and security concerns are focused on individuals, communities, and societies. These securities concerns are caused to a large extent by the nature of post-colonial states and their failure to govern. Most of the post-colonial states, like their predecessors depend on coercion rather than consent. These tried to gain legitimacy through the excessive use of force. These states tend to terrorize the people and general masses. The hegemony and the domination of the governing elite depend largely on the disproportionate use of force. In the upsurge in communal/

sectarian violence and ethnic conflicts in the South Asian states, since the end of Cold War, small arms and light weapons have played a major role. The weaponisation of society in Pakistan and Afghanistan has not only sharpened the ethnic, religious and linguistic contradictions but made the lives of common men, women and children insecure. The oppression of the dominant groups, feudal lords and religious fanaticists has gone beyond control with these lethal arms. In several parts of India, particularly in the so-called *BIMARU* states, caste and class wars got violent and communal riots have taken ugly shape many a time. The easy availability of these weapons has threatened to destroy the social and political fabric in the states of South Asia by encouraging a culture of violence. Mumbai, the commercial capital of India, had experienced horrific serial bomb blasts in 1993 because of SALW, in which many innocent people had lost their lives. The proliferation and misuse of small arms, have, undoubtedly, endangered personal security and undermined good governance.

One of the reasons for persistent violence and failure to have successful dialogue and reconciliation in J&K in India and in Sri Lanka could be the large-scale availability of arms. It has been revealed by D. Sivanandan, Joint Director CBI, West Zone, Mumbai that more than 4500 illicit firearms had been seized from terrorist and criminal gangs in Jammu and Kashmir region in a period of ten years.[19] However, the army reports indicate that, during the period spanning January 1990 to November 2002, security forces seized 24,664 series of AK rifles, 51,048 magazines and 31.20 lakh rounds of ammunition, 9,377 pistols/revolvers with 8,998 magazines and 1.90 lakh rounds, 988 universal machine guns (UMG) with 1300 magazines and about 1 lakh rounds, 333 sniper rifles with 44,274 rounds, 4164 rockets, 737 rocket launchers, 2266 rocket boosters and 47,025 grenades/hand grenades. These recoveries also included 68 tonnes of RDX, 24 tonnes of explosives, 3761 Improvised Explosive Devices (lED), 5,228 anti-personnel mines, 497 anti-tank mines, 49889 detonators and 5501 electric detonators.[20] The recovery included most sophisticated and high-tech arms along with ammunition and explosives that could cause mass causalities. In fact, civilians, including women and children, have become the targets of violence. Such violence against the civilians and non-combatants is completely against International Human Rights Conventions as well as International Humanitarian Law. During war as well as in the post-war period, high percentage of deaths and casualities of civilians are caused due to the use of small arms, ranging from grenades attack to landmines and explosives.

Small arms play a very intricate role in human rights abuses against individual freedom and personal dignity. These resulted in loss of human lives[21] and cause irreparable damage to infrastructure. These are used to kidnap, to commit rape, to torture, to force disappearance and to recruit children as soldiers. The presence of small arms aggravates the problems of forced internal displacement. The targeted attacks with small arms by the militants against the civilians in Jammu and Kashmir forced a vast majority of Kashmiri Pandits[22] and a sizeable number of Sikhs[23] and even a few Muslims to leave the valley in 1990 and thereafter. It is impossible for any government in New Delhi to negotiate peace if illicit guns reign over the valley. The militants' attack on Indian Parliament on December 13, 2001 and the resultant military build up along the Line of Control and international border resulted in the displacement of large number of families from the border areas. About 30,771 families comprising 153,131 persons had been forced to migrate from the border areas/ Line of Control of the districts Rajouri, Poonch, Jammu and Kathua. More than 40,000 people from Pallanwala and other adjoining areas of Akhnoor district are still living in camps.[24] Heavily armed terrorists create an environment of terror with these small arms to commit all kinds of atrocities against people, for example to deprive them of their belongings, to make them hostage and deny them the basic amenities or hijacking a plane or bus etc. Victims are not only initially rounded up with these arms but also often killed to achieve the demands. The simple use of these weapons makes even small and young children into deadly killers. In recent years, many school children, even in developed countries like the USA and UK have killed their friends and classmates. The simple use and the easy availability of these weapons have made them so deadly and destructive.

The proliferation and increasing availability of small arms and light weapons make the task of post-conflict peace building and reconstruction more difficult. It is very much obvious from the example of post-Taliban Afghanistan, where different tribal leaders and groups continued to challenge the authority of Hamid Karzai's Government with all the arms at their disposal. For justifying their claims in power-sharing, several warlords and various ethnic groups not only kept their military strength intact with SALW, rather made all-out efforts to improve the quality and increase the number of these arms.[25] As in post-conflict situation, these arms remain in circulation, the traditional mechanisms of conflict resolution also get eroded and use of guns remains a norm. Moreover, with the large-scale presence of these arms in illegal hands, the power of the state that was traditionally conceived to be the sole agency of force and coercion is challenged and its legitimacy is undermined. This further affects the security of the community and individuals. Consequently, the marginalized and weaker sections of the society, who look towards the state for their defence, usually lose faith in the capability and authority of state. Indirectly, these arms contribute to the phenomenon of 'failed' state.

Like all other kinds of arms, small arms and light weapons affect the process of economic development adversely. More violence means less capital investment and low employment opportunities, thereby contributing to a vicious cycle of poverty and violence. In the age of globalisation, it is the better conditions that attract the capital, investors and the tourists—the fundamentals of any economy. Most of the conflict regions remain backward and underdeveloped and low in Human Development Index. The latest Human Development Report 2005 indicates that in South Asia 31.9 per cent people are still living below the poverty line, i.e. their income is less than $1 a day, about 95 children out of 1,000 die under the age of five, 42.3 per cent children are not going to school at the primary level.[26] For sustainable development and human security, all efforts should be made to improve the human development index in these countries. This is possible only when violence is checked and instruments of war are controlled.

Measures to Control the Proliferation and Misuse of SALW

The proliferation and misuse of SALW have dangerous implications and devastating effect on human security. Per se these cannot be banned because of their legitimate use by the security forces. In ideal conditions, state should have the sole monopoly over these weapons, but because it failed to guarantee security to all individuals, groups and various communities living within it, the state, therefore, cannot deprive them of their legitimate right of self-defence. However, it is necessary to make a distinction between legal and illegal weapons so that action could be taken strictly against the latter. However, national efforts alone will prove to be inadequate to tackle this problem. In order to get desirable results, action must be taken simultaneously at both levels, i.e. national as well as regional.

At the national level, awareness campaigns against these weapons should be launched intensively in all the countries. Laws relating to curbing and controlling the production and proliferation of small arms must be implemented seriously. For addressing this problem, both the demand and supply of SALW have to be regulated. The demand for small arms is concerned with a broad range of issues, including structural and deep-rooted problems, such as poverty, socio-economic inequalities, unemployment, imbalanced regional growth, corruption and bad governance. These are the problems whose solutions cannot be found in the short-term, but serious efforts must be made to address the genuine grievances to avoid further aggravation and prevent any situation to turn violent and volatile. In short, there are no quick measures with the help of which the need/demand of small arms can be controlled. In the given situation, it is only the supply that should be regulated effectively and monitored by the state agencies closely.

As far as supply of SALW is concerned, it covers the production, illegal trade and transfer, air and sea droppings, smuggling, seizure and theft from security forces, etc. Stringent measures are required to put an effective control on all the channels of supply by making the administrative machinery active and efficacious. For evolving a holistic perspective and dealing with it at different levels and dimensions, a National Commission against SALW should be constituted. In this context, the role of NGOs and civil society against these weapons is most crucial. In fact, it is the supply and availability of weapons itself that raise the threshold of violence. Conversely, decline in their availability can lower the level of violence. Of course, SALW control will not by itself solve the conflicts and political issues. But certainly a peaceful and non-violent environment will be conducive for dialogue, negotiations and a political process. It will help in generating trust and building confidence, necessary for finding solution to any political problem.

National efforts are to be supplemented with the regional ones in South Asia. All the countries in South Asia had signed SAARC Convention on terrorism, but it has been rendered meaningless in view of its non-implementation by the member states. So what is required is not only a Convention to control SALW in South Asia, but also a commitment by all states to cooperate in order to contain illicit trafficking. Moreover, if South Asian Convention against SALW has to be effective and successful, it must be binding for all the states to act against non-state actors operating within its jurisdiction. Further, the Convention against SALW should focus on ammunition and explosives. As alluded to earlier, since these arms are small, they are quite easy to smuggle and difficult to detect. On the other hand, ammunition and explosives tend to be heavy and easy to detect. Weapons are useless without ammunition. Therefore, an emphasis on ammunition will be helpful in tackling the problem. ■

Notes & References

1. Steve Smith, "The Contested Concept of Security", Ken Booth, ed., *Critical Security Studies & World Politics*, New Delhi, 2005, pp. 27–62.
2. Jim Coe and Henry Smith, *Action Against Small Arms*, International Alert, Oxfam G B, 2003, p. 5. Also see UN Doc., A/52/298, August 1997.

3. "Counting the Human Cost", *Small Arms Survey*, A Project of the Graduate Institute of International Studies, Oxford, 2002.
4. Ibid.
5. Jim Coe and Henry Smith, n. 2, p.6.
6. For details see K. Kaur, "Soviets in Afghanistan: Strategic Implications", K.S Nagar & Gautam Sharma, eds., *India's Security: Superpower Threat*, Delhi, 1989, pp. 171–180. Also see John K. Cooley, *Unhold War: Afghanistan, America and International Terrorism*, London, 2001, pp. 81-106.
7. During the War in Afghanistan, more than half the weapons, notably stringers, originally meant for *mujahideen* in Afghanistan were found untraceable and were later sold in open markets in Pakistan. For details see http://www.rcss.org/policy_studies/ps_7_2html.
8. http://www.jammu-kashmir.com/insights/insight 9901-5 html.
9. For details see, Mohammed Ayoob, "South-West Asia After the Taliban", Ramesh Thakur & Oddny Wigger, *South Asia in the World: Problem Solving Perspectives on Security, Sustainable Development and Good Governance*, New Delhi, 2004, pp. 373–394.
10. Report of the Panel of Government Experts on Small Arms, UN Doc., A/4/298, August 1997, p.2.
11. Salma Malik and Mallika Joseph, *Small Arms and the Security Debate in South Asia*, Colombo, 2005, p. 19.
12. For details see World Bank, *World Development Report, 2003*; Arun Chaturvedi, "Issue of Human Development and Human Security in South Asia", Gopal Singh & R.K. Chauhan, *South Asia Today*, New Delhi, 2005, pp. 41–51 and R.S. Ghuman, "Uneven Economic Development and Discontent in South Asia: A Regional Analysis", Gopal Singh & R.K. Chauhan, pp. 52–68.
13. Sarah Hiddleston, "Can the UN Summit on Poverty Deliver?", *The State Times*, September 16, 2005.
14. For Details see Tara Ashtakala, "Huns and Guns : Small Arms in South Asia One Year After the UN Conference", http://www.Sikhspectrum.com/082003/guns_andhuns.htm.
15. The Afghan *Jihad* has led to the production of opium and by the end of the anti-Soviet *Jihad*, the Central Asian region produced 75 per cent of the world's opium, worth billion of dollars. For details see Salma Malik and Mallika Joseph, n. 11, pp. 37–38. For example, Bangladesh, India and Nepal provide a major route for drugs from South East Asia and traffickers have amassed extensive arsenals of firepower to protect their goods.
16. http://www.cobrapost.com/documents/smallarms.htm.
17. For details see Kanti Bajpai, "Human Security: Concept and Measurement", Kanti Bajpai and Siddharth Mallavarapu, eds., *International Relations in India*, New Delhi, 2005, pp. 275–332 and UNDP, *Human Development Report*, New York, 1994.

18. 'Cooperative Security' encourages a constructivist approach and tends to connote consultation rather than confrontation, reassurance rather than deterrence, transparency rather than secrecy, prevention rather than correction and interdependence rather than unilateralism. For details see Dipankar Banerjee, "Approach to Comprehensive and Cooperative Security" Dipankar Banerjee, ed., *Security in South Asia,* New Delhi, 1999, pp. 294–295 & P.R. Chari, "Towards A New Paradigm for National Security", P.R. Chari, ed., *Perspectives on National Security in South Asia: In Search of a New Paradigm,* New Delhi, 1999, pp. 421–422.
19. http://www.iansa.org/action/sasa_pr.htm.
20. http://www.satp.org/satporgtp/detailed_news.asp?date1=12/6/2002.
21. During the militancy in Jammu and Kashmir, more than 12,000 innocent civilians were among the 30,000 who lost their lives according to the Indian government official estimates. However, Kashmiris, including All Party Hurriyat Conference estimate between 80,000 and 1,00,000 deaths. The truth may be somewhere between these two extremes and most neutral observers estimate the figure around 60,000 deaths, mostly civilians.
22. The Kashmiri Pandits claims that more than three lakh people left the valley after the eruption of violence in the late 1980s. According to government of India estimates there are 56,487 migrant families of Kashmiri Pandits, For details see Government of India, Ministry of Home Affairs, *Annual Report 2004–2005.* http://www.mha.nic.in/AR 2004-2005/AR04-05.
23. The Chittisinghpora massacre wherein about 35 Kashmiri Sikhs were killed led to another displacement from the valley. The incident forced many Sikhs to move to the safer places, though earlier also many of them had left the valley. In May 2001, as many as 1903 displaced Sikhs were registered with the Relief Commissioner in Jammu.
24. Government of India, Ministry of Home Affairs, *Annual Report 2004–2005.* http://www.mha.nic.in/AR2004-2005/AR04-05Eng.pdf.
25. Since the fall of the Taliban, the warlords outside Kabul have constantly extended their military power. Despite the talk of disarmament of political economy of arms has emerged. For details see Rangin Dadfar Spanta, "Afghanistan : Nation-building in the shadow of the Warlords and the 'War on Terror" Jochen Hippler, ed., *Nation-Building : A Key Concept for Peaceful Conflict Transformation?,* London, 2005, pp. 75–80.

26 UNDP, *Human Development Report 2005,* New York, 2005, Chapter 1.

---

* The author expresses her gratitude to Air Commodore Jasjit Singh, Ex-Director IDSA, New Delhi and Ms. Binalakshmi Nepram, Safeworld for creating an interest in the subject.

Section IV
Regionalism and Regional Cooperation

Political Economy of Indo–Pakistan Trade Relations and SAARC

Ranjit Singh Ghuman*

The partition of the Indian subcontinent in 1947 into India and Pakistan was a tripartite package deal among British rulers, and Indian and Pakistani political leadership. However, the transfer of power from the Britishers to India and Pakistan culminated into mass exodus of population and large-scale bloodshed as the partition was on communal lines. Punjab and Bengal, inter alia, were the worst sufferers as the division was mainly of these two provinces of the erstwhile British colony. Punjab was divided into East Punjab and West Punjab and Bengal was divided into West Bengal and East Bengal. East Bengal came to be known as East Pakistan, which became Bangladesh in 1971. It was a strange combination of joy and sorrow as on the one hand independence was being celebrated and on the other, people were being forced to leave their age-old places of residence. In the process nearly one million people were killed and many more millions were rendered homeless, resourceless, jobless and even orphans. The traumatic memory of unparalleled suffering is fresh in the minds of the people even after 58 years of partition. The division was so rigid that the newly demarcated national boundary-lines cut asunder the transport network, rivers, canals, mountains, the residential houses and even families.

Bird's Eye View of both the Economies

The Britishers developed India as an integrated economic unit. This aspect was brutally ignored at the time of partition. The partition was mainly governed by non-economic considerations such as religious majority, religious fundamentalism,

---

* Professor, Department of Economics, Punjabi University, Patiala, Punjab.

communal considerations and vested political interests. Economic rationale was sadly ignored while carving out the two sovereign states. Its effects were widespread and extremely damaging to the social, natural, political and economic fabric of the Indian subcontinent. The partition, in fact, played havoc with the economic, political, social, religious and cultural network of both the regions.

Pakistan emerged in 1947 with scarcely any manufacturing capacity except an oil refinery in the western region, a few cotton textile plants and some units of sugar refining, tea processing and cement production. Most of the manufactured goods were initially being imported by Pakistan from India. The region, which after independence came to be known as Pakistan had been mainly developed as a source of industrial raw material and agricultural commodities. The industrial development of British India took place mainly in the territory which later constituted India. In fact, India possessed a little more than 90 per cent of total number of factories.[1] As regards major establishments, more than 96 per cent were in Indian territory; the share of workers employed in industry was even larger. Thus, in terms of industrial units, commercial establishments and natural resources, India was more favourably situated than Pakistan at the time of partition. As a result of partition, India lost its food granary and sources of raw materials while Pakistan lost its source of processed/manufactured goods, whatever little it had.

On the eve of partition both the dominions were among the poorest in the world. Both continue to be among the low income countries even after 58 years with per capita income of US$ 470 (India) and US $420 (Pakistan). In terms of Human Development Index (HDI) Pakistan and India ranked 144th and 128th respectively in descending order in 2004. As a consequence of partition, India comprised 81 per cent of total population and 77 per cent of the total area of the undivided country.[2] India, even now, comprises nearly 79 per cent of the total population of India, Pakistan and Bangladesh. The population of India and Pakistan was 1049 million and 145 million respectively in 2002. Their surface area was 3287 thousand square kilometres and 796 thousand square kilometres. The respective size of their GNI is US$ 494.9 billion and US$ 60.9 billion.[3]

The economies of both the countries were mainly agrarian at the time of partition. Pakistan's agricultural sector contributed about 54.50 per cent towards its gross domestic product during 1949-50. The share of manufacturing output in gross domestic product of Pakistan was 7.9 per cent during 1949-50. In the case of India the share of primary, secondary and tertiary sectors in its net domestic product was 61.3, 14.5 and 24.2 per cent, respectively, during 1950-51.[4] The respective share of agriculture in the GDP of India and Pakistan was 23 per cent in 2002. The corresponding share of industry was 27 per cent and 23 per cent and that of services was 51 per cent and 53 per cent.[5] The average annual growth rate of India and Pakistan during 1980-90 was 5.7 per cent and 6.1 per cent, respectively. India improved marginally with average annual growth rate of 5.8 per cent, whereas Pakistan experienced a deceleration, with 3.6 per cent growth rate, during 1990-2002.

About 35 to 40 per cent of their population is still living below poverty line. Nearly 8 to 9 per cent of their labour force is unemployed. Approximately 31 per cent of adult Indian males and 54 per cent of adult females are still illiterate. In the case of Pakistan the corresponding figures are 42 per cent and 71 per cent. More than 60 per cent of their workforce is still being employed in the primary sector. Compared to high expenditure on defence, the public expenditure on health in both the countries is just 0.9 per cent of their respective GDPs. Similarly, public expenditure on education in India and Pakistan has been 4.1 per cent and 1.8 per cent of their GDPs. The proportion of capital expenditure in central government expenditure in India declined from 11 per cent in 1990 to 8 per cent in 2000 and in the case of Pakistan it declined from 12 per cent in 1990 to 9 per cent in 2000. It is really disappointing to note that Pakistan's per capita GDP growth rate in 2000-01 was just 0.3 per cent. There was a time (around 1700 A.D.) when India's share in world GDP was nearly 22 per cent and now in 2001 it was just 1.5 per cent.

Wars and Political Relations Between India and Pakistan

As the two dominions could not make a smooth transition to independence, their relations with each other as sovereign countries, became strained right from inception. In fact, their relations with each other were based on hatred and fear psychosis. The political and religious leadership on both sides of the border were suspicious of the designs of each other. The fight over Kashmir in 1948 added fuel to fire and till now Kashmir is being raked up as the major bone of contention. The two countries again engaged in war in 1965 and 1971. After the 1965 war they signed Tashkent Agreement and after the 1971 war the Simla Agreement was concluded in 1972.

As a result of 1971 the war the East Wing of Pakistan became an independent country and came to be known as Bangladesh. There have been occasional happenings of cross-border firing by both the countries since then. In fact, the international border and the LoC between both the countries had always been live, the culmination of which was Kargil problem and the massive movement of forces to the border. The alleged cross-border terrorism in Jammu and Kashmir became another serious problem between India and Pakistan. In fact, Pakistan never reconciled to its defeat at the hands of India in the 1971 war and the consequential emergence of Bangladesh. Pakistan firmly believes that '*Mukti Bahini*' which eventually led to the creation of Bangladesh, was created by India.[6] At his press conference on July 2001, President of Pakistan, General Musharraf, justified the Kargil aggression and asserted that Pakistan's support to '*Jehadis*' in Kashmir was like India's arming the '*Mukti Bahini*' in the erstwhile Pakistan. The half-page advertisement titled 'in remembrance of Kargil heroes' in a Pakistan daily by Sheikh Mazhar-ul-Haq, a senior office bearer of the Pakistan Federation of Chambers of Commerce and Industry leaves nobody in doubt about the involvement of the Pakistan Army in the Kargil conflict.[7]

The not-so-good relations, political immaturity, fundamentalist approach to solve the problems and fear psychosis on both sides resulted in a huge loss of men and material during all these years. Both the countries are still continuing with hatred and enmity towards each other. As a result they have been spending huge amounts on defence. In 1999, Pakistan spent US $3650 million on defence which was nearly 5.7 per cent of its Gross National Product (GNP). The per capita annual expenditure on defence in Pakistan comes out to be US $27.[8] Contrary to it, Pakistan's public expenditure on health was 0.9 per cent of its GNP during 1990-99. During the same period its public expenditure on education has been 2.7 per cent of its GNP.[9] India spent US $12380 million on defence in 1999, which is 2.8 per cent of its GNP. The per capita annual expenditure on defence in India was US $12.5 in 1999. Compared to this, India's public expenditure on health and education during 1990-98 was 0.6 per cent and 3.2 per cent of its GNP, respectively. It is clear from the above facts that Pakistan's military expenditure is 1.67 times more than its combined public expenditure on health and education, so vital for human development.

Evidently both the neighbouring, but poor, countries have been spending very heavily on defence. A major proportion of this may be attributed to the threat perception from each other and the fear-psychosis. A Pakistani scholar[10] wrote that three basic schools of thought have been structuring the Pakistan's discourse on Kashmir. They are: (i) *The orthodox school of thought* which sees India as unconditionally hostile, arguing that India had never accepted the reality of Pakistan nor was willing to consider it as an 'equal' in the region. (ii) *The Islamists School of Thought* holds that there is vast international conspiracy against Islam by Hindu India, the Christian West and the Jewish Israel. As such, it was Pakistan's religious and moral obligation to support

'Jehadis' in Kashmir and elsewhere (iii) *The moderate/liberal elements* in the Pakistan's decision making circles do not consider India to be unconditionally hostile to Pakistan. They plead for Pakistan's economic reconstruction rather than following the first two lines of thought. The policy-making elite, in Pakistan, however, comprises two main groups—conservatives and ultra conservatives—the first two schools of thought cited above. The former believes that India wants to dominate the South Asian region while the latter subscribes to the view that the bigger neighbour would not lose any opportunity to further damage or destroy Pakistan. Unfortunately, the Pakistan's military and civil bureaucracy represent the ultra-conservatives.

It is because of this factor that Islamabad has been making consistent efforts to maintain the defence budget at such a level so as to match with India. Looking at the comparison of two economies, Pakistan's Gross National Income (GNI) is just 12.57 per cent of India's GNI but she is maintaining 50 per cent of the Indian army and defence equipment. Pakistani President, General Pervez Musharraf, claims that his government would procure major weapon systems to minimize the conventional military-technological gap with India.[11] The gap would be narrowed down if Islamabad could spend about US $10 billion over the next seven to eight years. Pakistan's defence budget has been between 5.5 per cent and 7.2 per cent of its GNI between 1981-82 and 1998-99. India, too, has been spending between 2.3 percent and 2.5 per cent of its GNI on defence during the same period. The recent 'Operation Parakram' might have costed about Rs. 20,000–25,000 crore to India and Rs. 15000-18000 crore to Pakistan. The cost of developing a balanced nuclear deterrent programme would be around Rs. 7000 crore, spread over 10 years for Pakistan and even higher to India. Poor economies like them can ill-afford such a "luxury". Both should understand that real might and security of a country lies in its economic strength and stability and not merely in its military strength. It is worth mentioning that both India and Pakistan have already fought three and a half low intensity wars with each other besides numerous skirmishes. They could not solve any longstanding problem between them through wars and violence. The complexities of problems have gone from bad to worse.

Genesis of Trade Relations between India and Pakistan

Though it is difficult to discuss trade relations between two hostile neighbouring countries, an effort has been made to do so. The discussion has been divided into three phases: phase first, from partition to 1965; phase second, from 1966 to 1974; and phase third, from 1975 to 2004.

Phase 1: 1947–1965

Prior to partition, preparations were started at the official level for partition. The two countries (which were still to come into existence) were given the status of two dominions. An expert committee, consisting of the representatives of both the dominions, studied the problems of inter-dominion commercial relations and made certain recommendations, which were approved by the partition council.[12] Keeping in view the broad interests of both the dominions, the expert committee on trade recommended: "the two governments should agree to maintain as far as possible the status quo regarding the matters affecting trade and movements between the two dominions up to February 29, 1948.[13] This arrangement is generally referred to as the "Standstill Agreement". The normal licencing and tariff restrictions on trade between the two countries came into force on the expiry of this standstill agreement, i.e. w.e.f. from March 1, 1948. After that trade between India and Pakistan was conducted on the basis of bilateral trade agreements. Up to 1965, about twelve trade/payments agreements were signed between India and Pakistan.[14]

To normalize the political relations between the two countries and to solve the Kashmir problem, six rounds of talks were held between India and Pakistan during December 1960 and May 1963. The Indian team was led by Swaran Singh, the then Minister for Railways, and the Pakistan team was led by Zulfikar Ali Bhutto, the then Union Minister of Industries. However, nothing came out of the talks, mainly for two reasons: Pakistan demanded at the beginning the whole of the Kashmir Valley and subsequently the whole State of Jammu and Kashmir whereas India offered 1500 square miles more than what Pakistan already occupied. Pakistan was prepared to concede only the district of Kathua to India. The second reason was the partisan attitude of Britain and the United States in support of Pakistan[15]. The Sino-Indian conflict of 1962 and the then newly formed Sino-Pak friendship marked a major setback to Indo-Pakistan trade relations. The Indo-Pak war of 1965 resulted in the imposition of trade embargo which remained into force up to 1974.

It was really strange that a short bout of war in 1965 resulted in a trade embargo for nine years. It is unparalleled in world history. The 1971 war reinforced this embargo on trade. As a result, there was no trade between India and Pakistan from 1966 to 1974. There were no diplomatic relations during this period between the two countries. It speaks volumes of political immaturity and irrationality. In fact political immaturity and irrationality have been governing the trade and other relations between India and Pakistan all through.

The relations between India and Pakistan have all through been influenced by the USA and China. The main plank of the US policy in this region has been to combat communism. During 1949–50, the USA tried to win over India in order to use her as a frontal state against communist China. When India did not fall prey to the US designs, America chose Pakistan for this purpose. In fact Pakistan became an American satellite in 1953 and as such it could never establish as a stable state. In return, Pakistan continued to receive a huge military and economic aid from the US. However, Pakistan's rulers used that aid to strengthen its defence forces against India. The role of China too was not favourable to Indo-Pakistan relations.

Phase 2: 1966–1974

As a result of trade embargo there was absolutely no legal trade between the two neighbouring countries from 1966 to 1974. The 1971 war further aggravated the situation and the trade embargo remained in force till 1974. Politically both the countries remained hostile to each other throughout this period. Even the diplomatic relations were severed on December 6, 1971 which were resumed on July 24, 1976.[16] All this happened in spite of the fact that several efforts were made to revive trade during this period. Even the Tashkent Agreement in 1966 offered restoration of trade relations, but unfortunately they could not be resumed till 1975. India made certain efforts to revive trade relations with Pakistan during this period but to no avail.[17]

The compulsions of national reconstruction and development did not allow acute belligerency between the two immediate neighbours for a long period. The two countries signed an agreement on July 2, 1972 known as Simla Agreement: the main objective was to establish durable peace in the sub-continent by putting an end to the atmosphere of conflict and confrontation between the two neighbouring countries and working for the promotion of friendly and harmonious relations.

The Simla Agreement paved the way for normalisation of relations between India and Pakistan. However, it took more than two years to sign a trade protocol in pursuance of Article 3 of the Simla Agreement. In fact, the Simla Agreement replaced the old UN-mandated "Ceasefire Line" with a new line of control (LoC) based on ground realities. A trade protocol was singed in New Delhi on November 30, 1974 lifting the embargo on trade between the two countries with effect from December 7, 1974. Protocol on resumption of shipping services between India and Pakistan was signed on January 15, 1975. The signing of this protocol paved the way for resumption of shipping services between the two countries which had remained suspended for about a decade. These two protocols were followed by a trade agreement between the governments of India and Pakistan.[18] The trade between the two countries was actually resumed in January 1975.

Phase 3: 1975–2004

Though the trade was resumed between India and Pakistan, the relations between them and for that matter trade relations between the two, passed through many highs and lows from 1975 onwards. Several rounds of talks at administrative, defence and political levels were held during this period.[19] Since 1983, not many serious efforts were made by the two countries until 1985. However, the institution of South Asian Association for Regional Cooperation (SAARC) in 1985 was a major step to normalise relations among the members of SAARC and promote trade and other economic relations. The normalisation of relations between India and Pakistan is of utmost importance and a prerequisite for the development, success and survival of SAARC. It may be noted that both India and Pakistan account for nearly 87 per cent of population, 91 per cent of surface area and 88 per cent of GDP of the seven SAARC countries. One of the major hurdles in the way of SAARC's journey towards higher levels of regional cooperation has been strained relations between India and Pakistan.

At the political level certain efforts were made to normalise the relations between India and Pakistan during the late 1980s when India and Pakistan had two young Prime Ministers—Rajiv Gandhi in India and Benazir Bhutto in Pakistan. The first half of the 1990s also raised hopes for normalisation of relations between the two countries. The efforts were made by Indian Prime Minister V.P. Singh and the Pakistan's Prime Minister Nawaz Shariff. Later, Indian Prime Minister Inder Kumar Gujral and Pakistan's Prime Minister Nawaz Shariff also made efforts to normalise and strengthen relations between two neighbouring countries. They even visited each other's country. Interestingly the birth place of Gujaral is in Pakistan and that of Nawaz Shariff is in India. However, all these efforts could not attain any substantial results.

Then came the historic bus journey (popularly known as bus diplomacy) from Amritsar to Lahore in early 1999, undertaken by the Indian Prime Minister Atal Behari Vajpayee, when Nawaz Shariff was Pakistan's Prime Minister. As a consequence of Bus Diplomacy, the Lahore Declaration was made and it raised the hopes quite high. However, all these efforts were shattered by striking against the 'rock' of Kashmir. Nevertheless, the Lahore Declaration commits both the countries to abide by the Simla Agreement. Even the much publicized Agra Summit in 2001 fell victim to the Kashmir problem.[20]

Indian Prime Minister Atal Behari Vajpayee's unilateral announcement in Srinagar for extending a 'hand of friendship' to Pakistan had once again shown a silver lining in the otherwise eclipsed relations between the two neighboring countries. All concerned with peace and prosperity in the subcontinent welcomed this bold initiative. After India's unilateral announcement of friendship, Pakistan, too, gave an indication of a 'paradigm shift' in its priorities and has spoken of "trade first" and "Kashmir later". Pakistan's offer of duty exemption on 600 Indian items is a positive gesture though she is yet to accord most favoured nation (MFN) status to India. On the contrary, India has already accorded MFN status to Pakistan though the same was withdrawn after the Kargil conflict. Pakistan has also accorded tariff concessions on the import of 1194 items from the SAARC member states under South Asian Preferential Trade Agreement (SAPTA). Islamabad's willingness to provide all necessary security guarantees to New Delhi, with regard to $4.5 billion (2500 km long) proposed Indo-Iran gas pipeline to be laid through its soil, is also an encouraging move. Both would gain immensely from this.

Numerous writings in various newspapers and periodicals have been highlighting different aspects of Indo-Pak relations since then. One, however, finds that discussion on trade and economic relations has been conspicuously missing in all those writings. In fact promotion of trade and economic ties could play a formidable role in normalizing and strengthening the relations between India and Pakistan as trade occupies a strategic importance for both the countries. Apart from having trade with each other, both India and Pakistan could resort to joint ventures and joint marketing of the goods and services in which they are now competing with each other in the global market. Besides, they could have transit trade through each other's territory, sea and air routes to other countries. For example, India could have trade relations with the Middle East, newly independent countries from the erstwhile Soviet Union, and other Central Asian countries through Pakistan. Similarly, Pakistan could have its trade with Bangladesh and Nepal through Indian territory. Thus, both the countries can approach to the solution of waxed problem by promoting and strengthening the other ties, such as trade. We have already witnessed that both India and China have bilateral trade relations on a significant scale while still negotiating on other complex and waxed issues.

The more recent meeting between Manmohan Singh, Prime Minister of India, and General Pervez Musharaff, President of Pakistan, in New York has further raised the hope for normalization of relations between the two neighbouring countries. The increasing people-to-people contacts and track-II diplomacy may prove to be another positive contribution towards normalization of relations. It is matter of satisfaction that the Indian Prime Minister and President of Pakistan resolved to continue bilateral talks to find peaceful and negotiated settlement on Kashmir and all other issues.

Rationale for Mutual Trade

The study of trade relations between these two neighbouring countries is of special significance against this background. Their mutual trade relations have been governed by various trade agreements and political relations and considerations ever since their independence. This is clear from the ever-decreasing share in each other's exports and imports. India's share in Pakistan's total imports and exports was 50.6 per cent and 23.6 per cent respectively during 1948–49. The corresponding shares in 1964–65 were 1.1 per cent and 5.9 per cent, respectively, during 1964–65 and 0.45 per cent and 2.46 per cent in 1979–80. India's share in Pakistan's exports and imports was nearly 0.75 per cent and 0.86 per cent in 1998[21]. As compared to this, Pakistan's share in India's imports and exports during 1951–52 was 1.06 per cent and 2.21 per cent. These shares came down to 0.17 per cent and 0.67 per cent in 1960–61 and to 0.40 per cent and 0.06 per cent in 1981–82. Pakistan's share in India's imports and exports during 1999–2000 was 0.15 per cent and 0.25 per cent, respectively[22]. The full potential of their mutual trade has never been realized so far, mainly owing to the predominance of political irrationalities over the economic rationalities. The mutual exports between the two countries during 2001–02 were worth US$ 212 million whereas their global exports were worth US$ 52,853 million, just 0.4 per cent of their global exports were between them. It is far below their mutual trade potential, being estimated around US$ 7,000 million per annum. An unofficial trade worth nearly US$ 2,000 million per annum is taking place between India and Pakistan. If this unofficial trade is routed through official channels, both the countries could earn a lot in terms of custom duty, etc.

Ever weakening trade ties and non-exploitation of trade potential between India and Pakistan have caused immeasurable financial loss to them. Both the countries would have gained somewhere between Rs. 15,000 and Rs. 20,000 crore during the last five decades, had they fully exploited their mutual trade potential. The gains were mainly in terms of lower prices compared to the global prices and much lower transport and transshipment costs due to proximity with each other. It is something strange that trade between two neighbouring countries has been mostly through Bombay-Karachi routes whereas on the eve of partition most of the trade used to be through land route via Wagah-Attari

Border. The distance between Amritsar and Lahore is just about 50 km. It is irrationality of the highest order that goods are first transported to Mumbai, then to Karachi and then to Lahore and other surrounding regions and vice versa. It involves huge transport and trans-shipment costs. More so opening up the Wagah-Attari Border for trade, *inter alia,* can give a boost to border trade also. Had there been strong trade ties between the two neighbouring countries, they would have also gained from their trade with the Middle East and Central Asian countries and from intra-SAARC trade. Pakistan, too, would have also gained a lot from the transit fee on Indian trade to third countries via Pakistan and vice versa.

Clearly, the trade dependency on each other has come down to negligible over a period of time. The situation has reached such a stage not because of the lack of potentialities but because of the hostile and hatred-loaded political relations, historical mistrust and fear psychosis. Another important fact which becomes clear from the foregoing discussion is that India's importance in Pakistan's exports and imports has been higher than that of Pakistan's in India's exports and imports. Both the countries, after partition, made deliberate efforts to reduce trade dependence on each other and develop trade relations with other countries. In the process, they have grossly ignored the fundamentals of trade theory. The post-partition international trade between India and Pakistan, in fact, was the direct outcome of partition. To a large extent inter-regional trade between the two regions, which now constitute Republic of India on the one hand and Islamic Republic of Pakistan on the other, became international trade. In fact the internal trade between these regions turned out to be international in character after the partition.

Kashmir Issue

Since every effort to normalize the relations between India and Pakistan and for that matter, bringing peace to the whole of South Asia could not surmount the Kashmir problem, there is a justification to give some space to it. Right from the very inception of Pakistan, Kashmir has been a bone of contention between India and Pakistan. It continues to be at the centre-stage even after three and a half wars and a death toll of nearly 30,000 during these wars and conflicts. Even the Nehru-Gandhi family's dominance in India and that of Abdullah family in Jammu and Kashmir have been unable to solve this problem. It became more and more complex over a period of time. Perhaps India was in a better position to solve this problem in 1948, at Tashkent in 1966 and at Simla in 1972. India, under the leadership of Indira Gandhi, was in a commanding position in 1972 and could clinch the issue by converting the Line of Control (LoC) into an international border[23].

In January 1948, Pakistan invaded Kashmir, forcing Indian intervention at the request of the then ruler of Kashmir Maharaja Hari Singh. The Maharaja signed the Instrument of Accession and Jammu and Kashmir became part of India. As compared to it, the status of 'Azad Kashmir' (Pakistan occupied Kashmir-POK) has never been defined. This area constitutes about 1/3rd of Kashmir and is alleged to be under the illegal occupation of Pakistan in the name of 'Azad' Kashmir. The UNCIP resolution stated that 'Azad' Kashmir is not a sovereign state, nor a province of Pakistan but rather a "local authority" with responsibility over the area consigned to it under the Cease Fire Agreement.

Pakistan has been demanding the implementation of UN Resolutions of 1948 and 1949 pertaining to plebiscite in Kashmir. However, according to Indian understanding these UN Resolutions have become irrelevant and UN Secretary General Kofi Annan supports India's viewpoint. At the same, it is important to note that Jammu and Kashmir is a pluralistic State. Besides being a Muslim majority, it has diverse communities such as Gujjars, Kashmiri Pandits, Bakkarwalas, Dogras and Ladhakhi Budhists.

The positions of India and Pakistan on Kashmir are diametrically opposite. To Pakistan, Kashmir is a disputed territory and cannot be accepted as part of India. Contrary to it, India has a firm position that Kashmir is an integral part of India. Indian Parliament, in 1994, had unanimously adopted a resolution reiterating, "all of Kashmir, including the region beyond the Line of Control (LoC) now occupied by Pakistan, is an integral part of India". The fulfillment of this resolution seems next to impossible without a full-fledged and long drawn-out war. And even if India succeeds in capturing PoK, it would have to deal with two million hostile Muslim population of PoK, who will have no loyalty to India. At the same time, Pakistan does not seem to have any capability to capture the province of Jammu and Kashmir by force. General Musharraf also admitted in New York in September 2004 that there can be no military solution to the Kashmir problem.

Concluding Comments

Evidently, India and Pakistan could not achieve any success in shedding mistrust, hatred, fear-psychosis and thereby normalizing their relations with each other. The Kashmir problem has gone from bad to worse. In fact, the Kashmir problem always becomes an insurmountable hurdle whenever there is any effort to normalize and strengthen mutual ties in trade, economic, cultural and other areas. It does not allow them to proceed further. But something would have to be done. Either find a satisfactory solution to the Kashmir problem or strengthen economic and other ties to such an extent that economic rationale compels the people and rulers on both the sides to come to terms. Strengthening of SAARC may further add to such a pressure. Under no circumstances, should this problem be allowed to linger on any more. It is neither in the interest of India and Pakistan nor in the interest of the people of Kashmir on both sides of LoC. There is an urgent need to save them from the immeasurable loss of resources, both human and material. Given the poor condition of their economies, abject poverty and massive unemployment, no country can afford to continue with such a political irrationality forever. Let economic rationality prevail upon political irrationality.

In such a scenario both the countries should make sincere and serious efforts to normalize relations with each other and thereby reduce their defence expenditure. Instead of wasting their energy and resources on perpetuating and nurturing conflict with each other, they should rather focus on peace, stability, growth and development and thereby on their pressing problems of unemployment, poverty, illiteracy and deprivation.

The Kashmir problem has done incalculable damage, in terms of both men and material, to both the countries over the past 57 years. They cannot afford to continue with this problem for too long. It would be altogether irrational to continuously hostage nearly 1330 million people in India and Pakistan for the sake of about 23 million Kashmiri population on both sides of the LoC (rather, international border).

Both India and Pakistan have been paying an extraordinary heavy price for their procrastination on Kashmir and other core issues. As such, Pakistan's singular pre-occupation with Kashmir and India's rhetoric for 'no talks without stoppage of cross border terrorism would not solve any problem between them. They should rather engage themselves in continuous dialogue as the eventual solution would emerge out of dialogue and an attitude of give and take rather than 'war' and 'violence'.

Promotion of trade relations, joint-ventures, joint marketing joint study groups on trade and other issues, permanent trade councilors in each other's High Commission, strengthening of SAARC, joint patrolling of LoC, end to propaganda war and hatredness, frequent meetings of civil and political bureaucracy and political leadership, track-II diplomacy and people to people contact, etc., could be some formidable steps towards confidence building exercise before the eventual solution to the core issues. The eventual solution, of course, would be a political solution to Kashmir problem that may either be the acceptance of LoC as an international border or allowing the Kashmiris to decide and determine their own future. Converting LoC into permanent border is the best solution according to Muttahida Quami Movement (MQM) Chief Altaf Hussain[24]. But the resolution of Kashmir issue, according to Hussain, will leave the Pakistan Army with no excuse to stay in power; they will have to make way for a democratically elected government. Under the circumstances, the solution to the Kashmir problem will have to be found by India and Pakistan themselves. Nevertheless, it will require a considerable amount of political will, sincerity and statesmanship of the highest order. The durable peace in the subcontinent can take place only after the satisfactory solution to the Kashmir problem. India, being a bigger country, has much more responsibility than Pakistan. The saner political leadership and people in both the countries must prevail upon the fundamentalists on both sides of the border. Both Indian and Pakistani leadership must transcend the past syndrome and march jointly towards the betterment of their people, including the Kashmiris, (earlier the better), otherwise posterity would curse them.

The normalization of relations is the only way to establish peace in the region that is the pre-requisite for growth and development. Development and prosperity is highly dependent on peaceful, normal and stable relations between the two countries. This is the only way to make use of their resources for peace, prosperity and development of the region and the only solution to their more pressing problems such as poverty, unemployment, inequality, illiteracy, under nutrition and malnutrition. ■

Notes & References

1. Altaf Zafar, *Pakistani Enterprises,* London, 1983, p.3.
2. P.T. Wadia and K.J.Merchant , *Our Economic Problems,* Bombay, 1959, p.85.
3. World Bank, *World Development Indicators,* 2004.
4. Griffin Keith and Azizur Rahman Khan, eds., *Growth and Inequality in Pakistan,* New Delhi, 1972, p.4.
5. World Bank, n. 3.
6. Ashok Kumar Mehta, "Musharraf's Shrewed Call to Jehaddis", *The Tribune,* July 23, 2001.
7. *The Hindu,* "Advertisement on Kargil Embarrases Musharaf Govt." July 28, 2001.
8. World Bank, *World Development Report,* 2001.
9. World Bank, *World Development Indicators,* (2000).
10. Yasmeen Samina, *Economic and Political Weekly,* February 16, 2002.

11. *Dawn*, June 24, 2002.
12. *The Partition Council* was set up in June 1947 to carry out the division of India and Pakistan, which arrived at a partition settlement on all affairs of the undivided country.
13. Government of India, *White Paper on Indo-Pakistan Trade Relations*, New Delhi, 1950, pp.3–4.
14. Ranjit Singh Ghuman, *Indo-Pakistan Trade Relations*, New Delhi, 1986, pp. 47–48.
15. R. Gharekhan Chinmaya , "The LoC and Kashmir", *The Hindu*, May 19, 2001.
16. The Government of Switzerland had been looking after the interests of India in Pakistan and that of Pakistani in India during this period.
17. For detail see Ranjit Singh Ghuman, n. 14, pp. 48–49.
18. Ibid., p.50.
19. Ibid., pp.51–56 and 84–88.
20. Pakistan President, General Musharraf gave a four point proposal in 2001 Agra Summit, *The Tribune*, July 15, 2001:
    (a) begin talks to resolve the disputes between India and Pakistan.
    (b) accept reality of Kashmir and resolve Kashmir issue.
    (c) 'eliminate the solutions that are not acceptable to India and Pakistan and to the people of Kashmir.
    (d) clinch a solution that is acceptable to all.
21. DGCI&S, Calcutta and *World Development Report, 2000-2001.*
22. DGCI&S, Calcutta, 2000–2001.
23. Rajeswar, T.V., "Dealing with a Military Ruler: India's difficulties and world opinion", *The Tribune*, July 30, 2001.
24. *Hindustan Times* (2004), 10 October, p. 1. Mohammad, Khair A. (1962), *United States' Foreign Policy in the Indo-Pakistan Sub Continent*, 1940-45 Ph.D. thesis, Michigan, USA), p.109.

Contours of Conflict, Co-operative Regimes and Critical Mass: A Study of the South Asian Region

Anand Aditya*

A Region at Risk

South Asia is restless today. Its restlessness, born out of frustration of the failures of decades of development efforts, fear of a nuclear holocaust and of a certain sense of fragility, because the seams of the past imperial divisions—faultlines of history—that are coming apart in the form of contours of conflict, now litter the region's whole map with killing fields instead of the peace that the veterans of independence struggles had envisioned for the region decades ago at the dawn of political freedom.[1]

In place of the prosperity that various development plans were expected to bring, millions today hang on to the tenterhooks of poverty. Babies are silenced to death by curable diseases, infants grow stunted, children are condemned to illiteracy and ceaseless work, mothers die during delivery, girls remain fettered to brothels, workers are sold for bonded labour, and fires, floods and famines keep stalking the villages of the region. All this has left the region the world's poorest, most illiterate, most malnourished and one of the most poorly governed as also most conflict-prone[2] and risky as well.[3] The failure of traditional paradigm of development in this part of the world was a foregone conclusion, not only because the roots of the problem lay in the structures of the very political regimes that emerged at liberation and remained unaddressed, but also because two forms of fundamentalism set the process from the very beginning on the path of failure—fundamentalism of faith, of both religion and ideology that the Afghan upheaval clearly brought to the fore,[4] as also of force that states on various occasions used to dictate development.[5] Development,

---

* Executive Director, Pragya Foundation, Kathmandu, Nepal.

however, is not a matter to be dictated and if the past half century of world history is any guide, dictatorship in any form, be it of princes, of priests, or of proletariats, is bound to fail.

Rationale and Study Outline

The situation in South Asia is a signal that the traditional order of co-operation, growth and security has failed. Partly, it is this failure and the challenge that it has brought to the fore that prompts this exercise to take a close look at the malady. But there are three more assumptions behind this undertaking. First, unless a rational ruling regime evolves in the region, the situation is likely to deteriorate further. Most of the conditions that Stephen Van Evera outlines in his paper 'Hypotheses on Nationalism and War' can be discerned in the region's context, such as profusion of stateless state-seeking nationalities, minority oppression, divergence in nationalist beliefs along with other structural, political, environmental and perceptual factors. Structuring a rational regional order will, however, demand a sustained exercise to promote the positive elements and countervail the negative factors at work. Second, the region offers ample opportunities for regional cooperation for the sustainable development of resource use and management patterns, linking trans-boundary cooperation and disaster prevention and mitigation. Third, a sea change is evident today in the traditional approaches to cooperation that can facilitate the implementation of new modalities of regional collaboration.

In the context sketched out above, this study proposes a brief conceptual framework profiles the security situation in the region, outlines the course of the region's developments in security followed by a features analysis and comparison of three co-operation regimes, does a SWOT analysis, presents an overview of the shifts under way and the potential stakeholders involved in new emerging order and sets out a course for future strategy.

Conceptual Framework

South Asia is a region of vast potential. It is also a region of multiple diversity. It has shown in the past its achievement capability in its world class wisdom, literature and cultural heritage and with its immense reservoirs of natural resources and extensive reserves of capable people, it can do so again. We successfully mid-wifed liberation from colonial rule. We saw the invention and implementation of the revolutionary impact of non-violent struggle in two other continents, North America (in the USA through Martin Luther King) and Africa (in South Africa through Gandhi and Nelson Mandela). It was South Asia that made definitive success of the Green Revolution despite its cycles of unceasing fires, floods, and famines, and of all the countries in the Third World, it was South Asia again that somehow was able to institutionalize the largest democracy keeping it kicking and alive in spite of the occasional hiccups. And at the regional level, South Asia is the only region that boasts of two nuclear powers.

There is, thus, little reason to despair. In economic terms, the signs of accelerated economic growth are already on the wall: Pakistan is reported to be set to exceed 5.3% growth target with India geared for over 8 per cent. The news of the day, however, is the transformational politics that has gripped Pakistan and India, the hub of South Asian relations since the end of the 1990s that is not only being seen as having a direct bearing on the global struggle against terrorism, but has somehow begun to radically alter the tenor of the whole region's traditional scenario. The events of the post-Islamabad summit are witness to that long-awaited change as is India's changed stance toward SAARC. Whereas India was opposed to SAARC expanding its activities to areas beyond the economic and non-political issues, it decided in 1991 to join cooperative efforts at the level to the extent and the tempo acceptable to other partners of SAARC. All this certainly marks a sea change raising new hopes and new possibilities.

However, if South Asia is to strike its own path of progress from poverty to prosperity, it will be essential to restructure the traditional mode of cooperation, reconsider the existing paradigm of regional governance, and revitalize the roles that individual states have so far been able to play in cultivating their mutual ties and relationship vis-à-vis the region as also the world at large. All this demands a new vision, new missions, new goals and strategies—goals that can be achieved and strategies that deliver.

In developing the argument, this paper makes the following points:

- A sustainable threshold of cooperation has to be crossed to make the new cooperative regime viable in the long run. This premise is based on the belief that meaningful and permanent collaboration cannot be enforced through institutionalizing international relations by principles and conventions, but by organizing international activities according to needs (a Mitranian framework of collaboration, 1946). The likelihood of progress is determined by needs, which means that cooperation is likely and sustainable where the need is greatest.
- For the new South Asian order, it is essential to promote the idea of regional governance.
- The countries in the region can and must adopt a proactive approach in restructuring their existing relationship and reconsolidating their roles in the region.

- To break the decisional logjam, resulting from institutional overloads at the national level, the decisions must be redistributed both upward and downward from the national governments at the centre to the regional and sub-national levels.
- The existing model of regional co-operation is a non-starter and if it is to deliver, a certain critical mass of co-operation has to be attained mutually by the ruling regimes, which means SAARC has to cross the threshold of sustainable co-operation.
- The political and economic parameters of South Asia stand significantly below those of the European Union and any transposing from the successful European or ASEAN model calls for careful caveats, particularly in view of the weak level of economic co-operation and mutual interactions.[6]
- Seventh, despite such caveats and the setbacks suffered so far in making a headway, SAARC does have immense scope for progress, given the changed and still changing environment of the day, the geopolitical compactness of the region[7] and the resources harnessable from the ocean.[8]
- There is a radical shift in the paradigm of values, goals, and approaches to traditional modes of defence, democratization, and development, each of which is likely to aid the process of the regionalist movement in the future.
- Finally, the situation demands a triadic strategy.

Security Profile of South Asia

The aforementioned contradictions throw up three questions: (i) How do the various countries of the region fare in human and military security? (ii) Where does the region as a whole stand in that regard? (iii) How does the public view the issues at stake? The curiosities prompted the development of a comparative profile of the seven countries of the region (Table 1A and 1B).

While considerable diversity is evident among the states in the physical aspects, such as area and population, on a number of other parameters related to value distribution and development (GNP per capita, docile ratio, wealth of nation, HDI, GDI), the indices appear comparably close, usually below the acceptable level, save in one or two cases. In the percentage of people without access to basic services (item 15) such as healthcare, sanitation, drinking water, and education, the situation is miserable, with a substantial share of each country's population denied access save the Maldives and Sri Lanka in a couple of instances. The human distress profile (item 13) offers no better picture either except in Nepal's case, which has declined in the past one decade with social crime spiralling upward. Almost none of the region's governmental regimes, for

Table 1A : A Comparative Profile of South Asian Countries

		Bangladesh	Bhutan	India	Maldives	Nepal	Pakistan	Sri Lanka
1.	Year the State was founded (or became independent)	(1971)	(1907)	(1947)	(1965)	1768	(1947)	(1948)
2.	Area ooo km	144	47	3,288	0.3	141	796	66
3.	Population million 1998	12.6	0.8	980	0.3	23	132	19
4.	Technical Hydroelectric Generation	2,520		75,905		277	9,137	1,289
5.	GNP billion dollars 1998	44		421.3	.323	4.8	63.2	15.2
6.	GNP per capita at ppp	1,100		1,770		1,090	1,560	
7.	Population below $ 1 a day			47.0	47.0	50.3	11.6	4.0
8.	Ratio of highest decile to lowest (income)	5.8		6.1		9.3	7.4	6.6
9.	Wealth of Nation per capita	3,100	6,500	4,300	8,800	1,600	6,800	9,400
10.	Civil Disorder Index (N=134), 1948 - 77	41 (101)		4,146 (7)	31 (105)	237 (66)	1,093 (21)	186 (73)
11.	Deaths from Political.Violence (N = 125), 1948 - 77	1,490 (48)		7,596 (26)	2 (121)	133 (82)	34,446 (4)	5,583 (3o)
12.	Number killed in Police Encounter, 1997-98	23		756		93	702	32
13.	Human Distress Profile							
	a. Cases Pending in Courts	14.5		6.3		1.0	1.4	
	b. Reported Rapes	33.0		11.0		1.0	7.0	20.0
	c. Armed Robberies	2.3		3.7		1.0	7.2	33.3
	d. Murders	1.0		1.6		1.1	1.3	3.7

14.	Govt. Stability (1 lowest, 9 highest)	4	6	6	6	9	5	6
15.	Percentage of People without Access to							
	a. Healthcare	55	35	15	25	58	45	7
	b. Sanitation	65	30	71	34	80	70	34
	c. Drinking water	21	42	19	4	52	40	43
	d. Education	62	58	48	7	72	62	10
16.	War State (1 peace, 9 war)	1	1	2	1	1	2	2
17.	Military Environment Index (0 highly unfavorable, 9 highly favorable for military operations)	7	4	3	8	2	5	4
18.	Three Top Priorities for Govt. Budget	Defense Education Gen. Adm.		Education Inflation Empl-t		Education Health Empl-t	Defense Education Gen. Devt.	Inflation Soc. welfare Gen. Devt
19.	Human Development Index	.440	.459	.545	.716	.463	.508	.721
20.	Gender - related Development Index GDI 1997	.428	.444	.525	.711	.441	.472	.712
21.	Human Governance Index HGI	.462		.577			.502	.465
22.	Freedom Rating FR (7 lowest, 1 highest)	3	7	3	6	3.5	4.5	3.5
23.	Political Freedom Index PFI (O lowest, 100 highest)	69		71.5		57.3	64.3	58.3
24.	Gross Human Rights Violation GHRV (1 lowest, 5 highest)	4	3	4	2	2	3	4

Note: Figures in parentheses are rankings with 1 highest or first in the scale.
Source: Human Development Report, 2000.

that matter, can boast a record of stability (item 14). Even the picture on the freedom and human rights front is mixed at best, skewed to the lower side of the scale (items 22, 23, 24). While in terms of real inter-state war (item 14) the countries show a positive trend, except for the two cases of India and Pakistan which are in a state of negative balance with three wars fought in the last 50 years and the priority given to defence (item 18), the internal situation except in the Maldives remains turbulent everywhere. On a number of other human security items, too, the situation is hardly flattering (items 10,11,12) (Table 1A).

All this can help in explaining the patterns of citizen perception on issues such as faith in the political system, political party, legal order, political leaders, judges, police officers, and corruption. One survey shows that a consistently high proportion of the respondents feel negatively on all these issues which is no good news (Table 1B).

Table 1B South Asia-wide Citizen Survey on Governance (in percentage)

QUERY ITEM (N =)	Bangladesh (524)	India (516)	Nepal (500)	Pakistan (500)	Sri Lanka (490)
1. Faith in the political system	45	29	31	63	75
2. Political Party does not represent our interests		49	15	48	82
3. Legal program is not just protective of people's rights	65	36	49	64	70
4. Non-profit organizations make an important contribution to people	43	39	62	37	67
5. Political leaders are corrupt	76	65	83	88	45
6. Judges are corrupt	61	30	55	67	44
7. Police officers are corrupt	86	67	64	94	83
8. Problem of corruption has worsened in the last 5 years	36	42	55	62	38

Sources: Table 2A : Items 2,3,5,6,7: *The World Development Report 1999/2000*, Tables 1, 4.
8. *Human Development in South Asia* (HDISA) 1999, Table 6.3.
9. Press Release, World Bank, Washington D.C., 17 Sept. 1995.
10, 11, 14, : George T. Kurian, *The New Book of World Rankings* (New York: Facts on File, 1984).
12. HDISA 1999, Table 6.1.
13. ——————, Fig. 6.1.
15. ——————, Table 4.2.
16, 17: James F. Dunnigan & Austin Bay, *A Quick and Dirty Guide to War*, New York , William Morrow, 1986.
18 : HDISA 1999, Technical Annex B.

20 . *Human Development Report* 1999, Tables 2, 3.
21 : HDISA 1999, Table 2.1.
22 : A Karatnycky, ed., *Freedom in the World,* Table of Independent Countries : Comparative Measures of Freedom, pp. 600- 602.
23 : Mahbub ul Haq, *Reflections on Human Development*, 1994, Annex 5.1.
24 : Ingomar Hauchler & Paul M. Kennedy, eds., *Global Trends : The World Almanac of Development and Peace*, Table 5.

Table 2B: Human Development in South Asia 1999, Technical Annex B.

The issue matrix, which presents a perspective on the issues that have dogged relations between the countries of the region, moreover, suggests there are certain dimensions common to the relationship between a number of states (water, migration, insurgency, and treaty) generating the most recurrent and most controversial debates.

Figure 2 Issue Matrix for South Asia

	Bangladesh	Bhutan	India	Maldives	Nepal	Pakistan	Sri Lanka
Bangla-desh			• Water • Migration • Insurgency				
Bhutan			• Water • Migration • Insurgency		• Migration		
India					• Security • Border • Migration • Insurgency Trade & Transit • Treaty	• Water • Migration • Insurgency	• Migration • Treaty
Maldives							
Nepal							
Pakistan							
Sri Lanka							

Blank cell indicates a situation of non-contiguity due to geographical distance minimizing scope for issues developing into conflicts

A huge democratic and developmental deficit is thus evident in the social order of the subcontinent. Compounding that deficit in the realm of gender and child equity, but even otherwise, so long as there is destitution of a whole mass of humanity, so long as there is disablement of a large part of the subcontinent's population and so long as there is undeserved discrimination and preventable deprivation of its people on the basis of race, region, or religion, the work on security agenda will remain. A new form of security orientation to improve human and societal security thus becomes important because there can be no citizen freedom, or even civil security, worth the name in its absence. Even the basic minimum of civic literacy in society can hardly be conceived in the absence of the rudiments of adequate security education. In that sense, at least, the issue of civic education programme on security emerges as a higher order agenda than many other freedoms of the political domain. It is the primal social force that can be conceived in the natural human yearning for freedom from backwardness and the political predicament into which the region has landed itself, because if it becomes effective, it cannot only facilitate the process of development, but also accelerate it by unhinging the many impediments that have held that process at bay.

A number of reasons could be offered to explain why such a situation has developed.

- The lack of differentiation of the political sphere from social and personal relations and the ascriptive and communal base of the ruling elite hamper a rational cognition of the issues related to security and development. Part of the explanation lies in the subsistent culture that tends to produce survival regimes.
- The totalistic nature of the political parties discourages a secular interpretation of the issues, just as the dominance of political cliques encourages factionalism, a situation that is hardly conducive to the formation or accumulation of robust social and political capital.
- The high level of personal freedom exercised by political leaders allows them to ignore policies and principles in deciding on matters of conflict resolution and security and the tendency to see issues in a black and white form radicalizes the context.
- A dual communication system maintains the cultural divide between the generations and urban and rural Nepal complicating issue comprehension further.
- There is an obvious mismatch between the pace of recruitment of the

various elements into political roles and the rate of the development of the political system's capacity to address the rising demands, interests, and needs of the various constituencies. Both conflict management capacity and insecurity coping capacity in such a circumstance remain hostage to the power incumbents' intentions and interests.

- Weak consensus over the fundamental national goals and values as also the legitimate means to materialize them inhibits the development of a unified approach to resolve the security crisis when it appears.
- The volume and quality of political discussions under way hardly match the political decisions needed to handle the structural conflicts and crises when they appear. There is, for instance, considerable heat and noise, but little light so far on the Maoist movement itself in Nepal. The explanation may lie in the scarcity of political capital.
- The inability of the SAARC forum to devise a regional mechanism to mediate on security issues: it is hard to understand why the regional association is shying away from setting up a mechanism such as the Regional Security Consultative Council suggested by Bhabani Sen Gupta.

Evolution of Regionalism and Security Developments

Between 1945 and 2002, one can notice a number of regional forums and agencies making their appearance, not each of which has been equally successful (see Box). But as the pace quickened, virtually every region on the face of earth now has a regional forum, among whom EU, NAFTA, OAU and ASEAN have emerged as trend-setters with CICA, APEC and ACD beginning to take lead role recently in Asia. Among them, given the geopolitical background and history, SAARC made its appearance relatively late and almost equally late and slow seems to have been its progress over the two decades of its conception and existence.

Box 1: Strategic Developments In South Asia

1947	Asian Relations Conference (Delhi)
1950	Nepal-India Treaty
1951	Indian troops in Nepal Tarai to quell uprising
1953	Northern Tier Strategy of USA to build up defence capabilities of frontline states in West Asia to contain Soviet influence
1954	Pakistan joins SEATO and in 1955 CENTO

1955	Bangdung Conference
1960	Tibetan influx and its potential to aggravate Sino-Bhutanese relations leads Bhutan to close border with China bringing cross-border trade to a standstill
1961	Goa taken over by India
1962	Chinese foreign minister extends his firm pledge to stand by Nepal's side in case of a foreign attack
	War between India and China
1963	Bhutan, for the first time, accepts India's concept of a broad security perimeter, and trains the Royal Bhutan Army through the Indian Military Training Team
1965	IDSA (Institute for Defence Studies and Analysis); New Delhi-based think-tank of the Ministry of Defence of India
	Arms Assistance Agreement between Nepal and India
	Indo-Pak War
1966	Armed revolt started by Mizo National Front (organized in 1960)
	US acquires Diego Garcia from Britain
1971	India supports Sri Lanka with military forces to curb political violence
	Indo-USSR strategic pact for 20 years
	Indian troops in East Pakistan
1972	Pakistan-India agreement on non-use of force in bilateral disputes
	Nagas agree for a ceasefire after liberation of Bangladesh and Indian forces overrun their base in former East Pakistan
	Hill people of Bangladesh organize under the PCJSS (Parbatya Chattagram Jano Shanghati Shamity) with a military wing Shanti Bahini
1973	CPR (Centre for Policy Research) set up as a think-tank in New Delhi to study national policy ISS (Inst. for Strategic Studies) set up in Islamabad; publishes Strategic Studies and Strategic Perspective
1974	Nuclear explosion at Pokhran by India; Land Demarcation Agreement between Sheikh Mujib and Indira Gandhi defines the midstream of the Muhuri (between East Bangladesh and Tripura State) as the permanent boundary
	Sikkim merges into India

1975	Shillong accord of Nagas
1977	President Carter suggests the Indian Ocean should be completely demilitarized
1978	BIISS (Bangladesh Institute for International and Strategic Studies) founded in Dhaka for Studies on foreign policy, military strategy, and regional security
	Both US President Carter and British PM Callaghan during their visits to South Asian countries promise economic help for multilateral cooperative projects with indications for the whole of the South Asian region being declared as a ZOP
1979	Soviet intervention in Afghanistan1980 (March) West Bengal government hoists Indian flag over the Purbasha (Talpatty) island
1981	Pakistan proposes a 'No War Pact' with India
1982	India proposes 'Treaty of Peace and Friendship' with Pakistan
1984	Operation Blue Star; Indira Gandhi's assassination in October incites communal frenzy, Siachin conflict
1985	Agitation started by GNLF (Gorkha National Liberation Front)
1987–1990	IPKF in Sri Lanka; more than 1150 Indian officers and soldiers killed
1988	India provides security relief to the Maldives threatened by mercenaries
1989	SAARC Chamber of Commerce and Industry set up by SAARC nations and their apex business federations to promote economic cooperation and to ultimately establish a SAARC Union
	South Asia Human Rights Documentation Centre set up in New Delhi to maintain an informal network of partner organization for human rights in the region
1990	Pressler Amendment prohibits military and economic aid to Pakistan
1991	SAARC Law set up (a network of 1500 eminent lawyers, judges, and legal activists from the region); Journal *SAARC Law Magazine*; advocates establishment of a SAARC arbitration centre and tribunal to resolve regional disputes rather than in larger international fora; funded by private

	sources and donations from legal associations, it has 5 affiliated country chapters
	SAMA (South Asian Media Association) established to help in resolution of conflicts in the region
	USSR dissolved
1992	PM Benazir Bhutto invites all opposition leaders in South Asia to discuss a common vision for the region
	Speakers of the Houses of South Asia meet in Sri Lanka and Nepal to form Association of SAARC Speakers and Parliamentarians
	Logang massacre in Bangladesh (army and settlers alleged to participate jointly), previous massacres - Kaukhail (1980), Dewan Bazaar (1986)
	Neemrana Initiative on Indo-Pak dialogue
	Indo-Pak agreement to provide prior notification of military exercises involving more than 10,000 troops and for establishing No-Fly Zones along their borders
	ICES (International Centre for Ethnic Studies) with branches in Colombo and Kandy set up with focus on ethnic and communal conflict in South Asia; human rights, peace, and security; and election monitoring
	RCSS (Regional Centre for Strategic Studies) set up in Colombo as a link between the region's scholars
	South Asian Forum for Human Rights (SAFHR) founded with a secretariat that rotates every few years
	India-Pakistan declaration on prohibition of chemical weapons (not to develop, produce, acquire or use)
	MQM reported working for Jinnahpur—a state comprising Karachi and Hyderabad separate from Sind
1993	Bombay riots; Russian Federation's Foreign Policy publication accords South Asia 7th place in its list of 10 priorities
	Yeltsin restores ties with India in a 20-year treaty India and China sign Agreement on the Maintenance of Peace and Tranquility along the Line of Actual Control
	India and China sign arms control agreement on Panchsheel basis of mutual and equal security
	Bombay blast kills more than 300
	CPD (Centre for Policy Dialogue) in Bangladesh

1994 ICPI collaborates with Parliamentarians for Global Action and the International Peace Academy for their program of workshops in peace-making and preventive diplomacy for parliamentarians in South Asia; 1st workshop held in May 1994 in Kathmandu; 2nd in Maldives May 1995

CASAC (Coalition for Action on South Asian Cooperation) formed around a nucleus of journalists, academics, business people, politicians, and administrators with secretariat in Kathmandu and national chapters around the region; works through its Executive Committee, and funded by FES and donations; a leading network for policy dialogue

UN Conference on Human Rights (Vienna) proclaims Right to Develop as a fundamental human right

UNCLOS (UN Convention on the Law of the Sea) comes into force making large areas of the sea responsibility of littoral and island states (EEZ of one state or another now covers 30% of INOC, expected to increase further when the present 200 nautical mile limit from the coastline extends to 350 by the year 2004)

1995 Pakistan-India People's Forum for Peace and Democracy started by activists, trade unions, and intellectuals to put pressure on the governments of India and Pakistan to improve relations; with chapters in various cities

4-day international conference in New Delhi on creation of an *Indian Ocean Community*, represented by 20 littoral states of the Indian Ocean and 4 SAARC members; ends up divided on approach to be taken—security-political vs. economic

Planning workshop held in Singapore on Conflict Resolution through Cooperation in Energy and Environment, a meeting of Indian, Nepalese, and Pakistani teams of two politicians and two experts from each country for cooperation on energy; funded by UNDP

1996 India-China Agreement on Confidence-Building Measures in the military field along the Line of Actual Control

IMO convenes a conference on maritime SAR (Search & Rescue) and Global Maritime Distress and Rescue System (GMOSS) that agrees to cover the area between Africa and Australia

	IPCS (Institute for Peace and Conflict Studies) set up in New Delhi; holds IPCS Seminar on South Asian Futures Conference in 1998 in Islamabad and Delhi, another at the same time on Global Security and Nuclear Disarmament; funded by American foundations, it is the coordinator for the Shanghai Dialogues
	CASAC holds a workshop for MPs on measures for conflict resolution and confidence-building in South Asia
1997	Male SAARC summit recognizes significance of good neighbourhood relations in promoting peace and cooperation and role of informal political consultations; sets up GEP (Group of Eminent Persons)
	IOR-ARC (Indian Ocean Rim-Association for Regional Cooperation established.
	Travelling Seminar organized by USIS and the International Center for Peace Initiatives (ICPI) for indigenous-language journalists early in the year, but with majority of participants from English language press
1998	Bilateral Bhutan-China agreement to maintain peace and tranquility along the Sino-Bhutanese border signed
	Decision taken to establish Regional Peace-Keeping Training Centre as a project of BIISS, funded by US Pacific Command
	Indian Coast Guard intercepts a large consignment of weapons on Long off Islands in the Andamans, possibly destined for militant groups in the Indian northeast (in March 1997 the Royal Thai Navy seizes arms shipment destined for a militant group in India)
	After nuclear tests, India categorizes China as its main adversary; Pakistan goes nuclear
	Pakistan advances comprehensive proposals for establishing strategic and conventional restraint regimes in South Asia including avoidance of nuclear and missile arms race, measures for nuclear risk reduction, moratorium on nuclear testing, establishment of strategic stability at minimum level of credible deterrence and balanced reduction of conventional forces and armaments; India does not agree and comes out with its own proposal on no first use of nuclear weapons agreement

	National Media Centre organizes India-Pakistan dialogue in Delhi centred around the English language press
	Informal proposal for 'Strategic Triangle' among Russia, China, and India comes from Russia; Russian Premier Y. Primakov visits India; extends military and technical cooperation to 2010 A.D.
1999	*Jang* group of newspapers organizes a meeting of MPs from India and Pakistan
	Lahore Declaration; a conference of Indian and Pakistani MPs in Islamabad earlier in 1999 creates a favourable atmosphere for Bus Diplomacy
	Kargil Battle: history's first direct combat between two nuclear powers; direct intervention by US and strong international pressure makes the Mujahideen and Pakistan's paramilitary forces withdraw to LoC
	North-South Security Programme of King's College (London) and SAMA (Sri Lanka) in cooperation with ICPI (Mumbai) and Citizens' Media Commission (Karachi) convene a gathering of press from 9 languages around the region that agrees on setting up a South Asian Editors' Forum to formulate guidelines to develop South Asian ethics in the press
	Military takeover of government in Pakistan
	Hijacking of IC-814 plane from Kathmandu to Afghanistan
2000	President Clinton's visit to South Asia underscores the region's growing significance in UN policy
2001	Madaris Ordinance initiated: Pakistan government imposes strict measures in early 2002 to regulate Madrassas
	De-weaponization program launched by Pakistan to flush out illegal weapons blamed for fuelling sectarian violence extended to religious and academic institutions; 215,000 weapons surrendered up to October 2002 compared with 18 million illicit arms floating around Pakistan
	Agra Summit fails
	Parliament in New Delhi attacked
2002	General Musharraf announces a ban on 5 extremist organizations
2004	12th SAARC Summit at Islamabad

Comparison of Regional Cooperation Regimes

What can explain the glacial pace of SAARC's progress? A comparison of the EU, ASEAN, and SAARC shows that whereas in area and population all the regions show some diversity, in economy, Human Development Index and political features—civil liberties, political rights, press freedom, and corruption perception index, the members of the European Union manifest far more uniformity than do either the ASEAN or SAARC states. The indices, moreover, are also at a significantly higher level. In each of these dimensions, ASEAN states usually exceed the nations of SAARC. Looked at another way, an analysis of the distribution patterns of NGOs and soldiers per area and population unit also brings out the differences between the three regions quite clearly (Table 2): The Population/NGO spread of EU, for instance, exceeds that of ASEAN by over ten times and of SAARC by 33 times and the population/soldier ratio for the same comparison sets are 1.2 and 2.5.

Features Analysis of South Asian Security Regimes

1. Since its very inception as an independent geopolitical region, South Asia has existed as a virtual 'zone of war' (K.J. Holsti's term), a typical insecurity community where more than four million people are officially carrying arms and where all the major developments in the area of defence and state security have almost invariably tended to contribute to the insecurity of the citizen, community, state and the region.
2. The span of the region's diversity in terms of most of the natural features (space, population, and resources) is the widest one could imagine (see Table 1) ranging from geo- and bio-diversity to the ethnic and social spheres, a feature which bears implications of crucial significance to security policy planning.
3. Most of the security issues of the region are chronic and common to a number of the countries (see Issue Matrix). Some of them are rooted in historic memory reaching back centuries, others decades. Any meaningful solution of these issues is therefore going to demand a series of measures in a long-term framework.
4. The only state contiguous to five states of the region, India, is the largest state of the subcontinent outpacing all its neighbours in population, area, economic strength and military power by a wide margin. Globally, it has the fourth largest army, the sixth largest navy (the only state in the region with blue water navy and the eighth largest air force.
5. The race for militarization between India and Pakistan in South Asia

Table 2: Comparison of EU, ASEAN, and SAARC

		Area '000 sq km 1999	Population million 2000	GDP PPP billion US$ 2000	GDPC PPP US$ 2000	Wealth of Nations '000 US$ 2000	Population at US $ 1 a day	National Poverty Line	HDI 2000
		1	2	3	4	5	6	7	8
A. EU3,247		**376.3**							
1.	Austria	84	8.1	217.1	26,765	394	.	.	0.926
2.	Belgium	33	10.2	278.6	27,178	384	.	.	0.939
3.	Denmark	43	5.3	147.4	27,627	463	.	.	0.926
4.	Finland	338	5.2	129.4	24,996	347	.	.	0.930
5.	France	552	59.2	1,426.6	24,223	413	.	.	0.926
6.	Germany	357	82.0	2,062.2	25,103	399	.	.	0.920
7.	Greece	132	10.6	174.3	16,501	142	.	.	0.879
8.	Ireland	70	3.8	113.3	29,866	212	.	.	0.917
9.	Italy	301	57.5	1,363.0	23,626	373	.	.	0.907
10.	Luxembourg	2.6	0.4	21.9	50,061	651	.	.	0.914
11.	The Netherlands	41	15.9	408.4	25,657	100	.	.	0.933
12.	Portugal	92	10.0	173.0	17,290	141	.	.	0.876
13.	Spain	506	39.9	768.5	19,472	265	.	.	0.906
14.	Sweden	450	8.8	215.3	24,277	496	.	.	0.904
15.	UK	245	59.4	1,404.4	23,589	324	.	.	0.932

B. ASEAN		**4,482**	**521.3**						
1.	Brunei Darus	5.8	0.3	5.4	16,779	165	.	.	0.856
2.	Cambodia	181	13.1	17.4	1,446	3.5	.	36.1	0.543
3.	Indonesia	1,905	212.1	640.3	3,043	12.0	7.7	27.1	0.684
4.	Lao PDR	237	5.3	8.3	1,575	6.7	26.3	46.1	0.485
5.	Malaysia	330	22.2	211.0	9,068	56.0	.	15.5	0.782
6.	Myanmar	677	47.7	..	..	14.0	..	..	0.552
7.	The Philippines	300	75.7	300.1	3,971	15.0	..	36.9	0.754
8.	Singapore	1	4.0	93.8	23,356	360.0	.	.	0.885
9.	Thailand	513	62.8	388.8	6,402	34.0	2.0	13.1	0.762
10.	Vietnam	332	78.1	156.8	1,996	2.6	..	50.9	0.688
C. SAARC		**4,488**	**1,331.9**						
1.	Bangladesh	144	137.4	209.9	1,602	3.1	21.1	35.6	0.478
2.	Bhutan	47	2.1	1.1	1,412	6.5	..	..	0.494
3.	India	3,288	1,008.9	2,395.4	2,358	4.3	44.2	35.0	0.577
4.	The Maldives	0.3	0.3	1.2	4,485	8.8	..	..	0.743
5.	Nepal	147	23.0	30.6	1,327	1.6	37.7	42.0	0.490
6.	Pakistan	796	141.3	266.2	1,928	6.8	31.0	34.0	0.499
7.	Sri Lanka	66	18.9	68.3	3,530	9.4	6.6	25.0	0.741

Civil Liberties 2000	Political Rights 2000	Press Freedom 2000	Law and Order 2001	Corruption Perception Index (CPI) 2000	Adult Literacy 2000	Urbanization 2000	Military Expenditure % GDP 2000	Armed Forces '000s 2000	Pop per Unit Soldier 2000	Area per Unit Soldier 2000	R & D Expenditure%GNP 1990-2000	Scientists Engineers per million 1990-2000	Number of NGOs 2000	Population per NGO 2000
9	10	11	12	13	14	15	16	17	18	19	20	21	22	23
								1,633					41,891	
1	1	14	6	7.8	.	67.3	0.8	74	109.5	1.1	1.6	1,605	2,684	3,018
2	1	9	5	6.6	.	97.3	1.4	39	261.5	0.8	1.6	2,307	3,162	3,226
1	1	9	6	9.5	.	85.1	1.5	22	240.9	2.0	1.9	3,240	2,806	1,889
1	1	14	6	9.9	.	59.0	1.3	32	162.5	10.6	..	..	2,647	1,964
2	1	21	5	6.7	.	75.4	2.6	294	201.4	1.9	2.2	2,686	3,551	16,671
2	1	13	5	7.4	.	87.5	1.5	221	371.0	1.6	2.3	2,873	3,505	23,395
3	1	30	3	4.2	97.2	60.1	4.9	159	66.7	0.8	0.5	1,045	2,137	4,960
1	1	18	6	7.5	.	59.0	0.7	12	316.7	5.8	1.5	2,132	1,996	1,904
2	1	27	6	5.5	98.4	66.9	2.1	251	229.1	1.2	1.0	1,322	3,257	17,654
1	1	10	6	8.7	.	91.5	0.7	1	400.0	2.6	..	..	1,175	340
1	1	15	6	8.8	.	89.5	1.6	52	305.8	0.8	2.0	2,490	3,203	4,964
1	1	17	5	6.3	92.2	64.4	2.1	45	222.2	2.0	0.6	1,583	2,289	4,369
2	1	20	4	7.0	97.6	77.6	1.3	166	240.4	3.0	0.8	1,562	3,116	12,805
1	1	10	6	9.0	.	83.3	2.1	53	166.0	8.5	3.8	4,095	2,975	2,958
2	1	17	6	8.3	.	89.5	2.5	212	280.2	1.2	2.5	4,103	3,388	17,532
								1,862					6,307	
5	7	74	6	..	91.5	72.2	7.6	5	60.0	1.2	..	..	184	1,630

6	6	61	..	..	67.8	16.9	2.4	140	93.6	1.3	..	..	136	96,324
4	3	47	2	1.9	86.9	41.0	1.1	297	714.1	6.4	0.1	..	1,033	205,324
6	7	69	..	..	48.7	19.3	..	29	182.8	8.2	..	..	107	49,533
5	5	70	3	5.0	87.5	57.4	1.9	96	231.3	3.4	0.4	154	1,065	20,845
7	7	100	3	..	84.7	27.7	1.7	344	138.7	2.0	..	..	207	230,435
3	2	30	2	2.9	95.3	58.6	1.2	106	714.2	2.8	0.2	156	1,071	70,682
5	5	68	6	9.2	92.3	100.0	4.8	60	66.7	0.02	1.1	2,182	1,039	3,850
3	2	29	5	3.2	95.5	19.8	1.6	301	208.6	1.7	0.1	102	1,028	61,089
6	7	80	4	2.6	93.4	24.1	7.9	484	161.4	0.7	..	274	437	178,719
								2,223					4,435	
4	3	60	2	0.4	41.3	25.0	1.3	137	1,002.9	1.1	..	51	593	231,703
6	7	76	..	..	47.0	7.1	..	6	350.0	7.8	..	..	64	32,813
3	2	42	4	2.7	57.2	27.7	2.4	1303	774.3	2.5	0.6	158	1,718	587,253
5	6	65	..	..	96.7	27.6	..	..	..	..	..	..	82	3,659
4	3	57	..	..	41.8	11.8	0.9	50	460.0	2.9	..	..	398	57,789
5	6	57	3	2.3	43.2	33.1	4.5	612	230.9	1.3	..	..	873	161,856
4	3	74	3	..	91.6	22.8	4.5	115	164.3	0.6	..	188	707	26,733

Human Development Report

confirms the premise that every increment in the military security of one state is paid for by insecurity of another. The ultimate outcome is thus the exact opposite of what was anticipated.

6. The key initiatives on most of the programs for peace and cooperation in the region have so far been taken by small states of the region: by Bangladesh for SAARC, by Nepal for the Zone of Peace and by Sri Lanka for the Zone of Peace in the Indian Ocean region.
7. The two largest states of the region—India and Pakistan—were born as twins, but rival twins, through a baptism of blood and fire and have fought three wars and are now nuclear powers. Their congenital hostility is symbolized in their missile nomenclature: India's 'Prithvi' and Pakistan's 'Ghauri'.
8. The 1999 battle over Kargil remains history's first direct combat between nuclear powers.
9. At a time when defence spending is generally declining, military budget is being hiked up in India and Pakistan.
10. In the context of South Asia, the argument that nuclearization leads to reduced expenditure on conventional forces has been proved to be an illusory concept. (In other words, nuclear deterrence does not necessarily relegate conventional deterrence.)
11. South Asia remains one of the poorest regions in the world where the population below the absolute poverty line is 45 per cent. Despite the stark poverty and misery this entails, a substantial part of the region's precious resources is being diverted to military purposes, of which India and Pakistan account for 90 per cent. No rationalization by the military strategists is going to justify the escalation of tension and mass insecurity psychosis it engenders at four levels—the panic caused among the small states, the enormous socio-economic burden it brings on state budgets, the opportunity costs claimed on national development and the war psychosis generated among the mass public, particularly of the two rival nuclear states.
12. Along with the balance of nuclear terror in place, there is a noticeable increase in the tendency of insurgents and sub-nationalist groups of the region to take recourse to small arms. As a result, small arms proliferation is already under way with long-range implications for state and inter-state insecurity.
13. The roots of a large share of insecurity in the region lie in the mal-development brought about by human interventions into nature causing land, water and food insecurity. One calculation puts the number of people displaced by big dams in the last 50 years alone at 3.3 million. The case of the Kaptai dam in

Bangladesh is just one stark reminder.

14. The traditional majority-centred policy, decision-making and implementation in the region has meant security only for the majority whose leverage on power and the military order has tended to sharply alienate and deprive the minorities. In the domain of security, it is often the pride and prejudice of the ruling majority which have ended up displacing, disabling, or preempting the opportunity access of the minorities and disadvantaged groups, the main reason behind the rising refrains for secession, division, and emergence of new political formations.
15. South Asia at present is also witness to intensive criminalization of its society and politics through corruption, drugs, arms trafficking, or rampant impunity and rise in violence.
16. Heavy politicization of all the major sectors in South Asia has polarized the society including the civil society, which tends to decrease societal security generating what has been termed a migrant milieu—the tendency to emigrate.
17. In South Asia, the conventional nation-state project is falling to pieces. That its seams are coming apart is clear from more than one evidence. The failure of the project was written into its very roots; conflict, crisis, violence, and insecurity were built into the constitution through some of the basic policies and principles of the state itself—majoritarian representation and adversarial mode of parliamentary opposition. The classical form of the South Asian state has thus turned out to be a futile exercise in caricature for an imaginary future that ill fits both its illustrious past and potential future. Trying to evolve a unitarian command state where diversity is the rule, was a fundamentally false start. It was less a product of consent or social contract and more an accident of colonial history, a manufactured reality surviving through the use of force, often exercised in egregiously violent ways.

Scope for Regional Cooperation

The foregoing review prompts the curiosity: What scope does South Asia offer for regional cooperation? For an assessment, Figure 2 lists the strengths, weaknesses, opportunities and threats in the region's context. Whereas quite a few weaknesses can be noticed along with some threats lurking behind, the region's environment does proffer some strong points and opportunities which can be beneficially utilized to promote cooperation in the region.

Figure 2

STRENGTHS (S)	WEAKNESSES (W)
• State commitment: Decentralization Act 1997; 60% of local revenue set aside for local spending • Increased presence of UN and other international agencies and INGOs in support of development • Rapidly growing civil society and NGO strength • Freer media environment • Holistic restructuring of concepts and strategies for peace, security, and development	• Endemic poverty: 45% of population below poverty line • Poor professional skills in teaching and research • Low levels of communication and interaction • Weak implementation, institutionalization, incentive mechanism • Poor monitoring, evaluation, and feedback system • Inadequate information and data banking system * Skewed concentration of agencies and resource distribution at the center
OPPORTUNITIES (O)	**THREATS (T)**
• Growingly assertive Local Self-Government • Increased IT and physical infrastructure for development • Growth in awareness of human, gender, ethnic, and rights of Dalit in support of larger local ownership, participation and decision-making • Globalization increases the potential for privatization and education marketing (students, teachers, and experts) at the domestic and international levels	• Threats emanating from political violence (insurgency) • Threats to environment • Threats to national heritage, social culture and norms • Risks rooted in unmediated globalization • Risks engendered by political instability and policy and planning discontinuity, particularly on the education front

Changing Regional Scenario

That regionalism is on the rise in South Asia can be concluded from more than one signal:

- The growing intensity and magnitude of the debate on the issue.
- A slow but steady and obvious change in the patterns of mutual attitudes and perceptions in the region. Recall the initiatives taken by Indians and Pakistani citizens recently hardly conceivable till yesterday.
- Changing modes of interactions between the various people, forums and organizations. Even a casual look at the chronology of events that have transpired will suggest that relations in the region are now changing and changing in a positive way (see Box 2).
- The emergence of public groups, professional bodies and civil society organizations that increasingly advocate issues and work for agendas at the regional, trans-national level.
- The proliferation of regional regimes and the growth of overlapping regional blocs along with sub regional bodies. Figure 2 offers a schematic overview of the overlapping regional blocs in and around Asia and the Indian Ocean region lending perspective in the South Asian context.

All this, of course, does not mean that the regionalist movement is going to be a cakewalk. On the contrary, South Asians are now on a ladder of steep learning curve where the progress forward in lessons of solidarity and partnership comes only at a price.

Along with all these changes, there is also a clearly evident shift in the perceptions:

- From conventional defence to nuclear deterrence in the past couple of decades.
- From neglect to prominence of the threat of non-state actors and militants.
- A distinct shift in the patterns of mutual hostility perception between the two countries, particularly after the Lahore dialogues, coinciding with the Sino–Indian and Indo–US détente. The ability of the erstwhile opponents to make concessions, some of which looked unfeasible till yesterday, shows the scope for further improvement.
- Proportional increase in the internal security problems, increase in the number of militant organizations, as also in sectarian violence.

The most critical role in changing the region's scenario, however, comes from the transition of ideas, approaches and values, a kind of shifting paradigm that is under way. This is evident from Table 3.

Table 3: Shifting Focus in the Process of Security Transition

SHIFT FROM	SHIFT FROM
State as prime actor Army Militarization Territorial Security and Sovereignty Power, Force (Protection function) Bilateralism Centre/Capital (Core) Leadership, Power Elite Paternalistic Mobilization Parochialism Centralism Majoritarianism Oligarchy/Hegemony/Dominance Clandestine transactions Arbitrariness, PersonalizeNationalism Large States (Fusion)Stability (Law and Order)	Individual citizens People as a whole Civic Education (Peace & Development)Livelihood and Environmental reform Welfare MultilateralismRemote AreasMass Public Participation Universalism Localism Pluralism, PR, Consociationalism Broader OwnershipTransparency Accountability Regionalism, Globalization Small States (Fission)Development

Stakeholders in the Region's Security

Redefining security means redefining the stakes and identifying those who hold stakes in the security of the system, be it at the local, national, or regional level. But since stakes are not fixed and keep evolving, the concept of stake holding itself needs to be reinvented in a dynamic framework. Seen thus, the security community in tomorrow's South Asia would possibly include a fairly wide range of actors:

- The conventional agencies authorized to use force and coercion: Army, police, paramilitary units, intelligence services.
- Political management bodies: Ruling Executive, Legislature, Judiciary, ministries, commissions, committees.
- Civil Society Groups: Professional bodies, non-governmental organizations, community groups, research organizations, media.
- Non-statutory security forces: Insurgency groups, private or political militant outfits.
- Regional organizations and forums: Agencies set up to oversee security and strategic functions at the various levels.

In the South Asian context, the latest arrival obviously is the SAARC. But one may expect more agencies and forum of strategic nature related to security to appear in the future. Their role is likely to grow and what they do and how they do it may prove crucial in deciding the destiny of the region as a whole. The roles and relationships of the actors at all these levels are bound to change, for unless they change, the idea of cooperative security will remain in paper.

Approaches to Cooperation

Each region can approach cooperation in its own way. But a look at the past shows that most of the cooperation regimes have been either state-centric or alliance-based. To bring out the best in the idea of cooperation, a three-track cooperative regime is proposed at this point. Table 4 makes a comparison of these three types on ten variables.

Table 4: Three Approaches to Regional Cooperation

Variables	(State-Centric) One-Track	(Alliance-Centric) Two-Track	(Cooperative Regimes) Three-Track
1. Population Affected or Involved	Rulers	Elite	Mass
2. Strategy for Action	Command (Top-down) Hierarchical	Mobilization	Participation
3. Time Dimension	Short-term	Mid-term	Long-term
4. Sectors Involved	Political and Military	Political, Military, Bureaucratic	Inter-sectoral involvement (Inter-Disciplinary) Holistic
5. Nature of Mechanism	Authoritarian, Exclusive, Opaque Closed Deterrent Mechanical Military (Rival States)	Partially open, Poor accountability Denying Physical legal Political (Alliances, Collective Security)	Democratic Inclusive, Transparent, Accountable, Mass Ownership Open Facilitative Structural Behavioral Social, Cultural (Region-States, Sub regional Triangles)

6. Level of Centralization of Decision-Making and Resource Distribution	Highly Centralized	Relatively Dispersed	Pluralistic, Decentralized
7. Dependency Framework (Nature of Regime)	Domination, Regiment Monopoly	Patron-client-relationship	Co-Dependence and Pluripolistic Order
8. Efficiency in Resource Use	Low	Low to Medium	High
9. Number of Networks and Linkages	Few	Growing	Large
10. Level of Trust (Social Capital) Generated	Very low	Low	Medium to High

Spokes of Regionalization

Given the rationale for the three-track mode of regional cooperation, the next stage of analysis can proceed in terms of the various spokes that the wheel of regionalization can be anticipated to comprise. Figure 3 illustrates the process of regionalization in terms of the seven spokes—here attitude, trust, solidarity, human capital, political capital, natural resources, and capability representing respectively the cultural, social, psychological, noological, structural, physical, and ethological dimensions of the process. The assumption is that the farther out a state moves from the centre of the diagram from the local level toward the global one along any of the seven spokes, the deeper the commitment and the drive and the stronger the pace and momentum of the process of regionalization.

The discussion so far offers the background to propose a triadic strategy to expedite the momentum of SAARC; that is, to accelerate the pace of regionalization in South Asia. It is triadic in the sense that it consists of three components—participation, approach and dimension. In the context of participation, it demands a three-track strategy of involving the power elite, professionals and people at the

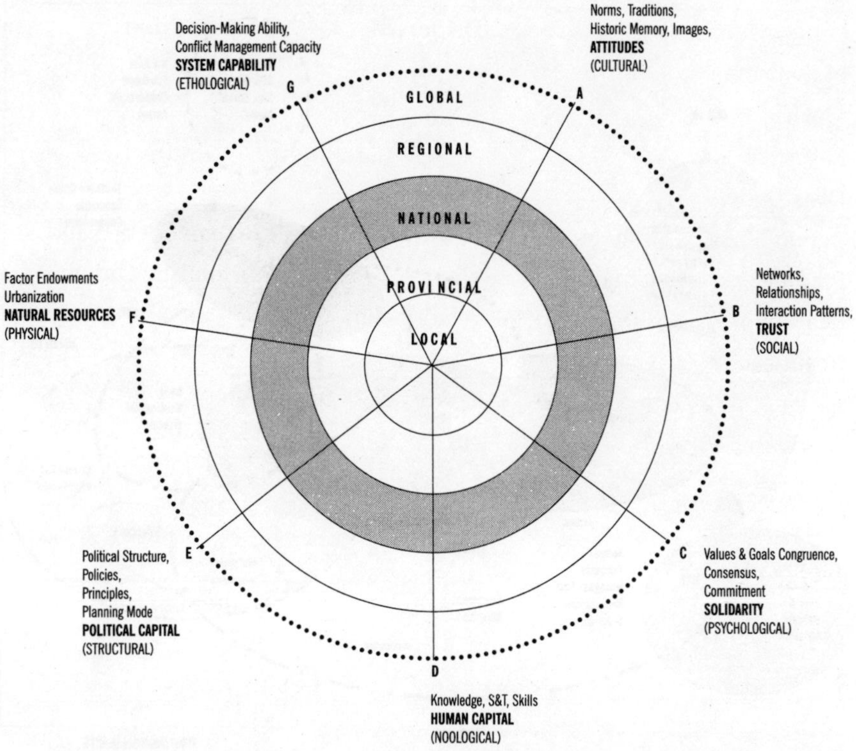

community level. Approach-wise, apart from the conventional punitive (remedial) and preventive approaches, a more positive approach has to be adopted. In terms of dimensions, defence, democracy, and development each must be stressed to harmonize progress. One may also add to it the temporal aspect, which calls for including the best practices and lessons from the past in the policies and plans that cannot afford to forget their implications for the future generations.

Conclusion: South Asia's Second Tryst

South Asia is at the threshold of a new change. A new order seems to be in the making, signalling the rebirth of this ancient subcontinent. More than five decades ago, when the leaders of the region involved in the independence movements were making their tryst with destiny, the tryst they struck was for political freedom of the land. The present restlessness around the region heralds a new kind of movement: the movement for the four other freedoms which are yet to appear here—freedom from fear, freedom from ignorance, freedom from

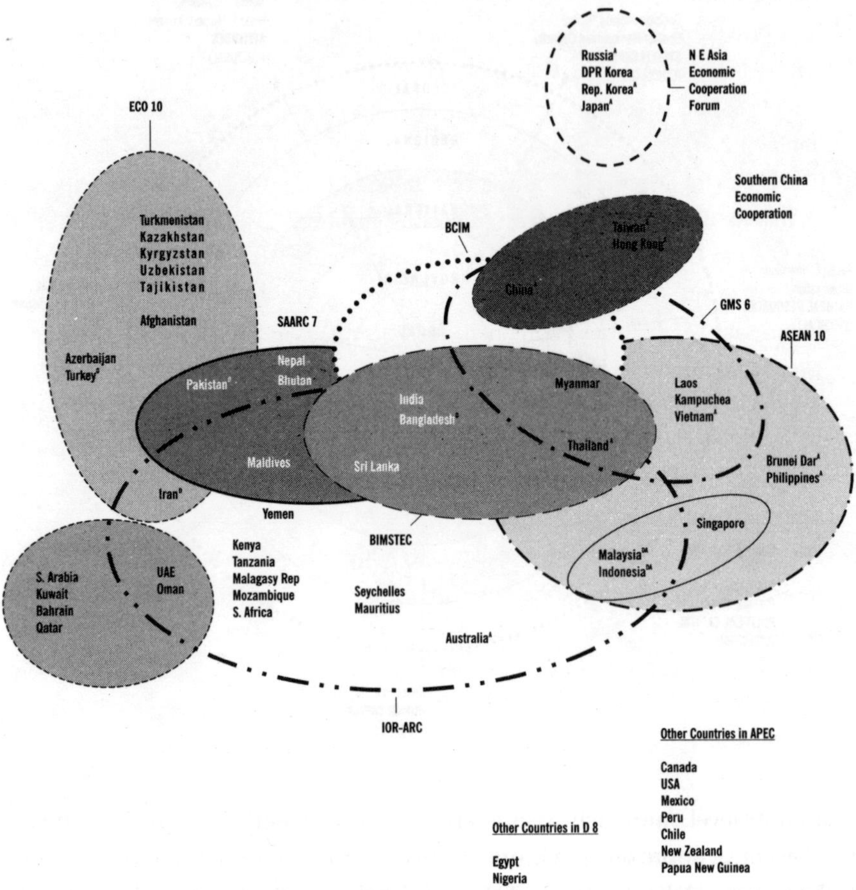

hunger, and freedom from disease—not just for a few and the fortunate in the society, but for all. Only such freedom will make the new tryst truly meaningful. It would be a tryst of the people in the real sense, that is, for the development of the whole region, but one which can be struck only by region-wide solidarity and is attainable only through the critical mass of co-operation. ■

Notes & References

- The chronology on security interactions in South Asia is partly based on Ilmas Futehally, "Conflict Management and Confidence-building Measures in South Asia", K.K. Bhargava and Sridhar K. Khatri, eds., *South Asia 2010: Challenges and Opportunitie*; Delhi, 2001, pp. 220-245.

- Data for table 1 were taken from the *Human Development Report 2000*. Col. 1 - WDR 2000/2001 Table 1; Col. 2 – HDR 2002, Table 5: Col. 3 – Table 12; Col. 4 – Table 12; Col. 5 – World Bank Press Release, September 17, 1995; Col. 6 – HDR, 2002, Table 3; Col. 7 – Table 3; Col 8 – Table 22; Cols. 9, 10, 11, 12, 13 – Table A1.1; Col. 14 – Table 1; Col. 15 – Table 5; Col. 16 – Table 17; Col.17 – Table 20; Cols. 20 and 21 – Table 11; Col. 22 – Table A1.2.
- The Scales for Democracy indicators in Table 1 Cols. 9, 10, 11, 12, 13 are respectively as follows (from negative lowest to positive highest): Civil Liberties: 7 to 1; Political Rights: 7 to 1; Press Freedom: 100 to 0; Law and Order: 0 to 6; Corruption Perception Index: 0 to 10.

1. Varun Sahni, "Fractured, Frightened, and Frustrated: South Asia after 11 September," Dipankar Banerjee and Gert W. Kuek, p. 86.
2. *Human Development Centre* (HDC), pp. 2–3.
3. Bhabani Sen Gupta, "Changing Patterns of Conflict in South Asia," *Asian Perspective*, Vol. 9, No. 2, Fall-Winter 1985, p. 241.
4. *The Times of India*, August 3, 2003, p.13.
5. For a discussion on the theme, see Anand Aditya, "Revolutionary Change and Social Resistance: Afghanistan in the Aftermath of the Soviet Intervention,' *Nepali Political Science and Politics*, Annual Journal, Vol. 3, 1994, pp. 1–14.
6. For an explanation of the failure of force as a state policy, see Anand Aditya, "From Nuremburg to New York: Clandestine Covenants and the Changing Role of Force in the Postwar Transition of Treaties," *Nepali Political Science and Politics*, Vol. 2, 1993, pp. 1–15.
7. Anand Aditya, *Indian Tourists in Nepal*, UNRISD Project Report, July 1998, Patterns of Regional Interaction, pp. 36–45.
8. For a geopolitical discussion of the region, see Anand Aditya, "South Asia: A Space Perspective," *The Nepal Council of World Affairs*, 1997, pp. 63–64; also Anand Aditya, "Small State Syndrome: Does the Small State Really Matter for the World at large?" *Strategic Studies*, Vol. 1, No. 1, Spring 1991, pp. 55–69.
9. The prospects of cooperation on resources of the sea in South Asia are covered in Toran B. Karki, Umakant Roy, Anand Aditya, *Resources of the Sea and Regional Cooperation: Country Study for Nepal*, Kathmandu, 1983.
10. Bob Wall, Robert S. Solum, and Mark R. Sobol, *The Visionary Leader*, New Delhi 1994, pp. 21–22.

Acknowledgement

The author gratefully acknowledges the timely help in the course of preparation of this draft by Mr. J.K. Tater, Mr. Prashu Ram Ghimire and Ms. Mona Aditya.

Prospects of Regional Cooperation Through SAFTA: An Indian Perspective

Jasbir Singh and Aroon Sharma*

Introduction

In order to ensure regional cooperation in South Asia, the South Asian Association for Regional Cooperation (SAARC) came into existence in December 1985. The SAARC charter[1] was adopted at the Dhaka Summit. Till date, 12 summits of the heads of states/governments have been held. The first summit was held on December 7–8, 1985 at Dhaka and the last summit held in Islamabad on January 4–6, 2004. The 12th SAARC summit held in Islamabad is considered a path-breaking and historic attempt in the area of economic cooperation in the South Asian region. It may be treated as a victory for common sense, for moderation, for statesmanship, for India, for Pakistan and particularly for the poor people of South Asia. The Islamabad Declaration ushered in a new era of cooperation in the region. Earlier SAARC was held hostage to Indo-Pak relations.[2] Now both sides have shown flexibility to make history.[3] With this summit two countries moved from a dead-end to a silver lining.

Reasons for Immediate Cooperation

In the post-cold war era and at a time when almost all countries of the world have undergone structural adjustments in the major economic structure of their economies and the globalisation particularly, WTO has given a new direction to the international trade relations and many countries have started looking for local or regional associations or unions to forward their economic interests collectively. Emergence of the European Union and more effective ASEAN has made it desirable to have an effective South Asian Association for Regional

* Readers, Department of Economics, University of Jammu, Jammu.

Cooperation. It is required to deal with regional and international problems like terrorism and regional economic imbalances in an effective way. The latest attempt made by the Bhutanese government to crack down on the Indian insurgent groups operating from her land is a classic case in point. The same is expected from Pakistan and Bangladesh. It would go a long way in tackling problem of terrorism at the SAARC level.

Positive Initiatives Taken Before the Summit

Before the Islamabad Summit, India and Pakistan took various positive steps which had impact on the proceedings of the summit.

1. Declaration of ceasefire in November (2003) by Pakistan and positive response by India.[4]
2. The bus service started between both countries.
3. Air services between two countries are in operation.
4. The bus service between two countries through Srinagar and Muzzafarabad opened.
5. The opening of Khokharapar and Munnobao road link is proposed.
6. The rail link between two countries has been revived.
7. A change in the enthusiasm among people of both the countries and the level of confidence shown by their leadership to put terrorism and hostilities behind them had been a very positive indication of the success of this summit.[5]
8. The RSS in India and even opposition leaders in Pakistan like the Jamaat leader Mulana Fazlur Rahman endorsed the better relations between two countries.
9. Pakistan agreed to extend MFN status to India.
10. It was an important step in the direction when Pakistan agreed not to raise the Kashmir issue in the SAARC summit and also assured not to allow its territory to be used for terrorism, violence and hostility against India. It was seen as a chance to set on positive trends in the Confidence Building Measures (CBMs)[6] through composite dialogue between these two countries.[7]

Areas of Common Interest

There is hardly any country among the seven (SAARC) countries that is not the victim of terrorism in one way or another. Terrorism has been duly recognised as the regional problem faced by all member countries. Not only words of condemnation and pledges of cooperation are required, all leaders stressed regional cooperation. The then Prime Minister of India, A.B. Vajpayee stressed for adoption of additional protocol to the 1987 SAARC Convention on Suppression of Terrorism, which would bring the region in line with international efforts at combating terrorism. The then Prime Minister of Pakistan, M. Zaffarullah Khan maintained that such an act would further manifest our determination to remove the sources of terror from our region. The Bhutanese Prime Minister, Lyonpo Jigmi Y. Thinely asked for will to root out the menace of terrorism from the region. Surya Bahadur Thapa, Prime Minister of Nepal, also voiced his concern in this regard. Sri Lankan President Chandrika Kumartunga appreciated the efforts of the Indian and Pakistan leadership in cooperating with each other to combat terrorism. The Prime Minister of Bangladesh, Khaleda Zia believed that the terrorist threat is great and assumes special significance in this summit. Commenting on the seriousness of terrorist threat Maldives President Maumoon Abdul Gayoom stressed for regional convention on terrorism to effectively deal with the trans-national threats of terrorism.[8] These leaders signed the additional protocol to deal effectively with financing of terrorism. This will help to eliminate all forms and manifestations of terrorism from South Asia. This protocol empowers the states to take appropriate measures, in accordance with their domestic legal principles for the identification, detection and freezing or seizure of any funds used or allocated for the purpose of committing the offences as well as the proceeds derived from such offences for purposes of possible forfeiture. It also envisages promotion of cooperation on immigration and customs control between the SAARC member countries consistent with their respective domestic legal and administrative regimes.

Exchange of information in order to improve immigration and customs control measures to detect and prevent the international movement of terrorists and their accomplices and trafficking in arms, narcotics and psychotropic substances or other materials intended to support terrorist activities is also envisaged in this agreement. All this should be carried out without any prejudice to applicable international commitments in relation to free movement of people and the facilitation of commerce.[9]

In order to promote the welfare of the people of South Asia and accelerate economic development in the region the key issues of poverty alleviation, promoting status of women and population stabilization were taken up for consideration. All these measures covered under the social charter. A ten-point charter was signed which include the highest priority given to the poverty alleviation programmes. It was agreed to ensure that disadvantaged and vulnerable sections were included in social development and the elderly persons lead meaningful and fulfilling lives while enjoying the rights without discrimination.

To meet the basic needs of the people living below the poverty line, it was agreed to guarantee access to basic education, adequate housing, safe drinking water and sanitation and primary health care in legislative, executive and administrative provisions. It was also agreed to share information regarding the outbreak of any communicable disease among their population. The member countries decided to share the capacity for manufacture of drugs and other chemical as also these products when sought by member nations. Realising that health issues were related to livelihood and trade issues which are influenced by international agreement and conventions, it was agreed to hold prior consultations on such matters to arrive at a coordinated stand.

It was agreed to provide free education to all children between the ages of 6 and 14 years. The steps would be taken to reduce low birth weight, malnutrition, anaemia among women and children, infant, child and mother morbidity and mortality. All forms of discrimination and violence against women were treated as violation of human rights and dignity and must be prohibited through legislative and judicial actions.

It is expected that the Islamabad Declaration would facilitate free trade, which is the other area of common interest in this region. This agreement was signed in 2004 and came into force on 1 January 2006. Tariffs have been brought down to zero per cent from 50 per cent but in stages. The whole system of free trade would be completed over a period of ten years. In the first stage, the tariffs rates shall be brought down to 20 per cent by India and Pakistan in two years while other countries shall achieve this objective in three years. In the second stage, India and Pakistan shall further bring import duties to 5 per cent or below in next five years. This will be achieved by Sri Lanka in six years while other countries can do it in eight years' time.

The major areas covered under SAFTA are provisions for dispute settlements, BOP exceptions, safeguard measures and special and differential treatment to least developed countries of the region like Bangladesh, Bhutan, Nepal, and the Maldives. Under this agreement provisions have been made to take care of the disputes settlement. It envisaged amicable settlement of all disputes pertaining to interpretation and application of SAFTA provisions regarding rights and obligations of member countries through bilateral consultations under the auspices of SAFTA forum, also working for economic cooperation and integration of economies.[10]

The removal of barriers to intra-regional investment, harmonising of customs classification, transit facilities for free intra-regional trade, simplification of procedures for business visas, customs procedures, import licensing, insurance and competition rules. Under SAFTA a total of 5550 tariff lines[11] have been earmarked for concessional tariffs by all member countries and value addition norm has been reduced from 40 to 30 per cent for least developed countries and from 50 to 40 per cent for other countries of the region. The SAFTA treaty also paves the way for creation of SAFTA Ministerial Council (SMC). It would be the highest decision-making body responsible for administration while the Committee of Experts (CoE) would act as dispute settlement body.

Before discussing the possibility of economic union, it is required to note the basic economic realities like Bangladesh with a population of 133 million, Gross National Income $49 billion and per capita income $360, Bhutan with a population of 0.82 million, Gross National Income $0.5 billion and per capita income of $640, India with population 1032 million, Gross National Income $477 billion and per capita income of $460, Pakistan with population 141 million, Gross National Income $60 billion and per capita income of $420, Nepal with population 24 million, Gross National Income $5.8 billion and per capita income $250, Sri Lanka with population 19 million, Gross National Income $ 16 billion and per capita income $880 and the Maldives with population 0.28 million, Gross National Income $ 0.59 billion and per capita income $2090.

Before or even after the 12th SAARC Summit, many hopes were raised with regard to creating a monetary union for South Asia on the patterns of the European Union. For that it was assumed that one monetary system is required. Are these the hypotheses that we are considering for the union and unified currency? Let us think about the requirements of this kind of union. With free trade a free exchange of goods and services would take place. For that all member countries would have to maintain a fiscal discipline, stable exchange rate and interest rate. This requires the introduction of a common currency. In this process all countries have to replace their local currencies with a common currency. This would depend on the economic and monetary cooperation among the SAARC countries. As mentioned earlier, for monetary union it is important to have a common fund, a common bank, a common currency and the value of exchange in international market. For this purpose it becomes very important to have a South Asian Reserve Fund on the lines of central bank which should introduce a common currency—South Asian Rupee (SAR). All countries have to trade in SAR. According to one estimate[12] about ten per cent of the region's reserve— around $11 billion—can be used to create the fund and all countries have to contribute into it. Not only this, SAR has to be used to fund all intra-regional projects (infrastructure development and research and development), for trade and other purposes. This can be used by the less developed countries of the region to tide over their balance of payment problems.[13] Thinking of an economic union at this point of time may seem too ambitious but discussing such hypotheses may lead us to fact in future. We should not forget that the European Union took 40 years to come up. This kind of union would basically be an economic union with political interests. There are at least four requirements for such kind of union:

Creating of a Free Trade Area: An important step in the direction of union is to create free trade in the region by removing tariffs and quantitative restrictions. The trade efficiency should be able to attract other countries away from the SAARC. Intra-SAARC regional trade stands at 5 per cent against intra-ASEAN regional trade at 63 per cent. The average GDP growth in the region ranged between 4 to 6 per cent. In 2002 the GNP of SAARC countries was $632 billion out of which India alone accounted for $501 billion. The total exports from the South Asian region had grown from $35.8 billion in 1991 to $76.8 billion in 2001, growing at an average rate of 10.3 per cent annually.

Common Custom Union: It is also expected that all member countries should adopt a single customs union. The custom union can help to remove any possibility of countries importing goods from low tariff countries and exporting to higher tariff countries.

A Common Market: Under this a common market is required where there should be no restriction on the foreign investment, transfer of technology, sharing of capital resources and movement of labour. A situation has to be created where all countries have confidence and peace should be long lasting.

Political Union: Encouraged by recent development, it can be suggested that a political union is also required for the success of such kind of union. All member countries have to come to a compromising point where they can maintain their own sovereignty and participate/cooperate with each other.

Positive Outcomes

Adopting the Islamabad Declaration and landmark agreements committing the member countries to elimination of terrorism in all forms and manifestation and providing for free trade in the region. The landmark of this declaration is adoption of the additional protocol on the review of the SAARC convention on suppression of the terrorism of 1987, which pledges itself to elimination of terrorism in the region.The South Asian Free Trade Agreement (SAFTA) is considered to be watershed of the summit, which would help to reinvigorate regional cooperation. In this context South Asian Preferential Trade Agreement (SAPTA) would also help the people of the SAARC countries.

Encouraged by the positive atmosphere many other problems like the controversy on Baglihar project were discussed by the officials from India and Pakistan to resolve the differences over the 450mw power project built by India on the river Chenab in Baglihar in J&K. It is being objected by Pakistan that this project is built in violation of the Indus Water Treaty 1960. Under this treaty India has full rights to utilise the river waters of the Ravi, Satluj and Beas while Pakistan has the riparian rights to utilise the waters of the Indus, Jehlum and Chenab.

The positive thing which one can find in this initiative was that the Pakistan army has also supported the moves of President Musharaf in his commitment not to allow the terrorist activities from the soil of Pakistan.[14] Apart from this, South Asian countries agreed to conduct a study for the creation of South Asian Energy Cooperation and to setup a South Asian Development Bank.

The year 2005 was designated as South Asia Tourism Year to develop tourism within the region to bring economic, social and cultural benefits to the region. Tourism has been identified as a common endeavour to attract tourists from other parts of the world by improving air links. All agreed to coordinate and to adopt a common position on various issues including WTO.

What should be done?

In the last couple of years the trade in SAARC has increased from \$1.59 billion in 1990 to over \$6.54 billion in 2001. As a percentage of South Asia's world trade, it has recorded an upward trend from 2.42 per cent in 1990 to 4.56 per cent in 2001. This increase can also be attributed to trade liberalisation under the WTO, bilateral trade arrangements and SAPTA, i.e., SAARC Preferential Trading Arrangement initiated in 1995.[15] In order to achieve the macro-economic targets the region will require an annual growth rate of 9.1 per cent, doubling of per capita income from \$300 to \$600, lowering of incremental capital–output ratio from 4:1 to 3: 1 and increasing the marginal savings rate from the current level to 27 per cent or more.

- Two countries should establish political, cultural, economic and social relations so that they might approach their bilateral differences with the sprit of accommodation and compromise rather than with suspicion and hostility.[16] The issues of poverty, hunger, health care, education, trade and sharing of the natural resources other than terrorism should be addressed. India has to build confidence among the member nations that her big-brother status will help them all to take advantage of her industrial, economic, scientific, defence power for their own benefits.

- Extradition treaty between India and Pakistan should be signed.
- The past years should not be kept in isolation. In fact, we have to learn from past experiences like poverty eradication measures recommended in 1992 were not implemented up to 2002, which was the deadline fixed for the implementation. Many other areas of cooperation have not been covered which were agreed under the previous agreements.
- Tulbul navigation project, Siachen, etc. should not be forgotten.
- Hydro potentials of the region have not been harnessed.
- Each member country should have a ministry for SAARC Affairs to concentrate on the SAARC issues only.
- Interests of the least developed nations of the region should be protected.

Of course, caution and restraint should be exercised to avoid needless rhetoric to weaken the new spirit of understanding and cooperation. The region should develop a composite area in which common trading centre presenting a common commodities and a unified brand of the quality product should be promoted. A basket of goods can be identified like IT brain power, tea and textiles from India, carpets from Nepal, tea and tourism from Sri Lanka, silk saris from Bangladesh and pepper and tourism from the Maldives. This can attract countries outside the region also as it would be easy for them to trade or travel with single currency with quality products.[17]

Benefits for India

India's trade in the SAARC countries has shown an increase during 2002-03. There was 21 per cent growth in India's trade in the region.[18] (The composition of India's exports and imports can be observed from Annexures A & B). India's trade with Pakistan has recorded an increase of 22 per cent as compared to the previous year. India's export to Pakistan went up by 45 per cent whereas imports from that country into India went down by 30 per cent to the previous year.[19]

India's trade with Bhutan has also improved during 2002-03 by 109 per cent. In absolute terms India's exports to Bhutan have gone up from Rs. 36.2 crore in 2001-02 to Rs. 189 crore in 2002-03, showing an increase of 422 per cent. However, India's imports from that country have also increased from Rs. 114.1 crore in 2001-02 to Rs. 125.4 crore in 2002-03, an increase of only 10 per cent.

Which is satisfying that our exports are increasing in the region, efforts have to be made to encourage other countries to export to India and enhance their access to expanding Indian market.

Though it is considered that India shall benefit from such a union, at the same time non-interested partners may exploit this as India plays a dominant role. Before we can think of any benefit one has to keep in mind that India has to have a balanced approach where she should not look like a dominant partner and at the same time she should not forget to be a competitive global economy. At large, India is going to be benefited.

The tea sector of India can benefit from free trade. Price competitiveness and easy transportation will help India to increase her tea exports to the Pakistan's market. At present India is exporting about 4 million kg of tea to Pakistan. This export goes through an indirect route via Colombo, Singapore and Dubai to Karachi, making Indian tea costly. The automobile sector of India would also get a boost by exporting auto cars to Pakistan.[20] According to the estimates made public by PTI, the illegal trade between India and Pakistan was not less than $1.5 to 2 billion[21] while official trade between these two countries was $262 million in 2002-03. This can also be to the benefit of both countries if they could convert this illegal trade into a legal one. India can also find a market for its pharmaceuticals in the region. Not only this, India can make available cheaper and quality drugs to her neighbours.

India has three projects for gas pipelines each from Iran[22], Turkmenistan[23] and Bangladesh[24]. Two out of these are to pass through Pakistan. Not only India but Pakistan's interests are also at stake. If India is to get cheaper gas from Iran pipeline, Pakistan is going to receive $580 million per year as transit fee. This project is expected to transport an estimated 20 million cubic metres of gas per day and Pakistan is expected to buy almost a third of this gas if it becomes an investor. The Turkmenistan pipeline project, which has to be routed through Afghanistan to Pakistan, is to benefit India with the supply of 1.6 billion cubic feet. At the same time, Pakistan is to be benefited with a supply of 0.6 billion cubic feet gas. Pakistan is expected to use most of the gas for generating power and also charge $350 million a year as transit fee. The third project is through Bangladesh which is expected to earn $300 million per year.

In the recent agreement between Indian Oil Corporation (IOC) and Bangladesh Petroleum Corporation (BPC), Bangladesh is to import at least half a million tonnes of diesel from India per year valued at $150 million. With this import Bangladesh can save up to $1 per barrel in cost.[25]

Trade

The main components of exports from India to other SAARC countries are tea, readymade garments, cotton yarn, chemicals and allied products, machinery, transport equipments, engineering goods, metal products, iron and steel, cotton, iron ore, fish and fish preparations, pharmaceuticals, leather and leather products, handicrafts, gems and jewellery and so on.

The main components of India's exports to Bangladesh were cotton yarn and fabrics. They amounted to Rs. 31655.28 lakh, which was nearly 39.1 per cent in 1991-92. The other main items of export to Bangladesh (during 1991-92) were machinery and instruments (8.9 per cent), fruits and vegetables (8.7 per cent), spices (6.2 per cent), man made yarn and fabrics (5 per cent), pharmaceuticals and drugs (3.9 per cent), rubber-manufactured products (3.5 per cent) and transport equipments (3.1 per cent).

The main components of Indian imports from Bangladesh in 1991-92 were newsprint, organic chemicals, metaliferrous ores and metal scrap, textiles yarn and fabrics, transport equipment, non-ferrous metals, pearls, precious and semi-precious stones. The most significant items among these were newsprint (29.1 per cent) and organic chemicals (4.7 per cent) constituting a major part of the total imports. On an overall basis India has substantial trade with Bangladesh. Its exports stood at $159 million and imports were $26 million in 1991.

The main component of India exports to Bhutan was transport equipment which amounted to Rs 124.48 lakh, which was nearly 42.1 per cent of the total exports to that country in 1991-92. The other items of export to Bhutan in 1991-92 were miscellaneous processed items (14.1 per cent), primary and semi finished iron and steel (9.9 per cent), machinery and instruments (3.1 per cent), manufactures of metals (3 per cent), tea (2.1 per cent) and ores and minerals (1.8 per cent).

The share of wood and wood products was nearly 39 per cent of the total imports from Bhutan in 1991-92, the share of inorganic chemicals were in total import from Bhutan was 38.9 per cent whereas coal, coke and briquettes constituted about 6.9 per cent of the total import from that country. On an overall basis India has substantial trade with Bhutan. India is the only country in SAARC which had more than 90 per cent trade with Bhutan.

The main components of exports to the Maldives were cotton yarn, fabrics make-up. It amounted to Rs. 267.87 lakh, which was nearly 22.8 per cent in 1991-92. The composition of other items and their respective shares in the total exports were manufactures of metal (9.4 per cent), fruits and vegetable (8.2 per cent), drugs and pharmaceuticals (7.8 per cent) and raw-cotton and accessories

(6.1 per cent). India has substantial trade with the Maldives also. India–Maldives had a Joint Economic Commission in January 1990, which is working for expanding trade between the two countries.

The main component of India's exports to Nepal was transport equipments. It amounted to Rs. 3,485.12 lakh, which was nearly 17.7 per cent of total exports. The composition of other items and their respective shares in the total exports were pharmaceuticals and drugs (11.9 per cent), machinery and instruments (8.8 per cent), glass, glassware, ceramic and cement (8.8 per cent), paper and wood products (6.8 per cent), un-manufactured tobacco (5 per cent), wheat (3.4 per cent), coal (2.7 per cent), processed items (3.5 per cent), cotton yarn, fabrics, and make-up (2.7 per cent) and rubber manufactured products (3.4 per cent).

The major items of import in India from Nepal in 1991–92 were printed books, newspaper and journals (17.11 per cent), vegetable oil (7.7 per cent), oil seeds (4.3 per cent), and cereal preparations (1.5 per cent). The other components of imports were crude minerals, wood and wood products, sugar, cereals, etc. Out of total imports of India from SAARC countries about 15.40 per cent imports are from Nepal alone. However the share of exports from India to Nepal declined during the 1990s.

The main components of exports to Pakistan were iron ore. It amounted to Rs. 2,077.68 lakh, which was 21.1 per cent of the total exports to that country. The composition of other items and their respective shares in the total exports were oil reeds (13.8 per cent), dye, tar and chemical (9.6 per cent), spices (9.2 per cent), paint, enamel and varnish (7 per cent), ore and minerals (5.3 per cent), pharmaceuticals and drugs and fine chemicals (4.8 per cent) and machinery and instruments (2.8 per cent).

The main components of imports from Pakistan in 1991–92 were fruits (20.8 per cent) and textile yarn, fabrics and make-up articles (9.2 per cent). The other components of import from Pakistan were metaliferous, ores and metal scrap, crude minerals, wool, pearls and semi-precious stones. Due to strained relations between two countries the trade could not grow to the desired extent. Though exports from India were to the tune of 10 per cent in the 1980s but these declined to less 5 per cent during the 1990s. Imports from Pakistan were higher than its export from that country. This was all due to discriminating policy followed by the Pakistan towards India (not according MFN status to India.).

The main components of exports to Sri Lanka in 1991–92 were cotton yarn fabric and make-up. Amounting to Rs. 10,409.49 lakh, which was 12.9 per cent of the total share of exports to that country. The composition of other items and their respective shares in the total exports were sugar and molasses (7.3

per cent), pharmaceuticals, drugs and fine chemicals (6.8 per cent), paper and wood products (3.9 per cent), man made yarn, fabrics and make-up (4.4 per cent) and machinery and instruments (4.6 per cent). Recently, India has also signed a contract with Sri Lanka to export 30,000 tonnes of diesel and 10,000 tonnes of jet fuel.

The main components of imports from Sri Lanka in 1991–92 were metaliferous, ores and metal scrap (25.3 per cent), organic chemicals (13.3 per cent), natural rubber (11.5 per cent), iron and steel (9.3 per cent 0, machinery (2 per cent), manufactures of metals (1.5 per cent), pulp and waste paper (1.5 per cent) and synthetic and reclaimed rubber (1.3 per cent).

India has significant trade relations with Sri Lanka. Though imports from Sri Lanka remained stagnant exports have increased with 2.2 per cent annual growth rate during the 1990s.

Benefits for Pakistan

Pakistan would be able to import tea, auto parts, consumer durables, pharmaceuticals and films from India at cheaper rates.[26] Apart from imports of these items from India, exporting cotton and textiles to India can benefit Pakistan. The tax evasion through illegal route followed by the traders will be plugged which will increase revenue receipt of Pakistan. Pakistani traders can increasingly trade Indian goods with their neighbours like Afghanistan, Iran, and CIS. In Pakistan, the unit cost of imports would be much less as compared with the import made by Pakistan from other countries.

Pakistan could not get entry into ASEAN Regional Forum of 23 members (the ASEAN Regional Forum has 23 members including 10 ASEAN members and 13 dialogue partners comprising India, the US, Russia, China, Australia, Canada, the EU, Japan, New Zealand, Magnolia, North Korea, South Korea, and Papua New Guinea). This group was established in the year 1994. Pakistan can use this opportunity and support of the SAARC nations to get an entry into ASEAN group and even make re-entry into the Association of Commonwealth countries.

Apprehensions

It is the third time that a date for setting up of free trade has been fixed. On all previous occasions political compulsion outweighed the economic requirement of the region. But a positive outcome can be observed this time, i.e. the thaw in Indo-Pak relations, outlining of tariff reduction with time schedule, addressing the problems of least developed countries of the region. This time frame and identification of the areas of concern gives new hope.

In order to make this agreement a success, both India and Pakistan have taken a few more steps to build confidence among the smaller nations. This can be done by providing some trade concessions to small nations, the momentum in Indo-Pak relations has to be carried on permanently, economic infrastructure is to be developed, the care should be taken that the major sectors of the economies do not feel threatened. Pakistan's continuous support to terrorists and many such outfits being allowed to work from her territories may raise some eyebrows despite assurances. India needs a cautious approach.

For a union it is required that there should be some minimum common line for arranging minimum compatibilities. Politically all member countries are different—Bangladesh, India and Sri Lanka are democracies in the region, Pakistan a dictatorship, Nepal has a palace-dictated democracy, the Maldives autocracy, and Bhutan a monarchy they have to find ways to be in a long-lasting union.

The peculiar geopolitical feature of the region gives India a lead position. All member countries border with India while they don't border with each other. Therefore, India may geographically and economically cast too large a shadow over South Asia. Countries outside the region should not exploit this. Many a time India has to bend backward to accommodate other countries of the region; at the same time she has to watch her interest by Free Trade Agreement with individual countries as has been done with Sri Lanka. It should be done with Bangladesh, Nepal and other countries of the region. Such bilateral tie-ups and faster Indian economic growth would discourage Pakistan to overact.

Conclusion

From the foregoing discussion, it can be inferred that the future of SAARC depends on the peaceful interaction of all member nations. On the economic front India, particularly after twelve years of liberalisation, is equipped to play the role of an economic powerhouse that can drive the region to a new era of prosperity. It would be in the interest of everybody to cooperate and benefit. One should not come out with jingoism that one country has scored a point over the other. This may invite suspicion. This summit should not be taken as over, rather as the beginning because the composite dialogue is to be followed.

The commitments made by the leadership of both countries are not possible without the help of each other. Therefore, it is important for both countries to give due credit to each other in facilitating the process. Be optimistic, don't recall the failures of the past Lahore and Agra summits. One should look forward for a people-to-people interaction and more transparency between the two countries. ■

Annexure A

1. Tarun Basu, "SAARC can Make South Asia Economic Power", The Financial World, Chandigarh, Vol. III (243), January 5, 2004.
2. CMIE, "Foreign Trade & Balance of Payment, Mumbai", 2003.
3. John Cherian, "Looking Ahead", Frontline, Vol. 21 (2), January 17–30, 2004.
4. Nisha Taneja, "Indo-Pak Trade Relations: Opportunities for Growth", Economic and Political Weekly, Vol. XXXIV (4), January 24, 2004.
5. P.K. Vasudeva, "SAFTA- for Growth of SAARC Countries", The Financial World, Vol. 123 (351), December 20, 2004.
6. Anthony J. Venebles, "Regional Integration Agreements: A Force For Convergence or Divergence", World Bank Paper, Series No. 2260, the World Bank, Washington D.C., 2001.

Notes & References

1. The charter includes main objectives: to promote the welfare of the people of South Asia and to improve their quality of life; to accelerate economic growth, social progress and cultural development in the region and to provide all individuals the opportunity to live with dignity and to realise their full potentials; to promote and strengthen collective self-reliance among the countries of South Asia; to contribute to mutual trust, understanding and appreciation of one another's problems; to promote active collaboration and mutual assistance in the economic, social, cultural, technical and scientific fields; to strengthen cooperation with other developing countries; to strengthen cooperation among themselves in international forums on matters of common interests; and to cooperate with international and regional organisations with similar aims and purposes.
2. The scope of economic cooperation under SAARC remained limited to certain relatively non-controversial areas owing to the existing of wide disparities in the resource potential among the member countries. Trade, technology transfer, industry, investment and monetary cooperation are some of the areas, which were not taken into consideration in right spirit. Among member countries particularly Pakistan remained wary of the inclusion of core economic areas in the SAARC activities on the ground that such a course would lead to greater dependence on India.
3. Adopting of the Islamabad Declaration is considered containing the road map for South Asian cooperation.
4. The ceasefire along the International Border, the Actual Line of Control and the ground position at Siachen maintained by India.

5. The visits made by the prominent academicians, lawyers, artists, journalists and many other people have contributed to initiate people to people contact. Even Indian spectators were allowed to watch the recently concluded cricket series in Pakistan.
6. In the local daily of Pakistan *The News*, the Prime Minister of Pakistan claimed that ice has broken with recent spate of Confidence Building Measures initiated by India and Pakistan. *The News*, January 2, 2004.
7. It was in 1997 that the last composite dialogue between two countries was held. Though it failed it had identified eight major subjects for discussion including the Kashmir issue and Confidence Building Measures. Again an effort was made to resolve disputes at the Agra Summit in July 2001 but it also failed.
8. *Daily Excelsior*, January 5, 2004.
9. G.K. Sharma, "Signing of SAFTA", *Daily Excelsior*, January 18, 2004.
10. Of these 5550 tariff lines, 2927 tariff lines have been from India.
11. Ramgopal Agarwal, Research And Information Systems for the Non-aligned and other developing countries.
12. Nagesh Kumar DG, Research And Information Systems for the Non-aligned and other developing countries.
13. *The Dawn*, January 15, 2004 – "Army Commander backs Peace Moves". The top military leadership declared that Pakistan would not allow its soil to be used for any terrorist activities.
14. Mahendra P. Lama, "Add Spark to SAARC", *The Times of India*, January 6, 2004.
15. *The Times of India*, January 3, 2004.
16. *The Times of India*, January 4, 2004.
17. India's exports to the SAARC countries has have increased from $1.70 million in 1996–97 to $2.60 million in 2002–03, an increased of 52.94 per cent. The imports from SAARC countries have increased from $241.78 million to $497.76 million, an increase of 105.87 per cent.
18. PHD Chamber of Commerce and Industries, India, *The Times of India*, January 4, 2004.
19. According to one estimate Suzuki Mehran—the Pakistani equivalent to Maruti 800 is one of the most popular cars, which is being sold at prices double than Indian Maruti, *Daily Excelsior*, January 5, 2004.
20. The Federation of Export Organisations (FIEO) put this figure at $1 billion.—*The Times of India*, January 7, 2004.
21. This is a $5 billion project, which would cover a length of 2670 km from

Assaluyeh, Bandar Abbas in Iran and will pass through Pakistan before entering India. It will have a capacity to transit 66 million cubic metres a day.

22. This will be $3.5 billion project covering 1,635 km from Daultabad (Turkmenistan) and passing through Pakistan before entering India. It will have a capacity of 2.2 billion cubic feet per day.
23. This will be $1.4 billion project covering 1,350 km, entering India from Biblyana through Bengal, Jharkhand, Bihar and Uttar Pradesh. It will have a capacity to carry 500 cubic feet per day.
24. This would be possible from lower transportation and handling charges.
25. At present Pakistan has one of the highest per capita consumption of tea. It imports about 150 million kg of tea from outside particularly from Kenya.

Regional Cooperation in South East Asia: Lessons for SAARC

Gurmeet Kaur*

Regional cooperation or collaboration for the resolution of common problems and achievements of mutually shared goals in the region is generally accepted as an important mode of interaction across the territorial boundaries of nation-states. The underlying idea is that regional cooperation promotes greater interaction and understanding, builds across pressures, increased mutual relevance and interdependence among the states of a region.[1]

There has been a perpetual quest for regional cooperation in South-East Asia and South Asia in the recent past. Both the regions have civilizational ties that are many centuries old, though their political growth has tended to differ, especially with the onset of different colonial rules in their states. Each country has its individual problems and each is trying to settle them in its own way. But in an inter-dependent international system, on occasions they do interact. Whether it is monarchy or dictatorship, a democracy or communist rule, these counties do have common problems and there is a compulsion of inter-nation or inter-regional cooperation to settle them.[2]

The foundation of ASEAN marked a landmark in giving concrete shape to the quest for regional cooperation among the non-communist South-East Asian countries. It was born in 1967 amidst underdevelopment, chronic instability, inter-state conflicts and all other legacies of long colonial exploitation. When the original five members of the organization (Indonesia, Malaysia, Singapore, Thailand and the Philippines) signed the Bangkok Declaration in 1967, they had little in common apart from climate and natural resources and somewhat similar

---

* Lecturer in Political Science, R.R.M.K. Arya Kanya Mahavidyalaya, Pathankot.

ideological orientation. Apart from the diversity in language, religion and ethnic identity these nations were isolated from each other politically and economically despite geographical and cultural bonds.[3] ASEAN is well established now with 10 ASEAN members, namely Indonesia, Malaysia, Thailand, the Philippines, Singapore, Brunei, Laos, Cambodia, Myanmar and Vietnam. Although from the outset, ASEAN was conceived as an organization for economic, social and cultural cooperation and consideration in these fields was no doubt central, yet it was the fact that there was a convergence in the political outlook of the five member nations, both with regard to national priority objectives as on the question of how best to secure these objectives in the emergent strategic configuration of East Asia, which provided them the main stimulus to join together in ASEAN. By the time of ASEAN's birth, the nations of South-East Asia were all intent on restoring stability and ensuring progress in their region after centuries of stagnation of strife. But they were also aware of the compulsive inclination of outside powers and especially the major powers, to continue to insert their interests in the affairs of this vitally important part of Asia. Viewed within this inevitable pattern of external influences and conflicting interests, the shaping of a coordinated approach among the nations of South East Asia towards the problems of peace, stability and development had, therefore, become an urgent necessity.[4]

Following the establishment of ASEAN in 1967, India took the initiative by bringing up the theme of great economic cooperation among Asian countries, when the Indian Prime Minister, Indira Gandhi, talked of regional cooperation among Pakistan, Afghanistan and India during her visits to Burma, Afghanistan and Indonesia in May 1969.[5] India's role in the emergence of Bangladesh in 1971 ruled out any meaningful regional cooperation in South Asia for several years to come. However, after change of government in India, Bangladesh and Pakistan in 1977 and 1978, there was a renewed stress on mutual cooperation and it was against this background that Bangladesh took the initiative to promote regional cooperation.[6]

Four smaller regional countries, namely, Nepal, Sri Lanka, the Maldives and Bhutan endorsed the proposal without hesitation. However, India and Pakistan came up with reservations for different reasons. India, which had political differences with all its neighbours, feared that this was a move to isolate her. Pakistan had the impression that the move would establish India's hegemony in the region in an institutionalized manner. Pakistan was also worried about deeper involvement in the South Asian region since it might cast doubt on the credibility and seriousness of its efforts to develop closer ties with the Islamic countries of West Asia.[7]

However, the seven countries of South Asia joined hands for the first time in 1983 in New Delhi to establish South Asian Regional Cooperation (SARC) to enlist the cooperation of the countries of the region. In 1985, it was decided in the Summit meeting at Dhaka that SARC would be known as SAARC (South Asia Association for Regional Cooperation). The members of the SAARC decided to cooperate not only in the economic sphere but also in agricultural, scientific, educational and literary fields.[8] SAARC is the creative will of South Asian countries to lessen conflicts and transfer great resources for the attainment of shared objectives of development. Before SAARC, the countries of the region had cooperated mainly on international forums like the Non-Aligned Movement (NAM). But at the regional level these states had largely experienced tension, conflict and even open warfare. Thus, the formation of SAARC heralds a new dawn, which has given rise to a new set of expectations of cooperation, peace and eventual prosperity in the region. It works on the basis of the principle of unanimity, exclusion of bilateral and contentious issues. Its overriding emphasis is on the socio-economic framework for cooperation.[9]

The guiding factor in this sub-region is a commonality in threat perception not in political and security implications but in terms of challenges emanating from the shared problems of poverty, disease and underdevelopment. Dictated by the imperatives arising from sensitivities in political relations, non-congruity in foreign policy orientations and perceptions, it has been considered prudent, not only to keep apart political cooperation beyond the agenda of SAARC but also to keep apart bilateral and contentious issues from SAARC deliberations is an attempt to insulate the regional cooperation process from their deleterious impacts. Instead of including political matters in the agenda of SAARC, the architects of SAARC perceived it as an instrument to promote and strengthen collective self-reliance which is nevertheless viewed to be catalyst in establishing mutual trust, understanding and appreciation of one another's problems.[10]

It is important to note that in selecting the non-political areas of cooperation, there has been an element of consciousness in the sense that only those areas of socio-cultural economic and technological cooperation have been included in the Integrated Programme of Action (IPA), which have been found to be non-controversial. The acceptance of the South Asian Preferential Trading Agreement (SAPTA) at the seventh SAARC summit in Dhaka has opened new ways of economic cooperation among the SAARC members. Inclusion of more goods and higher concessions within the domain of SAPTA agreement can also help trade expansion. SAPTA must consider a concept similar to ASEAN's

Common Effective Preferential Tariff (CEPT) scheme, which is laying the foundations for the ASEAN Free Trade Area (AFTA).[11]

The cooperation in the area of economic and trade relations under the framework of SAARC began with the preparation of a regional study in 1991 entitled "SAARC Trade, Manufactures and Services". This study provides an analysis of the status of intra SAARC trade and identifies various hindrances including trade barriers in expansion of economic and trade relations with SAARC. It also contained several practical suggestions and remedial measures to accelerate intra-SAARC trade. The Inter-Governmental Group established in 1991 held two meetings during 1992 and finalized a draft agreement regarding South Asian Preferential Arrangement (SAPTA), which was subsequently approved by the Committee on Economic Cooperation and other higher SAARC bodies. It was later signed by the member states on 11 April 1993 in Dhaka during the Seventh SAARC Summit.[12]

SAPTA is an important attempt of South Asian countries to expand intra-regional trade among the countries of this region. Under this arrangement, the constraints affecting intra-regional trade are sought to be removed through reduction in tariffs, non-tariff barriers and by direct trade measures.[13] SAPTA provides for special and more favourable treatment exclusively for the least developed contracting states[14] in order to assist them in deriving equitable benefits from the agreement. Article 10 of the agreement gives details of the special treatment for the LDCs for achieving reasonable levels of sustainable exports. The other member states are called upon to have special consideration in favour of exports from LDCs while duly applying safeguard measures. LDCs can also have greater flexibility in introduction and continuation of trade restrictions provisionally and during critical circumstances.[15]

SAPTA made a modest beginning with the conclusion of the first round which became operational from December 7, 1996. The concessions were exchanged in respect of 226 commodities of which 100 were for LDCs. The maximum number of products offered concessions, were made by India (106) constituting nearly half of the total number of products offered concession by all countries. Of the total number of products offered concession by India, 62 were offered in favour of the LDCs.[16] India's ratification of SAPTA is due to the fact that it has adopted the policy of liberalizing its trade. Thus it has taken steps to make its economy externally competitive and reduction of important tariffs through SAPTA is such an instance.[17] Bangladesh offered tariff concessions on preferential terms on small list of 12 items to the other six member of SAARC.[18] Bangladesh's ratification of SAPTA is indicative of its commitment to liberalized trade aimed at making a dent in the global market. The small list of commodities was due to the narrow export base of Bangladesh, which is a major impediment in this regard. Accompanied by its huge trade imbalance at the regional level, South Asia appears to be a lucrative market for Bhutan. As an LDC member of SAPTA, Bhutan has been induced by this factor to ratify the agreement. It offered a list of 11 items for tariff concessions on preferential terms. On these 11 items, 7 were included for LDCs.[19]

Long-term gains from regional trade encouraged the Maldives to ratify SAPTA. The Maldives is a follower of free-market economy, which is likely to act as a stimulus to its liberal trade policy. It gave concessions on 17 items to the rest of the SAPTA members.[20] The Maldivian business community also stands for SAPTA and the Maldivian Traders' Association has become a member of SAARC Chamber of Commerce and Industry.

Nepal strongly endorsed SAPTA because over 30 per cent of the total volume of Nepal's foreign trade is with SAARC member states, which could increase more through SAPTA.[21] Nepal allowed 10 per cent tariff concessions to all goods imported from SAARC countries. It offered concessions on 14 items, including four for LDCs. Initially, Pakistan was hesitant to ratify SAPTA on account of its hostile relations with India and its fear that India's giant industrial base might be a threat to Pakistan's industry and trade. India's emphasis on bilateral trade cooperation rather than on multilateral added a further element of doubt for Pakistan.[22] Later on Pakistan also signed the SAPTA agreement due to the consensus that without an agreement on trade there is little possibility of pushing the SAARC process forward. It agreed to offer concessions on 35 items, including 15 for LDCs with the concessions ranging from 10 to 15 per cent.[23] Sri Lanka was the initiator of the SAPTA proposal. It offered concession on 31 items of which 12 are of LDCs with concessions similar to those of Pakistan.[24]

Under SAPTA-II as many as 2013 products were offered concessions of which 764 had been exclusively in favour of LDCs. India has offered the maximum number of concessions numbering 911 products (favouring mainly Bangladesh), followed by Pakistan 386 products. In return India has received concession in respect of 474 products. The largest number of concessions has been in favour of Bangladesh followed by Pakistan. India and Nepal have not exchanged any concessions under SAPTA-II, since they have exchanged deeper concessions under a bilateral trade agreement.[25] This list of products offered concessions under SAPTA-II were to be impressive considering a handful of products negotiated under the first round. However, it is the concept of trade coverage rather than product coverage that is of crucial importance in determining the effectiveness of the negotiations.[26]

The 12th SAARC Summit in Islamabad has become a turning point in the history of South Asia. With all humility India has made it known to its neighbours that it can share its fortunes with others. With SAFTA (South Asia Free Trade Area) becoming a reality by 2006, tariffs and quantitative restrictions will be abolished in the region. Once SAFTA becomes operational the region will become more attractive for foreign investors. International players will even invest in cross border projects in the region. Free movement of labour across the borders may cause some problems but unrestrained flow of goods, services, technologies and investments would create million of jobs. Economic development of South Asia would mean reduction in poverty, unemployment and higher indices of human development.

On January 7, 2004 Pakistan announced that it was ready to discuss grant of Most Favoured Nation (MFN) status to India. The latter has already accorded MFN status to the former. The WTO guidelines require all the members to adopt a non-discriminatory tariff regime with their trading partners and neighbours. Once MFN status is accorded the scope for input of goods and services from India would rise tremendously. Official trade between the two countries is estimated at $700 million but illegal and indirect trade has been thriving and was estimated at $1.5 billion to $ 2 billion in 2002. Experts predict that Indo–Pak trade will reach the $ 10 billion mark within five years of free trade agreements in the regime.

Mutual distrust is something deeply ingrained in inter–state relations in South Asia and progress in SAARC would certainly be inhibited to that extent. What is needed is that an objective and comprehensive appreciation of needs and capabilities.

At the 12th SARC Summit on January 4, 2004 the members of the SAARC have realized that it was high time that they buried the differences of the past. Both the countries agreed to start the composite dialogue in the near future. Pervez Musharraf going out all the way assuring the Indian leadership that he would not let the terrorists use the territory of Pakistan against India. India has given its full support to Sri Lanka and has emphasized that a solution to the Tamil problem has to be found within the framework of unity and territorial integrity of Sri Lanka. The latest example of SAARC solidarity was the steps taken by Bhutan to flush out extremists groups of North Easter India operating from Bhutanese territory. Resumption of air links between India and Pakistan has given the signs of good relations between the two countries.

It is a reality that most of the political disputes in South Asia relate to India. India's pre-eminence in SAARC keeps the smaller members in a fear psychosis. The net result is mutual suspicion and misunderstanding which prohibits the political elites of SAARC countries from massing for free trade. India being the largest country in the region should take initiative for holding confidence among member nations of SAARC. The unequal size of markets, the fear of Indian economic domination over the economies of smaller countries, the competitive nature of these economies, dependence on west for technology, capital and expertise and informal trade or unofficial trade, regional transport and communication system are some important hindrances in the way of good trade relations among SAARC nations.[27]

In the presence of so many political and economic hindrances, it is the South Asian political leaders who would make policies for the future of SAFTA. Whatever the schemes formulated by state bureaucrats, the actual business of buying and selling of foreign collaborators for joint venture is largely in the hands of the private sector, particularly as state enterprises are being gradually privatized in practically all SAARC countries. The government can liberalize its trade policy and thus provide support to private sector. The practical efforts in the adaptation of SAFTA will move forward in a peaceful environment. Political interests are hampering trade interests. So there is a need of political understanding among the political elites in South Asia in order to operationalize SAFTA in true terms.[28]

However, experiences—both successes and failures—are of relevance to the late starters. In cases where the regional organizations are more or less similar in terms of values, socio-cultural trains, civilizational heritage and geo-political situation, the experiences of the regional organizations with longer experiences are expected to have relevance for the newly emergent ones. Even when the organizations are different in their political settings, motive forces and causes of development, an objective analysis and assessment of the experiences of the organizations may provide useful insights and perspectives for other organizations in deciding on their respective courses of development.

Comparing the process of development in SAARC with that in the ASEAN, it may be argued that both SAARC and ASEAN emerged as an extension of national efforts for development through cooperation primarily in the socio–economic, technical and cultural fields. For both the associations the central goal is the furtherance of the cause of peace, harmony and stability in their respective regions and to concert and harmonise efforts in accelerating economic development. And for both, the immediate goal of socio-economic and technical cooperation is viewed as a catalyst to the realization of the ultimate goal of regional peace, stability and harmony. In the process, both the organizations, as and when they deem fit, include new areas of cooperation in addition to the so-called agreed areas and also adopt new strategies.

Although the aims and purposes of both the organizations are similar, SAARC as a newly emerged organization will define its own course in its quest for mutually beneficial cooperation for its member states. The reason is too obvious: conditions are different in SAARC than that in ASEAN and conditions in the 1980s were different from those in the 1960s and the 1970s when ASEAN institutions were developed. Some of the ASEAN experiences will, however, be an interest to SAARC, in some cases as positive knowledge while in others as kind of the things to be avoided.

SAARC can learn the lesson from ASEAN that strained inter-state relations would not stand in the way of initiating regional cooperation and socio-economic development. ASEAN was born and nourished at a time when the political-strategic environment and inter-state relations in South-East Asia were seriously distorted. The strain stemmed not only from bilateral disputes but also mistrust and suspicion toward each other. The South East Asian leaders at the time of launching the association were all intent on coming out of the morass of tensions and instability. The driving force was provided by the desire to ensure peace and stability in the region to pay the way of unhindered national socio-economic development. The quest, no doubt, was backed by commonalities in threat and security perception from both within and outside the region. But the real motivation emerged from the appreciation of the evils and futility of mutual mistrust, tension, confrontation, which forced the states to negotiate and eventually go in for cooperation under the ASEAN. Similarly in the case of South Asian states, the driving force appeared to lie in the realization of the cost-benefit implications of mutual mistrust, tension and confrontation. The SAARC nations must have the faith in the argument that the regional cooperation in socio-economic areas would itself create a congenial political atmosphere, first, by the gradual and incremental process of cooperation and second, by the self generating compulsions of maintaining political stability or at least easing tensions in inter-state relations in order to facilitate cooperation in socio-economic fields.[29]

The ASEAN experience of regional cooperation shows that the association appears to have concentrated more on cooperation in politico-security and strategic matters. It would be pertinent to observe that even within the socio-economic areas, the success has been to a lesser degree in cases where schemes or projects were apparently too ambitious, whereas in the cases of issue-based and modest scale schemes and most importantly, in the case of specific result oriented ones, progress has been considerable, like tourism, food security and the like. Cooperation in these areas has not merely been successful in its own way but has also contributed to the strengthening of the popular base in favour of the association.

In relation to cooperation in the more vital areas like trade, the main problems have been linked to issues of 'economic nationalism' like market sharing and protectionism. Disparate levels of development coupled with divergent national interests lead to a search for national solution to the problems. Member states have tended to develop and intensify extra-regional linkages independent of the interest of the grouping as a whole, sometimes, adversely affecting the basis of confidence in the usefulness of regional cooperation. The problem is further compounded by the structural linkage of the economies with the west on the one hand and relatively low level of mutual complementarity on the other. The private sector performance in cooperative ventures has also not reached the desired level in some of the economic sectors.

Despite the low level of performance in some of the economic sectors, ASEAN has continued to move forward while apparently aware of the limits to what regional cooperation arrangements can be expected to achieve in the specific context, terms of reference and time span. The level of expectation in ASEAN seems to have been pragmatic so that not too much was expected too soon. Regional cooperation is viewed as one of the many other ways that member states endeavour collectively to resolve the problems facing them nationally, bilaterally and regionally. SAARC must adopt the basic approach admitted by ASEAN to 'go slow' so that activities and programmes do not have any 'grand design' disproportionate to regional preparedness.[30]

In terms of modality, ASEAN approach has been fairly informal. The process of decision-making and deliberations has been almost exclusively on the basis of mutual consultation. There has been a tacit understanding of avoiding any disputable and conflicting situation on matters both within and outside the preview of ASEAN. Problems of bilateral and contentious nature have been regarded as part of the reality and member states did recognize their impinging potential on the process of multilateral cooperation. It appears that ASEAN member-states have followed a deliberate policy of keeping the bilateral discords below a level that might lead to a crisis.

It is also important that although bilateral and contentious issues are not formally within the ASEAN agenda, the member states are not precluded from using the forum for informal discussion on any such subject. In the absence of any ASEAN mechanism for setting disputes amongst the member state, this was done through informal channels purposefully keeping the association aside. Often the member states settle disputes amongst themselves bilaterally. Such an informal mechanism could deal with inter-group conflicts so successfully that in the first summit held in Bali during February 23–24, 1967, ASEAN formally assumed the responsibility of conflict management and came out with a formal mechanism for the same.[31] In the process of its development ASEAN had to deal with a number of crises, which even threatened to shatter the very foundation of the association. The most severe conflict that ASEAN had to deal with was the dispute over Sabah. At times, it has been as severe as Kashmir dispute in the context of SAARC. The unity shown by the ASEAN member countries in the Cambodian crisis is an example before the SAARC nations. They have tackled the issue very well, in spite of individual differences.

In the case of SAARC, such innovations had hardly been witnessed. They must follow the same method of deliberate policy by keeping aside their national interests for the sake of development of SAARC as an association. In a regional grouping where the process of cooperation is strictly segregated from the management of intra-group conflicts, such innovative approaches on the past of its members are indispensable for the effective functioning of the grouping.[32]

In the context of asymmetries and divergences and concomitant disputes, member states of ASEAN have demonstrated a remarkable degree of understanding of each other's problems, aspirations and limitation. It appears that there was in ASEAN a consensus that disputes at bilateral level are part of the reality in inter-state relations and whilst there were attempts at settlement of such disputes, failure to do so, was never allowed to impede the process of cooperation under ASEAN.

So far as SAARC is concerned, it is not intended to deal with bilateral and contentious matters. In the backdrop of ASEAN experiences and even from what has happened so far in the SAARC forum, there seem to be two aspects to this problem. First, although such issues are also excluded from the formal agenda of the SAARC, member states are not precluded from raising and discussing these informally when they assemble for meeting within the SAARC forum. Indeed, some bilateral issues have already been picked up by member-states on more than one occasion and the forum has to that extent been found to be a tension-diffusing platform. The 12th SAARC summit is a recent example of taking the advantage of the frequency of high political-level meeting and member states have found SAARC a useful forum with an opportunity to iron out difference, the way their ASEAN counterparts have done.

The second aspect is linked with the asymmetry and consequent to that is the role of India, as the largest and most powerful country in the region. Among the concrete issues is the persistence of a big-power small-power syndrome. It is an objective reality that the asymmetry of panes in the region cannot be changed. What can be changed in India's perception towards its neighbours and vice versa? There is need of the development of spirit of mutual understanding, accommodation and trust amongst the South Asian countries[33].

Indonesia's policy towards its neighbours at times has been even more abrasive than the Indian policy. Nevertheless, ASEAN could devise a common ground where Indonesia's regional ambitions and consequential security concerns could be accommodated. In this regard, the role of Indonesia, particularly the far-sightedness and political acumen as displayed by its leadership, played a decisive role. Particularly in dealing with intra-group conflicts, Indonesia played a high degree of restraints and caution so as to remove the deep-seated suspicion in the minds of its ASEAN partners with regard to Jakarta's hegemonic ambitions in remarkable political ballast from the very outset and contributed significantly to the normalization of the politico-security environment in the region.[34]

A similar role played by India is likely to produce identical results in the context of SAARC. In this regard, the recent changes in the Indian policy, its reconciliatory stance on disputes with its neighbours are positive signs. To transform the current policy into a long-standing on the cultivation of elite cohesion in its support is indispensable. Similarly, the smaller South Asian countries also need to reconsider their policy towards India. First of all, they need to remain prepared to respond to any radical change that may be taken in Indian policy towards the region.

South Asian reality and the ASEAN experience amply suggest that the management of inter-state conflict and their ultimate resolution require considerable sacrifices on the part of all the parties concerned. While pressing for concessions from India, smaller South Asian countries will also have to find ways and means of accommodating some of India's regional aspirations. Indonesia's smaller neighbours have conveniently accommodated some of its regional aspirations without sacrificing their core concerns. In the changed circumstances, highly vigilant smaller South Asian countries need to be more visionary in dealing with India.[35]

It is evident from the experiences of ASEAN states that the domestic context played a crucial role in the radical transformation of the foreign policies of these nations. ASEAN countries adopted ambitious programmes during the late

1960s and 1970s to face the challenges of poverty, under development, inequality, deprivation and socio-political turmoil compounded by the communist threat from across the border. In order to concentrate upon the successful implementation of these programmes, the member states have to show willingness in relation to bilateral conflicts. Thus, the approach of ASEAN states with regard to conflict and cooperation was determined by their task as the domestic front.[36]

In terms of socio-economic development, the conditions in South Asia have been much worse than in South-East Asia. With no large-scale programme of socio-economic development, South Asian countries have no or very little stake in a friendly neighbourhood. In such a situation, conflict or cooperation makes little difference. Second, South Asia's failure in socio-economic development and consequential socio-political turmoil has created a constant pressure on the ruling elite to redirect mass grievances.[37] Therefore, in order to initiate a decisive shift away from conflict to a course of cooperation in the region, it is imperative for the SAARC countries to undertake radical programme of socio-economic development capable of shifting the focus of attention from political to economic at the national level. This would create a high stake in a friendly neighbourhood.

ASEAN is certainly a success story in terms of its experience in inter-regional cooperation, particularly the way it has offered the member states the possibility of establishing closer linkage and cooperation with Third World countries, group of countries and other regional and international bodies. ASEAN inter-regional cooperation has been effective not merely in obtaining aid or assistance packages but also in building up long-terms complementary economic relations. Particularly notable has been the ASEAN success in terms of projecting the region as an ASEAN entity whereby it has been possible to strengthen its bargaining position.

The prospects of cooperation between SAARC and ASEAN are promising and are likely to be beneficial to each other. There should be long-term planning and vision in this respect and pragmatic approach. Cooperation between the two associations can take off only or a 'go slow' strategy on the basis of a clear-cut vision of both the sides for each other's benefits and should necessarily be complementary to existing bilateral or multilateral relations. Inter-regional cooperation should also complement each other's capabilities. However, the hindrances that impede growth of trade between the two sub-regions will have to be handled with care. The infrastructural facilities including product development, marketing and sale promotion and facilities of transport and communication will have to develop in order to increase the meaningful economic linkages between the two regional groupings.

India, which became a sectoral dialogue partner of ASEAN in 1992 and a full dialogue partner in 1995, has increased the prospects of trade expansion between SAARC and ASEAN. India will now participate in post-ministerial conferences and specific dialogue committees and ASEAN Regional Forum, and annual security meeting of ASEAN that include important leading countries of the world. India, indeed, had a surprise development in the course of the ASEAN Bali Summit held on October 8, 2003. India's 'Look East Policy' is indeed a turning point in India's foreign policy and trade relations. This has certainly increased relations of India with ASEAN countries and in turn upon the way of increasing relations between two associations. Again, the inclusion of Vietnam as a member of ASEAN has ended the historical clash between communist and non-communist countries of South-East Asia. The end of communism in Vietnam and its membership of ASEAN have opened a new era of cooperation among the countries of South-East Asia. The historical friendly relations between India and Vietnam can also help to give a big boost to the trade and investment ties of South-East Asian nations with the South-Asian nations. By coming together the nations of diverse social and political system and levels of development can learn to raise the threshold of mutual tolerance and cooperation. ■

Notes & References

1. Hasan Aksari Rizvi, "Problems and Prospects of South Asian Regional Cooperation", *Regional Studies*, Vol. 2, No. 2, 1983–84, p. 13
2. Ganganath Jha, *South East Asia and India*, New Delhi, 1986, p.1.
3. *ASEAN Experiences of Regional and Inter-Regional Cooperation-Relevance for SAARC*, Dhaka, 1988, p. 11
4. Adam Malik, "Regional Cooperation in International Politics", *Regionalism in South East Asia*, papers presented at the First conference of ASEAN students of Regional Affairs (ASEAN-I), Jakarta, October 22–25, 1974, Centre for Strategic and International Studies, Jakarta, March, 1975, p. 161.
5. S.D. Muni and Anuradha Muni, *A Regional Cooperation in South Asia*, New Delhi, 1984, p.12. Also see *Jawaharlal Nehru on Internal Cooperation Ministry of Information and broadcasting*, Government of India, Faridabad, 1966, Jawaharlal Nehru, *India's Foreign Policy: Selected Speeches*, September 1946–April 1961, Ministry of Information and Broadcasting, Government of India, 1971, p. 38, I.N. Mukherjee, "India and Regional Cooperation", Akhtar Majeed, ed., *Indian Ocean Conflict and Regional Cooperation*, New Delhi, 1986, p. 12. Also see, Surendra Chopra, "The

Emerging Trends in the Non-Aligned Movement", *Indian Journal of Political Science*, Vol. 47, No. 2, 1986, pp. 161–177.

6. *Foreign Affairs Record*, Vol. 17, July 1972, pp. 192–93, Surendra Chopra, *Post Simla Indo-Pak Relations: From confrontation to De-escalation*, New Delhi, 1988, Srikant Paranjpe, "India South Asia and SAARC", *Asian Profile*, Vol. 15, No. 1, February 1987, p. 70, S.D. Muni, "India's Beneficial Bilateralism in South Asia", *India Quarterly*, Vol. 34, No. 4, December, 1979, pp. 417–33, "Founding of South Asian Association for Regional Cooperation (SAARC)", *SAARC perspective*, Kathmandu, May 1987, p. 9.
7. For details, see S.D. Muni, "Reagan's South Asia Policy: The Strategic Dimensions", *IDSA Journal*, Vol. 16, No. 2, October–December, 1983. Also see, *Holiday Weekly*, January 27 and June 15, 1980. *The Patriot*, November 17, 1986, Rajendra Sareen, "Pakistan", U.S. Bajjpai, ed., *India and its Neighbourhood*, New Delhi, 1986, pp. 194–216. K. Raman Pillai, "Tensions within Regional Organization: SAARC-A Case Study", Rama S. Melkote, ed., *Regional Organisation: A World Perspective*, New Delhi, 1990, pp.169–170, And S.D. Muni, "SAARC: Building Regionalism from Below", *Asian Survey*, Vol. 25, No. 4, April, 1985, p. 393.
8. SAARC, *Lok Sabha Secretariat*, New Delhi, 1988, pp. 10–16.
9. Pradeep Bhargava, "Political Economy of Regional Cooperation in South Asia", Bhabani Sen Gupta, ed., *Regional Cooperation and Development in South Asia*, Vol. 2, New Delhi, 1986, p. 132.
10. Iftekharuzzaman and Nilufar Choudhry, "SAARC-ASEAN Cooperation Perspectives and Issues", *Indonesian Quarterly*, Vol. 16, No. 1, 1988, p. 34, See the "Charter of SAARC", *SAARC, Lok Sabha Secretariat*, No. 8, p. 71
11. *SAARC Lok Sabha Secretariat*, No. 9, pp. 31–49, Hamdan Amjad Ali, "SAPTA: Panacea for SAARC's ills?", *Pakistan and Gulf Economist*, Vol. 13, No. 22, 1994, Minam Jafri, "SAPTA: Can They Evolve a Community of Compromise?", *Pakistan and Gulf Economist*, Vol.13, No. 22, 1994. Also See "Afta: A Bold New Approach to ASEAN Cooperation", *Economic Bulletin*, Vol. 21, Nos. 5–6, March 1992.
12. *SAARC information Handbook*, SAARC Chamber of Commerce and Industry, Office of the President, Dhaka, p. 46, Also see the details of SAPTA in a Paper presented by R. M. Roy, SAARC Secretariat, Kathmandu, May 10, 1994, Karachi.
13. Indra Nath Mukherji, "SAPTA: New Trade Opportunities", *World Focus*, Vol. 14, No. 7, 1993, pp. 22–24. Also see the "Declaration of the Seventh SAARC Summit", Dhaka, April 10–11, 1993, *Strategic Digest*, Vol. 23, No. 5, 1994, pp. 732-740.
14. As per the UN classification Bhutan, Bangladesh, the Maldives and Nepal have been classified as Least Developed contracting States.
15. R. M. Roy, n. 12, also see Sabbir Ahmad, "SAPTA - A preliminary Analysis", *Regional Studies*, Vol. 14, No. 2, 1996, p. 4.

16. Indra Nath Mukerji, "Transisting of SAPTA to SAFTA: Instruments and Modalities", a paper presented at SAPTA seminar held in November 1995, p. 7. Also see *Financial Express,* October 1, 1995 and Vijay Shukla, "New Frontiers of SAARC", *Indian Quarterly,* Vol. 52, No. 1–2, 1996, p. 91–93.
17. Ibid., also see Sabbir Ahmad, n. 15, p. 11.
18. *Financial Express,* November 6, 1995. Also see Sabbir Ahmad, n. 15, pp. 9–10.
19. *Financial Express,* October 1, 1995
20. Ibid.
21. *Bangladesh Observer,* May 25, 1994.
22. Rashid Ahmad Khan, "Indo Pakistan Trade: Prospects and Constraints", *Regional Studies,* Vol. 13, No. 1, 1994–95, pp. 50–55.
23. *Financial Express,* October 1, 1995.
24. Ibid.
25. I.N. Mukherji, "Healing and Wound-Prospects of SAPTA", *Mainstream,* Vol. 35, No. 23, May 17, 1997, p. 13.
26. Paper on "Guidelines for India's Offer and Request list in the Second Round of Negotiations", presented at the SAARC Brainstorming Session (Workshop), *Research and information System for Non-Aligned and other developing countries,* New Delhi, September 17–18, 1996 (being part of the results of a research project sponsored by the International Development Research Institute, Ottawa, Canada.
27. Rashid Ahmad Khan, n.22.
28. R.M. Roy, n.12.
29. A.K.M. Abdus Sabur, "Management of Intra-group Conflicts in SAARC: The Relevance of ASEAN Experiences," *South Asian Survey,* Vol.10, No.1, January–June 2003, pp. 86–89.
30. K.M. De Silva, " The European Community and ASEAN: Lesson for SAARC," *South Asian Survey,* Vol. 6, No. 2, July–December 1999, p. 273.
31. A.K.M. Abus Sabur, n. 29, pp. 89–90.
32. Ibid., p. 91.
33. Saman Kalegma, "A Need for New Direction for SAARC: An Economic Perspective," *South Asian Survey,* Vol. 9, No. 2, July–December 2002, p.172.
34. Ibid.
35. A.K.M. Abus Sabur, n. 29, p. 95.
36. Ibid.
37. Ibid.

Regional Cooperation in South Asia—Emerging Trends

Parmjit Kaur Gill*

I

Regionalism is an important trend in international relations. The term regionalism refers to close interaction between that particular area which possesses geographical contiguity along with common socio-cultural and economic proximities, whereas regional organisation stands for the common arrangement among the states. It includes sovereign states within a region, which have common interests[1]. Generally regional cooperation is pursued through regional organisation but it is not essential or a pre-condition for cooperation. The regional organisation is an instrument to make the idea of regional cooperation operative. It is based on certain conditions, for example: (a) formal agreements among governments, (b) possessing diplomatic forums, and (c) assisted by an associated international bureaucracy[2]. Regionalism is concerned with continuous mutual relationship among different sovereign entities geographically proximate to each other. There are different grounds for regional arrangements: security or military alliances like NATO, SEATO, CENTO and the Warsaw Pact; cooperative alliances which are basically for socio–economic cooperation like the EU, SAARC, ASEAN (SAARC not existed then) or recently established African Union (AU) on the lines of EU. Millier argued that the Arab League, Organisation for American States (OAS) and Organisation of African Unity (OAU) are cooperative arrangement to deal with socio-economic issues including the problems related with security of their respective members[3]. Apart from this, the idea of new regionalism has become

* Lecturer in Political Science, Department of Correspondence Courses, Punjabi University, Patiala.

very popular in the post-Cold War period. The various efforts like the formation of the EU, NAFTA, AFTA and SAFTA have been made to give practical shape to this new idea.

In the late 1980s attempt of the European Community to complete its internal market integration by the end of 1992 had induced a new global wave of regional integration; most notably: (i) the US–Canada free Trade Agreement and subsequent incorporation of Mexico in the North American Free Trade Agreement (NAFTA); (ii) the entrance of Austria, Finland, and Sweden into the European Union; (iii) the entrance of former communist states of central Europe; (iv) the Mercosur customs union among Brazil, Argentina, Paraguay, and Uruguary[4]; and (v) the recent formation of African Union (AU) 2003 on the lines of EU. However, there is a tremendous gap in the level of development between Europe and Africa. There has been a surge of Regional Trade Agreement (RTAs): about 162 RTAs are in force as of 2002 with over half of those coming into existence after 1995. The WTO estimates indicate that over 300 RTAs will be in effect by 2007, including the RTAs being negotiated between the EU and Latin America, and between the US and ASEAN. It reflects a trend of trade liberalisation outside the traditional regional boundaries[5]. Besides, Free Trade Area of the Americans (FTAA) is the most ambitious regional trade agreement proposed to date. Negotiating countries include every nation in America except Cuba with a total population of 800 million and a market of $13 trillion. Traditional views concerning the state-centric regional system are being challenged by the concentration of political and military power at the top as well as by a transnational network build around economic ties and cultural identities[6]. Early post-Cold War expectations that regions and regional concerts would form the foundation for a new international order have proven untenable. Instead, regions appear to arise either through the dissemination of various transactions and externalities or as protection against the hegemony of capitalist globalization and great-power politics. The old conception of regionalism need, to be redefined and reintegrated into current international relations theories. Vayrynen's views are a little confusing because the earlier formations of EEC or ASEAN were also against hegemony. European integration was largely in response to the US or former USSR's hegemonistic interest and ASEAN took birth against the Chinese or Japanese hegemonistic designs.

Somehow, history can be repeated. Regions were divided due to European colonialism and imperialism. Europe itself was the first victim of emergence of nation state and it flourished and established this Western orientation in the other parts of the world especially Asia and Africa. Now, Europe is first to integrate on socio-cultural-economic lines and is being followed by others.

No doubt, globalization is supporting the regional movements and new regionalism in many ways. In the era of rapid globalization, regionalism might seem a notion better suited to the nineteenth century than the twenty-first. Yet, regionalism has actually flourished in the second half of the twentieth-century. An increasing number of conflicts is based on territorial identities, while new regional-based political, economic, cultural and religious groupings have emerged. The most important theme emerges that regions are social and cultural constructs[7]. Therefore, the future world order is largely affected by regionalism. Bibek Debroy viewed that three nascent or emerging poles, perhaps through a hub and spoke kind of arrangement, can be detected in this process of bloc formation. First there is a pole centred on European Community, spilling over into elsewhere in Western Europe and some of the former socialist countries of East Europe. Second, there is a pole centred in North America, with potential spillovers into South America. Third, there is a possible pole centred on ASEAN. The only parts of the world that are not yet likely members of any of these poles are Africa and South Asia[8]. The argument here is that South Asia and Africa are able to create new poles for their significant role to play in the future world order.

Globalization has been affecting movements of regionalism both negatively and positively. According to Lange (1999), to understand the connection between the two phenomena, globalisation must be operationalised in a way that helps to identify aspects which could influence the state' capacity for territorial management as well as regionalist motives and goals. The result of Lange's empirical study shows that globalisation can support regionalist movements and at the same time restrict their options, depending on their ability to adapt. However, whether they are able to exploit the changing opportunity structures is highly dependent on internal factors and, therefore, path-dependent. Globalisation will support only certain types of regionalism, leading to pronounced asymmetrical challenges for the nation-state.[9] Wilfred Ethier viewed that in the late 1980s attempts were made for regional market and different types of arrangement came into existence during this time. In new regionalism, the small countries are linking up with a big country. The degree of liberalization in new regionalism is typically modest and we can say that the arrangements are one-sided or in favour of rich or big countries.[10] Whatever the benefits and losses incurred by large or small states, major powers or weak states, developing or developed economies, one aspect of regionalism is clear regionalism is on its resurgence.

II

Regionalism or Regional Cooperation in South Asia is also the impact of regionalism in other parts of the world, like EEC-EU, ASEAN (1967), OAS (1945), OAU (1963), etc. A brief description of theoretical perspective regarding South Asia Regional Cooperation will be important. Mukherjee Reed identifies four broad approaches to study the international relations: (a) the realist or state-centric approach; (b) the economic or firm-centrist approach; (c) the institutional approach; and (d) a historical and political economy approach. He said that in contrast to state-centric approaches, the firm-centric approach argues that the demise of cold war politics has rendered redundant the purely political basis for international relations and has allowed firms to play an important role in shaping foreign policy.[11] The firm-centred approach works when firms are interesting in cutting across the boundaries of one region, instead of multilateral and/or free arrangements. It led to the core-periphery model which is applicable to the East Asian region. Wherein Japan constitutes the core; Korea and Taiwan are constituting semi-periphery and less-developed countries such as the Philippines and Thailand are at the periphery. This model seems to assume the necessity of hegemonic stability. Reed applies a historical political-economy approach to regional cooperation in the South Asian region.[12] The South Asian experiment with regional cooperation, i.e. SAARC is not a success story in comparison with the EU and ASEAN. The EU is purely a functionalist model with the collaboration of institutionalism. According to Nisar-ul-Haq the functionalist, neo functionalist, theories of integration are based upon the traditional customs union theory with its famous typology of free trade area, customs union, common market, economic union and complete economic integration. This theory was developed and applied in the context of European Economic Community—a community of developed economies with a pluralistic democratic political set-up.[13] Reed argues that one important element in political-economy approach is the notion of structural power of capital, which primarily determines state-capital and interstate relationships. The parties to this new arrangement are states, domestic capital and transnational capital, where the structural power of transnational capital is the greatest at present.[14] The politico–economy approach is applicable to South-Asian cooperation because the forces of globalization gear-up South Asian Cooperation in a positive manner. The potential of socio–cultural cooperation already exists in the area, which is providing the base for political economy not only the structural power of transnational capital.

The partition of the Indian subcontinent has proved a major setback to the process of regional cooperation in the region. It mutilated and distorted the socio-cultural fabric of the divided land. Greenberg strongly opines that in each case, partition involved the creation of new boundaries and borders: new lines on a new way, new citizens of new states. But geographical division severed the already tenuous fabric of social relations and unprecedented political achievements arrived with overwhelming human catastrophe.[15] More than five decades are over but the division has not ceased to generate pain and trouble.

South Asia is a natural geo-economical integrated area. Cemendtaur supports this argument when he says, 'a person is generally referred to as an Indian if he is from India, Pakistan, Bangladesh, Sri Lanka, the Maldives or even Nepal and Bhutan'[16]. Moreover if we look at the map of South Asia, there are no physical boundaries. Geography defines South Asia as one region. All South Asians are the same people. Peace in South Asia is a necessity for all the countries of the region. The need for cooperation becomes imperative when we look at the problems, opportunities and threats prevailing in the region. As a region South Asia is the poorest and the most overpopulated one in the world. About 40% of the region's population lives below poverty line. India alone represents 80% of the region's population as also its GDP. More than 1/6 of world's labour force is in South Asia. Despite the huge difference in physical and demographic factors, all the South Asian countries have low incomes, high population densities (except Bhutan), poor health and literacy rates. Within the region there is a duality of economic structure. 'India, Pakistan and Sri Lanka could roughly be clubbed into a developing category while four others—Nepal, Bangladesh, Bhutan and Maldives—fall under the least developed category'.[17] There is population below $1 a day: India-44.2%, Nepal 37.7%, Pakistan 31%, Sri Lanka 6.6%[18], notwithstanding India's booming economy eclipsed by 44.2% population below one dollar a day. Key indicators of development are continuously alarming in South Asia after sub-Saharan Africa. The so-called strong economy engulfed in poverty, India the world's largest democracy with Pseudo nationalism of saffron *Jehadis*. Mukehrji Reed considers following features of SAARC economies: (a) every SAARC country relies heavily on the OECD (Organisation for Economic Cooperation and Development) countries for both imports and exports; (b) the area is predominantly agricultural; (c) all SAARC countries are major importers of food and technologies-intensive machinery, and exporters of primary commodities, textiles and certain labour-intensive manufactures.[19]

The South Asian Regional Cooperation had been a victim of cold war politics. Cold War encouraged the 'state-centric' politics between the member countries. Super powers, particularly, the USA was only concentrating upon 'containment of communism'. Pakistan has been instrumental in enhancing American interests in West Asia, which gave Pakistan an opportunity to make Kashmir a 'zone of contention'. South Asian Cooperation was a distant thing to think over. 'Zingel describes that SAARC is a marriage of convenience rather than love.[20] All the South Asian states have tried other alignments, Pakistan joined various defence alliances as a partner of the West in the early days of the Cold War and later turned to the Islamic, South West and Central Asian States while India was a leading member of NAM. There is a strange discrepancy in South Asia between regional cooperation on the one hand and open hostilities on the other. With the exception of the smallest members, they have all been experiencing strained relations with the largest one. In South Asia, India and Pakistan are involved in nuclear activities for both constructive and destructive purposes. Both are justified on the basis of national security, whereas nuclearization of this region is posing a major threat to its security. Such extravagance increases deterrence. It gives air to undue and pseudo nationalist-centric forces while a known fact is that South Asia needs comprehensive security which is multi-dimensional and comprises security against narco-traffic, international crime, environmental degradation, biodiversity loss, emerging diseases, over population, poverty, political unrest along with territorial security. Ashis Nandy rightly remarks that South Asia is a civilization against nation-state.[21] Idea of South Asia is partly artificial and so is its nation-state. That does not make the states fragile, but it makes them behave as if they were fragile to the extent that they believe they are so and seek to remove the fragility by being hardboiled national-security states. The idea of South Asia is actually a response to successful regional groupings like ASEAN and European Union. Because of the history of 'state formation' in the region the ethos of separatism is very strong. A number of secessionist conflicts continues in this region, like the Sri Lankan conflict, the Indo–Pakistan disagreement over Kashmir, the terrorist separatist movement in Punjab, etc.[22] One major reason of failure of institutionalism is anti India perceptions of rest of the states in South Asia. Cohen points out that Pakistan considers South Asian cooperation as the Indian hegemonic ambition.[23] Pakistan seeks larger regional interests by countering the Indian threat. Pakistan has been demanding multilateral, extra regional powers' help in ensuring containment of India. Bangladesh, Nepal, Sri Lanka raise voices against Indian domination and arrogance. Smaller states are trying to prevent hegemonic designs of India. India is trying to establish its hegemony and to mobilize collective behaviour for increasing strength in forums like the GATT and the WTO.[24] Since India's relationship with most of its neighbours was less than brotherly, these neighbours disliked names that seemingly endorsed Indian pre-eminence. They tried to imagine a new entity called South Asia.[25] Therefore the primary concern of the South Asian State, is nation-justifying state creation within the set territorial boundaries inherited from colonial rule. Socio–economic considerations are no doubt important, but important as an aid to nation and state creation[26]. Due to these reasons, there is only 5% intra-regional trade in South Asian region while it has reached 35% in ASEAN, 65% in the EU.

The geography of the region is integrated, which paves the way to harness the natural resources. Common socio–cultural bonds transcend the borders because South Asia is the region of regions[27]. These different regions within the sub-continent are socio-culturally and geographically integrated. The areas for immediate cooperation are agriculture, communication, education, prevention of drug trafficking and drug abuse, rural development, terrorism, crisis control management particularly in case of natural calamities, joint projects specially hydro-power projects. Cooperation in these areas will definitely reduce the tensions. Economic cooperation has become essential for establishing peace in the region. There are immense avenues in agriculture sector like spices, sugar, wheat, cotton, jute, spices, etc. where private sector could also come forward. Tourist and transport industry, leather and jute industry will be highly benefited. Bibek Debroy visualizes that now Nepal can become the hydroelectric capital for South Asia providing cheap electricity for itself and for other states of the region. Bangladesh with its large natural gas resources and seabeds could provide the resource base for fertilizers and petro-chemical industries. India can emerge the main supplies of capital goods and medium-tech consumer goods and can provide new technology for the whole South Asian region.[28]

III

Emerging trends for South Asian cooperation seem bright because the end of the Cold War and 9/11 incident are largely responsible for creating a conducive environment for cooperation in the South Asian region. Apart from this, globalization has opened tremendous avenues for regional cooperation in South Asia. Its preference of economic issues over the military one leading regional organisations on a worldwide scale to the proliferation of civil society, and decline of nation-state's role to control economies. It is bringing people of South Asia close to each other. Global market pressures are not only opening the channels for economic trade and interdependence but also introducing the people to each other, exploring their socio-cultural capabilities. Eduardo Faleiro argues that countries do not grow strong when cheap and quality products are denied to millions of consumers, when profitable opportunities are refused to thousand of producers and scope for revenue generation is left un-availed[29]. India and Pakistan have a great deal to learn from the global experience where trade is increasing being used as a prelude to political reconciliation. Rao also supports by saying that two structural changes in the world economy underway over the past decade and half have exerted enormous impact on the regional process[30]. One is the growth of economic regionalism and the other is globalisation. The twin global economic processes at work are rationalization and globalization of economies[31]. All this reveals that economy is preceding political or geo-strategic issues. The contentious issues between India and Pakistan are not the core issues. Pervez Musharraf, President of Pakistan, himself declared that the peace process is irreversible. In his recent visit to India Musharraf talked to media that the time of geopolitics is over and geo-economics has begun. In a way it can be considered as 'melting of ice' between the two countries. Both countries agreed to enhance the trade and to launch more bus routes on different points including J&K.[32] In the changing economic order of the world today, sustained economic growth and development depend on intense competition through increased productivity and technological innovations. Human resource development is central to the pursuit of sustainable economic growth. We are now in the age of knowledge-based economy. The world has made tremendous technological advancement[33]. These emerging trends of regionalisation and world economy pushing 'core' issues on the back burner. The progress of ASEAN, which was constituted in 1967, was also based on these factors. There were serious conflicts among major ASEAN countries—Indonesia, Malaysia and the Philippines. With the passage of time and successful ASEAN trade relations, disputes were 'managed' if not solved. A study analyses that ASEAN's primary focus was on learning to live with conflicts through effective measures of conflict management[34]. This was done through consultation/negotiation, largely at the bilateral level using numerous channels of communication. There was absence of any ASEAN mechanism for settling disputes amongst the member states. This was done through informal channels purposefully keeping the association aside. The main purpose was to focus on efforts for the fulfillment of ambitious programmes of socio-economic development. The ASEAN model is significant if not 'essential' for South Asian cooperation. SAARC can be rejuvenated on certain ASEAN strategies.

Another very important emerging trend is the process of Confidence Building Measures (CBMs) between India and Pakistan. To achieve peace, CBMs have a special importance in the international system. CBMs are conceived as an arrangement for building trust in order to create conditions for the management and resolution of conflict[35]. CBMs are not only military, though these are essential to avoid unexpected conflict. Political and economic CBMs provide the foundation and stability and allow a move towards strengthening interdependency, which is important to sustain other measures[36]. Though the concept of CBM, which is considered to be of Western origin, is not entirely new to South Asia as there are several bilateral pacts regarding trade, water and physical boundaries, like 'new regionalism' there is substantial change in the 'form and 'areas' of CBMs. 'The present program of CBMs both in the military and non-military sphere dates back to 1988, as a result of various crises and near war situation faced when there were reports of India's alleged plan to attack Pakistan's nuclear installations[37]. After 1997 there is a chain of military or non-military CBMs between India and Pakistan from 'Lahore Declaration 1999 to April 2005. Every military or non-military issue has been under process of discussion. Starting from Siachen Glacier, Sir Creek to Wullar Barrage, CBMs involves trade and bus diplomacy. A significant development happened between India–Pakistan relations when the Delhi–Lahore Bus put on track on 11 July, was once again hailed as a historic step on the long road to Indo–Pak peace and CBMs. Sushant Sarean agrees that the bus service between Srinagar and Mujaffrabad is not only a major political breakthrough but a CBM with far-reaching consequences.[38]

Multi-track diplomacy is also an important aspect of emerging scenario of cooperation. Track-I diplomacy is limited to the official level talks between two countries and is used for conflict resolution. Track-II is unofficial, informal interaction between those groups and individuals, who can develop the strategies, influence public opinion and organize human and material resources in ways that might help to resolve their conflict. Track-II diplomacy comes in the preview of CBMs. Track-II was started between India and Pakistan in the 1970s. But it was limited up to quasi or semi-government level—a handful of people, generally retired bureaucrats, army personnel, etc. They have been talking in terms of their respective countries on basic issues more than on socio–cultural economic issues. Therefore, in recent years, there has been more thrust on people-to-people contacts. We can name it multi-track diplomacy, which includes educationists, businessmen, sportsmen, art groups, partitioned families, etc. Multi-track diplomacy is bringing desirable fruits for peace and cooperation in the region. The flood of people seems to be excited to cross the borders between India and Pakistan, especially within both the Punjabs.

In the present scenario, it can be concluded that there are strong movements and forces of socio–cultural ties along with the pressure of market economy, which are demanding more and more trade relations. The emerging trend is that increasing interdependence will push the core issues aside. In the recent future, it seems there will be 'loose' or 'soft' borders among the South Asian states. There will be no alteration in the borders but their nature will certainly change. Eventually, these processes will strengthen the regional cooperation in the region. ■

Notes & References

1. Norman Hill, *International Politics*, New York, 1963.
2. Joseph Nye, *Peace in Parts: Integration and Conflicts in Regional Organisation*, Boston, 1971.
3. Lyne H. Miller, "Regional Organisations and Subordinate System", L.J. Steven & L. Spiegal, eds., *International Politics and Regions: A Comparative Approach*, New Jersey, 1970.
4. A.C. Theodore and H.W. James, *Introduction to International Relations*, New Jersey, 1978.
5. Wilfred J. Ethier, "Regionalism in a Multilateral World", *Journal of Political Economy*, Vol. 106, No. 1, 1998.
6. Raimo Vayrynen, "Regionalism: Old and New", *International Studies Review*, Vol. 5, No. 1, March 2003.
7. Lothar Honnighausen et.al., eds., *Regionalism in the Age of Globalism*, Vol. 2: Forms of Regionalism, http://www.wisc.edu/wisconsinpress/books/2910.
8. Bibek Debroy, *Regional Integration*, Paper Presented South Asia Beyond, 2000.
9. Niels Lange, *Fragmentation Vs. Integration: Regionalism in the Age of Globalisation*, ECPR Joint Sessions of Workshops, Mannheim/1999.
10. Wilfred J. Ehtier, n.5.
11. Ananya Mukherjee Reed, "Regionalisation in South Asia: Theory and Praxis", *Pacific Affairs*, Summer, Vol. 70, No. 2, 1997.
12. Ibid.
13. Nisar-ul-Haq, "Regional Cooperation in South Asia: A Theoretical Perspective and Prospects under SAFTA", *Indian Journal of Asian Affairs*, Vol. 17, No. I, June 2004.
14. Ananya Mukherjee Reed, n.11.
15. Jonathan D. Greenberg, "Divided Lands, Phantom Limbs: Partition in the Indian Subcontinent, Palestine, China, and Korea", *Journal of International Affairs*, Vol. 57, No. 2, Spring 2004.
16. A.H. Cemendtaur, "Peace in South Asia A Mirage?", *South Asian Politics*, Vol. 1, No. 3,

New Delhi, July 2002.

17. P.V. Rao, "Globalization and Regional Cooperation : The South Asian Experience", B.C. Upreti, ed., *SAARC: Dynamics of Regional Cooperation in South Asia,* Vol. 1, New Delhi, 2000.
18. *World Development Report,* 2003.
19. Ananya Mukherjeet Reed, n.11.
20. Wolfgang-Peter Zingel, *On the Economics of Regional Cooperation in South Asia,* Paper presented at the 15th European Conference on Modern South Asian Studies, Prague September 8-10, 1998, www.sai.uni_heidelberg.de/abt/intwep/zingel/prha98tml.
21. Ashis Nandy, "Imagined Homeland", *The Times of India,* March 9, 2005.
22. Ananya Mukherjee Reed, n.11.
23. Stephen P. Cohen, "South Asia: The Origins of War and the Conditions for Peace", *South Asian Survey,* Vol. 4, No.1, January–June 1997.
24. Ananya Mukherjee Reed, n.11.
25. Ashis Nandy, n.21.
26. A.P. Rana, "New Directions in the Study of SAARC: Evaluating the Bases of Regional Cooperation in South Asia", *South Asian Survey,* Vol. 10, No. 1, January–June 2003.
27. Bhupinder Brar, South Asia : A Region of States or Region of Regions, *South Asian Survey,* Vol. 6, No. 1, January–June, 1999.
28. Bibek Debroy, n.8.
29. Eduardo Faleiro, "South Asian Economic Cooperation", *Mizzima News,* July 18, 2003, www.mizzima.com.
30. P.V. Rao, n.17.
31. *The Times of India,* April 18, 2005.
32. Nisar-ul-Haq, n.13.
33. A.K.M. Abdus Sabur, "Management of Intra-Group conflicts in SAARC: The Relevance of ASEAN Experience", *South Asian Survey,* Vol. 10, No. 1, January–June 2003.
34. J.D. Dennis & Sandolo, *Conflict Resolution: A Unique US Role for the 21st Century*/USIA, U.S. Foreign Policy Agenda, December 1996.
35. Dipankar Banerjee, "Confidence Building Measures in South Asia: Role of Research Institutions", Moonis Ahmar, ed., *The Challenge of Confidence Building in South Asia,* New Delhi, 2001.
36. Salma Malik, "Nuclear CBMs in South Asia : A view from Islamabad".
37. *The Tribune,* August 17, 2003.
38. Sushant Sareen, "Politics of the Bus", *The Tribune,* April 23, 2005.

Index